D0992179

Everything / Nothing / Someone

Everything / Nothing / Someone

Alice Carrière

S&G

Spiegel & Grau, New York
www.spiegelandgrau.com

This is a work of nonfiction that includes the author's present recollections of her experiences over many years. Names and identifying characteristics of some people have been changed.

Jacket design by Strick & Williams; front jacket photograph by Gregory Lattimer
Interior design by Meighan Cavanaugh

Library of Congress Cataloging-in-Publication Data Available Upon Request

ISBN 978-1-954118-29-4 (hardcover)
ISBN 978-1-954118-30-0 (eBook)

Printed in the United States on 30 percent post consumer recycled paper

First Edition
10 9 8 7 6 5 4 3 2 1

For Gregory

Wo aber Gefahr ist, wächst das Rettende auch. /
Where danger is, grows that which saves also.

—Hölderlin

To be mad is to be enraged is to be insane is to
be uncontrolled is to commit violent action is
to be fashionable, as of wind or as of sea.

—Jennifer Bartlett, *History of the Universe*

I / Everything

1.

My mother's disembodied voice came through the intercom. "Alice. Alice."

Or maybe it was "Alice! Alice!"

Or maybe it was "Alice? Alice?"

If I couldn't get to the phone fast enough, she'd hang up and then I couldn't call her back because she kept her phone on privacy mode. She could reach me, but I couldn't reach her. I had to go looking for her to find out what she wanted. By the time I found her she didn't seem to care why she had called me in the first place. Maybe my mother was just a voice in my head. Maybe I was just a figment of her imagination.

She had put her bed in the third-floor pool room, which had a fireplace and views of her lush garden. During the day she was below me, painting in one of her two downstairs studios, and at night she was above me in the pool room with her bottle of white wine and her books. My bedroom was below the pool room, on the second floor. The pool held ninety tons of water and I could feel it all balancing over my head. As I lay in bed at night, I pictured the ceiling giving way. I wondered at the shape that water would take once it was cut loose from its parameters, violently free.

The intercom connected us within the massive house in New York City. Our address was 134 Charles Street, between Greenwich and Washington Streets, in the West Village. We never got the numbers put on the door, so there was just a torn piece of paper with *134* written on it taped to the inside of the glass. It was a seventeen-thousand-square-foot, three-story building with a concrete facade, large windows, and steel doors. The building used to be a factory for manufacturing train parts back in the days when trains ran along the west side of the island.

On the ground floor was an office and a gigantic studio, which led, via a spiral staircase, to an even bigger basement studio, where my mother painted every day from 6 a.m. until 7 p.m., with a two-hour nap in the middle of the day. Between the office and the upper studio was a small room where my father lived after my mother kicked him out of her bed and before she kicked him out of the house. It was also where my uncle Roy came to die, where Max hemorrhaged, and Michael wept. It was where people came to lock themselves in and fall apart.

The building had huge windows that let the world see us as we moved through the house. Once, for one of her lavish parties, my mother had the staff light hundreds of votive candles and line them along the windows. In the middle of the party, firemen in full gear stormed into the house thinking it was burning down. A neighbor had misinterpreted the chic flicker of tiny candles as a deadly blaze, or perhaps they had seen something in us, identified a threat, that we couldn't see ourselves.

On the second floor was my bedroom; a second room, which I called "my study"; Nanny's room; the library with a fireplace and rolling ladders that extended to the ceiling for access to the walls of books; the kitchen where Katy the cook prepared our meals; and the living room with another fireplace and a wall of windows that looked out onto a garden. Nanny was Eileen Denys Maynard, who went by Denys but was only ever called Nanny. She existed to everyone like a paper doll Mary Poppins, two-dimensional, her life beginning and ending as the British governess paid to raise me. To me, she was a mother, but one who could be fired and disappear at any moment.

The garden on the second floor had fruit trees and a koi pond and a spiral staircase covered in roses that ascended to another garden with a grape arbor and apple trees. My mother liked to be surrounded by things that were growing because she always felt she was killing things, that if she touched something, it would die. There was a tool shed, like on a farm—I'd never been to a farm but I imagined that's what a farm was like—but right on top of the building in the middle of Manhattan. I liked to go in there and smell the fecund fustiness of the shed. The bags of fertilizer, rusting tools, and drying twigs created a tranquilizing fog that curled itself between me and the city below. Our world had all the disparate components of the world from which we were disconnected—steel and trees, fire and water, soil and decomposition.

There were no locks on the doors inside the house. The doors were just sheets of opaque glass in steel frames. Not even the bathroom doors had locks. Nanny once walked in on me masturbating and said, "Oh dear, I forgot you are a woman now," and walked out. Nanny once walked in on me cutting myself and cried. No locks meant I couldn't say, "KEEP OUT!" When I was six, I put a No Smoking sign on my door. It didn't work. My parents were both chain-smokers and their smoke entered the room before they did, making my eyes water and my throat itch. Only mythic beings could do that—make their presence known inside another person's body. The boundaries were porous.

In this house one could not tell the difference between fantasy and reality, art and object, parent and child. In this house, I couldn't tell what I was to my mother. In this house, I couldn't tell if I was my father's daughter, wife, or mother.

The bathroom attached to my bedroom had two entrances, one from the hallway and one from my room. When my mother had parties and I was in my room, people sometimes didn't notice the door connecting to my bedroom and didn't close it, so I could hear them pee. Sometimes I could even see them if the mirrored door reflected into my bedroom. I liked to watch them and I liked the moment when they realized they had been seen. There would be a fat pause as they tried to remember what sounds they had made or what parts of them had been exposed. They would clear their throat before they zipped or yanked up their pants, before fabric fell back over knees. In this house, our most secret selves and our most private moments were meant to be spectated and thought about. The toilet flushed with an intensity that made me jump every time. The taps of the sink and bathtub and shower were marked with *C* and *F*, for *chaud* and *froid*—the French words for "hot" and "cold." People unfamiliar with the house often scalded themselves when they washed their hands. The house forced you to move differently. It could be a bewildering, even harmful place if you didn't know its rules.

It was as if I lived inside my mother's mind. Everything had been designed especially for her and her alone. The space was built to accommodate the particularities and peculiarities of her gestures and habits. The house had many horizontal surfaces—daybeds, kitchen counters, spacious hearths, hardwood floors on which she could assume her typical recumbent pose: on her side, arm cocked to prop up her head while smoking or reading or talking on the phone. She spread herself out on these domestic plateaus like Manet's *Olympia*, and life lived itself around her. She had transformed this place from a factory into a fortress, an irresistible nexus of strangeness, luxury, and niche functionality—the architecture of my mother's desires. Everything around us had her in it. She designed her own jewelry (a gemologist who rode a unicycle and had worked with the Hope Diamond was her collaborator), the pieces so elaborate that they tested the limits of engineering. She designed her own very uncomfortable furniture. She designed and commissioned our drinking glasses, handblown cylinders so light you could hardly tell there was anything in your hand. The concept behind them was to create something as close to nothing as possible but still be functional. I hated them because I couldn't stop breaking them. And I had to use them because they were part of the fundamental routine of my life. Which meant destroying them would also have to be a fundamental routine of my life. Even the most utilitarian aspects of our lives were impossible to negotiate—conceptualized beyond utility, aestheticized beyond the physics of living.

Nothing on the walls of my room was my own, nothing had been selected by me. There were no posters or drawings, only my mother's art or her friends' art. Every year my mother redesigned my room as a surprise for my birthday. She hung things up or took them down, added or took away, rearranged and reconfigured until the room was new and unrecognizable. Every year I would identify the changes from a master list and note what had been taken away or added. This new room had new rules, demanded new ways of living. This was the new place I would be doing my homework, the new direction I slept, the new view I had when I opened my eyes, the new me, curated by my mother. I felt the excess of it—the new teddy bear, rocking chair, computer, vanity mirror, canopy bed, and glow-in-the-dark constellations stuck to the ceiling in the correct configuration by my mother's studio assistants. It set me trembling with excitement but also panic, the trepidation of meeting the girl this unfamiliar room belonged to.

Roaming through the house was the purebred Welsh terrier, Charlie of Charles Street, my mother had bought me. She had sent him away to be trained at a fancy pet boarding school, where he was abused, and he returned to us a broken animal with a behavioral repertoire of biting, cowering behind the toilet, and eating his own excrement. I learned quickly that I could not touch or go near him while he ate or he would turn on me, snarling, and try to bite me. I'd encounter him in the hallway shitting on the floor and I'd edge by him as he growled, knowing if I tried to interfere with him feasting on his feces he'd attack. I tried to be affectionate with him, but he seemed consumed by the imaginary war that waged inside of him.

The house was full of people. There was a cook, a housekeeper, a house manager, a gardener, a fish man who looked after the koi pond, a studio manager, the studio manager's assistant, three studio assistants, and a studio assistant intern who cleaned the brushes. They were like family, especially the studio assistants. They worked with my mother in her most intimate space—her studio. They knew her way of thinking, discussed math, patterns, what came next in a series of paintings. Their jobs had no clear parameters. They worked in the studio but they also decorated the house for Christmas, organized my birthday parties, played with me. When my uncle was dying in the downstairs bedroom, Nancy, one of the assistants, got him his marijuana. Ricky, the studio assistant intern, sat with him as he was dying. These people existed for my mother. To keep things moving, to keep things clean, to keep me tended to, to keep paint fresh and canvases stretched and the whole operation going with my mother at the center, head down, brush up, painting.

I would stand in her studio and look up at the massive canvases: a wall of fire devouring a tartan square, playing cards, a skeleton; the shape of a house made up of thousands of small dots; a man holding an axe. She had a real human skeleton in the studio named Lucy. I would hold Lucy's excarnated hand, caressing the bumps and curves of her fingers in a morbid mother-and-child tableau. I wondered at the fact that my mother could casually own a human skeleton. Just because she wanted it, she could summon a whole dead human to hang out in the studio, to be named and petted and painted. Later, when my friend's father, a war photographer, was crushed by the second tower on September 11, my mother was given the film from his camera, and she rendered his final moments in paint, huge and bright. My mother was powerful. She could take over someone's remains, own the imprint they had left on the world, the imprint the world had left on them, and make that imprint even bigger, immortal. When my mother became the only Westerner commissioned to paint a temple ceiling in Japan, she let me put paint on the soles of my feet and walk across a square of paper. The idea that my feet would be walking across a ceiling in a temple in Japan made me feel like my mother could perform magic. She could make me everlasting; the feet that would only be tiny for a fraction of time, those feet would run forever across a ceiling where prayers were being chanted. I looked at the square of paper after the painting was done and saw for a brief moment how my mother had seen me, that my mother had seen me.

I spent most of my time in 134 Charles Street alone in my room listening to audiobooks. I didn't have many friends. I didn't know how to behave around children. I listened to audiobooks all the time. I listened to them to go to sleep at night, while I showered, while I did my homework, while I played in my room, on my way to school. The words slid down my ears and lit me up, helped me recognize where everyone else ended and I began. They taught me the right words for things; if I had the right word for things, everything could feel okay. I populated my life with the Watsons in 1963, with Marty and Shiloh, with Louis the swan, with Jonas and his memories. When I listened, I recognized my friends, I recognized myself. I had mastery over these spaces, these rooms built out of language. I could invite words in and I could say, "KEEP OUT!" I knew these worlds and I knew their rhythms and rules. I knew how Ron Rifkin pronounced certain words, where he paused to breathe, the exact inflection that came before the big reveal, and even though I knew to expect it, it thrilled me every time. I could say, "Aw, man!" in unison with LeVar Burton. These were disembodied voices too, but they didn't hang up if I couldn't get there fast enough; they let me turn them on and off again whenever I wanted. They could reach me, and I could reach them.

When I wasn't listening to audiobooks, I thought in the third person. Walking down the street to school I would think, "She is walking down the street. It is raining. The rain falls on her jacket." I turned myself into words and my life into a story. Years later, when I didn't recognize my own face in the mirror, when my body didn't feel like my own, I would again recite myself to myself, narrating myself into existence, trying to locate myself in my story.

The characters in the story of 134 Charles Street were rich, brilliant, loud, drunk, high, beautiful, careless, reckless, genius, gluttonous, well-dressed. Anna Wintour dropped off clothes, Steve Martin joked at the table, Wynton Marsalis played trumpet in the first-floor studio, Joan Didion sipped vodka-on-the-rocks in the garden, Al Gore won votes in our living room after bomb-sniffing dogs determined it was free of explosives, Merce Cunningham shuffled gracefully through the upper studio, Susan Sarandon and Julia Roberts compared colonoscopy stories over brunch at the dining room table. Starting at the age of seven, it was my job to tell the story of 134 Charles Street. "Would you like a tour?" I would ask in my Bonpoint dress to every guest who arrived at the extravagant parties my mother threw. I brought them through the studios, the gardens, and the pool room, naming the artists and designers for them. I was good at talking about where and how we lived; I just had no idea who I was talking about.

I first cut when I was seven. My mother would throw pool parties for my entire class of twenty kids, all of whom made merciless fun of me in school and out. I only ever hung out with adults. I'd stay late after school to visit with my teachers, asking them questions about their lives. I was excellent at anticipating what adults wanted from me, but I just couldn't read my classmates. Every year, they would descend on my house, invading my fortress. One year I walked into my room to get away from them and everything that belonged on my shelves was on the floor, much of it broken. We had just gotten Charlie and all my stuffed animals had been crammed into his crate. I couldn't see the floor. I felt woozy and faint. Adrenaline burned the underside of my skin, heating up the surface of me until it pulsed. I held my breath and felt an immense pressure against my entire body and an unfolding outward from deep within, as if I could be crushed and explode at the same time. I was angry, I was sad, I was terrified at how anger and sadness felt inside me. I needed to get the feelings out. I found the Swiss Army knife my father had given me. I pried open the biggest blade and pressed the edge of it against my palm. I pressed and dragged until I saw blood. Instantly my heartbeat receded from my ears, tucked itself calmly back into my rib cage, and my mind folded itself into a neat origami brain—clean, calm lines. The wild pitching was replaced by a thick stillness, the laceration a hot horizon, steadying and orienting me. It had come to me so easily, so naturally, and it had worked. I didn't know how I had known to cut myself to feel better; I had never heard about self-harm. With a tiny, shiny blade I learned I could unlock a doorway that led to a place that was entirely my own, even if I could only stay there for a moment within those seconds of pain. I didn't yet understand that the rage and sorrow I felt were not from mean kids. The feelings emerged from deeper deposits, cavernous compartments where the disembodied voices of my parents echoed, telling me things I shouldn't know, chanting the desires and fears that ruled them, until I couldn't tell the difference between my voice and theirs. Each cut organized into legible symbols the confusion of cravings—my father's, my mother's, my own—that made me feel like too much and eventually nothing. As a teenager, when I started cutting regularly, it felt like a passion, like a calling. Me upstairs, crosshatching my skin with a razor blade, my mother downstairs, crosshatching canvases with oil paint, each of us telling our story.

It was hard to know what was true in my house. There were no absolute truths because there were endless ways to say something, innumerable angles from which to see, so many media with which to transform things. At any moment something could be what it was and also the exact opposite. 134 Charles Street was a place of abundance and of absence. The kitchen had a pantry that was stocked with extra everything. Four bags of Cape Cod Potato Chips next to five bottles of maple syrup next to four boxes of Walker's Shortbread. I'd stand in the laundry room and stare at the repeating orange jugs of Tide detergent that stretched out along the shelves, a promise that things never ended. I didn't recognize this muchness for the extraordinary privilege it was. I didn't realize not everyone else had what we had, or that what we had was not an inherent quality of who we were. The excess felt like an exoskeleton, an impermeable shell that was naturally part of us. It never occurred to me to feel grateful, just like I wasn't grateful for the skin stretching across my bones.

My mother was, in her chronic extravagance, somehow always almost broke. Once, she came into my room, sat on my bed, stared over my head, and told me she had made two million dollars. Months later she came into my room, stared at her lit cigarette, and told me we were broke. She was a woman who didn't know her own social security number, how much money she had in the bank, the grand total of all the bills for all her extravagances. She didn't know how to manage the resources that, in the '70s, '80s, and '90s swelled and swelled and would later, from her profligacy, drain away. She only knew how to paint. She worked constantly, unflaggingly, and that meant that at any moment we could have everything or we could have nothing. Everything could change at any moment. Money, a parent, a mind, could all disappear.

I wasn't taught anything about real life. I knew the locations of Fra Angelico frescoes, I could recite all the lyrics to Kurt Weill's *The Threepenny Opera* in German, I could name all the famous examples of Gothic architecture. At fifteen, I still didn't know how to use a tampon because no one thought to tell me and I hadn't thought to ask. There were no lessons or tips or admonishments. My bed was made for me every morning, a towel was whisked away and washed every time I used one, my underwear was ironed. I floated around 134 Charles Street and didn't leave a trace. Not in creases in my clothes, nor on the walls or floors of my room, where even my mess couldn't stick. Later, I would do everything I could to make something stick to me, to the walls of my body and the sloping, slanting floors of my mind, until I finally understood the place that could contain me was the page.

Once, at my mother's Christmas tree decorating party, when I was old enough for the subsequent reaction to be inappropriate, embarrassing, strange, I dropped an ornament and it broke. I stared down at it, paralyzed. The only thing I could think of to say was, "What do I do?" My mother's assistant and a family friend were standing next to me. Their eyes widened with confused alarm. There was a pause, a heavy silence saturated by the colors of the lights and the density of my ignorance. "You get a broom and clean it up," one of them said. I could hear the amazement glazing her voice. My mind was blank. Destruction came easy, but what to do after, how to clean it up and move on, was a confounding proposition. In a house with no locks, in a family with no rules, in a mind with no limits, it was in the moment of demolition that I felt most at home.

The house that had been a structure for putting things together turned into the place in which we slowly came apart. In her work, my mother was obsessed with the archetypal house image—a square with a triangle on top. The most elementary, identifiable shape that indicated so much more: house, home, family, history. My mother rendered this silhouette in ink, in pastel, in Testors paint, in charcoal, in oils. It was big, it was small, it was crosshatched or composed of dots. It was chopped in half, it was dissolved, it was splintered. It was repeated over and over, as if she were trying to learn the meaning of the word, decipher its secrets.

My mother's muchness was matched by a grandiose but remote generosity. Our house became a repository for people fallen on hard times. Whether dying of AIDS, escaping an abusive parent or partner, facing poverty, or descending the spiral of manic depression, people would show up at our house and stay. I would be excited and curious about each new addition to the household and would focus all my thoughts and feelings on them, growing to love them as I walked by their rooms while they slept or wept. I liked to sit and talk to these people about their pain and their fears, nodding my head and thinking how big and unwieldy life could feel. I loved these people who seemed so lost, and I hoped our house could keep them safe. My mother cared from far away. She was not the person to bring the soup; she paid someone to bring the soup. But that was her way of showing that she wanted you to have soup. Later, when I would require ministration, my mother would lavish this care-by-proxy onto me in the form of psychiatrists and their pills, with the instruction to take them unquestioningly. Later, in the moments when I felt like I was disappearing, I wanted my mother to talk to me, to sit with me, to touch me. I craved a warmth that existed so deep inside her that it couldn't reach me. It couldn't even reach her. I wanted her to say, "Alice?

Alice?" and mean it, unspooling the question mark until it made four walls and a triangle roof where she would finally invite me in. I wanted her busy hands that built everything that surrounded me to help me prop up the walls of myself. Maybe she thought 134 Charles Street would magically protect us, that nothing could get to us. Except she didn't realize that the thing that wanted me dead was already inside the house.

2.

My mother, Jennifer Bartlett, broke onto the New York art scene in the 1970s. She was born in 1941 in Long Beach, California, to a bitter, beautiful, emotionally closed off mother, whose career in fashion illustration had been thwarted by my mother's arrival, and a charming alcoholic pipeline contractor with a secret second family. At five, she stood on the beach and declared to the expanse that she would be a great artist. She had always wanted to get away and she succeeded, graduating from Mills College then moving east to get her MFA at Yale. She married a handsome psychiatry student and then divorced him to move to New York City and pursue her career. She took a teaching gig at the School of Visual Arts and rented a loft on Greene Street in SoHo, joining a social milieu that came to include the artists Jonathan Borofsky, Joel Shapiro, Richard Serra, Barry Le Va, Alex Katz, Brice Marden, Lynda Benglis, Susan Rothenberg, Elizabeth Murray, Chuck Close, and Jasper Johns. "I was just crazy about New York," she said. "I remember the first time I got there, being knocked down by a big, fat woman when I was trying to hail a taxi. For some reason, this appealed to me enormously." She was catapulted to art world fame in 1976 with a piece called *Rhapsody*. In the *New York Times*, the art critic John Russell called it "the most ambitious single work of art to have come my way since I moved to New York." The piece, he said, "enlarges our notions of time, of memory, of change, and of painting itself." It was over 150 feet long and composed of 987 one-foot-by-one-foot steel plates with a baked enamel grid silk-screened onto them, a medium she had invented, inspired by New York subway signs. *Rhapsody* was enormous—in size and ambition. When it later hung in the Museum of Modern Art atrium, it took up all three walls. She wanted to make a piece that "had everything in it."

After hitting it big, Jennifer Bartlett bought her first mink coat, slapped on giant sunglasses and lipstick that was always crooked, sprayed on too heavily the Fracas de Robert Piguet perfume she ordered directly from Paris, and was dubbed "the Joan Collins of SoHo" by *New York* magazine. A 1985 twelve-page profile in the *New Yorker*, appropriately titled "Getting Everything In," described her "disconcertingly direct manner, her helmet of close-cropped dark hair, and her habit of cracking jokes at her own expense" and wondered how California could have "produced an artist of her energy, analytic rigor, and undissembled ambition." She had become, at that time, "one of the most widely exhibited artists of her generation." Her best friend, the artist Elizabeth Murray, described her as "sort of a brat. She was outspoken, and she seemed very sure of herself, and she made people angry—especially men." Another friend described her as "a monster pain." An article written by Joan Juliet Buck in *Vanity Fair* declared that "there is no actress glamorous enough to play Jennifer Bartlett. She believes in hot lunches, good clothes, and champagne. And she never stops working."

She was beautiful in a smudged way, crooked bottom teeth behind imperfect lipstick, short dark hair, and crystalline blue eyes that had an unexpected softness to them. She brought her own atmosphere with her wherever she went—a cloud of perfume, a cloud of smoke, a cloud of utter fucklessness. She had a loudness that came not just from the amplitude of sound waves, but from an orogenic pressure that brought the hilt of her desires—for something to stop or continue, to be given or leave her in peace—thrusting up through the moment, separating what was not about her (not much) and what was about her (more). She was the center of attention all the time, but the way she tugged on the spotlight seemed protective, as if she were trying to conceal herself with the glare. There was a vulnerability about her that revealed itself precisely in the moments most marked by crassness, by will, by stubbornness; a clumsiness to her attentional gluttony. She was extremely guarded. There was no one she opened up to. And she couldn't figure out affection. I received the occasional awkward pat, as if she were checking to see that all parts of me were still there, adjusting or confirming me, but never reaching me. When we did hug, she would cough out a laugh as our bodies touched, or a sarcastic "oh" would loop out of her, and I felt it, an overstuffed pillow between us, blocking the contact, the connection. She had zero ability to speak about emotions and often bit off the moment with the glib announcement that she "felt like working" or "felt like not feeling," amputating the sentiment at the joint. The *New Yorker* quoted her as saying she "developed an infinite capacity for work and none for reflection." She worked all the time, and it was all she wanted to do.

I watched my mother as she lived her life around me, passing by on her way down to the studio or up to her bedroom and down again in her fog of perfume and smoke to work or attend a party. I read her traces like letters. I knew this story; I was familiar with the narrative of her goings-away. She was downstairs or upstairs doing and thinking about special, mysterious things. Maybe, if I became special and mysterious too, she would turn her eyes to me. But later, when the mysteries of my own mind proved nearly lethal, when I became special with madness, she would avoid my gaze even more.

My father was a European sex symbol. Mathieu Carrière had been working in film and television since he was thirteen years old, acting in English, French, German, Italian, and Spanish with Orson Welles, Isabelle Huppert, Brigitte Bardot, Marlon Brando, Romy Schneider, and Antonio Banderas. After a brief career as a teenage equestrian vaulting champion, he left Lübeck, a small town forty-five minutes outside Hamburg, Germany, in 1969 to live in Paris, performing in drag in cabarets, bedding Princess Caroline of Monaco, attending philosophy classes at the Sorbonne, and becoming the protégé of the famous philosopher Gilles Deleuze. He tripped on acid in front of Visconti and Alain Delon at Domaine de Monthyon. He and Andy Warhol drew different shaped penises on the backs of Polaroids at Angelina's in Paris. "Some are curved," said Andy, "and maybe some are even like spirals."

My father spoke six languages, wrote a book about the poet Heinrich von Kleist, and was awarded the Légion d'Honneur, the highest French order of merit. He was six-foot-one and thin, had wavy light-brown hair that would turn white at forty, penetrating blue eyes, and puffy lips that gave the impression of sensuality and innocence. He was never still, always smoking, drinking, playing speed chess, inhaling cocaine, exhaling outrageous stories or wild theories. His body couldn't handle inertia; he rolled his thumb over his fingers over and over, as if compulsively checking that they were still attached to his body. He was loud, explosive, disruptive. He left people jarred and exhilarated, offended and compelled. He asked personal, invasive questions, and people would respond by telling him the worst things that had ever happened to them, things they had never told anyone before.

My parents met at a dinner party in New York in 1980, when my mother was thirty-nine and my father was thirty. He made her smoked salmon sandwiches and piled them onto her plate. She lit a Marlboro Red and inhaled as she ate.

"Shouldn't you do one at a time?" my father asked.

"I like to smoke and eat at the same time," my mother replied, pungent oil and thick smoke on her lips.

At dinner, she was seated next to another man named Matthew. My father fixed his attention on her and asked, loudly from across the table, "Which Matthew do you want?"

"You," she announced, and brought him back to her SoHo loft.

After my mother's success with *Rhapsody*, there was only one goal left to achieve. As the psychiatric files from my later hospitalization explained: *Alice was born to a mother with two driving ambitions: to be a successful artist and to have a child.* After years of trying to get pregnant without success and a failed adoption attempt, my mother learned, at forty-three, she was pregnant.

As the doctor performed the cesarean, my father played a word game with my mother.

"Name a French writer who has the same name as a piece of meat," he said.

"Colette," said my mother.

"Not bad, but that's côtelette," he said.

"Chateaubriand," the surgeon said and pulled me out, as if I were the answer to every riddle.

We spent the first four years of my life in Paris, with many trips across the Atlantic on the Concorde. My mother would hold her Abyssinian cat, Kanga, on her lap and feed her caviar. The apartment was a spacious penthouse on Rue Vavin, with terraces and a skylighted studio where my mother painted. A spiral staircase led up to my parents' bedroom. It was steep with huge gaps, making it impossible for me to access their room, but I didn't live there anyway. Nanny and I lived in a small apartment next to theirs. I spent my days with Nanny. She took me to the Jardin du Luxembourg, where she'd watch me ride the carousel. We pushed wooden boats across the pond in the center of the park and named the ducks that swam there. We watched the old men smoke cigars and play boules, listening to the tock of the metal balls and their rough laughter. She brought me to La Coupole, where I sat at the bar, my legs swinging, and pulled cold, booger-like snails out of their tiny black helixed homes with a pin and ate them. One day, my father brought home a crab as big as my head and put it in our bathtub as a joke. I was terrified of crabs and wet my pants because I refused to pee next to that monster that waved its claws and made skittering noises as it tried to escape.

While Nanny and I went about our routines, in our little apartment, with our little delights and disappointments, my father and mother tried to exist together. My father watched her paint and direct her assistants to build a giant replica of a house, cut it in half, and then put it back together again. He was in awe of her. It was entirely her world, he'd later say, occasionally visited by him and me. Everything she did, she did alone. He watched her neutralize everything with work—her feelings, her environment, her moods. My father, busy playing speed chess and doing cocaine, would disappear for days, returning home irritable and wired. He wrote, produced, and directed a film about a German pianist addicted to cocaine and gambling and married to a successful architect. In the movie, called *Fool's Mate*, the wife, named "Alice," kicks him out to protect their daughter, "Isabelle" (my middle name), and he confesses to a murder he didn't commit to get out of his debts. He told me later he made the movie so the ending wouldn't happen in real life, a creative prophylaxis, bending life into art to bend life. I played his daughter, Nanny played the nanny, and in the role of the main character's mistress my father cast the woman he had been having an affair with. My mother designed the costumes, which meant she had to dress the woman my father was fucking. When my mother found out, they sat at Le Select, the bar around the corner from the apartment, and weighed their options. My mother decided they should stay together and never mention it again.

3.

We moved to New York City and into 134 Charles Street in September 1990, when I was five years old. My father spent his days writing screenplays and playing chess in Washington Square Park, making friends with his opponents—the drunks, hustlers, and unhoused who spent most of their lives curled up on the benches or hunched over the concrete chess tables. My mother's crowd found him very cute, and her friends joked that she had married him because he was so photogenic.

My mother started therapy with Dr. Viola Bernard. She drank too much, had relationship problems, and had a troubling memory about walking in on her father fucking a family friend. Under Dr. Bernard's care—intense psychotherapy sessions and hypnosis—my mother began to be flooded with what Dr. Bernard told her were repressed memories, horrific scenes of ritualized abuse and murder of children at the hands of a couple, Bertie and Russell, who were family friends from her youth. Dr. Bernard encouraged her to "remember," disclose as much as she could, and write about it in journals. My mother, haunted, hunted for clues in her past. She hired a private detective who couldn't find anything. She tracked down Bertie and Russell's phone number and confronted them over the phone. She was convinced that her parents had been complicit and confronted her mother, Joanne, who told her it was all nonsense. She believed her younger sibling, Jessica, had been raped by Bertie and Russell as an infant. She asked Jessica, a trans woman, if her gender dysphoria could have been a result of the abuse she believed they had both endured. Jessica said no but remembered having sleepovers at Bertie and Russell's and that there was not an extra bed for her, so she had slept in their bed. She also remembered their mother telling her that she could never go over there again. Something could have been happening, but no one could confirm any of my mother's claims. My mother told her friends what she had discovered in therapy. They recalled her matter-of-factly describing child rape and murder in a flat affect as she sipped glass after glass of white wine. When speaking to me years later, my godmother Paula would wonder, "If all these children were going missing, where were the news articles? Where were the missing persons reports?" "How could they have been so well-organized and keep it so secret?" another friend wondered. "It didn't seem possible or plausible. But she really believed it."

I learned my mother's story when I was eleven. I was spying on her for my father. She had filed for divorce when I was six, starting a custody battle that would last six years. When we were all in the middle of it, my father told me to look for a list of witnesses that my mother might call to testify. I looked in her closet and found a journal. I read an entry about my mother giving my father a blow job and that, in the middle of the act, she'd had a "flashback" to being on a boat with Bertie and Russell. Russell had pushed her head under the water as she threw up and he said, "You're feeding the fishes." The sides of my mouth twitched into the inappropriate smile I made when I felt the barbed worm of unease twist around inside me. When my mother came up from the studio to have her lunch, I told her what I had found. We sat in my bedroom, and she told me how a married couple who were friends of her parents had used her in a sex cult. They had raped her and her one-and-a-half-year-old brother. They took them on trips on their boat, where they had orgies with other children. They used the Black children of maids who worked in the neighborhood in ritualized sex games. They murdered a seven-year-old Black boy, who they called "Monkey Boy," through erotic asphyxiation and made my mother bury the body on the beach at night, telling her that if she ever told anyone she would be thrown into prison for life.

She told me this story in a very straightforward way and then went off to take her nap. She told me the story as if I already knew it, as if we'd been through all of this already, and I sat and listened as if it were one of my audiobooks. She didn't tell me how she felt about any of it or ask how I might feel about it. She didn't cry and her voice didn't strain against any feelings I could discern. I sat and stared at her, thrilled that she was sitting in my room talking to me. She told me that the series she had painted called "Earth Paintings"—some of which were hanging in our house—was about the abuse. My mother left me in my room thinking about my father getting a blow job and how to spell erotic asphyxiation.

I stood in front of one of the paintings. My mother had done several versions of each image—in oils on a large canvas, on a medium canvas, in gouache on paper, in pastels, in ink, until there were 108 of them. Over and over and over, she painted and drew and smeared and shaped and formed and brought to life these memories that had been brought to life inside of her. For days and weeks and months, she dragged her terrors into the world for everyone to see and froze them there forever. Maybe she was frozen in them too. I stared at the painting showing "Monkey Boy" being buried on the beach. I was suddenly able to see into my mother's mind. I could be there with her on the beach, being forced to bury a body. I could be her. I stood in front of that painting and imagined all the feelings she must have felt. I understood the power of not feeling, too. Of being able to tell your story with paint or with words and then just going to sleep.

I WOULD LATER LEARN that my mother was most likely a victim of the Satanic Panic, a moral hysteria that swept the nation in the '80s and '90s. Unsubstantiated claims of children being used in Satanic rituals involving sex and murder were leveled against daycare workers and parents. Patients in psychotherapy were persuaded by overzealous clinicians that they had repressed memories of unspeakable abuse involving incest, pedophilia, and murder, and needed to uncover them. The science of recovered memory therapy would be debunked but the damage remained—families torn apart by accusations, patients tormented by the continued belief in these persuasive inventions or the awareness of their fiction. My mother's memories were likely false, just stories. But "just stories" were powerful. Just stories led her far, far away from people, and killed off something inside her.

My father was negotiating his own indoctrination. For ten years, as the protégé of French philosopher Gilles Deleuze, he had been involved in the most anthropologically anarchistic, mind-boggling philosophical theories he had ever encountered in his life. It was not only a philosophy, he would explain, it was a militant activist movement to change the world based on a theory of desire. The only thing that existed was the constant production of desire, which was overflowing, and state and capitalism and laws were all ways to tame it and put it into oppressive structures. Deleuze and his students believed they were radical revolutionaries. In 1977, a group of influential French intellectuals penned an open letter to French Parliament calling for the decriminalization of sex between adults and minors. Among them was Gilles Deleuze. An excerpt from my father's journals, written when I was three, captured the type of thinking the movement fostered: *There is a possibility of a non-abusive, not traumatizing sexuality between children and grown-ups. Nakedness and tenderness and relaxation with the body of the other person is possible. My daughter does not excite me. I think the fear of the people who make the rules is that their own repressed desires could come up, which makes them see that area as an inappropriate field between a child and an adult. Maybe it's their way of keeping their own incestuous desires in check.* My father's flirtation with this ideology would soon encounter the full force of the American puritanism he reviled, and his attempts, in the face of this convergence, to shore up his identity with these theories would leave me ever more confused and abstracted.

My mother, in the care of Dr. Bernard, saw transgression everywhere. She became terrified of my father's behavior around me. One night, drunk, she came into my room and saw my father in bed with me under a blanket, reading me a book. Screaming, she ripped the blanket off and hauled him out of the room. The next day she banished him downstairs, to the small first-floor room between the office and the studios. The next night, I woke up and sneaked down the stairs to visit my father. I stood under the glowing exit sign, a remnant from when the building was a warehouse, which hung above the large steel door that separated upstairs from downstairs. The house was always kept very cold and I was chilly in my nightgown. I felt for the doorknob in the dark. The frigidness felt magical, the frosty bite on my palm marking the breaching of another world. I held my breath and turned the knob. As if my hand had exerted some powerful sorcery, alarms began screeching all through the house, convulsing the cold air around me. I felt the screaming in my body, the noise grabbing me by the arms and shaking me, trying to tell me something I wasn't listening to. I stood at the threshold of my mother's and father's worlds, a limen loaded with alarms, and shook with fear and confusion.

A few months later, my mother began the divorce proceedings that would last six years. Those years would be crowded with lawyers and witnesses and judges and forensic psychologists. My mother told me nothing about the trial. My father told me everything—what he was accused of, how everyone was out to get us, what to say to the judge. I stared at the stenographer in the judge's chambers while I recited what my father had told me, her face wooden, the chittering of her machine seeming to emanate from inside her, like she was a wind-up toy. I would keep the judge's decree in a manila envelope for decades, and it grew yellow and faded as I read it over and over, trying to figure out what was true.

My mother's lawyers charged my father with "a variety of inappropriate conduct," which included: climbing into my crib at night, lying on the sofa with his hand in my underpants, taking me swimming in the ocean beyond my depth and without a life jacket, putting me on a horse without a helmet, giving me a cartoon book with "inappropriate" images like "a man masturbating, a woman engaged in a series of salacious movements," keeping porn in his room, kissing me on the lips when we said goodbye, feeding me with his fingers as if I were an infant, exchanging chewing gum mouth to mouth, taking my underwear with him when he traveled, showing me films he had been in that were inappropriate for a young child, giving me knives and cigarette lighters as gifts, letting me, at seven, give him subcutaneous injections for a medical condition he had, and leaving me alone on Manhattan street corners while he went to buy cigarettes and a newspaper. Some of the charges I remembered and some I didn't. I remembered all the times—when I was five, six, and seven—when I stood awkwardly with a stranger who had been dispatched with my care while my father made a phone call or strode into a deli. I remembered that little gummy nugget being pushed into my mouth by his tongue, receiving it slick from his saliva, bursting with our liquids as I started to chew. I remembered bending over his stomach, sliding a needle into his flesh, holding my breath as I slowly depressed the syringe and injected him, the bruises that rose to the surface the next day. I remembered watching him pack the little square of my underwear printed with the days of the week or cat faces into his suitcase. I did not remember his hands down my pants. "No charges of sexual abuse were made," read the documents, but people started to view my father with suspicion, and reprobation and rumors clung like barnacles to our lives. A story began to circulate that my father had said that a daughter's first sexual experience should be with her father. According to my father, he had been at a dinner party speaking to an anthropologist friend of his who was telling him about an academic paper that described mothers in Japan giving blow jobs to their sons before exams. My father jokingly exclaimed, "Incest is best," which Nanny overheard and told my mother. From father to Nanny to mother to family friends, this story reached me as the edict "A daughter's first sexual experience should be with her father." It was something I would have lodged in my head for decades. My father fought the allegations. Some of them were misunderstandings or overreactions, and some were intentional exaggerations and fabrications by lawyers. The porn magazines that had been found by the housekeeper and reported to my mother were brought into court. The judge went through each one, concluding at the end of his inspection that since they were all images of middle-aged women (my father had a penchant for older ladies) they were okay but should not have been kept in the house. A forensic psychologist had to phone a colleague in Europe to confirm that Europeans did in fact kiss on the lips and sometimes took baths with their kids. But my father was coming apart under the constant scrutiny and condemnation.

My visits with my father—to the apartment he had rented nearby or to Europe every alternating vacation and half of every summer—were monitored by court-appointed supervisors. Nanny was the first court-appointed supervisor. Then came my babysitter Pem, who looked after me on Nanny's days off. Then came Pem's cousin. Then my mother's nineteen-year-old studio assistant whom no one knew very well. Then my third-grade assistant teacher who was allergic to all fruits and vegetables and who screamed at me for making faces when I was tonguing a loose tooth. The supervisors were the embodiment of that alarm system between my mother and father's worlds—constant reminders that we were not a normal family, that there was something wrong.

I didn't think anything was wrong with my father or how we were together. When he was with me, he told me stories all the time—stories he made up, stories from the books he was reading, stories from Greek mythology, stories from philosophy, stories from psychology, stories from history (of art, architecture, humankind). He seemed to know everything and wanted to share it with me. He played games with me constantly, something my mother refused to do because she was, according to her, "too competitive." He challenged me to come up with words in different languages with as many meanings as possible, to solve riddles, to say a sentence with the emphasis each time on a different word to change the meaning. He tipped matchsticks onto the table and told me to make a house by moving only one matchstick. He wanted to know everything about everyone, and I watched him ask strangers who lit his cigarette about their childhood, invite cab drivers and waiters to dinner, drill into the world and soak himself, and me, with what came rushing out. Along with his games and stories, my father told me everything about the trial. He told me often about American prudishness and my mother projecting her past onto him. I watched his face scrunch and slacken as he told me all the ways he was being accused and attacked, his features like an EKG, recording the electrical impulses of distortion that formed the rhythm of our lives. His eyes would fill with tears as he lit another cigarette and ran his thumb over his fingers. My mother told me nothing, asked me no questions.

My allegiance was to my father. I would follow my mother around the house as she poured her coffee or wine, as she worked in the garden, as she looked for a book in the library, and bombard her with questions and accusations. "Why do you hate Dad? Why do you want to take me away from him? Fuck your American prudishness," I'd say to her back.

"It's complicated," she'd say. "You sound like your father."

"Good," I'd say. I didn't understand that she was terrified, afraid to do the wrong thing, say the wrong thing, touch me the wrong way. So she just didn't. She withdrew into the places over which she had mastery, exiling herself to the worlds she reigned over with confidence—her studio and her bedroom. Downstairs in her studio, if she made a mistake she could just paint over it. And upstairs there was no such thing as a wrong book read or a wrong cigarette smoked. But her child was an entirely different medium; her child was a photogram—the interplay of object, light, and time resulting in an irreversible exposure. The things she believed had been done to her had marked her irrevocably, and she was sure that she would somehow, through proximity, mar me as permanently.

As the custody case continued, as I was brought to forensic psychologists and met with the judge, and had it all explained to me by my father, I became desperate. When I was seven, and my mother and I were visiting family friends at their house in Connecticut; I started shouting at her in their kitchen, telling her all the ways she was destroying my father's and my life. She stood, arms at her sides, helpless. Interpreting her helplessness as indifference, I grabbed a knife from the knife block on the kitchen counter. "If you don't let me have more time with Dad I'll kill myself," I screamed. She moved toward me, trying to take the knife away. I ran. I ran through the opulent rooms, the cream carpets so thick they muted the sounds of our movements, threatening to stab myself as my mother's friends looked on. My mother ran after me, begging me to put the knife down. Finally, she was pursuing me. And all it took was a knife held against my body.

Over my father's objections, I was sent to be observed by forensic psychologists who watched me play with anatomically correct dolls, took notes, and then wrote up reports about me. I was sent to a child psychologist for treatment. After my first session with Dr. Shore, I told my mother and father that the doctor had hit me. My father was furious. My mother didn't believe me and bribed me with an electric toothbrush to go back. I went back. And since I was back, I figured nothing bad had really happened, maybe nothing had happened, because I wouldn't be back there if it had. I was learning to doubt myself. The unbelievable story of being hit by my child psychologist felt so real—I could recall his arm whizzing through the air, the full dimensions of my smallness as he towered over me—but there would always be a part of me that wondered if I had fabricated the memory from the raw material of my father's recalcitrance. I had no idea what was true.

My father kept journals where he wrote down everything that happened every day. During disagreements with me he would take one out, flip to a page, and read out loud what had really happened. "No, you did not ask me to watch a movie in the afternoon," he would say, holding the pages open and gesturing to that day's entry. I'd squint my eyes and try to decipher his writing, which was sometimes in German, sometimes in English, sometimes in French. I'd search for the words to match the version of reality I had in my head and, not finding them, I'd doubt myself.

Nanny also kept journals about everything that happened when I was with my father. Her journals told the story of a seven-year-old who stayed up until midnight, drank beer, never took a bath (*not for a week straight*), and was at the mercy of her father's erratic moods and mercurial family. *I wish I could tell M what a blank blank human he is*, she wrote. *I have never disliked someone so much or had such little regard for them. Yet I have to deal with him. In my heart I am glad he is hurt because he has so little thought for anyone else, from his mother to the people he works with, unless it's to his advantage. Poor Alice. I can see her getting hurt and so cross. It is frightful to think one person can make life so difficult for so many people, yet we do nothing. That is the worst part for me. The fact M gets away with it. Such ego. I am so angry I cannot sleep.* Everyone told a different version of what happened, what I needed, and who I was. Everyone seemed like a credible narrator, but how could so many things be true at the same time? I was at the center of so many stories, piles of documents that would only grow larger—notebooks and court judgments and psychiatric files and eventually even a psychological case study—that claimed to tell me who I was, but in whose pages I disappeared.

There were moments that threatened my allegiance to my father. My mother took me to Japan when I was seven. She had been commissioned by the Homan-ji Temple, in Chōshi-shi, Japan, to design and paint their ceiling, and she brought me with her for the unveiling. I accompanied her everywhere she went, she in her blue and white yukata—a cotton summer kimono—and me in my white one with red cranes on it. We sat next to each other at the elaborate breakfasts the hotel served every morning—low tables piled with endless kinds of fish, raw and roasted whole, blue and white china, black lacquered bowls holding soup, large, rough-hewn bowls that looked like a giant had scooped them straight out of black rock. She took me to a hot spring near a famous noodle shop. We sat in the steaming water as people threw leftover noodles into the adjacent stream, the white squiggles of noodle a pop-art augmentation of the current's ripples. We got lost in a forest together before eventually emerging onto a mountain road and hitchhiking back to the hotel. I watched her closely as she navigated this foreign world with confidence, as she invited me to explore it with her. Far away from the site of our turmoil, in a place neither of us had ever been, wearing matching clothes, it was as if I were seeing her for the first time. Then my father arrived. His lawyer had called him and told him that my mother couldn't just unilaterally make decisions for me and my father should respond, so he bought a ticket and followed us to Japan. The monks had prepared a special ceremony for my mother, and my father insisted on being there. The monks chanted and scattered leaf-shaped pieces of thick paper painted in gold as we knelt on the floor. I watched my mother move through the ceremony. She knew when to bow and when to smile, when to speak and when to be quiet. I had never seen her follow rules and pay attention to the other people around her. There was a stillness and an ease in her that amazed and perplexed me as I watched her accept a string of carved prayer beads from a monk. She seemed content and competent, and I felt myself admiring her. Then something hit my leg. My father had started rolling Mentos across the floor to me while the monks chanted. We were kneeling in a line so he had to bend forward and roll the candy past my mother and her esteemed guests. I was very embarrassed. My insides seized every time I saw those fat white discs spinning toward me. I didn't want people to think that I condoned this game or that I was bored, but I was afraid that my father would be even more disruptive if I didn't try to catch the mints. I let them come to rest in the crescent of my palm, putting them in a little pile, each time hoping it would be the last. I could see the glances, near-bursting with acid disapproval, that my mother and the other guests were directing at my father. I felt very old and tired, as if my father were my ungovernable child. In that moment, I wanted to follow the rules. I wanted to separate myself from him, make it clear that his desires were not mine.

My father had rented an apartment near 134 Charles Street so he could be with me when he was in the United States. He got me a black hooded rat to keep at his place. The white spots reminded me of the reflection of clouds in water, so I named it Claude after Monet. We thought it was a fat male but Claude turned out to be a pregnant female and soon we had nine rats. I would put a rat in my sleeve and let it crawl up my arm, around my shoulders, and back out through my other sleeve. Nanny was alarmed when she watched me change clothes and saw bright red rat scratches all over my torso. One day, I was sitting on the sofa watching TV in my father's apartment with my rats crawling all around me. My father came and sat down. We watched some TV. I decided to put the rats back into their cage. I could only find eight of them. Edgar, named after Degas, wasn't there. I crowbarred my father off the sofa and yanked up the pillow he had been sitting on. Edgar lay on the sofa. He did not move. He had his mouth open, not wide, not like he was screaming, but like he was trying to interrupt someone who wouldn't stop talking. I screamed and started crying. I scooped Edgar off the sofa and he lay in my hand—he fit perfectly in my palm. He was warm—not just alive-warm, but over-warm from the weight of the pillow and of my father. I wept.

My father, not wanting to tell me my pet was dead, took Edgar from my hand and told me he would be fine. He held Edgar in his left palm and with his right pointer finger began massaging Edgar's chest. He said he could get Edgar's heart to start beating again by forcing the blood through it. I watched. Edgar did not move. My father told me now all we needed to do was put him in the freezer and he'd be fine in a few hours. He took Edgar into the kitchen, wrapped him in tinfoil, and put him in the freezer, next to the Pop-Tarts. I had never had a Pop-Tart before; my mother didn't let me eat food like that, but my father did and I knew it was what normal kids ate. We waited on the sofa for Edgar to come back to life.

A few hours later, I reached into the freezer, took Edgar out, carefully placed him on the counter, and slowly unwrapped him. Edgar did not move. He was frozen. I started crying. My father said now we just had to put Edgar on the heater and he would be alive again. He threw away the tin foil and wrapped Edgar in a clean towel and put him on the heater. We sat on the sofa and waited for Edgar to come back to life.

Later that night, I unwrapped Edgar and held him in my hands. He felt very warm, very alive. I knew that it had worked. He wasn't moving yet but I knew that he would. I put him in my pocket and could feel his warmth against my leg. I carried him around in my pocket, waiting.

Edgar did not come back to life. Over the course of that day, my father had scrubbed at the boundaries between life and death, between his power and the rules of existence, until the only things left were the force of my yearning and a warm rat carcass.

The adults around me, I would later learn, were bracing themselves for how I would turn out. My mother's staff would whisper predictions to one another. I was a hyper-talkative kid and had inherited my mother's loud voice, her stubborn will, and her need to occupy to capacity any room she was in. When words failed me, head swimming and heart pounding, I threw powerful tantrums, stomach on floor, limbs flailing. If my underwear creased under my tights, or my socks folded in my shoes, or the bows on my dresses were not tied breathlessly tight, I wept and screamed. Starting at seven years old I said that the only feelings I could feel were "guilt, regret, and nervous excitement." I didn't know the word "anxiety" so I called it "nervous excitement." My anxiety left me painfully indecisive. Every morning before school, my mother and I picked out my outfit for the day. I'd stand in my room, sweater sets and wool slacks, jeans and a flannel shirt spread out around me, struggling for air as I held a cardigan up to my body, weeping until I was an hour and a half late for school. Every day after school, at the corner deli, I'd hunch over the freezer and stare despairingly down at the frost-flecked Sundae Crunch Bars, the patriotic-hued Rocket Pops, the sophisticated mini-tubs of Häagen-Dazs, the frigid blast of air making my tears sting. I could not choose. I invented rituals and rules to feel like I had some control over my "nervous excitement" and my life. I'd gather my stuffed animals and pretend to remove stones from their stomachs, lining them up along the windowsills of my room in various stages of recovery after I had removed from them that hard lump of nervous excitement that I felt in my own gut. I hated going to bed. In order to calm down enough for sleep, I organized my stuffed animals in an arc around me. There were strict rules governing their arrangement, and every time one tipped over, I had to get up—disrupting and collapsing the entire structure—to make it inviolable again. Sometimes I had to do it many times a night, but it had to be done. Many nights, I wet my bed.

Nanny was with me all the time. My parents had hired her three months before I was born because of her "straightforwardness" and her ability to handle "unconventional problems." She was the one who tried to console me when the bows on my dresses weren't tight enough, when my socks or underwear bunched, when I was confronted with a decision. Despite her dyslexia, she read to me at night. She sat with me while I did my homework because I couldn't concentrate when I was on my own. She had her sister, Thelma, send me audiobooks from England: *The Peppermint Pig*, *The Animals of Farthing Wood*, *The Wolves of Willoughby Chase*. The narrators had the same accent as Nanny, and I sometimes felt like they were all related, that this was my family. Nanny was family but she was also not family. Sometimes I felt that division imposed by my family, and sometimes I felt it coming from her. Every Christmas, while we opened presents, Nanny would spend the morning cleaning the kitchen. That wasn't her job, and it didn't need to be done, but she did it. I would run from tree to sink, tugging at her apron, trying to get her to come and be with us. But she refused. Each time I ran back and forth it felt like I was trying to sew us together. She told me later that she had always wanted to do more, to protect me better, but she had been afraid. She was scared she would be fired and then there would be no one to protect me.

As Nanny witnessed, my mother worked in her studio and my father worked overseas. When he was away he sent me faxes—from the Lalitha Mahal Palace Hotel in Mysore, India, Gran Hotel Havana in Barcelona, the Hilton Luxembourg, the Vollererhof Kurhotel near

Salzburg—telling me everything he did and everything he saw, with drawings of creatures doing human things: an elephant on roller skates, a pig learning vowels sitting on a tortoise, a stork carrying a postcard, a rat with a paintbrush. He told me all about the movie or play or TV show he was in and the screenplays he was working on, that he looked forward to talking to me about movies and poetry and his screenplays because I was "so sharp and good with characters and plot." He wrote: *How I love your name, Alice, Alice, like a door to another, new world. You have helped me understand the world a little better. The world has become more beautiful because of you.* He was with me even when he couldn't be, and he made me feel seen and wanted in a way my mother didn't. I was a door to another, new world that only we inhabited. When he returned, it felt like all the pieces of me would rattle apart from the momentum of my excitement. I stared out the window and waited for him, trying to picture him first in the airplane, then in the taxi, then walking down the street. From the library windows of 134 Charles Street, I scanned the street below for his waves of white hair to come floating into view and hover below me as he rang the doorbell.

One evening, when I was seven and it was time for his visit to end, we stood in the foyer of 134 Charles Street saying goodbye. My father stood over me and looked down at me. His white hair made him look like one of those deep-sea jellyfish that possess the ability to glow, to make themselves alive with light in the pitch-black depths. He was crying and the tears and the fading light smeared his features into a disarray of shadow and pain. He stood over me and said, "Lick the tears from my eyes."

I hesitated. A low, humming current started to run through me, little flutters that left me queasy. It felt important, what was being asked of me. It felt strange but I trusted it was necessary. I stuck out my tongue and stood on my tiptoes. His skin was so thin and I could feel it crimp as I applied pressure with my tongue and dragged it up, following the path of his tears to their source. I smelled the stale cigarette smoke in his hair. I stopped when I felt the soft, flat triangle that meant I had reached the outskirts of his eyeball. I didn't want to hurt his eye so I withdrew my tongue. I had taken something of my father's into me, something intimate—his liquids and his lonely need. In the foyer, between the two sets of steel doors that kept the outside out and the inside in, the boundaries were blurring, smudged into confusion by a salty little tear. My father smiled through his tears, told me he loved me, and left. I stood alone in the foyer, tasting salt.

4.

I spent every alternating vacation and half of each summer with my father in Europe, accompanied by a court-appointed supervisor—first Nanny, then the revolving door of random chaperones, then my father's steady girlfriend. My father and I traveled to many places; film shoots took him all over the world. In Tunisia, when I was twelve, he told me stories about the Tuareg and the Berber people as we rode on camelback through the Sahara. We walked along the beach and ate the bright orange sex organs of the sea urchin, which young men sold out of plastic crates for one dinar. They cut the creature open with a pair of blunt scissors and handed me a spoon and a wedge of lemon. I ate eighteen in a row and felt sick. We drove out into the Sahara and stopped at a shack where an old man served us mint tea with pine nuts in it and, according to my father, offered to sell us his daughter. We walked through the souk and drank more mint tea in rooms piled high with carpets and kilims. In Madrid we bought two kittens off the street, which my father convinced the director to adopt when we left. In a small town outside Berlin, my father bought me a wild boar, which I named Obelix, and which also required rehoming when we left. In St. Tropez I sipped Bellinis and read Agatha Christie novels. In Rome I stood in front of the *Dying Gaul*, wanting to run my fingers across the weeping lip of his marble wound. We lay splayed on the stone floor of the Sistine Chapel and stared up at a white-bearded god who touched his animating forefinger to a muscled mortal, until security guards told us to leave. I'd accompany him on his movie sets or wait backstage at his plays, watching him fall onto a floor lined with blazing candles or sword fight his lover's husband. I was confronted with newness constantly, my only routine the instructions I knew so well—to buckle my seat belt and stow my tray table, or to be quiet when the director yelled "Action!" Traveling with my father was an adventure, but in that adventure was, like degrading dynamite, an explosive instability. He was impatient and had a temper. I'd watch him closely as we stood in line to walk through the metal detectors or waited for our bags at baggage claim, trying to identify the fizz of imminent rage that popped off him like bubbles off soda right before he exploded. He'd throw his bag down or abandon half our luggage and me and storm off. In those moments I felt accountable; I needed to get the situation under control. I would stammer apologies, swiveling back and forth between him and everyone who saw what was happening, drag our suitcases off the baggage carousel, and run after him, humiliation and panic rippling through me.

Each trip to Europe, we'd visit my grandparents, who lived at Weberkoppel 70 in Lübeck. My grandfather, or "Opa," Dr. Bern Carrière, was a handsome, clinically depressed psychiatrist whose mother, according to my father, had had one of the first "successful" lobotomies in Germany. Opa smoked a pipe and brought the dictionary to the dinner table. He played solitaire and saw his patients, some from a local jail, in his office in the house. My grandmother, or "Oma," Jutta Mühling Carrière, was a self-proclaimed "radical" with a passion for literature, politics, and conflict, who had, as my father described it, "a Jekyll and Hyde personality" marked by a foundational rage I was too little to recognize. I never fully understood the depths of her wrath until I heard about a letter my father had discovered. It was written by Oma in 1968, addressed to my father and his younger sister, Mareike. There was one word that my father couldn't make out: "If at the time the ___________ had existed this whole horror wouldn't have happened." Mareike deciphered the word. It was *pill*. If the birth control pill had existed, she would never have gotten pregnant with my father, she would never have married Bern, and she would have been a free woman. But that was not what had happened.

My father was born in Hannover, Germany in 1950. He spent the first ten years of his life in mental institutions, where his father worked and where doctors and patients lived together. The patients had jobs, which included looking after the doctors' children. Frau Feit, who only had one tooth, had been committed after she had tried to burn her two children alive in a psychotic episode. When Till, my father's one-and-a-half-year-old brother, was left in her care, she would sit by the window, with newspaper spread at her feet, and hold him naked over the pages as he shit and pissed. After six hours, she would fold the newspaper and throw it away. My father's babysitter was named Herr Lachs—Mr. Salmon. Herr Lachs had a hole in his forehead—an old war wound—which he could put a ping-pong ball into. He would put my father in the basket on the front of his bicycle and ride through the village. Children would run after them, taunting Herr Lachs with a chant made mean only by the repetition of his strange name, and Herr Lachs would take out his knife and throw it at them. When Oma asked if Herr Lachs would throw a knife at Mathieu if he teased him about his name, Herr Lachs said, "No, Frau Jutta. He reminds me too much of my corporal." Their other babysitter was a man who said that God was transforming him into a woman so He could have a child with him. He took my father downstairs to the coal cellar and fondled him. My father couldn't tell who was sick and who was sane; he just knew if they were nice to him or not. After spending his early years living side by side with mental patients, nothing in human nature would ever be strange to him.

The family later moved to Lübeck and into Weberkoppel 70, which became its own holding cell for damaged people slipping in and out of fantasy, denial, love, and rage. Jutta chased her children—Mathieu, Till, and now a daughter, Mareike—around the garden, hitting them with a carpet beater until they were bloody. My father, the eldest, tried to protect his younger siblings. Forced to accept the authority of his violent mother, he would fight against authority of any kind for the rest of his life.

Bern suffered his entire life from depression, which he treated himself, and when my father heard Bach coming from his closed office, he knew his father was having one of his episodes and that he'd soon have to talk him down from suicide.

"But I love you," my father said to his father, who hung limply in the doorway of his office, the air itching with violins.

"I hate you," my father screamed into his mother's face, thrusting out his ten-year-old chest as his little sister hid under the table and his little brother balled himself up in the corner, their hands clamped over the fresh burns from Jutta's hot iron.

By the time I was born, Weberkoppel 70 was a house of old things—old food, old people, old ghosts—revivified by smells: Nivea Creme on Oma's face, smoke from Opa's pipe, mildew in the kitchen, mold on the cheese, rotting compost and swan shit in the garden. That spiky bouquet—sprays of despair and hard buds of anger—released its fragrance as we moved among one another, among the things of Weberkoppel 70. These things were different from the things in 134 Charles Street. These things were crammed with feeling, brimming with the traces of people—whether dead or leftover from death. Each artifact oozed an essence that kept us in a chronic state of remembering that could sometimes replace living. At one end of the living room, across from her doll collection, Oma had built a shrine to her dead son. On December 19, 1979, when Till was twenty-six, Opa, Oma, and Mareike went to Oma's father's birthday party in a town two hours away. Till stayed behind. He had long suffered from mental illness marked by mood swings and psychosis, and that night, took the phone off the hook and made a cocktail of LSD, which he had with him, and sleeping pills, which he took from the chest of medicines that Opa had in his office. He wrote a note that said: "Here is the money I owe you. Thank you for lending it to me," and slipped seventy Deutsche marks into the envelope. He got hungry and wandered into the kitchen, where he passed out and choked on his own vomit. When the family returned and saw him lying there, blue and dead, Oma grabbed a knife from the kitchen counter and cut his throat, trying to get the vomit out. She would never forgive Opa for making her be the one to slit her son's throat, for giving up on their death-blue son. Mareike called my father, who was in Berlin, and he jumped in the car and drove as fast as he could. When he arrived, Opa was silent in his office, not moving, not talking. Oma was in a fury that never went away. Later, as they drove to the morgue, Oma screamed at Opa that he was driving too slowly. As if there were still time, as if the power of her mind and need could reanimate her son.

After Till's death, Oma commissioned one of my grandfather's psychiatric patients to make a doll that was an exact replica of five-year-old Till. This doll sat at the center of the shrine, below a large oil painting she had also commissioned of Till the year he died. Oma's kitchen, the place where Till died, was also a shrine to him. It was organized but famously filthy, as if the accumulation of all that had happened in that kitchen, the rage and sadness, like the grease and grit, could never be washed away. My head level with the counter, I could see the contours of sticky residue, rust like dried blood on the curves of the dish rack, the ring of scuzz in the sink, the cobwebs in the corners of the window. No one was allowed to use the kitchen except Oma. She screamed at anyone who rinsed a dish or changed out an old sponge for a new one. Till had lived in the attic, and Oma had also kept that room exactly as it was the night he died. His pipe lay on its side still full of half-smoked tobacco. His bed was not made and his pillow still had an indent in it.

Every Christmas I was there, we visited Till's grave. Oma brought buckets and brushes to clean the gravestone and candles and flowers to lay on it. No one touched. No one spoke. Oma filled the silence with the slurping sound she made whenever she exerted herself—a grating inhale followed by a wet hissing that puffed her cheeks out. She must have made that noise when she was chasing her children around the garden, when she beat and burned them. She must have made that noise when the inexperienced doctor ripped the head off her about-to-be-born baby as it was sliding out of her, another dead child. That disgusting and scary sound pinned me down and jammed my face into the tender, rotting center of all her heartbreak.

Underneath Till's attic reliquary was where I slept—in my aunt Mareike's old room, which had also been kept exactly as she had left it, half-used lipsticks and her stash of '70s *Penthouse* magazines still in her closet. The ceiling, covered in '60s-style wallpaper with giant swirls of color like the inside of a lava lamp, slanted so steeply that I could wedge my body between the ceiling and the bed, my nose squished by the ceiling-wall. On the slanting walls hung black-and-white posters of the famous mime, Marcel Marceau, his face painted white, his mouth a slash of black, too narrow for words. He terrified me and sent me looking for Nanny at night. Oma made Nanny sleep in the basement. In the journals Nanny kept, she described the sleeping arrangement: *I feel as if I have been completely neutralized as an observer in one very clever move by Mathieu and Jutta. My bedroom is about as far away from Alice and Mathieu as possible—downstairs in the cellar tucked away at the far end of the house. I did not know this room existed. Jutta said Mathieu came up with this idea.* To get to Nanny, I would have to sneak through the house in complete darkness, feeling my way past Opa's room, past Oma's room, down the stairs, through the hallway, to the basement door. I moved slowly. The darkness felt like flesh, an invisible body bear-hugging me, and with each step I tried to pry myself loose. The basement stairs were steep and narrow and my heart thudded as I made my way down. Sometimes I got too scared and froze, too frightened to move forward and too frightened to go back to my creepy room. Eventually I would admit defeat and slip past Oma and Opa and Marcel and back into my bed.

Nanny spent her days in Lübeck witnessing and documenting. She would silently sit at the round dining table in her long wool skirt and collared sweater, salting half a tomato, and observe: *Big argument at the table. Jutta, Mathieu, Bern all in German. Oh how I wish I could tell the lot to get lost. Good grief, four more weeks. What have I done to deserve this? What are Bern's thoughts as a doctor? He is a good one and respected but he sure has trouble with his own family.* The next night she wrote: *Oh what a life! Supper was eaten in silence. It's like walking on eggshells. Everyone has their own ideas as to how Alice is to act. Alice is being good and knows things are tense.*

Oma was often angry. She was angry at my father for not playing with me, for playing with me too much, at me for having eaten a yogurt, for refusing to eat a yogurt, at Nanny for not making the bed, for making the bed wrong, at Opa for talking when she wanted to talk, for not talking when she wanted to talk to him.

The next day Nanny wrote: *God the games people play. Mathieu and Jutta are control freaks. Mathieu is giving Alice such terrible ideas of ways of getting through life. I forgot one gem. Mathieu said to Alice when everyone returned at 6 p.m., "I've been with you six hours, give me a break." This is the kind of thing that makes me want to laugh at this man who pictures himself as such a wonderful father. He is only happy when he is drawing Alice into his world but when she wants to stay there he gets tired. He treats Alice like an adult and the next time like a spoiled brat then expects her to be quiet when he wants to do something. Mathieu kept saying "I know you are jealous" to Alice when at dinner last night he was speaking to a 13-year-old and her mother.*

My father could be very charming, but Nanny was immune. *M is playing the game*, she wrote. *But I still think he is acting. After all he grew up around Drs and knows their games of the mind.* Sometimes, she would be pushed too far. *I ended up having words with Mathieu*, she wrote. *Real words. He said I am the cause of him being ruined. That I am a spy for the court. He said he would tell me why I had ruined him but not in front of his daughter. I said "Why not? You have told her everything else."*

She described my own exchange of words with my father: *Alice is really getting angry with Mathieu and telling him why he does not protect her like a father should.* Finally, she reached a breaking point: *They are all such egos!!! I feel so degraded. How does one deal with it? As I look at them I see a bunch of egotistic, selfish, dirty muddle lot.* She could witness, but she could not intervene. She saw herself in a war, a constant battle she had to fight alone, for me. *I will be surprised if I can keep quiet much longer*, she wrote. *I keep being corrected in what I say and do. Talk about undermining a person. I keep thinking of being a POW and that I am stronger than my captors and after all in just over 3 weeks I will be free to fight another day on my ground.*

She was fiercely protective of me. The pen nearly broke through the notebook paper when she wrote: *ALICE MUST NOT BE MADE RESPONSIBLE FOR HER FATHER'S ACTIONS.* She defended me against Oma's accusations that I was spoiled. Nanny understood me and saw how my pain was often misunderstood as petulance. *Alice gave me her hand as if to make me know I am there for her*, she wrote. *Alice came to me and gave me a big hug while we were sweeping in the garden.*

Nanny was dyslexic and didn't like to write, but she was diligent about writing in her tiny, palm-sized notebooks. There was an urgency to her chronicle, as if words were the only way she knew to put up a fight. When I discovered her journals almost thirty years later, I would recognize that urgency, how things only became real when they were turned into language, how that language was often the only thing left when that reality fell apart.

FOR ALL THE CHAOS, there were things I loved about being in Lübeck. Weberkoppel 70 had its own special rules and rhythms. The day began with a breakfast of Müsli. I'd spend the morning running through the garden, swimming naked in the lake, or reading in the hammock. The big meal of the day was lunch. Oma would make potato pancakes with sour cream and apple sauce made from the apples that grew in the garden, which I helped her pick. She had a collection of plates with scenes painted on them: a farmer in a field, a woman stepping out of a wagon. I stood at the table picking each one up and examining it, trying to decide which would be mine for the meal. In the afternoon, I'd sit with Opa in his office, adorned with his spicy pipe smoke, and play solitaire or read Asterix and Obelix comics. For our supper, Oma scraped the mold off blocks of cheese and put them on a lazy Susan along with sliced tomatoes, a tube of liverwurst, a tub of quark, a tub of schmaltz, a tub of margarine, and some hard-boiled eggs. I liked to squeeze the liverwurst out onto a hot piece of toast and wait for the deep, rich aroma of the liver, activated by the heat, to hit my nose. Sometimes she made Rote Grütze for dessert, a kind of gelatinous cherry pudding, bright red with the consistency of mucus. I poured thick vanilla cream on top. Oma was proud of her cooking and proud that even her little American granddaughter asked for second helpings. Sometimes she treated me to Labskaus—the sailor's fare that was a hash of beets, beef, and potato, served with rolled herring—and laughed and patted my arm as I shoveled it into my mouth. As a concession to my Americanness, Oma kept a box of Corn Flakes in the cupboard. She offered it to me once, at the beginning of every trip, and reveled in my refusal as I reached instead for the Müsli. She kept the same box of Corn Flakes for twenty years. The day would end with Oma playing dice and drinking Schnapps as I sat next to her on a dirty beanbag watching *Mr. Bean*, which she had recorded for me on VHS.

The house had a sprawling garden that led down to Lake Wakenitz. In the winters, I'd walk on the lake's frozen crust. My grandparents' dogs would pull me on a sled so fast I could barely open my eyes for the cold wind. Neighbors set up tables on the ice and ladled hot wine with apple and cinnamon into cups. In the summer, I'd ride my bicycle down the country paths, pulling over to rescue slugs that had crept out after it rained. My father and I went frog catching in the ponds and brought them back to the garden so they could eat all the pests. We built a treehouse with a zip line. Every other year on August 14, my birthday, we had a giant bonfire in the garden. Oma spent all year collecting twigs and sticks and limbs and branches, stacking them on a stone circle at the bottom of the garden until the pile towered above me and I got to light it, running around the base, coaxing it into a mountain of flames. We had a big party around the bonfire and Oma made sausages and potato salad and plum cake and invited all the neighbors. We played charades in English and German. The swans, threatening and beautiful, would walk up from the lake into the garden. The party sparked a thrill and an unease inside me. I loved being surrounded by the eager, curious children who appeared every summer in my life as if they had been waiting for me all year. They treated me better than my peers in America. They didn't make fun of me, they were interested in me. They asked me genuine questions, and when I didn't understand a word they used, we'd embark on a collaborative journey to decipher each other. I looked forward to the mystifying moments with these kids, when we hunted for the right words. Each year I returned with my German a little better, bringing an offering of more shared words, lexical contributions that, like a bonfire, could blaze into understanding.

In the summers my father and I would take a rowboat out onto the lake and spend the day exploring, swimming, picking up the neighborhood kids, or just rowing back and forth. He would tell me stories—about history, things he made up, about his life. He told me about the poet who went mad and locked himself in a tower. He told me about the royal who bathed in the blood of children to stay young. He told me about the Borgias and Romulus and Remus and Gilles de Rais. I felt happiest when I was listening to my father's stories. One day when I was ten, my father was rowing us across the lake and telling me the story of the book he was reading called *Smilla's Sense of Snow*, and I was trying to figure out how it would end. He rowed us around the lake as I invented endings. After a while I'd exhausted my imagination. I felt good. The sun was hot and I trailed my fingers in the cool water. There was a huge old boat that had been abandoned in the tangled reeds. My father pulled our boat up next to it and we climbed aboard. I spent hours climbing all over it, looking out the windows and piecing together a mysterious history to this deserted vessel—pirates, soldiers, runaway children. As we rowed back, my father said, "I stuck my toe up your mother's cunt."

My mind felt like it was being pried open, hinging wide as the image of my father's toe up my mother's cunt stuffed itself inside me. I wanted to have the right words for this, to respond in a way that proved I was the perfect confidante. I looked at the skin of the lake and pictured all the information shut into it. All the lost rings and dead dogs and secret things done and seen and felt, sealed under the placid surface. My father was now telling me that one of his girlfriends had been "frigid," that she could only orgasm with a shower head, not through sex. It was my responsibility to take in these stories, swirl them around in my brain until a thought or an opinion formed at the edges that I could scrape out and offer as proof that I could think about and understand anything, whether it was a murdered boy or the sexual hang-ups of the people close to me.

"That's interesting," I said. "Then what happened?"

I was the receptacle for my parents' stories. My mother would eventually burn the journals that captured her memories of abuse, as if their physical incineration would wipe away the consequences too. But I would keep those stories alive, in my mind and in my body. Her silence was like a fire, too. A roaring, violent thing that spread through my life as my father's burning wall of information raced toward me from the other side. I tried to do my own documenting, tried to put down into words what I felt before it blew away. In August 1996, when I had just celebrated my eleventh birthday in Lübeck, I wrote in the journal I had gotten as a present from Oma: *Nothing sick happened today.* I never specified what I meant by "sick" or how I felt about it. The next day I wrote: *I guess it's good that nothing sexy happened. Although when I was massaging my Papa's shoulder I felt like more than his daughter, if you know what I mean!* When I discovered that entry twenty years later, I wondered about the exclamation point. Had I been shocked or amused or curious? At eleven, I had already become a dispassionate documentarian of my life.

My father had started letting me know I had "a great ass." I started calling him by his first name. It wasn't a fully thought-out alteration, but I needed to create distance between us, to add delineation to spaces that had none. Replacing "Papa" with his given name felt right, but it also left me feeling unmoored. I was no longer the daughter to his "Papa," I was something else, or I was a little bit of many things.

I had always been *more than* just me. To my mother, I was a symbol, proof that she could create anything she wanted to, against odds, against expectation, against nature. To my father, I was the mother who didn't regret him, the wife who hadn't left him, the collaborator who would never outgrow him.

That same year, my half-sister, Elena, was born. My father had been dating her mother, Bettina, throughout the divorce, and they lived together in my father's Hamburg apartment. After Elena was born, Bettina took over from Nanny as the court-appointed supervisor. With Nanny gone there was no expectation of order or routine, no tether to my mother's world, and I set about trying to situate myself alone in my father's newly reconfigured one. Bettina was a beautiful, big-assed blond with soft skin and a soft voice. She was tender and affectionate, and I liked her. I was excited to have a sister. I'd bounce Elena on my lap as I watched German MTV in the living room. I'd heft her onto my hip and take her for walks in the neighborhood. I fed her her first oyster, played her her first Beatles song. I loved my sister and I loved taking care of her. It also made me feel tied to my father in a way I couldn't articulate. When Elena was six months old, and I was eleven and a half, I picked her up from her crib and held her in my arms. I lifted my shirt as I had seen Bettina do and tried to get Elena to attach to my tiny nipple. She refused. I tried again and again and each time she turned her head away from me. She started to cry. I felt angry that Elena wanted someone other than me, that Bettina could give her something I couldn't.

Bettina was effortlessly maternal most of the time, but she vibrated at a high frequency, and my father was not an easy man to live with. They started having trouble almost immediately, and I would sit them down across from me in the living room and conduct couples therapy, asking them to list their grievances as I sat with my hands clasped, mimicking the therapists I'd been to. My father seemed to love these sessions and took them very seriously. He'd lean forward, nodding at everything I said.

"What are you feeling right now?" I'd ask Bettina, who looked uncomfortable.

I liked being at the center of their relationship, and I felt competent and useful.

The evening following a particularly stressful session, she and my father were having a fight as I sat on my father's lap. I couldn't understand what they were saying because they were speaking very fast and in German, but I could feel him getting angrier and angrier underneath me. I watched Bettina as she talked, then yelled, at him over my head. I felt invisible but I also felt powerful, nestled in between them, at the heart of their discord, observing. I felt lulled by the indecipherable acrimony happening all around me, and then suddenly I was cold and wet. Bettina had thrown a glass of white wine in my face. It was meant for my father, but it had hit me. My father threw me off his lap and screamed at Bettina. I stood to the side, licking drops of pinot grigio off my nose, wondering how I would address this in our next session.

That same summer, my father was on a reality show where *Promis*, the German word for "famous people," helped build houses for charity. He took me to the set. The celebrities mostly posed with power tools, smiling and laughing through their endearing incompetence. My father always wanted to put me in front of the camera. I assumed everyone would be captivated by a non-famous eleven-year-old saying not very exciting things in English on German reality TV. I thought hard about hilarious and clever things I could say. They filmed my father and me sawing something with a giant saw. My little body rocked back and forth and I yelled in German, "Better than sex!" They filmed us hammering some nails into a wall and I shouted, "Better than sex!" They filmed us digging a hole and I sang out, "Better than sex," and winked. In the backyard of the celebrity construction site there was a pit full of mud and water. My father took off his clothes and got in. I took off my clothes, leaving on my kitten-print underpants. We were very hilarious and spontaneous and wild for sitting in this hole of cold muddy water on TV. To break the silence that had settled over us I yelled, "Better than sex!" My father laughed.

5.

I was split between two kinds of lawlessness: there were no rules in my father's house because they didn't apply to us and were meant to be broken anyway; there were no rules in my mother's house because it never occurred to her to make them. Back in New York, I would sit at the butcher block table in the kitchen while Nanny made me breakfast and told me stories. Nanny loved to talk about her past. She was born in 1926 in New Cross, on the outskirts of London. Her family lost all their money when her uncle embezzled from the family business, and they had to move into a small apartment above a shop that sold linoleum and nails. She'd lived through WWII, recalling the sounds of the doodlebugs whirring through the air, and fought off a would-be rapist. Her aunt killed herself right in front of her. ("She asked me for a glass of water and I gave it to her. Then she took all her pills and dropped dead.") Nanny was dyslexic and not as pretty as her sister, and no one had thought she would make anything of herself, but other people's incredulity made her even more determined. She went to governess school, got her certificate, and left

England. By the time she retired, she had lived in Montreal, Telluride, Paris, and New York, had traveled the world and met all sorts of glamorous people.

As she stirred my Cream of Wheat in a pot or heated my clothes up in the oven on cold days, she told me about the families she had worked for. She told me about the Johnsons and how the father left the mother for another man. She told me about her time working for Edward Litchfield, the chancellor of the University of Pittsburgh, and how the entire family, including their two little boys, died in a plane crash over Lake Michigan.

"I was devastated," Nanny said. "But the rest of the family acted like I was irrelevant, like I hadn't loved those boys since they were born."

Nanny walked me to and from St. Luke's School, five minutes away. There were twenty kids in my grade and I tried to fit in with them. JP was my best friend and my first great love. We'd met when we were three at Tadpoles swimming class, would end up going to the same elementary and middle school, the same high school, and I would be the last person with him the night he died from brain cancer at twenty-seven. Everybody liked JP. He was a tap dancing prodigy who studied under Savion Glover. He was kind and funny and had the coolest flattop we'd ever seen with his initials shaved onto the back of his head with a crown on top. I'd go over to his house and we'd watch Michael Jackson videos and eat frozen mint Milanos and coffee ice cream. We'd play *Street Fighter* on his Nintendo and then play it for real out in his hallway. I was very interested in sex, and when we had sleepovers, I'd make JP take off his clothes and I'd lie on top of him.

All the other kids at school made fun of me. They made fun of the continental way I pronounced certain words. They made fun of my strange haircut—short like a boy's, like my mother's. They made fun of how much I raised my hand in English class and my long and rambling comments. They made fun of my outfits. My mother dressed me, and I went to elementary school in wool sweater sets and pearls. They made fun of my school lunches, prepared by our cook, Katy—smoked salmon with crackers, fiddlehead ferns when in season, bouillabaisse. The other kids' lunches were full of all the foods I had seen on TV—humanoid-shaped squeeze bottles filled with fluorescent liquid, cookies shaped like kangaroos that were dipped into icing, fruity drinks with tiny colorful globules floating around in them, soft gummies that exploded with tropical ooze, perfect circles of lunch meat and cubes of cheese in plastic compartments. I bought these snacks at the corner deli after school and forced myself to try them. I hated them and I hated that I had failed to tap into that common joy. I didn't get it. The other kids knew a lot about the popular music of the time. Green Day's *Dookie* had just come out, and everyone had a copy. I bought one and held it in my hands, staring at the colorful album art that reminded me of a Hieronymus Bosch painting I had seen. I forced myself to listen to it over and over, trying to love it. I had not been exposed to much music. My mother didn't listen to music, only audiobooks. From six in the morning until seven at night, my mother listened to audiobooks while she worked. When I walked by the upper studio on my way to school, I heard, over the audiobook I was listening to on my Walkman, Trollope or Dickens booming from Bose speakers. Words surrounded me, pursued me, as if I were a part of them they had lost and needed to reclaim.

I listened to my mother's audiobooks when I worked with her in her studio. She helped me with my creative school projects. I would meet her in her studio and we'd lay out all my supplies. She painted as I hunched over my replica of the Sahara Desert. Little wooden Bedouins crouched around a fire I had created out of tendrils of colorful blown glass my mother had leftover from a piece. We constructed a life-size Egyptian teenager named Nofret, complete with toys and games and a scroll covered in hieroglyphics. We didn't talk, we worked, the words of nineteenth-century novelists filling our heads.

My mother and I were a good team in those moments. I'd have an idea that impressed her, and she'd help me make it come alive. I worked hard on my projects—I loved learning and I was good in school—and my mother seemed to respect that. When we worked side by side, when our focus was trained on turning what was inside of us into something that would exist, beautifully, on the outside, I felt connected to her. Art and invention brought us together, bridged the gap between us.

She took me to Tuscany when I was twelve and we visited a tiny, ramshackle church, where inside, totally unguarded, was a Fra Angelico fresco. Even at twelve I knew how special it was to be so close and alone with something so spectacular.

"Isn't it extraordinary?" my mother said, her voice softer and quieter than I had ever heard it.

"Yes," I said, as awestruck at my mother's reverence as I was at the fresco.

I was close with my mother's sister, Julie, whose graphic design office was on the first floor of 134 Charles Street. I'd come home every day from school and go directly to Julie's office, where she would talk to me, show me the projects she was working on, and draw funny faces on the pads of my toes. Julie loved musicals from the 1950s and '60s, and she gave me a box of DVDs of *South Pacific*, *Gigi*, *Guys and Dolls*, *Singin' in the Rain, My Fair Lady.* I'd learn the songs and belt them out in her office. Every New Year's Eve I'd go to her apartment, where she and my uncle, Takaaki, would hide a new pair of pajamas and I'd have to find it. Julie and Takaaki seemed to really like each other. I would watch them move around their small apartment and study their interactions—how they made each other laugh or touched each other on the back or elbow. I had not seen anything like that up close, their easy intimacy a momentary correction to the vocabulary of love I was learning.

When I was twelve, my mother's younger brother, Roy, moved in to 134 Charles Street. He had lost all his money because of his gambling addiction and had been diagnosed with cancer. He was six two, almost bald, and very skinny. He moved into the room on the first floor that had been my father's room.

I first learned about Roy's existence one Christmas morning when I was nine. Under the tree, I found a Ziploc bag with *To Alice, From Roy* written on it in Sharpie marker. Inside the bag were pins with strange symbols, fabric badges with writing in different languages, and a man's watch with no wristband.

"Mom," I called across the room to my mother as she unwrapped a set of overly designed Moss oven mitts.

"What?" she answered, not looking up, unwinding a swathe of tulle that had wrapped itself around her arm.

"There's a Ziploc bag that says it's for me from Roy and it's got all this random stuff in it," I said.

"That's from your uncle Roy." She paused, distracted by a gigantic origami swan. "He probably won them from gambling."

"Why?"

"He's addicted to gambling. He lives in Las Vegas and works at Kentucky Fried Chicken."

She said all this without once looking up.

I sifted through the contents of the bag. My mother had never told me about Roy. I had never met him and had also never heard of him but he knew me and had thought of me enough to send me his hard-won treasures.

I liked Roy a lot. We played Scrabble almost every night after dinner. We sat in the library, on the green leather sofas, and slapped words onto the board. He was very serious about it. He never gave me hints and he always won. He helped me study for my tests, making up tricks and strategies to help me remember information. He gave me money for good grades and put it in funny greeting cards that he signed "Uncle Wiggly," which was a character from my favorite board game. We played the "gotcha last" game, where we teased each other or made puns and whoever said "gotcha last" first, won. One time, after he had won the gotcha last game, he typed up a very official-sounding letter that began with *To Whom it May Concern* and was signed *The Gotcha Last Board of Administrators*, informing me, in businesslike language, that I had to be his maid for a week.

Nanny, my mother, and I had always eaten our meals together, me reading aloud my school projects—the fourth-grade speech I had written in favor of legalizing gay marriage (which I was prohibited from reading at school assembly), the creation myth I had written where the sky made love to the sea (returned to me with a smiley face and a request from the teacher to please write another one that was "more appropriate" but declared "great and totally acceptable" by my mother). Now Roy was part of this routine, sitting across from me at the table and critiquing my projects like I was a grown-up. Then his dying began, and tracking its progress became my new routine. His vitality fell off him hard and slick and fast. He lost more and more weight. His limbs seemed longer for the weight they had lost, but unwieldy in their lightness. His weakness turned every movement into a different movement because he was too weak to carry it through. As the months went by, he grew sullen and stopped looking me in the eye, but I couldn't stop watching.

My babysitter, Pem, took me to the movies to see *Home Alone*. One of the previews was for *Edward Scissorhands* and it terrified me so much that for years after, I couldn't watch previews. I had to sit outside the theater doors and someone had to come and get me when the previews were over and tell me that it was okay to come in. Now, with Roy in the house—in the kitchen or climbing slowly up the stairs or in his room with the door open—always dying, I was being forced to watch those horrifying previews over and over. Every day when I entered or left the house, I would pass by his open door and see him sitting on the edge of his bed staring into space. Even if I looked away, the smoke from the weed he used to manage his symptoms slipped inside me. When I retreated to my room, I'd hear him shuffling around at night in the kitchen. I couldn't escape him and I couldn't just wait outside the door for it to be over because no one knew when it would end and no one told me anything anyway.

It was hard to know what to do for him. I made him macaroni and cheese from a box once and brought it to him in his room. I felt as if I wasn't supposed to see what was going on in there. There was only one window, which was closed, so the room was filled with cigarette smoke. The walls were yellow from it, the same yellow as his jaundiced skin. There was a twin bed, a La-Z-Boy, a TV, and a bookshelf. On the bookshelf were a lot of books and a bowl filled with packs and packs of American Spirit cigarettes. He liked adventure novels. On the covers were cowboys with huge hats. Suns were always blood red and skies were bruisy.

Roy was sitting in the La-Z-Boy, smoking an American Spirit and watching a boxing match on TV. I put the tray on his lap. I glanced at his face. He had lost so much weight that the skin just dangled, exhausted. It made me forget I was looking at a face.

"Thanks," he said, not moving his eyes from the screen.

"You're welcome," I said.

I stopped myself from saying the only thing that came to mind: "I'm sorry I'm not dying."

At this stage of his decline, there was no more Scrabble, no more quizzing, no more book report debates. I was a girl growing up, but I couldn't help feeling like I was supposed to accompany Roy, that in my youth and my health, I was betraying him.

6.

I was growing up. I put on makeup, I wore a leopard-print bra whose straps revealed themselves under my tank top. My hair had grown out from the short, fluffy helmet I had in middle school into shoulder-length ringlets. I was fourteen and in my freshman year of high school at the Dalton School on the Upper East Side. I was excited to be there and very friendly. I approached everyone with a huge smile and asked them how they were. One girl told me, "When I first met you I thought you were mentally challenged. But you're just really friendly." I was desperate for attention and friendship, but I was clumsy and confused about who I was. I still needed my mother to dress me. I couldn't decide if I liked something unless she told me it was good. Every day still began with the fraught hour it took for us to plan an outfit, which ended with me in tears.

Dalton was populated by the kids of the ultra-rich—fifteen-year-olds dressed head to toe in Chanel, or in a jersey from the football team owned by their parents, touting last names that appeared on hospital buildings and museum wings. These kids had the regular traits of youthful immaturity carved away from them by the shining edge of money, and Dalton felt like a sovereign nation ruled by small grown-ups. There were strict sartorial, linguistic, and aesthetic rules. All the girls owned the same Longchamp purse. They straightened their hair and wore pajama bottoms to school. The rumor was that most girls' parents gifted them a nose job the summer before freshman year. I watched and listened, adopting their "like"s and "literally"s, hoping to sneak into their ranks, even though I showed up one day wearing the same skirt as my history teacher. I wasn't bullied like I had been in middle school, but I didn't fit in.

Halfway through my freshman year, my father came to visit from Hamburg, where he was now living full-time in order to maintain his career and be closer to Elena. I was excited to see him. He had always been the person I could talk to about my thoughts and feelings. I could ask him anything, and he would answer me honestly. "Have you ever felt like killing yourself?" I asked him. We'd have long conversations about Till, about madness, loneliness, otherness. He spoke about sadness and compulsion in ways I could understand, and ways that made me feel understood.

But this night was different. Sitting at the table at a Chinese restaurant, I was tense and couldn't look him in the eye. I felt uncomfortable, and that discomfort confused and scared me.

"So what's going on in your life?" he asked.

"Nothing much. You know. A lot of work. The usual," I said.

"No, I don't know. I'm not really allowed to be too involved in your life," he said, his words echinated with contempt.

I jiggled my leg and he ran his thumb over his fingers, over and over.

I stared hard at the menu, studying the names of entrees, trying to soothe the nameless unease that was rising inside me. I could feel my father across the table, buzzing along with the fluorescent lights. I put the menu down.

"I hate making decisions," I said.

"I know," he said.

I felt attacked by his knowledge of me. Every awareness he had of any of the things that made me Me felt like a violation instead of the comfort it had previously been.

We finally finished dinner and my father hailed a cab. Inside, I was pressed up against the door and he had his arm around me. His long legs were spread and he was slid down the seat halfway. Our bodies were as close together as they could be. I felt the tight fist of heart in my chest, clenching as if it were trying to retreat from being inside me, who was inside his embrace inside this taxi inside the night. I wanted to run. I realized I was clutching the door handle.

"You two newlyweds?" the cab driver asked.

I turned my head to look at the reflection of this stranger's eyes in the rearview mirror.

My father laughed.

"No, I'm her father."

I looked away from the mirror to avoid the driver's eyes.

"I would never hold my daughter like that," he said.

My father laughed again. His fingers stroked my forehead. I felt their caress in my guts, turning my organs in a nauseating plowing. My face got hot and my chest smoldered. I opened the window. My father's hands, placed just so, could change entirely who I was, turning me from daughter to newlywed.

That summer my mother took me to Iceland for four weeks. We lay on the lava fields, our bodies leaving deep imprints in the thick moss that covered them. We set up a tent on a black sand beach and wild ponies nosed their way inside. The wind was so strong that it flattened the tent on top of us and we rolled out of it laughing. We ate Arctic char and bread as we both drew the landscape. I felt calm and happy as we sat side by side in a lava field, passing pastels back and forth as the landscape we were both sharing in formed under our fingers. We rode on Ski-Doos up a glacier, the fog getting so thick we couldn't see our hands in front of our faces. Over dinner every night, we talked. She told me how she felt like an "alien." How she felt a distance between her and everyone else, like she was watching them from behind a pane of glass and didn't understand the rules that everyone else was following. I told her I knew exactly what she meant, how unfamiliar even the most familiar things could feel. As we spoke, I hoped I wasn't included in the "everyone else," that I got to be on her side of the glass. I ate slowly and ordered two desserts, trying to stretch the evening as long as I could. As we deboned our fish in the endless Arctic day, our alienation brought us momentarily together.

We visited a man who read tarot cards at the base of a glacier. He performed our readings separately. After studying my cards, he asked me if I had been sexually abused.

"I don't know," I said. "I've wondered that."

Afterwards, my mother and I went to eat fish stew. I told her what the man had asked me.

"Do you think I was sexually abused? Do you think Dad did that?"

"I don't know," she said. "Maybe."

"Maybe what I feel is just because of what you went through. Maybe I've confused your experiences with mine," I said.

"I don't know. Maybe," she said and ate her stew.

I realized I was jealous of my mother's abuse. I was jealous of her for having it as an excuse for everything. She couldn't give me affection or talk about feelings because pedophile Satanists had ruined her. She drank because she had witnessed murder and endured torture. I couldn't have her, because the abuse had taken most of her away, and what remained belonged to her work.

. . .

By my sophomore year at Dalton I had developed an unexpected popularity for two reasons: I was skinny and I had gotten pretty, which offset my weirdness. I started performing in the school plays and made a best friend. Effie was a talented actor originally from Switzerland, who lived in the worst projects in all of New York. She was at Dalton on a scholarship. Effie and I would go to the Angelika Film Center and watch indie films, then roam the streets for hours discussing the plays we would write, composing Dada poetry from words on signs and billboards, and planning the naked photo shoot we were going to have with the fifty-year-old photographer Effie was corresponding with. Effie had struggled in ways that were both familiar and unfamiliar to me, and she had a reckless, radiant resilience. She had a dark sense of humor and could make anything funny, but would fall into steely seriousness if I mentioned thoughts of self-harm or waxed too romantic about suicide. Despite our different backgrounds, it felt like we shared the same rare disease, one that made us uniquely sensitive to the world.

Along with a best friend, I had a boyfriend. Nate and I started dating when I was fifteen and he was eighteen. We were both part of the theater crowd, and Nate would be voted most handsome in his senior yearbook. I was excited to be dating him. He and his friends seemed to possess the correct ratio of quirk and competence, unlike me. I was too loud, too talkative, too hyper, and tried too hard. When someone asked me how I was, I answered: "There is a smattering of novelty in my life." I used increasingly big words, some of which I didn't entirely know the meaning of, in casual conversation. I was terrified that unless I applied myself to the moment like thick oil paint with a palette knife, I would go unnoticed and unloved.

Nate noticed and then loved me. Things were going well with him, but I found myself unable to look at or touch his penis. Panic creaked inside me whenever I thought of trying to make my way around his genitals. Nate was patient with me. He surprised me with a giant, phallic candy cane, as thick as my forearm, in my locker to lighten the mood. Sometimes when Nate and I were making out I would hallucinate my father's face onto his. I would push through it, not wanting to have to explain why I had stopped. Every time we had sex, I felt angry and guilty afterwards. "Wow, your ass is incredible," said Nate. Yes, I thought, my father thinks so too.

As I was squirming inside the expectations of a cool group of teenagers and my handsome boyfriend, Roy was still at home dying. One night, Nate and I were in my bedroom having sex. I heard Roy's slippers shuffling around in the kitchen. It was dark in my bedroom, and dark everywhere else in the house, but the shuffling sound of Roy's slippers was like a searchlight slipping its glare all over me, lighting up the scene. Nate paused and said, "Shit, we should stop." He started to move off me, but I gripped his back and pressed him back down onto my body.

"No, it's fine, keep going," I said.

"But it's weird," he said. "He'll hear us."

"It's okay," I said. "He always walks around at night. It's okay."

The shuffling continued, and I tried to drown out the friction of Roy's footfalls with the friction of Nate's body on mine.

"Keep going," I insisted.

We kept going. The sound of Roy's slippers faded as he retreated downstairs.

As my relationship with Nate progressed, I spent time with his family. His parents seemed to adore each other, and he had a smart, pretty sister who was two years younger than me. I was fascinated by them. His parents loved art and also knew what a retirement account was; they read interesting books and also their children's report cards. I was especially struck by the way they loved one another—Dad, Mom, brother, sister, talking to each other, showing affection, with a clarity of emotion that confounded me to my core. My confusion translated to rage and paranoia. I became fiercely jealous of his sister. When Nate took me to a circus and bought me a T-shirt, I became enraged when he bought one for his sister too. I loved them, I envied them, I hated them, I wanted to be wrapped up in them, I wanted to tear them apart. Their uncomplicated love didn't seem possible or real, but more like a delusion that Nate needed to be cured of. My efforts to make him see his family as I saw mine failed, and, after sixteen months of dating, Nate broke up with me in my junior year. He was the first person to calmly admit they suspected I was "crazy." As if that word were air, I rushed up to the surface to breathe it in, huge gulps of "crazy" that found me sitting at my desk trying to focus on homework, pulling out my hair, cutting my thighs. My grades dropped. Teachers commented that I had been the star of the class and now they weren't even sure I was paying attention.

When I asked my mother to get me a therapist, she asked me no questions, but had her assistant make me an appointment with a woman uptown. I was also sent to a psychiatrist who diagnosed me with depression and put me on the antidepressant Paxil. Numbness thickened over me like scar tissue, pangs of anxiety, irritability, and hyperactivity breaking through. My therapy sessions felt like English assignments, opportunities to construct perfect stories about myself and wait for praise.

My mother never asked me how I was feeling or about the medication I was put on. We did get drunk together at parties and talk about books we were reading and gossip we had heard. Loaded up on red wine and hors d'oeuvres, we'd lie on the sofas in the living room and make each other roar with laughter as fancy people milled around us. I still gave the tour of the house as I had done as a child, now in a red Miu Miu dress my mother had bought me in Italy, leading actors, writers, politicians, models, and rock stars around the studios, the gardens, the pool. My mother and I were a good team at those parties.

She liked that I looked good and talked well. At that moment—when my damage was still inconspicuous—I was what she needed me to be. But that moment would soon be over.

Every year we'd go to Joan Didion's Easter party at her Upper East Side apartment. The year I was sixteen, we were seated in the living room, along with Patti Smith, the artist Brice Marden, and his wife, Helen. Helen was talking about superstitions. A lone word glowed in my brain: *imbrued.* I wanted to use that word because it was special and difficult. I wanted to impress these people. I started to say:

"It's interesting how these superstitions are imbrued with—"

"I think it's *imbued,*" my mother said, cutting me off.

I felt destabilized, wobbly, as if that *r* were structural and removing it would topple me. To steady myself, I pictured the dictionary I had been studying that week. I could see that *r* curving over the *u.* I felt its growl under my tongue, between that plosive and that rounded vowel. I knew it was there but my accomplished, brilliant mother was telling me I was wrong. I tried not to panic as Patti Smith and Joan Didion stared at us.

"Well, *imbrued* is also a word, and it means saturated with blood, so I mean it more as a metaphor," I said cautiously.

"I think she's right," said Patti.

I wanted to hug her. I opened my mouth to continue my thought, but my mother was telling a story. As we left, my mother grabbed an unopened bottle of white wine and told me to stick it in my purse. She didn't have room for it in her tiny clutch. We were going home in a car service. There was plenty of good wine at home. Why did she need to steal this bottle? But there was something in her gesture I recognized—an urgency, a thrill, a way to seize control. I had taken to carrying a razor blade around in my purse. Even if I wasn't going to use it, I liked knowing it was there. I understood why she was taking the wine, but I couldn't tell her that I did. In sharing this transgression, I chose to believe we were communicating.

. . .

I LEFT MY MOTHER and a dying Roy and went to visit my father and his family. In Lübeck, I spent a lot of time in Till's attic bedroom. I would sit there for hours and stare at the dead insects, the only sign that time was passing. On his desk were papers covered in his neat, loopy handwriting, and I would pore over them, convinced they contained valuable information that only I could understand. I liked to put his pipe to my lips and suck, plugging myself into him, into a cosmic source that only we could tap into, the ancient grit lining my tongue. Oma had always told me that Till and I would have loved each other, that we were very similar. We would have made each other laugh. We would have understood each other. I pictured him deciding whether or not to live anymore. My father told me that Till had believed it was simple. "If fifty-one percent of your life is bad," Till had said, "and forty-nine percent is good, then you have your answer. It all depends on that one percent."

My father was in his second custody battle. Bettina had married a Venetian and taken Elena to live in Venice. During that time—the summers I was fifteen, sixteen, and seventeen—my father and I drank and talked a lot, filling ourselves to bursting with booze, words, grandiose ideas, trying to still that hyper bird that lived in our chests, a thrashing bundle of unease. My father surrounded himself with a coterie of hard-partying, morally suspect middle-aged men who took an interest in me. Tim was a tabloid journalist who wrote for the *Bild Zeitung*, the most widely distributed publication in Germany. He was small and compact with a pointy nose, wore shiny shirts with the top four buttons undone, loved heavy metal music, and wrote dark, angsty poetry that he read aloud to me. My father introduced me to Tim when I was fifteen and he was thirty. He was instantly attracted to me and my father seemed proud of that. Whenever I came to Hamburg,

Tim would take me to heavy metal clubs. We'd drink Jägermeister, and he would back me into dark corners and kiss me. Then we talked about death and pain. Tim loved to hear me talk about all the ways I hurt and hurt myself.

"I don't like you as much when you're not in pain," he told me. I stood in those dark bars tasting the brown, herbaceous syrup and watched Tim as he shimmied around the dance floor, getting closer and closer, a smirk on his face. I was not attracted to Tim, but I found his interest in me compelling. It felt important to be liked by this man, however uninteresting and gross I found him. I was taller than him and would slip out of my heels so our mouths could meet. I wondered if my father knew about this, if he had matched me up with Tim to be pushed into corners and kissed. When Tim's eyes dug into mine, when his hands dug into my waist as he ground his pelvis against me, I felt like I was doing a good job. When he read me his terrible poetry, I knew I was in the right place at the right time doing the right thing. When I told him about cutting myself, he held my wrist and traced the scars with his finger, sometimes kissing them. My pain had a reason, and the reason was to entertain this man. His face softened and his body gyrated with desire, and in this dark club, where the Beatles played their first show, I found merit and meaning.

My father invited Jürgen Schmidt over to the Hamburg apartment, telling me, with great drama, that Jürgen had been the top mobster in Hamburg and the most successful and famous pimp. I couldn't wait to meet him. Pimp meant power. It meant deciding who was worth what. Jürgen Schmidt had a mustache and wore aviators and a fedora. The first few buttons of his shirt were undone and curls of chest hair wandered up to his neck. My father introduced me to him like he was throwing open the door to a room of secret splendor.

"Well, what would you charge for her?" my father asked.

I felt suspended over a deep pit in the pause before Jürgen's final valuation. What if he didn't assess me high enough? What number meant I was valuable? How would I ever know if I was worth anything? Jürgen gave a number. My father seemed satisfied, and we all laughed. We played darts in the living room. My father had told me Jürgen never took off his sunglasses so I hopped around him and draped myself on him and flirted and tried to get him to take them off. If I succeeded, it would mean I was incredibly sexy, irresistible, and valuable, and that would make my father proud.

We went to parties thrown by Udo Müller. Udo was an infamous denizen of Hamburg nightlife, renowned for his debauchery. He was in his fifties, with a dark tan, conspicuous veneers, and a glistening pompadour. One night, I was seated on a sofa with Udo, my father, and a handsome thirty-three-year-old actor named Johann. Johann was on my left and my father was on my right. We were smoking a joint. I never liked weed but I liked the idea of smoking it in a club with a handsome thirty-three-year-old actor and my father. I liked showing my father that I was a wild, untamable, riveting creature. I danced and I drank and I flirted with Johann, who wrapped his fist up in my long hair and kissed me. At 3 a.m. my father told me it was time to go. I pouted and refused. He grabbed my ponytail and yanked. I laughed and hid under the table. He pretended to drag me away by my hair, both of us laughing. I refused to leave. He threw his hands up and said to Udo and Johann, without looking at me, "Fine. Get her home safely, boys," and left. I spent the rest of the night making out with Johann on the sofa until Udo said it was time to go. He had located a pretty brunette sex worker and she, Udo, Johann, and I got into a taxi. I assumed they were taking me home. We drove along the water and the taxi stopped in front of a house, not mine, in a part of Hamburg I was not familiar with. It seemed that none of the adults had any money. The driver started yelling and Udo yelled back. I found some cash at the bottom of my purse and paid the driver, pushing the men out of the cab as they cursed at the driver over their shoulders. We were at Udo's apartment, and once inside the girl went to cry on the couch. The men got beers. I knelt next to her and comforted her in broken German. Udo and Johann stood behind us watching and drinking. Udo held out his hand, palm up. The girl got up, still crying, put her hand in his, and followed him to the back of the apartment. My father had told me that Udo had a special penis pump that he used when he had taken too much cocaine and couldn't get erect. I felt bad about what awaited her. Johann went to the bathroom. I took the opportunity to arrange myself, leaning into the doorway of the balcony, jutting out my hip, and tilting my head sideways. Johann came back into the room and said, "Who are you posing for?" He wrapped his arms across my breasts from behind.

"No one," I said coyly.

Johann led me into a bedroom. I lay down on the bed and faced away from him. My heart was racing, my breath catching in my throat. It felt like something was slipping away from me, fast. I gripped the sheet, pulling it up from the mattress. I heard Johann's belt buckle thud to the floor. He got into bed and put his body against mine. He was soft and warm, and his softness and warmth draped me in a grotesque humidity. I lay completely still and pretended to be asleep, trying to smooth my breath over the wild hopping of my heart. "Are you asleep?" he asked. I didn't answer. He rubbed himself against my back and sighed. And then he was still. I waited until I heard him snoring and then got out of the bed and locked myself in the bathroom. I sat on the floor, with my back against the door, waiting for the suffocating heat from Johann's body to dissipate off my skin. I stared at my phone and called my friend JP, who was in New York.

"I'm stuck in a bathroom and I don't know where I am," I told him, breathlessly. "I don't know what to do. I need to get out of here."

JP told me to call my father. We hung up and I stared at my phone. I called my father but he didn't answer. I managed to reach my German uncle who said he would pick me up. I didn't know the address so I walked outside and started reading street signs. I walked alone through the still, early morning streets. As I waited on the corner for my uncle to arrive, I stared at the river, blurred into inflexibility by the gray dawn—a steel ingot. I stared at my hands, leaden at the end of my arms. I closed my eyes and saw the image of me dancing in a club for my father and his friends. It had been fun, hadn't it? Finally my uncle pulled up and I got into his car. We drove to his house and I went to bed. When I woke up I called my father. He screamed at me that he had been calling every hospital in Hamburg. Johann had called him frantic because I was gone, informing my father that he had put me to sleep on the sofa and covered me with a blanket. I needed to apologize to Udo and Johann, my father said. When I got home my father dialed Udo's number and handed me the phone. I mumbled an apology and thanked Johann for taking care of me.

THAT WINTER, my father threw a New Year's Eve party in the Hamburg apartment. In every room I entered, my father's friends reached out to me, hands on my thighs, in my hair, up my skirt. Was this what my father wished he could do? I walked into my bedroom, and Karl approached me. Karl was a photographer in his forties with long, wavy hair, a pointy chin covered in blond stubble, thin, curling lips, and intense blue eyes. He brought his body close to mine and gripped my arms. His tongue in my mouth felt mushy and too wet. He was vigorous with it. His facial hair was tough and spiky in my mouth. The combination reminded me of a sea urchin—the glistening pile of soggy sex organs bordered by spikes. He removed his face from mine, peered down at me, and walked out. I spent the rest of the night positioning myself in his sight line. He and my father left to go to a club. It got late and I wanted to go to sleep. I got into bed and wrote in my journal, which had streaks of dried blood on the pages: *Dad's drunk. More ambiguous than when Mom is. Which is worse? Dad is so plastered. He tried something with me. I don't want to start out this year as an old-man-teasing sex object.* I didn't offer any more information about what I meant when I said that my father had "tried something"—whether the attempt was sexual or confrontational. *Maybe this is not a good world for me. Why do I feel so guilty?* I turned off the light and was beginning to fall asleep when my father's friend Detlev crawled into bed with me. I got up and left the room. I tried the doorknob of the guest room but it was locked. I went into the room I used to share with my sister before Bettina had taken her to Venice. People were having sex in it. I interrupted them long enough to remove one of the mattresses, and put it on the floor in the hallway. I managed to doze for a few hours.

The next afternoon Karl called to chastise me for kissing him. He warned me that he was far too old and though he knew it would be difficult for me, we couldn't do that again, much as he wanted to have sex with me. His voice had a placating, conciliatory tone that made me doubt my memory. Did these men know me, know my desires, better than I did? I apologized to Karl.

On the plane back to New York, I was reading *Crime and Punishment*, and a handsome, blond man in the seat next to me asked how I liked it. He introduced himself as thirty-three-year-old Captain Will Price. He taught literature at West Point military academy. I told him I was reading the book for my Russian literature class, and that I was sixteen. He told me that he had been a virgin until he was twenty-three because of God and that now, at thirty-three, he was determined to be a virgin again. We made out as the plane landed and it felt like something right out of a romantic comedy. Back in New York, we made a date to go out for sushi. He ordered two sakes and sneaked me one because I was underage. I brought him back to 134 Charles Street. The house was dark and still. I brought him into my room and closed the door. We kissed deeply and his hands made their way to my body. I knelt on my bed and he bent over me to meet my mouth. He still had his coat on and I held on to his lapels. He pulled away from me to look around, at the crossword puzzles I had taped to the walls, at the stuffed animal on my bed, at my backpack on the floor, at the teenage mess. I sucked him back into our kissing. I felt his crotch and he was hard. The next time he pulled away his face was bright red. His eyes darted around the room.

"Don't worry, my mom's asleep," I said. I wasn't worried. I suspected that if she walked in on us, she'd simply apologize and close the door.

He started stammering. He never said out loud that he was alarmed that he was about to fuck a teenager, or that he was scared my mother would walk in, mid-felony, or that he feared a wrathful god might deny him heaven. Instead, he muttered an apology and ran out of the room. I froze, kneeling in the center of my bed, wondering what I'd done wrong.

The summer I turned seventeen, my father and I were at the Kempinski Hotel in Berlin. When he wasn't on set, we spent our days by the pool, swimming, reading, and eating french fries. I read books in the steam room until the pages grew wet and glued together. We talked about movies and books, and he asked me for my opinions about the screenplay he was writing. We were sitting at a table near the pool, wet from swimming, our bathrobes open. My cuts itched under my swimsuit. I smelled french fries and chlorine. We had our notebooks open on the table. Water from my hair dripped onto the page, making the ink spidery and diluted. We were talking about filmmaking.

"It's always been my dream," said my father, "to make a movie that stars a father and daughter in the roles of the lovers and have a sex scene between them. It's never been done. It would be the first. It would be revolutionary. We would star in it."

We spoke all the time about art, about pushing the boundaries of art, about collaborating. And I loved it. Today's idea was that we fake-fuck on camera. Or maybe it was real fucking? I wasn't completely sure. I gripped the french fry in my hand, my body bracing for the impact as this image was dropped into me. But this suggestion of onscreen incest sank, its detonation muffled, as if I were an endless, bottomless body of water. The new banality of these comments made them more dangerous. They could sneak into my psyche, disguised as any other thought or feeling, and pollute the entire ecosystem.

Back in Hamburg, we decided we needed to do something transgressive before I turned eighteen and became an adult. "We should do naked photos while you're still a Lolita," my father suggested. This made a great deal of sense to me. I would only be a "Lolita" for one more year. I felt a nameless loss and wondered what time was taking from me. Karl the photographer came over. My father and I decided on an Amazon queen theme, based on Heinrich von Kleist's play *Penthesilea.* My father sat in the corner working the tip of a long stick into a point with a knife. This would be my spear. He gave me a small piece of gray cloth to wear around my hips tied with some rope. The three of us drove out into a forest, where my father had arranged for a horse. I jammed my bare foot into my father's cupped hands, pushing against them to hoist myself up onto the horse. I had never ridden a horse naked before and the vigorousness of the bouncing of my breasts surprised and amused me. I rode bareback and without underwear, for historical accuracy, and the thin, pilled pad I sat on rubbed against my vulva. The sensation of rubbing and motion and the rhythmic force and release of pressure against my crotch brought me from arousal to pain and back again, sensations that were not the same, but also sometimes the same.

I felt powerful. I felt exposed and exalted as the two men watched and directed me, my body telling a story. But underneath was a shivering disquiet, as if at any moment I could be thrown from this system, this fantasy these men had created, and break into meaningless, invisible pieces.

7.

I was trying to fulfill the basic milestones that were expected of me. My peers had been studying with private SAT tutors since freshman year. I had barely opened any of the big, glossy prep books. When I took the test, one of the questions in the verbal comprehension section was about my mother. There was a paragraph that discussed her being commissioned to design a garden for Battery Park City. I gaped and looked around, bursting to tell someone. But everyone's head was down, struggling to answer questions about my mother, about our life. I filled in the bubbles on the test sheet, hoping I had gotten the answers right.

My mother took me to visit colleges. I had wanted to take a gap year, but she disapproved of that idea. We drove to Yale and Middlebury and Vassar. She was a terrible driver, both aggressive and unsure, and I pushed my legs against the well of the car and my hands against the dashboard as she weaved back and forth, trying to change lanes. As we waited for AAA in the dark (she had driven up onto a curb and broken an axel), eating chocolate and trying to decide my future, I watched my mother's profile, studying the woman whose desires for me, whose desire for me, preoccupied and perplexed me. She took me shopping at Bed Bath & and Beyond for college supplies, and we deliberated over bedsheet patterns. It felt good to join her in picturing my future, to know that we both held in our minds an image of me walking across a quad or finally making my own bed with the plaid comforter we picked out. In the end, I applied just to Vassar because it was the only place I wanted to go. I lied to the college counselor, saying I had absolutely sent in the recommended number of reach, target, and safety-school applications. I made Till the subject of my college admissions essay. I was accepted.

I ARRIVED AT VASSAR COLLEGE in August 2003. I felt good. People seemed to like me, boys especially. I had long, over-excited talks with new friends who would appear at night and pull me from my bed for adventures. We walked the campus in our nightclothes—me in a pink satin slip with a tuxedo blazer thrown over it. I met interesting people from places I'd never been—like Bulgaria and Pennsylvania. We developed absurd inside jokes. I wasn't cutting. During orientation week I wrote in my journal: *Here I am at Vassar. I'm smiling as I write this. I'm hesitant to say it's been great. It's hard to believe I'm here all on my own. I feel so comfortable.* I bought my books. I wrote my schedule in my new planner. I convinced my roommate, a cheery, cherubic Texan, to put a poster of the porn star Jenna Jameson on our door. Classes began. I loved my Gothic literature class, and outlined hypothetical essays before they were even assigned. I even liked the cafeteria food. I went to parties, developed crushes. But my gossamered euphoria was fragile. I was afraid it would tear, and I wrote in my journal: *I don't want this to go downhill. I'm not quite sure how to pace myself to make sure that doesn't happen. I have to write. I have to have something to show for myself.* Over the following weeks I continued to raise my hand in class and swish into parties in my vintage dresses, trying to perform who I thought I was, but with each verbose answer or too-loud laugh, I felt more and more distant from myself and from everyone around me. I started to panic. I couldn't tell if there was a nascent someone huddled within the grandiose construct I had managed to assemble out of the loudest, brightest bits of my parents. As if the dial were being slowly turned on a radio, the lively tempo of my college life dissolved into static. I slept longer and later. I barely made it to class, and when I did I couldn't focus. I stopped doing homework.

I covered my minuscule dorm room with mess. I didn't wash my clothes. The unisex bathroom down the hall felt too far to walk to, so I urinated in mugs and emptied them out of the window at night. My roommate had started sleeping over in her friend's room, so I had more room for my mess to spread. On the ledge at the head of the bottom bunk, where I slept, were cups of old coffee, mugs of old tea, bowls of old ramen noodles. They sat there for weeks. I watched the mold change colors and grow and take on different textures. I coffined myself in the bottom bunk, zipped up in a sleeping bag I had bought so I wouldn't have to wash my sheets, asleep more hours than I was awake, surrounded by decay. Blood stains streaked my pillow. I wandered around campus in a somnambulant haze, wearing a bathrobe, blood soaking through the terry cloth, drinking vodka from a mug. I was cutting every day, numbering each cut with a pen, trying to impose meaning and order as my reason dissolved, as I dissolved. I wrote in my journal that *I have a fantasy of making a smooth cut along the outside of my body, up the side, under the arm, over it, around the neck, down the arm, under, down the other side, under my foot, end. Cut in half.* One month shy of the end of my first, and only, semester at Vassar, I brought myself to the campus medical services building and showed them my arms and legs. They locked me in the medical center—my every movement supervised—and called my mother. The next day, a friend of my mother's helped me pack my things and drove me back to 134 Charles Street.

Being back at home, I was able to pee in a bathroom and dress myself, but I felt like I was watching myself from far away. I resumed sessions with my therapist and continued taking the antidepressant my psychiatrist prescribed. A month after I returned from Vassar, Roy was taken to hospice to finish dying. I visited him only once, with my mother. As we got into the car, I handed her stories I had written over the last few years—about a man who builds a house just to burn it down, a funeral where the next of kin are required to eat the deceased, a doctor who performs an autopsy on the man he murdered.

"What's this?" she asked.

"They're stories I wrote," I said. "I want Roy to read them."

"Oh, he can't read anymore," she said, and handed them back.

On each side of the long hospice hallway were open doors, one after another, and in each room someone was dying. I felt like I was seeing something I shouldn't be seeing, something obscene and private. Every body in every bed made that pyramid where the sheet tented over the toes. The same shape over and over and over, in every room, all the way down the hallway, as if someone had pressed the wrong button and multiplied reality. We were there to find that one shape, to find the right name on the whiteboard next to each doorway. I watched as a nurse erased and rewrote a different name on someone's door.

Roy lay in his room with his door open, making strange, ugly noises. We sat in chairs next to him listening to his mystic growls and alien wheezes.

A rabbi came up to us.

"How do you know Roy? What faith was he?" he asked my mother.

"He wasn't religious," I said.

"Was he like a father to you?" he asked me.

I didn't know what to say because it didn't feel like I knew what that meant.

"I don't want to talk about him like he's not here," said my mother.

The rabbi asked me to help him clean up a small conference room. I followed him. I carried a plastic platter of stale, neon-orange cubes of cheddar cheese and tipped it into a garbage can. I asked the rabbi if there was more cleaning to do, but he said, "No, go and be with your family." I had no idea what me doing that would look like, how it would feel. I wanted to throw more things in garbage cans, scrunch up trash, wipe dust off tabletops. I wanted to keep moving.

A week later, my mother told me Roy was dead.

"I wasn't there when he died," she said. "I went to make a phone call and he died."

I didn't know what to say. I watched her face for signs of how one responded to this kind of thing. I wondered if I would see her cry for the first time. I didn't. I went with my aunt and my mother to the funeral home. I brought my journal with me because this was novel and this was information, and collecting that information seemed imperative. The funeral director led us into a thickly carpeted office with no windows. All around us were shelves with urns for sale and little peaked cards with prices written on them. I walked around the room writing down how much each urn cost.

We took the elevator to the third floor.

"In the last room to your left," said the funeral director.

The room was huge and fat with carpet. There was a long rectangular table against the back wall and on it was the corpse of Roy, his head sticking out from an enormous blue plastic bag. I didn't understand what I was looking at. I felt dizzy and far away. My mother and Julie left the room. I walked over to the corpse. I couldn't figure out if it was real, if I was real. I watched myself put out my hand and touch the forehead of the corpse. The forehead was so cold. The room was warm so I didn't understand why the head was cold. I felt the frigid ball of flesh under my hand. I was trying to understand, as the head cooled my fingertips, where the edges were, where he ended and I began. I imagined myself as a projection, the final image his brain had sparked before it had sputtered out. I felt like a dream being dreamed by the people around me, a reverie fading as it was dragged into wakefulness. I walked out into the hallway where my mother and aunt sat in high-backed, upholstered chairs, and was surprised when they looked up at me, that they could still see me. The funeral director appeared and led us into an elevator, down a hallway, and then into a small windowless room. The man stood in the doorway and said, "You can have a moment in here." He closed the door behind him. There was a water cooler in the room with tiny cone-shaped paper cups. Someone filled one for me and put it in my hand. The water was very cold and the cup was very thin. It felt like there was nothing separating the water from me, and that at any moment the water would lose its shape and just spill all over me. At any moment things would lose their shape and spill all over onto everything.

II / Nothing

1.

I moved blankly through unstructured days. I looked up stripping jobs in the city. I researched writing letters to death-row convicts. I sat in my room, wondering if lonely men waiting to die, in a club or in prison, could give me purpose. I didn't have the follow-through for either activity. Some nights I drank myself to sleep, other nights I cut myself to sleep. During the day, I sat in my room, trying to write and listening to Nanny talk to herself in the kitchen. Nanny, now seventy-seven, had retired, and my mother had invited her to live with us for the remainder of her life. Nanny was lonely, and her disembodied voice sneaked her loneliness into me, past my door with no lock, until I was crowded with both of our alienation, jam-packed with an emptiness that would grow bigger than I could have ever imagined.

I was trying to be normal, and what normal looked like was hanging out with a guy with a soul patch and taking a giant hit from a bong, which I'd never done. I inhaled deeply and held my breath for as long as I could. As I exhaled, I felt the smoke take everything I was with it. I heard myself say "whoa, whoa, whoa" over and over. I couldn't stop saying "whoa," as if the sound would somehow adhere me to the body I was now far, far away from. I crawled to the bathroom, locked myself inside, and lay on the floor. I stared at the warning on the side of a bottle of Clorox spray that lay under the sink a few inches away from my face. I tried to read the words over and over again but I had no idea what *contact with eyes* or *call poison control* meant, and the less sense they made the more panicked I became. My body boomed with heartbeats, an empty, shuddering shell on the floor of a bathroom. I touched my face, my arm, trying to convince myself that the membrane between inside and outside was still intact. The feeling of my skin on me made me sick and I began to vomit. I flushed the toilet, and it started to overflow. I slid slowly across the floor as the water inched toward me. When it finally reached me, I opened the door, ran through the living room, and out the front door. I ran barefoot through the streets, the guy with the soul patch running after me. A cop car drove by and I flagged it down. Soul Patch told them I had smoked weed and needed to go to the emergency room, could they take me? The cops told him that they could take me but they'd also have to arrest me. Take a cab, I was advised. Soul Patch hailed a cab as I sat in the fetal position on the curb. I was sent home from St. Vincent's Hospital with a piece of paper telling me about panic attacks, but I knew it was something more. I went to sleep that night hoping unconsciousness would reverse the horrifying depletion that had taken place. But I awoke the next morning and fell, breathless, into a room I could barely recognize, a body I could barely feel, and a mind I could barely follow into perception. The unmistakable arrhythmia of the "disconnect," as I had begun to call it, that had been disrupting my life, was now louder, more insistent, a second heart that beat along with my original heart, out of time, out of body.

. . .

THREE MONTHS AFTER ROY DIED, my mother was diagnosed with cervical cancer. I went with her and Julie to Sloan Kettering Cancer Center for her hysterectomy. As they prepped my mother for surgery, she looked scared. It was hard to identify; the expression was not at home on her face. I didn't like her looking like that.

While we were waiting, I got hungry. I always got hungry in the middle of crises. (On September 11, when Dalton went into lockdown after the second plane hit the Twin Towers, I went straight to the deserted cafeteria and devoured two plates of lo mein.) I now went to the hospital cafeteria and ate as much as I possibly could. I went back upstairs, and we were told we could go and see my mother. She had her eyes closed and was making noises.

I touched her. She was hot and soft, like melting wax.

The next day we visited again. I stared as the doctor checked the wound, even though he told me not to look. It was huge, the size of my hand, and deep. She contracted a MRSA infection and the wound would not close. Weeks passed and it still did not close, a mouth hanging open in the middle of her, as if frozen in shock or yawning in boredom. A team of surgeons prescribed and scraped and cut away but the infection would not abate. They sent her home with a wound VAC, a large suction cup that fit over the wound and was attached to tubes. The tubes extended from the vacuum device attached to her stomach, over her shoulders, and down into a canister she wore as a backpack, sucking and drawing the infected sludge out of the wound. She had to wear the wound VAC all the time. A sound like gravel under car tires filled up the space as the red-brown goo sailed across her chest, over her shoulders, and disappeared into the black-hole backpack. I could see her insides on the outside, the boundary between internal and external eroding. The more I saw of her, the less I understood. She was remote in her indomitability and she was remote in her frailty.

As she recovered up in the pool room bedroom, I didn't do anything for her. If she wanted to see me or needed something, I refused to go upstairs to her. I would not bring up her glasses, I would not come and talk to her. It felt too far away and too high up. But really I was confused. This was not how the story was supposed to go. And that felt scary. My mother was not supposed to be one of those sick strays who came here to die. She was not the person who lay in her room, in the dark, in weakness and uncertainty. She was the woman who ordered up other people's skeletons, who rendered the world and herself gigantic and powerful, who was the exception to every rule.

As my mother convalesced, I was having a hard time finding and then holding on to myself. I tried to describe to my therapist the feeling that I wasn't real, that I didn't exist. She didn't understand what I was talking about. She seemed to have been caught off guard by my cutting and now by my burgeoning unreality. I tried over and over to explain what I was experiencing. I couldn't look in the mirror because I didn't recognize my own face. I didn't know who or what I was. I couldn't remember being a person. I had memories but I felt no connection to them. I looked at my hands and I didn't understand that they were mine. Sometimes they felt very small and sometimes they felt very large. When I spoke, I didn't know where the sound was coming from, who or what was making it. Everything was too bright, very far away, and unfamiliar. Time stopped being linear, and instead curled in on itself in a lethal looping. Each moment was the first moment in the history of the universe, when things were just taking shape, though never forming something solid. At the same time there was a constant sense of déjà vu, as if everything that was happening had already happened. I felt far, far away. The thing that I was had crawled into the very back of my brain and was huddled there, squinting through a peephole at an unrecognizable world.

To get back to myself I was self-harming all the time. The self-harm did what nothing else could. The way I cut varied. Sometimes, I sucked in air and sliced at my flesh as quickly as possible, separating as much skin as possible, going as deep as I could. Sometimes, I drew the blade across my skin slowly, daring myself, seeing how much pain I could endure. It was a conversation. I asked my body a question and a red mouth opened on my flesh, answering me. If the answer wasn't loud enough, if I needed more pain, I would heat the blade of my Swiss Army knife with a lighter until it glowed red and press it sideways against my flesh, take a sharp breath, and listen to the skin crackle. After a few seconds I removed the blade and, hit with the rush of endorphins, felt wrapped in warm velvet. My mind and body unkinked and slackened. The burning lit up every neuron, set them singing in a barbershop harmony that revealed every pitch of injury—the shivering falsetto of pain, the rich bass of analgesia. The skin bubbled up and I popped the burn blisters and watched the liquid emerge. Sometimes I sampled the fluid issuing from my injured body as if it were a precious antidote. I loved those wounds, I revered them. My scarified body was a monument I was continually erecting for the confounding, darkly divine-seeming mind that felt so powerful, so alien. The scab that formed on top of the cut was the scarlet dome of a cathedral, the white scar lines left behind carvings on the facade. After each cut, after each burn, I was returned to my body, I touched the walls of myself again. It was also a way to mark time. Day one was when I hurt myself, and each successive day after, I healed. I knew then that I at least had the body of a human. I was alive and I could still move from the present into the future, whether I wanted to or not.

In March 2004, I was in the shower cutting, watching the water turn red, watching the blood streak down my legs like a second set of veins. I had dismantled a shaving razor and was using that keen, slim metal to slice up my thighs. On contact with the water, the blood, diluted, grew limpid, lighter, creating swift runnels of bloody water down my body. It stung when the water pelted the wounds. I sat on the floor of the shower and stared out at the world. I had been given a name, I had memorized all the semantic information having to do with Alice Carrière, but I was someone, something else. I was crying. Not from the physical pain, which no longer registered as pain, but from that collapsing feeling, so empty inside that the swollen world crashed in on me like a waterlogged ceiling. The weeping echoed in the bathroom, spread out over it, bounced off the walls and back at me. It was not me making that noise; the room was screaming at me, hollering warnings of what could happen if I kept this up—or what might happen if I didn't. I realized I couldn't stop cutting. The razor flitted back and forth across my skin. It felt like it was part of my hand, a disloyal extremity, a mutinous appendage. Somehow I managed to lay it on the rim of the bathtub next to the shower. The shower had steamed up the room, giving all my movements a dreamlike quality, as if I were a creature emerging from the mist. The water was so hot it had turned my skin pink, with streaks of deep red where I had opened myself up. I turned off the shower and dried myself, avoiding the cuts, and put on some clothes. I called my therapist and said:

"I think I need to go somewhere."

She told me to go to Lenox Hill Hospital.

I should let my mother know, I thought. On the phone the red light next to "bedroom" glowed: privacy mode on. I called my mother's secretary downstairs.

"I'm going to check myself into a psych hospital," I said.

"You should let your mother know," she said.

The secretary told me that my mother was in her room with two socialite friends. I felt like someone else had made the phone call to my therapist, someone else had made the choice to commit me. I needed to run. I grabbed cash, a change of shirt, a bottle of Chanel No. 14 perfume, and a toothbrush, and shoved them into my purse. I pitched out of my room, and there they were, standing in the kitchen. My mother's secretary must have gone upstairs and told them what I had said. All three of them were staring at me, silent as the sucking tubes of the wound VAC growled. I met my mother's eyes. I ran.

Outside, I didn't know which way to go because I didn't know why I was running. I ran down the street. The two socialites ran after me. One of them screamed at her chauffeur to stop me. He revved the engine and followed me. They caught up to me and cornered me. They were holding out their slender arms, their skin pale and smooth and glowing. Their hairstyles were the same—smooth and voluminous and shiny and curled at the ends, like fancy, looping calligraphy. Even the way their hair fell across their shoulders as they shifted back and forth, caging me with their arms, had a serenity, a calmness to it. They were ill-suited for these crazed postures, this urgent locomotion. Their eyes were not meant to be wild. I looked at them looking at me. They looked afraid, and I was the one making them afraid, and that scared me.

"It's Sally," said Sally. "Don't you remember all those clothes I gave you?"

"I know who you are. I'm not that far gone," I said. My brain stilled as it tried to figure out why it was being asked about borrowed clothes. In that moment of stillness, the soft, pastel urgency of these two women, trying to help my sick mother by trying to help her sick daughter, drained me of fight and I agreed to walk back to the house.

Back in the kitchen, my mother looked terrified, weighed down by those sucking tubes and her weakness. I went into my room, opened the tiny drawer where I kept my cutting kit—a shiny black LeSportsac pouch full of Swiss Army knives my father had given me, the sharp inserts of box cutters from my mother's studio, and the slivers of metal I had pried loose from shaving razors—brought it out into the kitchen and silently dropped it into my mother's hands. My gesture, pouring the sharp edges I used to flay myself into her soft, warm palm, contained a rage of such density that I flattened under it. I felt small and ashamed, and the force of regret knocked the breath out of me. I wanted to hug her and I wanted us to cry together. But I said nothing.

I went with my mother to Lenox Hill Hospital. She was silent as I filled out the forms. She said nothing as we rode the elevator to the eighth floor, the psych ward. We were buzzed in. A tech went through my bag, flipping through the pages of Sylvia Plath's *The Bell Jar* and Ken Kesey's *One Flew Over the Cuckoo's Nest* that I had brought with me, searching for razor blades I may have stashed inside. I felt oddly excited. A strange elation tickled the base of my spine as they stared at me, rifled through my belongings, tried to figure me out. This place was new. This place was unusual. To be a person in this place was new and unusual. This could be me. I could tape this identity over the busted-out hole of me.

"How do you know I haven't hidden something in my shampoo bottle?" I asked.

The tech eyed me with boredom and contempt.

"We don't," he said. "Did you?"

"No," I said.

He confiscated my shampoo bottle.

My mother left, and I was alone, eight floors up among strangers.

I was brought down a hall and into the second room on the left. An old woman was bent over one of the beds, her torso and face pressed into the mattress and her ass in the air.

"This is your roommate," said the nurse. "Elaine, this is your new roommate."

Elaine was making noises. Groans and mutters.

"I must have gained weight, these bloomers are killing me," she said into the mattress. "Everything is torturous."

Good word, I thought.

I wandered out into the main room that had tables and chairs, a broken rowing machine, and a tiny TV hanging from the ceiling. I started introducing myself to the people I would spend the next week with.

Evelyn had dissociative identity disorder—the new name for multiple personality disorder.

"I have ten different personalities with no dominant alter," she explained to me. Some were male and some were female, some were gay and some were straight, one was a baby.

"It's like cold water turning into hot water," she said about switching between alternate personalities.

Her scalp showed through her dry strawberry-blond hair, which was falling out because of her medication.

Ray always had rubber gloves hanging from his back pants pocket.

"What's your hobby?" he asked me and then answered his own question. "Ice skating. I read the obits voraciously. I just said ice skating to be sociable."

Rachel had survived Auschwitz. She was very old and her body was slight and gnarled. I felt drawn to nurture her as if she were an infant. I rubbed her back and spoke to her in hushed German. She rocked back and forth as much as her frail body allowed and murmured, "I hallucine. I hallucine." Marlene, who had also survived Auschwitz, walked over. Rachel looked up at her and asked if I had been in Auschwitz with them.

I played Scrabble with a young Russian man who was in hiding from the people who were trying to kill him.

"This place is like a vacation," he said. "Free food and safety." He tried to guess my birthday and said he would write a philosophical treatise about me. He also understood important mathematical equations.

A young female patient asked me many times a day, "How has your sleep been?"

"Fine," I answered over and over.

"So, how was your sleep last night?" she asked me. To her credit, it was a different question.

"So-so," I said, just to give her a different answer.

There was a schedule with activities so that we could separate the homogenous hunks of time that could jam up around us and crush us. We did aromatherapy. We did dance therapy. I swayed my hips and lifted my arms so my shirt rode up to my ribcage. The counselor tugged it down and said to the men, "You have to dance or turn away." The men stared, unmoving.

We did a flower-arranging session. Everyone took great care to select and tie the slim stems and the frilly blossoms together. I cut the blossoms off the stems, tied the green, decapitated stalks together, and put them in water. They looked like asparagus. Later, they would just look like anger.

That night they placed the flower arrangements on the tables where we ate dinner. All the bouquets were displayed except mine. I flew into a rage.

"What happened to my bouquet?"

"I think it was thrown out. It didn't have any flowers on it," said a nurse.

"That's how it was supposed to be. That was me expressing myself. Why is only what you think is beautiful beautiful? How dare you," I screamed.

Then it was time for dinner and I forgot my anger as a hunk of boiled chicken was placed in front of me.

I liked being here. The rules were clear and simple, their mere existence novel and diverting. Expectations were low—we were not here to get better, just not to get worse. The people were interesting. Patients introduced themselves with their diagnoses. They spoke casually about suicide attempts, about abusive parents, about hallucinations. A vinelike intimacy crept over and between us as we exchanged stories and showed each other our scars. Squeezed inside these hallways, eight stories up, it felt like we were the last people on earth. We had been selected, by magic or nature or divinity, to feel more, see beyond, hear maybe one too many voices. We each had something wrong, wrong enough to mark our skins, glaze our eyes, circle a hospital band around our wrists. In my mind, I hovered above the city not like a person but like an atmosphere, transformed into something enormous and powerful, making people stare up at me with wonder, making them sweat or shiver. I didn't feel like I was sick; I felt like I was special.

A nurse took me to the basement in a wheelchair for the medical workup every patient was required to get. When I walked back into the hallway afterward, the nurse was no longer there so I kept walking. I didn't have any shoes on, only hospital socks, though we were allowed to wear our street clothes. I took the elevator to the lobby. I walked outside in my socks, waiting for alarms to go off, for someone to notice the psych ward hospital bracelet on my wrist, tackle me, and bring me back where I belonged. But no one noticed me. The air on my skin, the strangers crawling around me, the sheer mass of other lives being lived in my proximity seemed otherworldly. Perhaps I didn't belong here anymore. I was a patient now. I belonged up there. There I had purpose. There I was accomplished. I could be the sexiest dancer, the angriest florist, and if I tried hard enough, the sickest patient. I went back inside the lobby and took the elevator back up to the eighth floor. When I approached the main door to the psych ward, Dr. Brune, the head doctor, was standing in the hallway. I knocked on the glass door. When Dr. Brune saw me, his eyes widened. I smiled wide and waved. He took long strides to the door like he wanted to run but was stopping himself.

"Did you come back up here alone?" he asked.

"Yes," I said. "They left me downstairs."

"And you came back?"

"Yes."

Dr. Brune didn't seem to understand.

On my third day there, my mother brought me chocolate from my favorite candy shop, Li-Lac. I ate greedily. I didn't think about my mother making an effort to bring me my favorite chocolate. I didn't think of her as housing such considerations, such care. I thought only that I had gotten something I wanted. Susan, who never spoke and rubbed scuff marks off the floor, glided over and removed three pieces of chocolate from the package and walked away. Anger enveloped me. I hunched over the chocolate defensively, trying to protect what I had, not wanting to share, unable to share the moment with my mother, the woman who was trying to give me everything she knew how to give.

The next day my father flew in from Germany and came to the hospital with my mother; it was only the second time I had seen my parents together in over a decade. He asked Dr. Brune how they would know I was well enough to be let out.

"When she stops cutting," said Dr. Brune.

"How will you know if she's stopped cutting if she's in a place where she can't cut?" my father asked.

"That's an interesting philosophical question," said Dr. Brune.

I was given the Minnesota Multiphasic Personality Inventory to fill out. It was composed of over five hundred statements I had to agree or disagree with, such as: "I like to pick flowers or grow house plants," "I am afraid of fire," "I like mechanics magazines," "Sometimes I feel like my soul is leaving my body." I felt so disconnected from myself that I couldn't decide what I felt from the list of choices. I let my father fill out the MMPI for me. The only moment I thought to intervene was when he reached the statement: "My father is a good man." But I just watched as he silently and without hesitation filled in the bubble marked "yes."

The next day, my mother and father sat across from me at a table in the main room. It felt like a strange weather phenomenon, as if three different fronts had coalesced in one spot. My mother sat silently as I tried to explain to them what I was experiencing. My father leaned toward me and scribbled notes. I jiggled my leg as I drew a picture of an outline of a body, like a crime scene, then drew a spiky aura around it and then small marks emanating from the head. I told them I felt disconnected from my body and my memories and my self. My father listened, nodding his head, writing down everything I said. He massaged my feet and hands, trying to see if I could feel it. I told him to press harder until it hurt but it never did.

"You seem manic," said my mother.

"I can't feel love anymore," I told them. "I have as much access to myself as I have to other people."

My father wrote down every word.

My mother wanted to hear what the doctor had to say.

When it was time for them to leave, my father pulled out a disposable camera and started taking photographs of me, the ward, and the patients. A nurse confiscated the camera, and I felt a pinch of loss as I watched the proof that we had all been here disappear.

Back in my room, the void began to unfold inside of me. The core of who I was was a tab of Alka-Seltzer dunked in water, its cohesiveness breaking up and effervescing into nothing, into oneness with what surrounded it. I wanted out of my mind and my body. At the same time I wanted to return to myself. I couldn't cut so I grabbed my notebook. I tried to write, which was how I spent my nights. My handwriting had become pudgy and loopy, like a child's. *I don't know what's wrong with me. It's become too pervasive. I think it's taken over entirely. I have no connection to myself anymore. It's as if I've memorized myself: my abilities, my proclivities, my tendencies, and I'm carrying them out by rote. Everything is too bright. It's a crystalline shifting, kaleidoscopic. If writing helps I would have to be writing all the time. I feel dizzy and hot. Weak. Shaking. Short of breath. I don't know who I am. What is this? Would I kill myself if I get crazier? Am I getting crazier? Yes.* I wrote nonstop for an hour. I begged the page to keep me safe. I wrote down a list of words: *insalubrious, surreptitious, spank, reek, lament, tacheometry.* I went into the bathroom that had no lock on the door and crawled under the sink. I drew my knees to my chest and caged them with my arms, hand gripping unrecognizable hand. I started to bang the back of my head against the wall. I said my name, my address, and my phone number over and over again.

"Alice Isabelle Carrière. One three four Charles Street between Greenwich and Washington. Two one two six seven five two four two one."

I had shattered into innumerable pieces and been scattered across immeasurable distances. Each particle had a part of me but no particle had enough of me to be me. I tried to pound the fragments back together with these words and the force of my head against the wall. The words got louder. They needed to be louder. They needed to be so loud that they flattened me back into myself. The words got fewer and fewer until I was just screaming my own name.

A nurse came in.

"You are frightening the other patients," she said.

She helped me up off the floor.

"Let's make your bed, and explain to me what's going on," she said.

"I don't know. It's so hard to describe. It's like I'm outside of myself and I don't recognize what I'm looking at. Everything feels unfamiliar, as if I'm seeing it for the first time."

"It sounds like you're dissociating," she said.

I had never heard that word, not even in therapy. The more I had tried to describe my disconnect, the more my therapist suspected I was schizophrenic, and the more alone I felt. Now, this woman I barely knew was offering me something very important. She was giving me the word.

"What does that mean?" I asked. The pumping of my heart felt like hands grabbing at a lifeline.

"You should talk to your doctor about it," she said.

"Can you get me a book or print something out for me?" I asked, gripping the bedsheet to my chest. "I need to know what this is."

The idea that what had been growing in me, the unnameable blankness, existed somewhere beyond me, in black and white on a page, gave me hope, made me feel like I could exist somewhere too. No matter how much I faded from existence and then roared back on crests of blood, I was still a person and there was a word for me.

After one week they released me. One week after that I lay in the bath, took a razor, and slid it up my left inner forearm, somehow missing all major vessels and arteries. The skin opened up and blood bloomed from the cut, the edges fading from opaque to translucent. I imagined my skin speaking, announcing the new word it had learned: *dissociation*.

2.

I was back floating around 134 Charles Street. I read all the books on dissociation I could find. I recognized myself in the flat repulsion of Sartre's *Nausea*. I understood the remote alarm, a nova raging in desolation, that seethed through Clarice Lispector's *The Passion According to G.H.* as she spent almost two hundred pages thinking about a cockroach, thinking about her thinking. I felt the same annihilating desperation in Octavia Butler's short story *The Evening and the Morning and the Night* as the characters tried to dig themselves out of their bodies. Along with dissociating, the boundaries between my moods had grown dangerously porous, happiness bleeding into despair, into euphoria, into desolation. When I felt good, it was an intense kind of good, hot steam spewing from a ruptured pipe. Then came sadness that turned vapor into liquid into stone, until my own breath drowned, then choked me. When I felt good, I spent hours reading the dictionary and writing down words. I spent days memorizing the capitals of all the countries in the world, making my mother's staff quiz me, pacing the floor muttering "Burkina Faso, Ouagadougou" under my breath. I wrote out an equation for death, pages and pages of nonsense graphs and charts and made-up mathematical symbols, with notes in the margins that said "Winnicott's aura" or "Schrödinger." The next week, I grew quiet. I stayed in bed and watched my favorite musicals, trying to locate in them what I had loved before and crying when I couldn't. I stood in the pantry reading the labels on boxes of cookies and the bottles of Diet Coke my mom was addicted to, trying to comfort myself with those concise lists of ingredients that disclosed what was inside. I'd get in the pool and see how long I could stay under water. Once I found a stray gemstone in the grout of the pool-side tiles, leftover from my mother's sessions with the gemologist, when she'd shuffle gems into lines with a credit card, like dazzling cocaine, often sending them skittering across the floor and the gemologist scrambling to corral an errant emerald. The pool room smelled of the perfumes she made with celebrity event planner Robert Isabell, rows of little black glass bottles reeking of musk and leather and bergamot lining the lip of the pool, her life up here so extravagant, so colorful, so fragrant, and in such contrast to how drained of life I felt.

I spent a lot of time in Nanny's room drinking Red Rose tea and watching TV with her. I would wedge myself next to her in her armchair, sometimes playing with the gold chain around her neck like I had when I was a baby, and we'd watch *Keeping Up Appearances*, *Antiques Roadshow*, and *Gilmore Girls*. She sometimes tried to ask questions about what was going on with me but she wouldn't know what to say, so we'd stay curled up together and wait to see how much that Victorian inkwell would go for at auction. Words were useless here, but the closeness of our bodies and the calm of her room reminded me of something solid and essential.

One night, she walked in on me cutting. It felt like she had walked in on me having sex, something so intimate.

"What are you doing?" she asked, squinting at me through the dark.

"I'm cutting myself," I said. It didn't occur to me to lie.

Pain swept over her face. She sat down on the edge of my bed and put her hand on my leg. The contact made me flinch.

"It's fine. It's fine," I said, the word turning into a moan. "You can leave."

"I'm not leaving you alone," she said.

"It's fine. I swear. I promise you can leave." The last word stretched itself out, as if trying to drag her toward the door.

She sat with me for a long time, until I fell asleep. In the morning, the razor blade and lighter I used to sterilize it were gone from my bedside.

Two weeks later, energized again, I sat at the dining room table stabbing at my computer, finishing the novel I had been writing. When I finished it, I gave it to my mother to read. She read it up in her bedroom, and when she finished it, I found a note in my room, written on a ripped-out page of a notebook with a circle of coffee stain on it. It read: "You are a success already—you have written this. Deal with it. Go to Kinko's and get it bound." I kept the note, framed it, and put it on my desk.

My mother had no idea what to do with me or what to say. The only time we spent together was Thursday nights when I'd meet her up in the pool room bedroom and we'd watch *The L Word*, a show about lesbians in LA. We'd sit on her bed eating potato chips and criticizing the fashion, the shape of their boobs, and the dramatic facial expressions they made while they fucked each other. Most days, I watched her trying to get away from me. When I tried to show her something, play her a song, or read her something, her eyes would go first: arms cocked, palms on table, gaze elsewhere. I would watch her leave.

"You're leaving?" I would say to her back.

"Yes," she would say, not looking back.

Sometimes I would try and force my way in. I walked up to her in the studio and told her I had given some guy a blow job.

"Ugh, I don't want to hear about that," she said, walking away.

I was a ghost and I tried to haunt my mother into recognition. I walked around for a week with a cut up my forearm, and she never noticed or at least didn't say anything. I would show her my cuts, shoving my arm into the path of her gaze, inviting her to walk through their openings and into me.

My mother hosted a fashion show for the designer Ronaldus Shamask. Before the party I hung out in the kitchen as cute cater waiters in starched white shirts and ties lined canapés onto silver trays. When my mother walked in to check on things, I approached her and held out my arm.

"What should I do about these?" I said, gesturing at the healing cuts on my arm. "How should I cover them up?"

I spoke louder than I needed to, making sure the servers and chef could hear me.

"Just put some makeup on them," she said, her voice low as she cast uncomfortable sidelong glances at the strangers around her pretending not to hear.

I didn't need her advice on how to cover up my cuts. I didn't want to cover them up. I wanted them witnessed. Then the party began and I gave the tour over and over, circulating like a blood cell through the halls of 134 Charles Street. After an hour, the guests moved down to the lower studio and watched as models wearing organza trapeze dresses streaked with colorful rubber paint stalked through the space and a man played a cello while reciting a poem. After the party was over, I lingered in the kitchen talking to the servers as they wrapped leftover slices of seared tuna in Saran Wrap. I didn't want them to leave. I wanted them to stay and talk to me, to offer me more food, to laugh at my jokes. I stood in the kitchen as they loosened their ties and put their coats on, and 134 Charles Street emptied out, until it was only the three of us left, my mother drunk upstairs, Nanny alone in her room with the TV on, and me in the empty kitchen, eating leftover hors d'oeuvres and drinking from the half-empty bottles of red wine.

I made my way into the library and scanned the shelves. I saw my mother's name on the spine of a book and slid it out. It was the fictionalized autobiography she had written and published the year I was born. It was called *History of the Universe*, and it was her history, which made her the universe. That felt right. It had been edited down to a modest 197 pages from nearly two thousand pages of journal entries. It was organized into five chapters—Family, Marriage, Career, Friends, and Death—and in them she described everything about everyone she knew, everything she thought, all the products she used—from Crest toothpaste to Clinique powder—and every single detail about her physical appearance. As I read her book late into the night, I was grateful for her near-compulsive meticulousness and her self-absorption. Because she believed that every thought she had was interesting, I got to know my mother; I was allowed access to her through the only way she knew how to communicate—her work. The only thing she did not describe were emotions, unless she was listing synonyms for rage. What did something so vast and powerful and mysterious as the Universe have to do with feelings? One line read: *I wish I didn't think I was the only person in the world.* I couldn't tell if it was the most arrogant thing I had ever heard, or the loneliest. The only person in the world had no one to talk to, nothing to counteract the persuasion of their own imaginings. The only person in the world got to invent reality, but was alone to suffer the consequences of its incoherence. And what about the child belonging to the only person in the world? Just another invention.

I had started snorting Dead Uncle Roy's leftover Dilaudid, the powerful opioid he had been prescribed when he was dying, that I'd found in my mother's bathroom. When the drug hit, I felt rooted. I felt my edges. Twelve days before my nineteenth birthday, I invited Effie and another friend, David, over for a swim while my mother was out of town. Effie and David watched me snort two pills and I poured us all vodka. We went up to the pool room and took off our clothes. David got in the water and Effie and I started dancing. I felt great. I was a giant bunny rabbit, all wiggles and heat and softness. I bent over and kissed David. Nausea began to insinuate itself into the warm fluff. I staggered downstairs, still naked, and lurched into the kitchen. I switched on the tea kettle to make some coffee. While I waited for the water to boil I got an English muffin from the bread box. I caught my reflection in the curved metal and it felt remote, my face just an extension of the appliance—a knob or a handle. I slid a serrated knife out of the knife block to separate the two sides of the muffin. Instead of cutting the muffin, I calmly slid the knife across my right forearm four times. It felt very natural, part of the rudimentary gestures of meal preparation. Coffee, muffin, skin. It felt reflexive, correct. As the blood started spilling down my arm, I slowly realized I had done something incorrect. I picked up the phone and called Effie on the intercom.

"Effie? Effie? Could you come down here for a moment, please?" My voice was oddly formal.

I stared at my arm as I waited for Effie. There was no pain. It had opened up so easily. I found a dish towel and wrapped it around my arm. Effie and David arrived in the kitchen. Effie gasped.

"What did you do? What did you do?" she said.

"We have to go to the hospital," David said.

I went to my room to put on some clothes and attempted to put on makeup, but David dragged me away from the mirror. We piled into his car and he drove us to Saint Vincent's Hospital.

On the way, David said, "Just say you cut yourself by accident."

I didn't want to lie. I'd tell the nurses and doctors the truth and we'd talk about it. We'd discuss how interesting it was and they'd nod and say, "Good point." They'd understand.

When we arrived at St. Vincent's, a man with a clipboard asked me what had happened. I chattered away about the pills, the vodka, the kitchen knife. A nurse took my blood and took my clothes and hooked me up to a saline drip. Someone called my mother, who was three hours away in the Hamptons. Effie left. David came in to check on me and then left too. I was taken into another room to get stitches. I watched a doctor stitch me up, embroidering my body, turning me into a decoration. She led me back to my bed. A young psychologist arrived, looking scared. She was petite and pretty and gripped a clipboard, as if it kept her from falling to great depths. She asked me why I did this. I announced, in a clear, too-loud voice: "I am not going to pontificate to you on the proximity of mortality." I may have smiled. She paused, wrote something down on her clipboard, and left. A man at the foot of the bed next to me turned to me and said, "Wow, you have a big vocabulary."

"Thank you," I said, and smiled.

The saline made me need to pee constantly. I walked to the bathroom in my thin blue paper gown, trailing my IV. The bathroom floor was covered in urine and my hospital-issued blue socks with the nibs of rubber on them soaked it up. I felt strangely capable, welcoming the unique challenges of being a patient once again.

After the sun came up, and the drugs and alcohol were flushed from my system, I started to get antsy. I demanded my clothes and was refused.

"You almost killed yourself in three different ways," I was told.

"What would happen if I ripped out my IV?" I asked.

The doctors finally reached my therapist. I convinced her to get them to let me go. She told me she would as long as I came to see her that day and that I agreed to be put on the waiting list for an inpatient hospital. I was given my clothes and I left.

Twenty days later, I was admitted to Austen Riggs, a psychiatric hospital. In his report, Dr. Palton documented his impression of me during the admissions interview: *Attractive, very bright, and verbal young woman wearing a dress that showed a little too much of her for the weather and the occasion, and with a seductive quality.* It was a warm fall day and I'd worn a knee-length yellow dress in a stretchy cotton that showed my collarbone and my arms, but no cleavage.

My mother had driven me to Austen Riggs and was waiting in the reception area. Dr. Palton invited her into the room to discuss payment. *Things broke down*, Dr. Palton wrote in his report. *The area of finances became a sinkhole in the consultation. Although mother and her secretary and Alice had all been told in writing and/or by phone about the financial terms of admission, Ms. Bartlett arrived at the consultation without her checkbook, without having given us her or her daughter's insurance information, without having filed the fee reduction we sent her.*

Dr. Palton told us that my insurance would not cover my stay. My mother couldn't afford the treatment at that time and had assumed insurance would cover it. I watched my mother sitting on the cream sofa. I could detect no power or mystery in her. She was small and scared. I understood for a moment what I was taking from her, what my existence demanded. As Dr. Palton chastised her, I felt protective of her. We both had a naïve belief in the endlessness of everything—of resources, of good graces, of exceptions—but the demands of my illness were straining that illusion. For a brief moment I glimpsed the reality of what was happening—of what my illness meant for me and for my family, what it would take from us. My failure to keep pace with my peers, with the expectations of the people around me, would have consequences. I ran crying into the bathroom, and my mother followed me. I told her I couldn't be admitted. It was too expensive and I wasn't worth it. She told me it was all right, that we'd figure something out.

My mother made a phone call as Dr. Palton watched her from his office door. I found out later that she had called a friend to borrow the money to pay the astronomical admissions fee. The German medical insurance my father had would end up enabling my stay at Riggs. I was admitted to Austen Riggs, and those momentary realizations—that I was not just owed everything, that the world would not heel at my feet—evaporated as I moved into the white columned mansion and became a full-time sick person for the next year.

3.

The Austen Riggs Center, located on Main Street in a small town called Stockbridge, Massachusetts, was a prestigious "open-setting" psychiatric hospital for "treatment-resistant patients." We could leave whenever we wanted. Patients walked in and out freely, went to the few restaurants in the area, shopped in Great Barrington, saw movies in Pittsfield, even traveled out of the state. The nurses didn't wear uniforms, and we could lock our doors. Our meals were cooked for us. For breakfast, we could choose from omelets, scrambled eggs, pancakes, French toast. There was an enormous refrigerator in the cafeteria that held Old Chatham Sheepherding Company sheep's milk yogurt, in plain and maple flavors, and Naked smoothies. We could take as many as we liked, whenever we liked. I decided I would make up for the cost of this place by eating as much fancy yogurt as I possibly could. Sometimes, tourists would mistake Riggs for a hotel and line up at the buffet with the patients.

The residential building was a weathered white mansion with a mahogany staircase with peeling lacquer, threadbare red and yellow patterned carpets, dusty floor-to-ceiling drapes, a chandelier with dull brass finishes and missing pendeloques, and a large community room with a shabby brown out-of-tune baby grand piano with a few broken keys. My room had a bay window, fireplace, and pink sink that, I was told, Judy Garland had installed when she spent time there. The staff boasted that James Taylor had written "Fire and Rain" during his stay. The place had an impressive pedigree. My peers now were: the daughter of an NYC mega-restaurateur, the daughter of a famous Native American author, the stepdaughter of a singer whose Christmas song haunted every North American store from October until January, and the daughter of the man responsible for the fragrances in most products. Angela was an ex-junkie dwarf and a movie producer who was afraid of unattached pieces of hair. Paula was a morbidly obese lesbian who threatened to throw herself out of her shrink's window (which was only six feet above the ground). Chad was seventeen and could make himself vomit on cue, without even sticking his finger down his throat. Beth rarely spoke and made strange, startlingly loud noises deep down in her throat. Bob was a middle-aged man who had been a patient for a solid decade and hit on all the girls, asking them repeatedly, "Can I check under your hood?" He claimed it was cheaper for his father to pay for this place than to keep having to bail him out of jail or pay for totaled cars. Brad was five five, told people that he was six two, and wasn't worried because he could always fall back on modeling. Steven kept saying he was going to start a book club and stashed a gun in his room. Derek had been in a cult and before that had been a Chippendales dancer.

At Riggs, the recommended stay was "indefinite"—patients were encouraged to stay for years, or at least until their money ran out. To fill the time, people fucked each other, smoked weed on the sly, occasionally overdosed on Tylenol or Klonopin, formed cliques, bullied each other. Our main purpose was to explain ourselves, over and over, to one another. Riggs boasted a high number of self-styled intellectuals, so we proved adept at this assignment. There were activities and events to keep us patients from languishing in introspective luxury. For Halloween there was a costume party. I dressed up as Vocabulary, with words like *insalubrious* written on my arms, and felt very cute and smart. For Thanksgiving, there was a pumpkin carving competition. I carved the image of a pumpkin into a pumpkin and titled it *Narcissism*, and felt very clever. There was a woodshop; a greenhouse; ceramics, visual, and fiber arts studios; and a black-box theater whose two productions a year were helmed by a Shakespeare & Co. director and included patients and local actors. There was also an endless supply of what we, naïve and bored and entitled and sick, interpreted as "drama." An unknown man called the phones in the rooms of all the female patients, posing as boyfriends or male friends in order to have phone sex with them. I fell for it, thinking it was my friend Hicham. A fifty-year-old patient convinced an eighteen-year-old patient to take a Valium so he could have anal sex with her. Someone wrote the word *kike* on a pizza box. One girl threw a TV down the stairs because she wanted to hear that satisfying crunch. The same girl took down the giant oil painting in the living room and, with a sign saying "Free Painting," pedaled it on Main Street in the snow. If the staff found out about any of these things, the community would sit and talk about it. There were barely any rules and no consequences, and rules and consequences were the two things I needed most. My room was a mess, and I repeatedly "failed" inspection, but failure meant nothing here. I was urged to go to group therapy sessions, but nothing happened if I didn't show up. It was assumed we would be here for a very long time, and I felt no urgency, no need. The doctors and counselors expressed no urgency, implied no need. The passivity and luxury that defined this treatment would later anger me. How could we grow when we encountered no resistance, nothing that encouraged us to change? The extreme bounty—of time, of chances, of yogurt—and the extreme luxury—chronological, spatial, psychic, culinary—were like sedatives. They made the reasons for being here, and the need to overcome them, fuzzy. I wondered why anyone would ever want to leave. We were important and special and cared for accordingly. My every move so important as to be recorded by staff, my every complaint listened to and wondered about, my every random thought met with a rapt audience. If this was what it meant to be ill, I didn't know if I ever wanted to get better.

My therapist at Riggs, Dr. Lampen, was a pretty blond woman who rarely spoke, with a face that didn't move. It was as if she had a special frozen face on top of her real face. I tried to imagine her inner life, the secret hiding place behind her motionlessness, but it was so extreme that I sometimes wondered if she was real. There was no desk in her room, only two chairs and a sofa. There were no photographs, no personal touches. This was intentional. This kind of therapy relied on anonymity—I wasn't allowed to know anything about her so that I couldn't project anything onto her. It was a familiar and infuriating feeling: another remote woman. She did have a hook from which she hung her coat. That coat was the only evidence that she existed outside of this room. It hung there, heavy with meaning. Sometimes it would be wet or there would be a leaf on it, and I felt I had glimpsed something I wasn't supposed to.

I began therapy by saying what I was not. "I am not human," I said. "I don't have feelings." "I don't have a history or an identity that belongs to me." After a few weeks, I was able to name myself. "I am depersonalized," I said. "I am an only child who lived in a big house." "I pretend everything is a novelty." "I turn pain into art, like my mother."

Dr. Lampen subjected me to long stretches of silence, which made her motionlessness even more eerie and pronounced.

"I don't like quiet because I'm afraid of my own mind," I told her.

She was silent.

I asked her why she was so quiet.

"I'm having a reverie about what you just told me," she said.

"I want that," I said. "I want to be able to have a reverie."

I grabbed on to that word as the one strapped-down thing in the deep space of my mind. I wanted my mind to be able to play, to wander without vanishing into the infinite, dark universe of my dissociated brain.

Every professional I spoke with insisted I describe over and over again what I meant by depersonalization—a type of dissociation I had learned about from the books and articles I'd read. It was a phenomenon most commonly brought on by trauma.

"I am incapable of knowing myself," I explained to Dr. Lampen. "I feel like I can't remember my past. I can't distinguish my thoughts about myself from my parents' thoughts about me. I feel like my arms and legs don't belong to me. I'm not real. I don't feel anything. I feel totally alien to myself."

"What does the cutting do for you?" she asked.

"When I see the blood, I feel better," I said. "It centers me and it re-establishes causality. When I cut I know I will bleed and then I know I will heal. I don't understand consequences, how one thing leads directly to another. I think that's because of my parents, how they believe we're an exception to the rules, that what applies to other people doesn't apply to us."

"What do you think the dissociation does for you? Do you think it also helps in some way?"

"I think it protects me the way hibernation protects an animal through winter," I said. I pointed to the back of my neck. "I'm located here," I said. "Silent and watching."

I felt virtuosic naming my ailments. If I didn't have an identity, I could be a rhapsody of vacancy. If the difference could not be told between me and my parents, I could be a triptych of disorientation.

There was non-mandatory group therapy, which was held in the basement, a dark, dingy-green room with overly cushy green sofas that made me feel as if I were in a stomach being digested. We were discussing the fact that Amy had taken a lighter to the phone in the hall.

"I just wonder what it means that Amy destroyed the place you speak into. Perhaps she feels she doesn't have a voice here," said one of the counselors.

"This was an act of tremendous hostility, and there is a way in which Amy isn't heard in this community," said another counselor.

"A cigar is never a cigar and I'm pissed at you," said Angela.

Amy said nothing and rolled her eyes at the floor.

"I feel as if you're burning us right now in refusing to talk about it," said one of the nurses.

I was sitting next to Kim, who had asked me three times that day how to spell *pomegranate*. For some reason, there was a tennis racket next to me on the sofa and I walked my fingers down along the strings like a ladder.

Now Amy was crying. She was telling a story about how her mother had set her bedsheets on fire one night when she was a kid. How maybe setting the phone on fire was connected to that memory. How maybe she was trying to do something like what her mother had done to her so that she could feel a sense of control over a moment when she had no control. The counselors were nodding very slowly, like their heads were applauding. Everyone said something. Everyone did the leaning-forward. Everyone looked intently at where the words and tears and feelings were coming from. I had been trying to figure out a word in the crossword puzzle that lay next to me on the sofa without anyone noticing. My eyes were hurting from looking sideways and down in the dark.

Dr. Shapiro turned to me.

"How do you feel, Alice?" Dr. Shapiro asked. He had a white close-clipped beard, white hair, and round glasses.

I looked up. "What?"

"Right now. How do you feel right now?" asked Dr. Shapiro.

I raised my eyebrows and didn't say anything. The question frightened me.

"I feel like you don't feel," said Derek, flipping his palms up in frustration.

"I've never seen you cry," said Angela. "You're so fucking cheery all the time."

They were right. I had gotten good at compensating for the emptiness by carbonating my personality until I fizzed with chipperness, then turned flat and tepid and locked myself in my room with plates of food to binge-watch my *CSI* DVDs.

How did I feel? I didn't know. I couldn't locate the mechanism responsible for generating feelings and I couldn't decipher the faint flickering of feelings that did manage to arise. But there were endless metaphors that I could mix to try to approximate awareness.

"Feelings are like nictitating tinsel caught somewhere in between where my mind has receded to and my brain kind of slumps nesciently," I said. "Feeling is me writing a sentence on a chalkboard and something following me with an eraser, erasing every letter as I write it down."

The room was quiet. I had started using huge words, often incorrectly, in every sentence I spoke, as if encrusting my speech with precious gems would blind people to its fundamental worthlessness.

"You're full of shit," said Derek, this time stretching his hands out with his palms like stop signs.

"I think it means a lot that Alice is here today. The fact that she came means that she wants to do the work," said Dr. Shapiro.

"You walk around here in those sexy outfits and you think you're so smart," said Angela.

"Who the fuck are you, really?" said Derek.

This was a good question. This was *the* question.

"I just say lots and lots of words, and then follow them with their synonyms, maybe to try and get at that one essential and preliminary thing or maybe to get as far away from it as possible," I said.

"What are you even talking about?" Angela said. "Amy is talking about how she feels and she's upset and you're just bullshitting around. Are you even listening to anything anyone else says?"

I looked over at Amy. I saw her crying. I had heard her story. It was just a story. I saw how she struggled through telling it but I didn't get it. I was so preoccupied with not feeling human that I couldn't recognize humanity anywhere else. The answer to twenty-four across was *whist*, which was an early form of the card game bridge and also an adjective meaning silent or hushed.

"How do you feel right now?" Dr. Shapiro asked again.

I knew that they were all waiting for something, but I didn't know what. I was silent for a while, and the silence sucked at the room.

"My mind is the mental colluvia at the base of the hill of my brain. It's insalubrious," I said.

No one said anything.

"I can't tell the difference between my mother and a remote control," I said.

No one said a word. Derek got up and left.

I DEVELOPED A CLOSE FRIENDSHIP with a girl named Carly. Carly was a pretty Jewish girl from the Upper East Side with eating and borderline disorders and cratered self-esteem. She had a sharp, morbid sense of humor, which contrasted arrestingly with her soft, deep kindness. She spoke in a girlish mumble, which she occasionally interrupted to spit brilliant absurdist freestyle raps. Her mother was critical and domineering, pushing her to injury on the balance beam installed in their apartment for her early gymnastics career, and the men she dated were ruthlessly narcissistic. Carly would sit on the floor of her room with Frownies (what looked like pieces of cardboard) taped to her face to prevent wrinkles on her twenty-year-old skin, and create—hand-painted phrenology skulls, embroidered journal entries, BDSM PowerPoint presentations. We spent all our time together. We drove around Massachusetts in Carly's Lexus visiting thrift shops, getting our ears pierced, singing karaoke at the local bar. She gave me my first bikini wax, the two of us sprawled on the floor of her room, laughing until we cried as we both tried to pry cooling wax off my genitals. We listened to The Modern Lovers' "Hospital" and Belle and Sebastian's "Get Me Away from Here, I'm Dying" as she dyed my hair black and we talked about how it felt when we hurt ourselves, what our mothers had done wrong, the blow job she had given fellow-patient Colin, and the sex I'd had with fellow-patient Nick while speeding down a highway at night.

I loved being a best friend. I loved being essential, being an intercessor between someone and their deepest revelations. But I was careless with feelings and information; I would get distracted or bored and turn away from these friendships with no thought for the person on the other side. I didn't know how to sustain relationships. I was still friends with Effie but now, without her right in front of me, I forgot our friendship existed. Riggs was its own world, and I forgot everything outside of it—my old friends, my sister in Europe, the needs and wants of other people. My friendship with Carly was the only friendship that mattered, until I decided it no longer did.

When a new girl arrived, I dropped Carly and spent every minute with Sophia. Sophia was a tall, gap-toothed California girl with broad shoulders and a wide, beautiful face who was less interesting and meaner than Carly but who liked me a lot. One year later, she would copy down my mother's credit card number and order three thousand dollars' worth of clothes on it. Sophia would make fun of Carly, and I would laugh along. I would pass Carly in the halls and both our gazes would drop to the floor. I felt bad but I didn't know how to fix it.

There was something repulsive but inevitable about how I treated people, something that reminded me of my parents.

I had many family therapy sessions at Riggs, sometimes with my mother and Nanny, sometimes with my mother and father, and sometimes just with my mother. When it was just my mother, she spoke about the bind she found herself in with her competing interests: her work and me.

"I'm making changes," she said. "I'm planning not to participate in any shows this year and to spend more time out in Amagansett painting."

I was hurt, but I didn't say anything. The social worker observed how we cautiously tiptoed around our needs.

We began to talk about our difficulty conveying feelings and communicating what we needed, and how we couldn't express our love and longing for each other. We noticed similarities in how we managed feelings—by withdrawing and avoiding—and we admitted that it left us feeling angry and isolated from each other.

My mother connected her inability to communicate feelings to her trauma.

"I can't cry," she said, "because it's too painful to go to that level of feeling. I was always afraid I'd damage you because of what happened to me, so I could never fully commit to parenting you."

Her brow was creased in a way that told me this was difficult for her, painful. She was trying.

"I'm jealous of your trauma," I said.

She looked confused.

What I meant was I needed something tangible to point to and blame. What I meant was I needed us to be the same, and I needed us to be different. What I meant was, I needed her.

When my father flew in from Germany for a week, we had many family sessions. "You both have such different stories," I said. "About what happened and about who I am. I can't tell what my own history is because I can't tell the difference between my memories and yours. That's why I can't make any decisions for myself. I feel like your world, your feelings, your ideas are all-consuming, and they become a bigger priority than anything I think or feel. I want you both to sit down in front of a witness and get your story straight so that I know what happened to me."

My father nodded over and over, saying "Yes, yes, yes." My mother stared into space.

"I kind of almost want you to kill each other," I said.

My father laughed and said, "Yes, yes, exactly. I can understand that."

"I need to separate from you," I continued. "Especially you, Mom. I feel confused by your history, the abuse. When I read your journals I almost believed your trauma had happened to me. I need to know what really happened to me." I turned to my father. "For instance, did you really say a daughter's first sexual experience should be with her father?"

"No, no I didn't," he said.

"Did you hear him say it?" I asked my mother.

"I don't know," she said.

My father threw up his hands. There was a limpness to my mother's gaze.

The social worker asked my parents questions about their childhoods. My parents both agreed that as the eldest children in dysfunctional, often violent households, they felt like they couldn't protect their younger siblings from death and abuse, which left them feeling helpless, anxious, and ineffectual as parents. They admitted that their drug and alcohol use played a role in blurring what we all agreed to call "reality." They were both afraid I'd kill myself, like Till. I resented the evocation of his name and that they were using him as a cautionary tale.

I had thought that watching my parents agree would shift something inside me, but their collaboration made me anxious, scared, and angry. I had only one memory of us together when I was little—I was three and they were leaving to go out, dressed in their fancy clothes, and I was dizzy from my mother's heavy-handed dose of perfume. I was weeping. I didn't want them to leave. When they left, I wept and wept, and when they came back, I thought it was because they had heard me from far, far away. It seemed I spent my life trying to manage distance, negotiate the intervals between: me and my father (his closeness a balm and a threat), my mother (her distance a challenge and a bereavement), my body and my mind (the cleaving I feared would kill me). Now that my parents were both in the same room with me, I couldn't correctly interpret their presence and their effort as the love and concern that it was. Instead, my body read their unity, however fleeting, as another threat.

I was put through psychological testing. For the first test, I had to draw a picture of myself. I finished and handed it to the doctor.

"Where is the body?" she asked.

I looked at my self-portrait. I had drawn a giant, blank oval surrounded by squiggles of curly hair. The head shape and hair squiggles took up the entire page.

"Oh," I said. I stared at my picture. "I guess I forgot."

For the Thematic Apperception Test I was shown a card with a neutral image on it and was asked to create a story about the image. In response to a card showing a boy holding a violin, I informed the doctor that the boy had dismantled the violin in order to exact revenge on his mother by fashioning an exact replica of his father's suicide. In response to another card, I explained that the "ultimate narcissist" finds another woman with her same build and hair and puts a mask on her that's identical to her own face in order to free herself of solipsism by essentially killing her version of herself in her.

"It's how suicide becomes murder when you separate yourself from yourself," I clarified.

I felt an immense pressure to come up with the most interesting stories I could possibly tell. I imagined my parents watching me, waiting for me to tell fascinating tales, to do what I was good at. I didn't know the plain language of feeling, the fundamental mechanics of observation, without the flourishes of violent imaginings. Stories were a coded language I was proficient in.

The therapist administering the tests summarized my responses in her files: *The temptation of psychotic fantasy is that it makes anything seem possible, and it distracts Alice from dizzying fears and deep sadness. She can tolerate very little stillness, softness, or passivity, instead favoring stimulating situations that provide a forum for grand ideas and imaginary scenarios.* The file summarized the testing results: *The testing diagnosis is of a narcissistic character in a psychotic state characterized by boundary disturbances, intermittently disorganized thinking, and disregard for consensually validated reality.* I was diagnosed with dissociative disorder and psychotic disorder NOS (not otherwise specified). The file concluded that:

> *Currently she cannot locate an outer psychological edge where she ends and something else—a desire for someone recognized as separate from herself, or a metrical world not subject to her fantasy—begins. Lacking a clear identity, she is nevertheless self-absorbed in the sense of being trapped in her own mind, where what little sense of relating she does have is intensely, even gruesomely sadomasochistic. Ms. Carrière lives in a world where little holds firm and everything is up for question, as if there were no limit to the power of her mind's capacity to create and destroy. She mentally turns convention on its head, and nothing is as it appears, not the structures of family or church, not the usual constraints of space and time, not even the categories of life and*

> *death. Her philosophizing reaches psychotic proportions and her thinking, though supported by a formidable intelligence and expansive cultural knowledge, is so fast and so fantastic that it speeds beyond easy contact with other minds.*

Had I read that then, I would have thought that all sounded beautiful. Reading it later, it sounded very lonely.

ONE SPRING DAY, I was downstairs in the computer room, where Angela was submitting her monthly order of boxes of lint rollers, jars of sauerkraut, and packs of Wolford stockings, and Chad was showing someone the NRA website. I went to use the bathroom. I finished peeing and wiped myself. As I pulled my hand away, I felt something dangling out of me. At first I thought it must be the string of a tampon, but I wasn't having my period and knew I hadn't put one in, and it didn't feel like whatever it was was in my vagina. I tugged on it and it slid out smoothly. I held it in front of me, pinched in toilet paper.

It was a worm. It was a worm—eight inches long with almost the girth of a pencil—that I had just yanked out of my anus. With my left hand I pulled up my overalls and buttoned them with difficulty. I went to the sink and laid the worm on the edge. It was moving. The worm was alive. It looked clean. It looked brand new. I bathed the worm with soap and water. I wrapped it in a paper towel and put it in my pocket.

I looked at myself in the mirror. My face looked as if it was about to make an unanticipated acceptance speech, mouth half open and eyebrows arched. My body was dead quiet and I was calm. Then I felt as if a wide, heavy peal of laughter was ballooning inside me. Something was happening that was too big to contain—things were coming out, things I could not control. I scrubbed my hands under hot water, so hot it steamed. I checked myself out in the mirror again. I rubbed underneath my eye to remove a smudge of makeup. I looked good.

I left the bathroom. Sophia was waiting for me outside the computer room.

"A worm just came out of my ass," I told Sophia.

I felt power. I felt pride. I smiled.

"No. No fucking way. Oh my god," said Sophia. She recoiled, screamed, waved her arms around.

I left Sophia and headed to the nurses' station on the second floor, the worm in my pocket. I walked down a long, twisting hallway covered with a light-brown carpet. My worm was the secret I didn't know I was keeping. I was my worm's secret that it was revealing to me. And the secret was that I had a body. And that body did, in fact, have something alive in it.

I walked up to the nurses' station.

"Can I help you?" asked Nurse Linda.

"I just excreted a worm," I said, voice smooth as a worm gliding through dirt.

The nurses said nothing. It seemed they were waiting for the punch line. I reached into my pocket and I took out my worm. I slowly unfolded the paper towel and laid it down on the partition between the nurses and me. There was silence. They looked at my worm. Nurse Linda's lips looked like worms. Nurse Brenda squinted as if worms were about to come out of her eyes. Nurse Debra held her breath as if her lungs were filled with worms and no air.

"I'm sorry, I've never seen anything like this," Nurse Brenda said.

"What do you want to do?" asked Nurse Debra, as if I were an expert at having a parasite ambulate out of my anus.

"I want to go to the emergency room."

I felt saner than I'd ever felt. I felt my body. I had a body. I was in that body. And inside that body there had been a worm.

"No," said Nurse Debra. "This is not an emergency."

I saw the word *emergency* in my head. *Emergency* contained the word *emerge*. A worm had emerged from my anus. Its emergence was an emergency.

"Take me to the fucking emergency room," I said.

"I'm sorry," said Nurse Debra. "This is not an emergency."

"I need to go to the emergency room."

"You are not in any immediate danger. You will have to wait until tomorrow. Then someone will be able to take you to the doctor."

I pictured an entire night alone with my worm, but also not alone because maybe there were more of them. My entire insides could be crawling with worms. I needed to know what was inside me.

"But I need to go now. I need to know what this is. Can you tell me what this is? No, you can't. You've never seen anything like this before. I need to know what this is."

"Do you feel physically ill?" asked Nurse Debra.

I felt ill with urgency.

"No," I said.

"I'm sorry, we can't take you to the emergency room," said Nurse Brenda.

I gave up.

"I want a Ziploc bag," I said.

A nurse cautiously passed the Ziploc bag to me. I tenderly put the swaddled worm into the bag. Sophia and I borrowed Derek's car and left for the hospital. I looked out the car window at Riggs at night. Riggs, lit up from inside, took on a surreal beauty. Maybe I'd be there for a decade, like Bob. Maybe I'd be happy there. But I had something in me after all, something that reminded me I had places to be, capacities I had underestimated and ignored.

We reached the hospital and smoked two cigarettes each outside. We went in and waited. The doctor called us into a room. He was perfect looking, like he was on a soap opera about emergency room doctors and he was about to take off his shirt. I told him my story, and he said, "Why don't you show me what we're dealing with?"

I unwrapped the worm and held it, my arms outstretched to the doctor, a sacred offering to a god.

I watched as he tried to conceal his alarm.

"I'm sorry. I've never seen anything like this," he said.

He left. I put on lip gloss. He returned.

"Have you been eating excrement?" he asked.

"Not that I can recall, but I wouldn't put it past me," I said.

"This is a roundworm. They are typically found in animals, not humans. I don't know how you got it and I don't know when. It could have been in there for years. I'm prescribing you anti-parasitics. Take these and give the nurses a stool sample every day for the next two weeks. This will kill any that might still be inside. You may pass a few more."

Back at Riggs, the nurses gave me a plastic seat that fit over the toilet for me to shit in, plastic containers, Ziploc bags, and brown paper bags. Every day over the next week, I defecated into the plastic contraption, carefully smeared my feces into the containers, placed them in the plastic bags, and then into the brown ones. Each time, I looked for worms. I never found another one. My worm was singular, unlike anything anyone had ever seen.

4.

I was feeling better. I felt calmer, clearer. I was on a small dose of an antipsychotic, Abilify, and that seemed to organize my thoughts and slow them down. I was able to have a "reverie," calmly linking one thought to the next. I was able to cry. I had stopped cutting. I performed, with absolute dedication and glee, in the plays put on at Riggs, worked at the woodshop, where Eduardo, a kind man in his seventies with vitiligo and infinite patience, talked to me about the songs of Nellie McKay and the books of Carlos Castaneda. I borrowed a camera from the photography studio and took black-and-white photos of everything I saw—a deserted playground, streetlight-illuminated snow, the headless reflection in a mirror of my aunt, uncle, Nanny, and mother, who had all come to visit. The nurses and doctors commented on my progress. We were getting somewhere.

Then I celebrated my one-year-anniversary of being at Riggs, and Sophia and I started going into New York City every weekend. I had earned some freedom, some latitude, I thought. We would get dressed in my room—it was bigger and I had more clothes. I'd put on my favorite outfit—a pair of thin leggings and a tight red T-shirt that had the words I AM A VERY SICK WOMAN written in yellow letters across the chest that I'd found at a nearby vintage store. I liked when people asked me what it meant and I got to tell them I was crazy. It felt like a uniform, announcing what my job was, or a convenient name tag. We'd put on makeup, pack an overnight bag, get someone to drive us to the train station, take the four-hour train to Grand Central Station, and then grab a taxi to 134 Charles Street to drop our bags. We'd go out to bars, get drunk, climb into my bed to get a few hours of sleep, take the train back to Riggs on Sunday night, and spend the next week avoiding group therapy and planning our next weekend.

One September night in 2005, a month after I turned twenty, we went to Joe's Pub in the East Village to see a friend's show. I wore a tight striped cashmere sweater that we joked made me look like Freddy Krueger. Sophia wore a vintage Harley Davidson T-shirt with holes in it and low-rise jeans. Halfway through the show, Sophia nudged me and whispered, "Oh my God, look who it is."

She pointed to a skinny guy in two pieces of a three-piece suit with a globe of frizzy curls around his head. I didn't recognize him. I shrugged and furrowed my brow. She explained to me that he was the guitarist from her favorite band, a famous indie rock group that had risen to fame four years earlier. I recognized the band name. I had first heard of them two years ago at a party thrown by my friend Josh in LA. At the party, I met Paul, who sat in the corner with sunglasses on. I asked him what he did.

"Nothing, I'm a dilettante," he said.

Paul was five years older than me, well-dressed and funny. He talked to me all night but made me feel like it was a special favor. He told me about his best friend who was a guitarist in a famous band.

He wrote down a list of bands I should listen to: Elliott Smith, Guided by Voices, Modest Mouse, Adam Green. I thought he was very cool. When I returned to New York, I wrote him an email about buying new socks. He wrote back that it was the best thing he had ever read. Two years and a mental institution later, I still thought about Paul, and here was his best friend from the famous rock band.

"Go say hi," I told Sophia.

We approached him.

"I am obsessed with you," Sophia told Paul's best friend.

The guitarist smiled and put his arm around the petite blond standing next to him, who had a luscious Bardot pout and looked bored. I watched the blond as Sophia waited for her ardor to penetrate her icon. The blond seemed so competent at just standing there, at fitting into this cool, famous guy's armpit, that I felt I could learn from her. Sophia was trying to convey the breadth of her obsession.

"Like, literally, your band is the soundtrack to my life," said Sophia.

"Thanks," he said.

Sophia was standing too close to the guy, and her hands, which she had made into claws in front of her face to emphasize the size and force of her love, were frozen in the air between them. She wanted to say more, get deeper, but didn't seem to know how.

"Hey," I said. "Do you know Paul Elroy?"

"Yeah," he said. His tone was different from the curt "thanks" he had offered Sophia.

"I met him years ago in LA," I said.

"He's actually on a train right now coming into the city. Let me call him."

He punched some keys on his Motorola Razr and asked Paul if he knew me. Paul confirmed and said we should meet him at a bar on the Lower East Side. At the bar, as I inexpertly poked pool balls around the table, I told Paul, the rock star, and his fiancée that Sophia and I were taking the weekend off from the mental institution we were in. Everyone thought I was making a joke. I laughed and assured them I wasn't being funny, I was certifiable. I felt cool and mysterious. I invited everyone back to 134 Charles. My mother was out of town and Nanny was asleep. Paul and I paddled face-to-face from one end of the pool to the other, and back again, talking. The guitarist played us the band's unreleased new album. Sophia, drunk, begged the guitarist's fiancée to let her be a bridesmaid at their wedding. It grew light outside. The party dispersed and Sophia and I went back to Riggs later that day.

Paul and I started talking on the phone every night for hours. We talked about film and middle school and pizza toppings, about betrayal and hair. He was staying at the East Village pied-à-terre of a famous actress descended from Hollywood royalty who had transitioned rehab-inflected child stardom into a long and successful career, and the next weekend I arrived at the actress's apartment for our first date. I was late because I had been straightening my butt-length, curly hair and covering my eyelids in black eyeshadow because Paul had told me he liked straight hair and lots of eye makeup on girls. I wore a silk blouse with a brown tweed vest, tight jeans and bright yellow Manolo Blahnik heels I borrowed from my mother, two sizes too big and stuffed with insoles. Paul seemed really excited to see me and offered me a drink. He had on a vintage T-shirt with a cheeky slogan and the shape of a southern state on it, a vest, tailored black Levi's, and Converse high tops, which he dirtied up in gutters before officially wearing to go out because clean Chucks were not cool. He had huge, round eyes and a weak chin that made it look like someone was turning the volume down on his face. He disguised it with stubble. He was very funny, and we sat on the sofa laughing. As I was telling him the story of my worm, he went over to the kitchen island and started laying out lines of powder.

"It's cocaine," he said, and snorted up the lines. I watched him and continued my story.

An hour later he laid out more lines and snorted them.

"It's actually heroin," he said, as if I had challenged him. "I just do it recreationally."

We sat on pillows on the floor, and Paul played me his favorite records.

We got in the shower, and I apologized for the water washing away my heavy makeup. We got in bed and watched infomercials, laughing at the strange contraptions and the over-eager barkers. We started kissing and after foreplay that involved a blow job and nothing else, he announced that he, as a rule, didn't wear condoms. I allowed him to shove his bare penis, only half hard from all the heroin, into me, and hoped my moans were convincing. I went back to Riggs the next day, thinking of nothing but the next time I could see Paul.

I continued having family therapy sessions at Riggs, but they had a new focus: Paul.

My discharge date was approaching and my therapist was concerned about my recent behavior and my lack of awareness around it, and didn't think I was able to live safely outside of Riggs. My mother was worried too, and frightened by my relationship with Paul.

"He has too much influence over you," she said.

I scoffed and rolled my eyes, now heavily lined in black.

She tried to be sympathetic, telling me about how she had used confusion to avoid feelings, how she had a history of inviting unhealthy people into her life too.

She told me she felt disrespected when I brought Paul and his friends over to do their drugs. She told me I was acting like my father. I couldn't hear her. I couldn't see that it was her house and her life. I was oblivious to everything but doing what I needed to do to become important to Paul, but I compromised and said I'd postpone my discharge by one month.

When my father called in from Europe for family sessions, he wasn't concerned about my relationship with Paul. He thought it was normal and good for me to do "age-appropriate things." He wondered why I was postponing my discharge. He was frustrated and wanted me to leave Riggs, come to Europe, and do more "age-appropriate things."

"I'm afraid for Alice to leave here without a solid foundation and no real plan in place. She should stay at Riggs," my mother said.

"I'm afraid for her to stay any longer," my father said. "She'll end up in a hospital forever. She should leave and come to Europe."

I ended up staying the extra month I had agreed to and then left Austen Riggs "against medical advice." I had been there a year and two months. My therapist wrote in my summation of hospitalization: *She is still attracted to the position of being the child "full of potential" to be a writer, and she fears damaging this "potential" by work or by entering a process of becoming "someone" in particular. Someone, that is, who is more limited than the girl who stimulated so much excitement in the adults around her.*

"We hope to see you back here," said Dr. Shapiro, at my final meeting with the staff.

"Thank you," I said reflexively.

I was referred to a psychopharmacologist so I could continue taking the antipsychotic I had been put on at Riggs. Upon meeting with me for the first time ever and for only forty-five minutes, Dr. Gilbert sent me home with a prescription for ninety pills of Klonopin, a powerful and highly addictive benzodiazepine for anxiety that was not recommended for prolonged use and would later be linked to an increased risk of dementia, and ninety pills of Adderall, prescription speed, for ADD/ADHD. He told me that Adderall wore off every four hours, and that I should take the Klonopin whenever I felt I needed to and to get to sleep at night. After my first dose of Adderall, I went from smoking five cigarettes a day to smoking a pack and a half of the Marlboro 27s Paul smoked. I sweat through my clothes and ground my teeth. My eyeballs felt peeled open and my blood felt like it was steaming. I became reactive, hostile, and unable to read social cues. I spoke too loudly and too much and too fast, trying to hear myself over the whomping of my heart and the whooshing of my boiling blood. Each dose of Adderall made me anxious, so I'd take Klonopin like the doctor had recommended. The Adderall made me unable to sleep, so I'd take Klonopin like the doctor had recommended. I was on so much Adderall that the Klonopin didn't make me feel high or relaxed, just woozy and ravenous and sloppy. It didn't occur to me that I could question the doctor. I had learned from my mother never to question the expertise and authority of doctors. This must be what becoming well felt like.

I spent most of my time at Paul's new apartment on First Avenue and First Street (paid for by his wealthy father), where he introduced me to good music and cocaine. Paul and I had no jobs, but we followed a strict itinerary. Most evenings started at ten, when we made our way to JP Ward's, a small dive bar on Avenue A with a pool table and identical twin bartenders. I took shots of Jägermeister and drank Amstel Lights (Paul's favorite) until I puked. I'd wash my mouth out and we'd walk a block to 2A, where Stephen, the gorgeous junkie bartender who chewed razor blades, made us shots that tasted like candy—Tootsie Roll, key lime pie with a cherry on top. After 2A, we'd hit Niagara and snort cocaine to a backdrop of '60s R&B and soul, and '70s punk and new wave. If we got hungry, we'd grab pierogi at Veselka and then finish the night at Black and White, where the bartender set out ashtrays and we'd cut lines on the bar. One weekend Paul took me to Benihana with his friends who secretly told the servers that it was my birthday, even though it wasn't, and I was served a scoop of ice cream with a candle in it and everyone sang happy birthday to me. Paul and I took a pedicab through Times Square to get home, scooting jerkily through traffic and streams of people as "Clocks" by Coldplay played on an old boom box. We went to a famous comedian's game night. Paul had spinach stuck in his teeth and I panicked about whether we were in a place in our relationship where I should tell him that he had something in his teeth. I didn't tell him.

My relationship with Paul had landed me squarely at the cool kids' table. Paul's friends were very cool. They were fashion photographers (one of whom claimed to be related to William Faulkner), young rock stars who now got to be friends with older rock stars, movie stars with checkered pasts, models who were also designers (usually of T-shirts), producers, a relative of a famous Motown singer. Everyone had an apartment in Manhattan and schedules that allowed them to show up for anything, at any time. I learned that the word *party* could be used as a verb, and that was all we did. I was anxious all the time. I wanted nothing more than to impress all these people and I was terrible at it. I did crossword puzzles in bars to appear unique. When I ran into people I knew, I theatrically exclaimed, "As I live and breathe!" At the threshold of every bar, I sprayed myself heavily with an extra layer of Chanel No. 19 perfume. I had no sense of how I came off, how false and desperate. But I *was* false and desperate. I was empty and out of my mother's house, and I needed someone else to weigh me down with their desires.

Paul had never called anyone his girlfriend before. One night we were shopping at the Asian market M2M, and he called me sweetheart across a rack of wasabi peas, and I felt carbonated inside. Then he told me he would be calling me his girlfriend, because he had liked how it felt calling me "sweetheart." He was hard to win over and prided himself on not forming attachments with women. It was thrilling watching him swing from detachment to attentiveness, seeing him zoom in on me with a mischievous smile on his face. I got to be Paul's girlfriend, and that came with certain conditions. Paul demanded that I straighten my curly hair. On New Year's Eve, he got furious because I left it a little wavy.

"Why would you do this to me, especially on New Year's Eve?" he said.

He suggested I dye it dark, so I did.

Paul liked girls who wore lots of makeup, so I covered my eyelids in black eye shadow and became afraid to leave the house if I didn't have my eyes properly outlined. I had to ask, "Are we going to have sex or can I take off my makeup?"

"Keep it on. I might want to later," he'd say as he poured a box of Nerds in his mouth, eyes glued to the latest Paul Thomas Anderson movie.

Paul didn't "believe in going down on girls," so I tackled his opiate-deflated cock with intense focus and a belief that my only chance at pleasure lay in figuring out how to fold his limp penis into me and make it fun for him.

Paul told me what to wear, picking out my outfits before every night out. He told me that it would be okay if I lost another ten pounds (I was a size double zero) and then told me it had been a joke. I did what he told me. I welcomed his instructions.

I'd return to 134 Charles to host drug-fueled pool parties when my mother was out of town, or crash there when Paul and I got in a fight. Sometimes, when I came home in the morning after a night out, I'd bring the newspaper up with me and encounter my mother and Nanny in the kitchen drinking their coffee and tea. Neither would comment on the fact that I had been out all night. Neither would ask where I'd been or who I was with.

Some evenings I'd catch my mother alone in the kitchen. I'd be happy to see her and I'd want to talk. I'd sit at the butcher block table, leg jiggling from the cocaine or the Adderall, and talk to her as she got another bottle of wine from the fridge. I talked to her about the people I'd met, ideas I had for the cover of my unfinished novel I hadn't looked at in months, books I'd heard were good.

"You seem hyper," she'd say.

"I had a lot of green tea," I'd answer.

She wouldn't respond and would leave the kitchen without looking at me to go and drink by herself.

One night, after another failed attempt to initiate a coked-up conversation, when she was on her second bottle of wine, I followed her out of the kitchen and cornered her on the stairs.

"Why are you always walking away from me?" I screamed.

"Leave me alone," she said.

"No, I want to talk to you. Why don't you want to talk to me?"

"Because I don't respect you," she yelled, and disappeared up the stairs.

I stood there, alone, shocked by the volume of her voice, the passion in it. I had never heard her raise her voice like that. It seemed the only thing that could enliven her, could turn up the volume, could get her to direct words, passionate words, my way, was my failure.

It didn't occur to me that I was supposed to be leading a different life. That people my age were becoming responsible adults, building lives. Doctors had taught me that my job was to take my medication and think about how to communicate my thoughts and feelings. My mother had taught me to obey the doctors. She didn't ask me what medications I was being prescribed. If I ever spoke of feelings, she asked me if I was making it to my sessions.

I was seeing a new therapist recommended by my team at Riggs. Dr. Hart called my words "jewel-like," and we sat in her office twice a week spinning stories and sculpting metaphors. Sometimes I'd hand over gram bags of cocaine to her, saying I wanted to cut back, and she'd praise me.

Meanwhile, Paul was doing more and more heroin and had started smoking crack. I was doing more and more cocaine, paid for by the money our parents continued to give us, and on good nights we'd stay up talking and listening to music until the following afternoon. One night, a week after Stephen the bartender died of a speedball overdose, I walked into the living room to find Paul slumped over on the sofa. I shook him and his head flopped back. As I dialed 911, he sat up, laughing. Paul's temper got worse and we would walk into bars screaming at each other, dropping the argument mid-sentence as soon as the bartender handed us shots. On Valentine's Day, Paul took me out to dinner at Lavagna, the Italian restaurant he and all his friends frequented. That night I drank champagne, followed by red wine, followed by white wine. As we left the restaurant I leaned against a discarded armoire standing on the curb and vomited. Paul started yelling at me.

"You manipulated me into buying you an expensive dinner and now you're throwing it up," he screamed.

We walked to Ace Bar to play pool. After a few silent rounds, we made our way to Horseshoe Bar and ran into his friend Lilian, whom Paul believed had a crush on him. We sat in the red vinyl upholstered booth and they talked. I interjected something, and Paul told me to shut up. I went silent. Then my body lurched forward, my forehead almost hitting the table. He had hit me in the back of the head, hard. My face went hot with shock. I slid out of the booth and started to make my way to the door. Paul got up and tried to corner me, his hands extended. The bouncer came over and asked if everything was okay, and I said no and slid out the door. I leaned against the building and called my friend Leah. Leah and I had met the first day of a group therapy I was attending, and she had liked me instantly because I had asked the counselor, after a girl had a benzodiazepine-withdrawal-induced seizure, if we could have a cigarette break. Leah told me to leave the bar. But I couldn't leave. I needed to take care of Paul. I was Paul's girlfriend. I was afraid he would eject me from his world if I didn't, black-lidded and emaciated, follow his rules.

I lingered outside until I saw Paul come out, swaying. I hung up my phone and slung an arm around him and he leaned on me. I walked us home, propping him up, trying to stop him from throwing himself in front of cars. He had told Lilian to meet us at his apartment. She arrived just as we did and I saw her eyes saucer as she took in the scene. On the floor was a month's worth of the *Daily News*, pieces of paper (Post-its; pages ripped out of notebooks, ruled, graphed, blank, some with writing on them; a song lyric; a grocery item; a phone number; something reminding us of something one of us was supposed to do but never would), the celluloid skins of Now and Laters, Skittles, Sour Patch Kids, and Starbursts, which were all over the bed, under the pillows, and stuck between the wall and the bed. Heroin addicts liked candy. There were no clean dishes or utensils or pots or pans or drinking glasses. These dirty items could be found: stacked along the edge of the kitchen sink, on the bathroom floor, on the bedroom floor, on the one living room windowsill, on the two bedroom windowsills, on the one bathroom windowsill.

Paul sat on the small sofa, lit a crack pipe, and said to Lilian, "I bet you've never seen someone smoke crack before." Lilian asked if I was okay to be alone and without waiting for my answer said goodbye to Paul and left. I sat in silence as Paul smoked his crack and after a few hours I helped him into bed. He crawled to the bottom of the bed, where I was standing, put his forehead against mine, and said, "You're nothing, you don't deserve to exist. I'll put a boot in your face."

"Go to sleep," I said, then pushed him down onto the bed and tucked him in.

I felt a strange competency, as if he were my child and I was required to manage his tantrums.

When I woke up later that morning, Paul was gone. I waited in bed until he stumbled through the door the next day. He slapped on a fentanyl patch designed for terminally ill people, got into bed, and we binge-watched *Flavor of Love.*

A few days later, I woke up early in the morning, hungry. Paul was still awake from the night before.

"I'll make you some pasta with Parmesan," said Paul, from the other room. He could be nice like that.

"Olive oil and butter, too," I said from the bedroom.

I listened to his noises. The thuds and sighs and grunts and plops and bangs and clinks created an auricular comic strip of his domesticity that I followed from the other room. Then the sounds stopped.

"I cut myself," he said from the other room.

"So get a Band-Aid." I did not get out of bed.

No sound came from the other room.

"Just put a Band-Aid on it," I repeated.

No response.

"Is it bad?" I asked.

"I think so," said Paul.

I got out of bed and walked naked into the other room. Paul was standing very still and held his left hand in his right. He held it up and close to him as if I wanted to take it away from him. Blood was pouring down his arm. Paul's hand looked nothing like a hand. Everything became two-dimensional and I couldn't see what was happening, only the words to describe what was happening. I saw the sentence: "The Grand Canyon filled with blood." Then the words "the flopping open of a neatly folded ream of tough velvet" appeared over Paul's shape. The letters of "a Fabergé egg spilling its rubied yolk" stamped themselves on the scene.

Things that can be described as anything but themselves and still be true are marvelous, I thought.

I shook my head, the metaphors scattering like droplets of water. I put my hands on Paul's shoulders and moved him onto the sofa.

I forced a dishtowel around his hand, and placed his other hand around it like a tourniquet.

"Squeeze it hard. Keep pressure on it. Keep the arm elevated," I said.

I found my dress from the previous night in between the bed and the wall and put it on. I walked back out to the other room, found my purse, and packed it with: two wallets, two pink Motorola Razr cell phones, two sets of keys, and one half-empty bottle of warm ginger ale in anticipation of blood loss and plummeting blood sugar. I turned off the stove. I turned the handle of the pot in which the water was beginning to boil and angled it toward the back of the stove because it was not safe to have the handle of a pot sticking out. I saw a half-shattered drinking glass on the counter with blood on it. He had been washing a bowl, and his hand had slipped and smashed into a drinking glass, which broke and split his hand almost in half. I turned from the stove and looked at Paul silently wilting in my arrangement of him, his fingers rooted in the squishy red dishtowel. I found a roll of paper towels, unreeled it, and crammed the pristine paper blossom into Paul's fist, red roots sprouting instantly.

"Let's get you to the hospital," I said.

I picked up my purse from the floor and Paul from the sofa and I exited us into the hallway. I locked the door with one hand, holding Paul upright with the other. I led us down the hallway, opened the door one-handed, and we fell into the morning. I ran ahead, my arm raised, trying to catch a cab. I looked behind me at Paul, and I watched as he began a slow-motion free-fall toward the ground, then swung his body at the last minute in a circus-act arc that kept him in his looping stride. I ran back and let him fall against me. I walked us down the block, keeping my right arm up, trying to hail a cab. No taxis stopped for us. I kept us upright until we reached the curb, where I let him slide down me and sit. I called 911.

"Yes, hello. I need an ambulance at the corner of First Street and First Avenue. Northwest corner. My boyfriend has a severe laceration of the left hand. It is almost completely severed and he is bleeding profusely. Please hurry."

A man approached.

"I called an ambulance. I saw you guys. He looks pretty bad," he said.

"Yes, thank you. Everything is under control. I called an ambulance. It's on its way," I said.

I turned away from the man and hoped my ambulance came first. I wanted it to be mine.

Paul was leaning heavily against my leg, bleeding. He stared at the pavement.

"Can you light me a cigarette?" he asked.

I looked down at the top of his head. His hair was greasy and stringy.

"I don't know if that's a good idea," I said.

He was asking my permission. I got to decide for him and that felt good.

"It'll make me feel better. I swear," he said.

"Okay. Fine. Just one," I said. I wanted a cigarette too. I lit two and gave one to him.

The ambulance slung itself onto the curb. Three EMTs hopped out and arranged themselves around us. One unfurled Paul's split fist. One EMT, into a walkie-talkie, said: "Yeah, it's pretty bad. He almost cut his hand off."

One of the EMTs pulled me aside. He came too close and spoke at me in weak bursts of aerosol spit.

"Has he been taking any drugs? Is he on something right now?" he asked.

Now I got to tell his story. I felt powerful.

"He has a long history of frequent and heavy drug use. He has a serious heroin addiction in addition to frequent crack and cocaine abuse. He claims he's clean at the moment, but he's an addict, so I can't confirm that with any certainty. I know he has been self-administering methadone to come down. He may be on it right now. I don't know the exact dosage, but I presume it's high, given the severity of his heroin use. I hope that's helpful," I said.

"I thought so. His pupils are pinpoints. And he looks dirty. You look clean," said the EMT.

"Thanks," I said, feeling like I had won an award, best actress in a crisis.

"Can I have a drag of that?" asked the EMT, pointing to my cigarette, as if we were close friends. I felt flattered and disgusted.

"You can have it," I said. I gave him the cigarette.

I left the EMT and walked around to the back of the ambulance. Paul had already been packed inside, quivering on the padded vinyl bench. I pushed past the two EMTs and sat down next to Paul. I intercepted the clipboarded forms as they were passed to him. I would fill out the forms because I knew all the answers and I had neat handwriting. I would be thorough.

The ambulance began its carnival of urgent lights and motion. Paul reached for my hand with his good hand. I let him hold my hand, even though I didn't want to. His hand was little and exhausted and wet. I could catch him before he nearly fell. I could elevate his arm and hold the phone to my ear and walk him upright down the street. I could remember to turn off the stove. I was indispensable. I was a basic need. My handwriting would be legible despite the reckless driving. The information I gave would reveal him. In this crisis, I felt alive. I did not want to sit and hold his little okay hand.

We arrived at St. Vincent's. I knew this place. I'd been here before. I knew the system. I was in the system. But we were not here for me. This time, someone else had cut themselves open.

We were taken to Trauma Room 3. Paul sat on the bed. He was limp and hunched over like a half-deflated pool toy. A doctor entered.

She numbed his hand with a large syringe and began to suture the wound. Left with nothing needing my white-knuckling, I exited the building and sat on the steps. In my purse was a pillowcase that said Saint Vincent's Hospital on it, which I stole from Trauma Room 3. Tiredness began to erode the spiky peaks of adrenaline. It started to rain. I lit a cigarette. Paul was okay. I had conquered this crisis. But this morning of over-full moments would pass, and I would be nothing again.

5.

When Paul's hand was healed, he flew back to LA, telling me every week he would return in a week. His aunt called to tell me she had found syringes in the trash. He came back to New York City on Valentine's Day and there were bruises on his forearms. We went to a fondue restaurant and he nodded out over the steaming pot of cheese. "Jet lag," he said. I believed him. Then he returned to LA and never came back.

That summer, my father came to New York for my twenty-first birthday. We sat at the dining room table at 134 Charles Street. He had written a screenplay and wanted the two of us to do a table read. The screenplay was about Dracula biting a "junkie prostitute" and getting addicted to heroin through her blood, and the prostitute getting addicted to drinking blood. Dracula and the prostitute fell in love. My father was going to play Dracula and he wanted me to play the junkie prostitute. When we reached the part when Dracula bites the prostitute and they fall in love, the words—writhing on a bed, kissing and sucking with urgency and desire became too much for me. I stopped reading.

"I'm hungry," I said.

I went into the kitchen and put a pot of water on to boil for pasta and my father followed me. He talked to me as I unboxed the spaghetti, found some pesto, and put it in a bowl.

"Every father secretly wants to sleep with his daughter," he said.

I was struck with numbness, as if I'd been bitten by something poisonous. My skin went hot. I couldn't speak. I forced myself to evaluate what he had said like I would a painting created by a long-dead artist with intentions muddied by time and context. Something that had nothing to do with me. *Just say something smart,* I thought. I heard the top of the pot rattle as the water boiled.

"I think the water's boiling," I said and turned away from him.

That same year, my father was crucified. A photograph of my half-sister, Elena, had appeared in a newspaper without her mother's consent, so Bettina sued. Instead of paying the 5,000-euro fine, my father decided to go to jail and used his imprisonment, in collaboration with the popular tabloid *Bild Zeitung*, to bring awareness to the rights of unmarried fathers and their children. In Germany, at the time, unmarried fathers often lost their custodial rights in separations. My father organized a coalition of three hundred people, mostly fathers who had lost children through separations and custody disputes, to gather in front of the Federal Ministry of Justice in Berlin to crucify him. My father, thin to the point of emaciation, was tied to a large cross, naked except for a piece of cloth around his hips and a "crown of thorns" on his head. Around him stood fathers dressed in old-fashioned prison uniforms, chanting and holding signs that read: END THE WAR AGAINST FATHERS, EQUAL CUSTODY FROM BIRTH ON, and FATHERS ARE ALSO PARENTS. My father struck poses—head thrown back, mouth open; head slumped lifelessly forward. He and his army of bereft fathers eventually managed to get the law changed.

The story was near perfect. It had villains and disenfranchised masses and a charismatic leader upon whom misfortune was repeatedly visited and a triumph over power. My father's mythologizing was complete. To the public he was father, martyr, Christ. To me he was slippery and far less noble. I never considered that he had his own reasons for doing this, for fighting. That he had another daughter he loved. That he had priorities beyond me. I saw the grandiose, public gestures he made to protect his relationship with my sister, and I felt angry and jealous and abandoned.

I DECIDED TO APPLY to Columbia University to finish my undergraduate degree. Paul's absence meant I had time to be something other than a girlfriend, and it also meant the end of our grueling schedule of bar hopping and narcotics. I was excited to be in school and threw myself into my classes. I felt hyped up—I was, after all, still on Adderall. My brain whirred with ideas and I'd shoot my hand into the air and quiver it until I was called on. I loved having to show my student ID, saying over and over to myself, "I am a student." I made the dean's list my first semester. Then I started seeing a new psychopharmacologist who diagnosed me with bipolar and generalized anxiety disorders, justifying the former with the observation that I dressed differently at each session—sometimes in a colorful sundress, sometimes in tight black jeans and a vintage band T-shirt. Along with my new diagnoses came more meds: the antipsychotic Risperdal for potential hypomania, the mood stabilizer Lamictal for mood swings, Trazodone for depression, more Klonopin, more Adderall, and the sedating antipsychotic Seroquel, because the Adderall made me unable to sleep. The Seroquel combined with the Klonopin made me insatiable. I stood in front of the fridge at 2 a.m. gouging out pieces of cold chicken from a carcass with my hands and shoveling them into my mouth. I woke up in the middle of the night and put a spoonful of chocolate pudding, which I'd left next to the bed, into my mouth and fell back asleep before I could swallow it, waking to my cheek glued to the stained pillowcase. Twice I fell asleep on a half-eaten Milky Way bar, and once on a wedge of brie. I started to gain weight. I was prescribed medications to counteract the side effects of the medications—Topamax and Liothyronine for the weight gain from the Seroquel and Klonopin, Lyrica and Gabapentin to file down the amphetamine teeth that lined my brain.

As I was prescribed more pills, I was diagnosed with more disorders, whose symptoms often resembled the side effects of the pills. I wasn't ruminating obsessively because I was on prescription speed, but because I had obsessive-compulsive personality disorder. My emotional lability was because of borderline personality disorder, not because my brain blazed into a chemical conflagration every morning only to be doused dead by downers at night. I started to think of myself as a machine that ran on pharmaceuticals, an appliance designed to obliterate feelings. I had learned from my mother that feelings were not welcome, and now I was learning they were pathological. There was no such thing as sadness, only clinical depression. Joy and motivation were only harbingers of hypomania. Feelings, good or bad, meant that something was wrong. If I felt sad, I called Dr. Sarini and requested a higher dose of my mood stabilizer. If I felt suspiciously okay, I suspected I was becoming hypomanic and called to get my antipsychotic increased. When I decided, after reading Kay Redfield Jamison's memoir of her struggle with bipolar disorder, that I should be on Lithium, I left a message for Dr. Sarini, and the next day a prescription was called in to my pharmacy. My hands turned purple and I felt swirly and deadened. I left another message saying I had decided to stop taking it. I was curious about the full potential of stimulants and requested every form—Ritalin and Concerta along with the Adderall. Prescriptions for all of them appeared and I would experiment with taking one, and the next day, the other. Dr. Sarini told me repeatedly that psychopharmacology was "trial and error" and that this haphazard prescribing was the way it was supposed to go. This was me taking care of myself. He told me I would need to be on medication for the rest of my life. My mother's belief in these doctors never wavered, and she still never asked about my medications or how I was tolerating them.

When I visited my father and grandparents in Lübeck, they asked me what medications I was taking. As I ate my liverwurst toast, I listed all the pills.

"So you have pills to wake you up and pills to make you sleep," said my father.

I resisted. It wasn't like that. There were good reasons. There had to be. Opa, a psychiatrist, shook his head and hauled out his giant reference books to look up the compounds.

"They bring you up and they bring you down. This is not the way," he muttered.

I got defensive. I thought they were trying to stop me from getting help.

My diagnoses explained and explained away every part of me. I held them aloft and visible like a sign at an airport, using them to identify myself even to strangers. My alleged bipolarity was often the first trait I announced about myself, opening myself up like my heavily highlighted *Diagnostic and Statistical Manual of Mental Disorders* (*DSM*). The medications were the necessary accessories to this identity. When I traveled and had to put all my pill bottles in a Ziploc bag to go through security, I felt a bolt of pride as TSA agents pried it from my bag and examined it. What must they have thought of me? Were they intrigued? Impressed? Intimidated? That they might think I was sick never occurred to me. I could not abide the simplicity of sickness. I was not just sick, I was special.

My sessions with my therapist reinforced this belief. We discussed nothing concrete. She was in constant contact with my psychopharmacologist but expressed no concern or thoughtfulness about all the medications. Twice a week, every week, we discussed the idea of me, the idea of my parents, the idea of being a human among humans. She praised my eloquence, asked me about my dreams, matched me metaphor for metaphor, helped me abstract myself further. I was always honest with her because I was talented at being a patient. I feared averageness, I told her. I feared limits, I feared the quiet in which I would be forced to confront that I might be average and be averagely limited. But the average person was not on nine medications with seven diagnoses. I was still exceptional.

Another doctor was added to my entourage. My mother and I started going to a family therapist. Dr. Kaufman's face was soft and bulbous, as if his features had taken shape from the mushy wax of a slowly melting candle. He would welcome us into his office, remove his shoes, put his feet up on a foot stool, and take a sip from his plastic cup of Orangina, which sat next to a fresh liter of the stuff. During the session, my mother and I sat on the floor in the hallway outside his office with the door propped open, so we could smoke cigarettes. Dr. Kaufman commented on my weight, congratulating me when I was skinny, then asking me why I had put on extra pounds. Hopped up on Adderall, I made long speeches about feeling neglected or having no identity of my own. My mother listened, struggled to find feeling words, and deferred to Dr. Kaufman, who decreed that every time she got drunk and criticized me, she had to buy me a dress. Nanny attended some of the sessions, and Dr. Kaufman used her as a witness, to confirm or deny the validity of our statements. The sessions were endless and useless, and I begged my mother to stop seeing him, but he was renowned and expensive, and she was convinced he could fix us.

. . .

MY MOTHER WAS HAVING a hard time. She was broke. Her extravagances had caught up with her.

"Should I sell this house?" she asked me one afternoon.

I was on my way upstairs.

"Sure, why not. It's full of ghosts," I said, and walked away.

The house was sold. We stayed at 134 Charles Street for six months, packing it up. The week of the move, my mother flew to the Caribbean with Nanny, leaving me alone to finish packing up the first twenty-three years of my life. I took my Adderall and drank Red Bull all day as I sorted through stacks of photographs, middle school French exams, my Silver Cross baby carriage, the desiccated jack-o'-lantern I had carved fifteen years ago and kept in a Ziploc bag. My very last night in 134 Charles Street, I sat in the empty living room at four in the morning, after having stayed up all night haphazardly throwing things into boxes, weeping, listening to "Hey Jude," and putting cigarettes out on the floor that was no longer mine. I stared at the living room, empty of my mother's uncomfortable furniture, the walls bare of her massive paintings. The house felt weak and afraid, and so did I. I lay on the floor on my side as if were cuddling 134 Charles. I was scared to leave the fortress that had defined me for so long.

In a trunk I found all the cards that my mother had written to me when I was a child. When I finished going through everything in the trunk, I sat down and read them, saving a letter she'd written on the occasion of my fifth birthday for last. It read:

Dear Alice,

You will be five tomorrow. Today you jumped, ran, all over the house being happy about being five. "I'll be five, I'm going to be five, when I'm five I'll . . ." You told me that when you became five you wouldn't wet your bed anymore and you'd be able to lift heavy things. You wanted a chocolate cake with chocolate icing; and strawberry icing, separate from the chocolate icing. You wanted your father (Papa, Mathieu, Daddy) to be here, and you will have both. You want many other things: rainbow ice cream, a locket, your dinner now, a story, 2 stories, a pretend game, 3 movies, all the way through. What you have is your father—Mathieu. Your mother—Jennifer. Your Nanny—Denys. All of us wish you the very best, with all our love for the beginning of your big girl life. You are pretty, intelligent, lively, sensitive, kind, gentle, fierce, wild, and strong. You are the great joy of my life. Congratulations at five.

Mom, Mommy, Maman, Jennifer

That night, alone in the house, I wrote my mother a letter:

Dear Mom,

Your letter, and my finding it, is really the culmination of a slow, necessary process—of me realizing you are a real person separate from me, and of finding my way to you. I remember when I first realized that I love your work. I remember when I first admired your style. I realize I have something not many people have. I have a role model, and I hate that word. I think I fight you so hard because you remind me of everything I am afraid I will never be. Maybe I accuse you of neglect because I neglect myself. I am so terrified by my admiration and love for you that I lash out at you. I find your love for me devastating and inexplicable. The more I realize how much you do for me and how much you love me, the more scared I am that I have depleted you. That I have misused and abused you. I am scared that I will never be able to be that person you wanted and believed I could be. I want to live up to your dreams for me. You need to know that you have lived up to my dreams for a mother. You wrote as if you were writing something(one) into existence. Even then, you spoke to me as a person. Now, we are negotiating what we mean to each other and how we express that. What we want from and for each other. Maybe I treated you so poorly because I didn't understand that you needed me too. I know I still fight you at certain steps, but I am starting to understand the value of the direction in which you are trying to point me. I am sick of wanting to be victimized, I am sick of being sick. I am trying to push away the guilt and regret and self-loathing. It's easier to feel damaged than it is to realize I've been lucky and loved. In you and Nanny I have had everything. I am sick of symbols. I don't want a life of metaphor and turns of phrase. I feel as if I have been talking my whole life. Talking around things, talking over people, talking myself in and out of things, talking myself up, talking myself down. I am ready to listen. I want a relationship with you. Maybe then I won't feel so scared all the time.

I love you,
Your daughter (and fellow alien),
Alice
December 2008

I closed the door of 134 Charles Street behind me for the last time and caught a plane to meet my mother on the island of Nevis. I arrived that night and handed her my letter. She took it to her room. I was at the bathroom sink when I heard her come back in. My breath caught and my heart quickened. My mother came into the bathroom.

"This is very nice," she said.

"Well, it's all true," I said, instinctively raising my arms for an embrace.

"Why don't you keep it for me?" she said. My arms found their place at my side again.

She handed the letter back to me and went back into her room.

After the sale of 134 Charles Street, my mother bought a house in Brooklyn. Nanny moved in with my aunt and uncle in Tribeca while it was being renovated, and my mother moved into her tiny cottage in Amagansett. I moved into my first apartment, on West Seventeenth Street. My mother and I, no longer held together by 134 Charles Street, drifted further apart. When I moved, she gave me a box of all the utensils she didn't need, so I arrived at my new apartment with a pizza slicer, an ice cream scoop, skewers for roasting marshmallows, and a set of grapefruit spoons, both of us hoping I was prepared for real life.

One evening, I got a call from Gregory. I had met him through the famous guitarist at Dangerous Studios in New York City. He was a music producer and songwriter who had been in a band that was signed to RCA in the '90s and was producing the guitarist's first solo record. Gregory was fifteen years older than me, handsome, charming, talented, funny, well-dressed, and had a shih tzu named Spike who wouldn't stop growling. When he lit my cigarette he told me to look away so I wouldn't look cross-eyed. I stared at his dimple. I went to pet Spike, but he growled at me. I tried to remember Paul was there with me. I'd see Gregory whenever Paul and I went out, which was almost every night. We liked each other immediately and had long, passionate conversations in the dark corners of bars. One night, we found ourselves alone together at 4 a.m. on the Lower East Side under a streetlight.

"All I want to do is kiss you," one of us said.

"Me too," said the other.

We stared into each other, the moment dilating with our desire and deliberation. It was thrilling to want that hard.

"We can't do this," I said.

I had to get back to Paul, and Gregory had to get back to his girlfriend of sixteen years.

Now, two years later, both of us single, I asked Gregory over the phone, "Do you want to come over and tuck me in?"

"Have you ever been properly tucked?" he asked, and I laughed.

That night, he walked up the stairs to my apartment and I greeted him at the door.

"I have to warn you, I'm a drunk," he said.

I heard: "I have to warn you, I'm drunk," so I said, "Don't worry, I'll catch up."

He was wearing a three-piece, taupe corduroy suit with a T-shirt that he had painted a tie onto. He had big, expressive eyes and shaggy brown hair and a huge, dimpled smile. In my apartment, I poured us drinks and dropped the needle of my vintage record player onto Elvis Costello and the Attractions' *Armed Forces*.

I settled on the sofa next to Gregory.

"So what have you been writing?" he asked.

"Well, I wrote a novel about the necessity of perverse relationships, how masochism is a kind of art," I said.

"What is the necessity of perverse relationships?"

I fumbled for an explanation. I hadn't expected him to ask follow-up questions.

"I'd like to read it," he said.

"How's the producing going?" I asked.

"It's good. I like to see how much I can do with as little as possible. Some of my best stuff was made in my kitchen with a cheap microphone. No one listening is going to know or care what mic I used or what compressor; they just know if they like it. I just want little

Johnny down the street to put on his headphones and go, 'I'm not alone.'"

"Were you little Johnny in his room alone?" I asked.

He laughed. "I still am."

He grabbed my neck and pulled me into a kiss.

That night we had sex. Afterwards, I lay on my back, laughing. "What the fuck was that? So that's what it's supposed to feel like?"

"You have a sex smile," he said, grinning. "You can't stop smiling."

I hadn't before known what it felt like to not be able to get enough of someone. I hadn't known what it felt like for someone to make my pleasure not only a priority but a party. After that first night Gregory just didn't leave. We collected his stuff from his friend's apartment, where he'd been staying since he'd broken up with his long-term girlfriend. We fucked four times a day, breaking my sofa, keeping us indoors for days. The rest of the time we talked, listened to music, wrote together, and drank.

We sat on my floor drinking whiskey and writing a song we titled "High Class Problems." I had always been afraid to sing, but he encouraged me.

"Just recite it, like Lou Reed," he said.

He strummed his guitar and I leaned toward the laptop speaker we were recording into.

"I got high," I sang. Gregory held up his hand for me to pause. I paused. Then he motioned for me to continue. "Class. Problems."

A car alarm started blaring in the street, and he harmonized with it. We did a few takes of the first verse and then got distracted by a red rubber ball, which we rolled back and forth across the floor at each other while he told me about his life.

He described how he was alone a lot as a kid and would spend days in his room listening to records, typing out the lyrics of his favorite songs. He'd spend hours playing a note on his little plastic organ, humming in unison, then altering his pitch so he could feel the dissonance in his body. He played in what he called the Me and Me band, where he'd record himself singing and playing on one boom box, then press play on that boom box while recording on another while singing a harmony with the first boom box. I told him how I had spent hours alone in my room listening to my audiobooks, how I'd recite my actions to myself like I was my own narrator.

He told me about his twenties: the band he had formed, getting signed to RCA, touring with the Verve Pipe and Lenny Kravitz, modeling for *L'Uomo Vogue* and doing runway for Issey Miyake. He told me how he had started ordering pain pills online from Málaga, Spain, and had moved on to snorting heroin, a habit he would keep hidden for years—a high-functioning and productive junkie—and would only break by becoming an alcoholic instead. I told him about my cutting, about my mother who didn't seem to like me, about my father who didn't seem to know the right way to like me. He wasn't awestruck and he wasn't shocked. He asked me many questions—about what I loved and what I feared, about what I actually was trying to say when I obscured my meaning with metaphors and big words. He listened hard, and it made me feel weightless, no longer heaving up the effigy of myself made out of pills and catchphrases and scars.

Infatuation developed rapidly, a superbug that put me down hard and fast. We created an intense, insular little world, in which each tiny gesture—a kiss, a laugh—felt huge, the magnification in a dew drop. I couldn't bear to leave him for any amount of time. I tried to go to class but turned around and ran back to my apartment just as the uptown C train pulled into the station. We flung ourselves at each other until the paste of us could mix, participating in the invention of a novel compound. We said "I love you" to each other right away, over and over, many times a day, as if our bodies, metabolizing the other's fervor too fast, required more and more and more sustenance.

Of equal vigor was Gregory's alcoholism. He was honest with me from the beginning about how far gone he was.

"It's like I'm trying to kill myself by jumping out of a first-floor window over and over," he told me.

I witnessed up close the grueling routine demanded by his illness. He drank a liter of vodka a day, and at night I'd wake to see him in front of the refrigerator, the freezer door open, drinking straight from the bottle to quell the shakes. My sheets became saturated in acrid alcoholic sweat. He dry heaved over the toilet in the mornings. As Gregory's illness blazed, the medications I was taking flinted the tinder of my pathologies.

"I'm going to scare you off," he said.

"I'm going to scare you off," I said.

"I'm on a grand adventure," he said, spreading his arms wide. "I know it's foolish and I know it's irresponsible and I don't care. And if ever you don't want me here, I'll leave."

"I want you here," I said.

Three months later, I had to fly to the Caribbean to meet my mother. In the middle of a blizzard, I dressed Gregory in his three-piece suit, put a MetroCard and forty dollars in his pocket, wrapped him up in his coat and a warm hat, and sent him into the snowy night. He had nowhere to go, but I, an oblivious rich kid, didn't understand what that really meant.

Gregory had continued to scrape together enough money to sustain his drinking and stay in youth hostels by producing the records of Manhattan brats impressed by his résumé, but the money had run out. He called an old friend who got him a ticket to Fort Myers, Florida, where he waited out the winter in his former tour manager's apartment, overlooking a trailer park. I visited him for Valentine's Day. We rode bikes around Fort Myers, wrote songs on a friend's pontoon, laughed when a parrot landed on my shoulder. We had such loud sex that neighbors would holler "oh god yes" at us from their trailers. When I arrived home, I opened my email to find an MP3 attachment titled "Carrière." From my computer speakers, in a voice about to collapse under the weight of its sentiment, Gregory sang: "Carrière, Carrière, I want to carry her away." By the end, as he repeated the lines "Without you I'm only half me. Without you I only have me," I could hear the sorrow in his voice.

Gregory was subsisting on baked potatoes and rice. His royalty checks and former tour manager paid for his alcohol. Once spring arrived, he flew back to New York, relying first on family, then on his charm to keep a roof over his head. He eventually ran out of favors. After detox in a hospital, rehab in Pennsylvania, a relapse, a bus trip back to New York, and a realization he really had nowhere to go, he ended up at Men's Educational Alliance PRIDE Site One—a sober-living center on the Lower East Side. Most of the residents were reluctantly sober convicts, mandated by the courts to be there. Gregory's counselor was a former champion whistler and his designated "big brother" was an ex–Barnum & Bailey Circus clown with a snaggletooth and an anxiety disorder, whom Gregory dubbed "Johnny Panic" after the Sylvia Plath book. At night, Gregory would lie on the top bunk in the twelve-by-sixteen-foot room listening to his three roommates snore. One guy gasped in his sleep and then made a high-pitched noise that sounded like a little girl calling Gregory's name from far away: "Greeeeeeg." The guy in the bottom bunk had a baritone snore that would vibrate the bed. Johnny Panic would exhale and then fall into a long silence that was exploded by a violent, gasping inhalation. These sounds formed a relentless sonic locomotive that tore through Gregory's sleepless nights. He didn't have any ear plugs or headphones, so he'd wad up toilet paper, soak it in spit, cram it in his ears, and wrap a pair of pants around his head. After 6:15 a.m. wake-up and breakfast, Gregory swept, mopped floors, and cleaned toilets. For the first seven days he had to be escorted at all times—even to the toilet for his withdrawal-induced diarrhea and dry heaves—by other residents. The residents were allowed to take a "med walk" four times a day, where they walked to Tompkins Square Park, rolled loose-leaf tobacco, which was the only kind they could afford on the ten-dollars-a-week stipend, and smoked. He tried to comfort himself with the fact that he was in his old neighborhood. To calm down, he would chant to himself, "I am in the East Village on East Tenth Street by Tompkins Square Park. I'm home."

One morning, after four months of sober confinement, Gregory walked out of Men's Educational Alliance PRIDE Site One, across Tompkins Square Park, and through the band-sticker-covered door of Doc Holliday's, where he asked the Bettie Paige look-alike bartender for two double whiskeys, paid for with the royalty checks that had continued to arrive and that he'd secretly cashed and kept waded in a sock in his drawer. To sleep, he found a flophouse, which was one giant room, the floor of a warehouse, separated by partitions topped with chicken wire to prevent people from crawling into other people's space. A man with white tufts of hair puffing like smoke from his open shirt handed him a can of bug spray and told him to spray himself and the room down because of the bed bugs. In eight months, Gregory would be curled up under a blanket in a small room in Brooklyn, unable to eat anything except flakes of salt, his hair falling out from malnourishment, his feet numb from neuropathy, drinking. In another eight months, he would be curled up on a bench in Tompkins Square Park, unrecognizable and waiting to die.

I tried to keep track of him. He wasn't allowed a cell phone at PRIDE Site One, so I resorted to calling his ex-girlfriend, who didn't know where he was. I called another girl he had been staying with, who refused to give me any information about him. When he regained access to his phone, he was too preoccupied with his slow suicide to pick up when anyone called. I called every hostel I could remember him ever having mentioned, including one called, unforgettably, "Lollipop," but they refused to release information about their guests. I thought about him all the time, but I would soon become distracted by a threat even greater than my heartbreak. As Gregory was folding in on himself like a napkin twisted into the shape of a person, my symptomatology—derived from illness or the medications allegedly treating that illness—was stretching, finding its legs, about to bound off to the very limit of where I thought my mind could go.

6.

That summer I visited my father in Berlin, where he was shooting a telenovela called *Anna und die Liebe*. I was twenty-three and I looked after my sister, who was twelve. We'd take the train to the suburbs where my father was shooting and spend the day in his dressing room. We'd run lines, eat snacks, and take selfies. We wandered the Berlin suburbs talking and singing songs—Regina Spektor's "Fidelity," an Italian lullaby, and a song by a Moldovan pop trio I'd heard on German MTV.

"You're going to be very beautiful," I said to Elena.

"I don't want to be beautiful," she said. "That doesn't interest me." I laughed. I respected that.

I loved my sister and I was impressed by her. She was confident and decisive and very diplomatic. When my father and I fought she'd silently place a note on the table that informed us of our bad behavior and instructed us to get along and then walk away. I wondered sometimes who I was to her. I wanted her to love me. I wanted to be important to her. But I was also jealous of her, even though she was only twelve. My father was protective of her and never yelled or threw tantrums like he had around me. When she'd misbehave or refuse to do something, he was patient.

"Why aren't you screaming at her?" I'd scream at him. "You weren't like this with me."

I was still being prescribed Adderall, which left me with a relentless, irrepressible boiling inside my brain and my chest that I needed to match with constant stimulation and movement on the outside. I dragged Elena all around Berlin, compulsively shopping with my mother's credit card and visiting tattoo shops to see if they could tattoo the first lines of my novel onto my forearm. My friend Leah was also in Berlin, and we went out one night with her friend Friedrich. We walked from bar to bar, trying to decide where to go. We'd walk in and I'd immediately say, "No, not here" and insist we leave. Nowhere we went felt right. I needed to keep moving, keep searching for that perfect, elusive place. I thought I was being discerning, that my indecision and insatiable need were relatable and they too were in search of something they could never find, but later that night, Friedrich said to Leah, "I hope your friend gets the help she needs."

To bring myself down, I drank alone at night, whiskey and vodka straight out of bottles I found in the apartment where we were staying. My sister, perhaps in an act of helpless defiance, took my phone and secretly documented my binges. Photos of me asleep with my mouth wide open clutching a near-empty bottle, photos of overflowing ashtrays and empty liquor bottles lining the windowsill would mysteriously appear in my photo library. One night, after my sister had gone back to Venice, I found a baggie of cocaine in a purse I had packed. My father used to tell me that when I turned eighteen, we could do heroin on a beach together, and I thought this would be the perfect opportunity to fulfill one of our fantasies. I also knew he used to love cocaine (which he had stopped using when Elena was born) and I wanted him to do it with me.

He declined so I laid out a line on the coffee table and snorted it.

"Isn't it so crazy I just randomly found this?" I said. "I had no idea it was in here and it crossed an entire ocean to surprise us, like a gift from the gods. Fucking wild, no?"

He was eerily quiet. I was used to him twiddling his fingers and sucking on a cigarette and following the little cards on the screen as he played Skat. But now he was completely still, lying on the couch. He stared into the distance. I bowed my head to do another line. He erupted from the couch, towered over me, and stabbed a finger into the air between us.

"Don't you ever fucking do that in front of me again." His words held a cracking force but were low and level.

I was speechless. All the images of our shared transgressions swirled around me. I thought this was what he wanted. Just the two of us getting into trouble, doing things normal assholes didn't do, because they couldn't understand, because they were too boring or stupid or prudish or American. I thought this was who he wanted me to be. But I had fucked up and he was rejecting me.

After years of sexualized words and gazes—my father's and other men's—I was concerned that my father was no longer sexually attracted to me. I had been tracking what I thought was his waning interest for a while. When the pills first made me gain weight I asked him if I was the same size as my mother when they got married.

"No," he said. "She was slim."

Something inside my chest collapsed. I had failed. I was watching a light in his eyes dim. The more my body changed, the bigger or smaller it got, pumped up or whittled down by meds, the more I worried about my fluctuating worth. I had at first thought it might intrigue him, as other facets of my sickness seemed to. When I was seventeen and we were visiting his friend Karl, my father walked into the living room and removed any remotely injurious object (pencil, stapler, lighter, sharp-edged picture frame) in a flamboyant performance of parental protectiveness. When I came to visit one year and showed him my Ziploc bag full of nine medication bottles, he made me pose with it and took a picture of me holding the bag aloft, smiling. But he seemed frustrated by the physical changes and I became attuned and sensitive to his irritation. Before flying to Berlin, I had lost twenty pounds and would overhear him on the phone telling people how great I looked and how much weight I'd lost. Every time I went to visit him I mapped the hills and valleys of my body, desperately trying to decipher if there was beauty still in its shapes.

It was a strange circuitry of worry and responsibility, pride and shame, pathways lighting up and crossing that should never have intersected. I had started to see the world differently, but I couldn't figure out why. Every movie I watched that contained a scene when a father was affectionate with a child, I anticipated a dark turn. Every time I saw a father be affectionate with a daughter in public, my bones ached with suspicion and a queasy trepidation. I interpreted every physical gesture, any moment when skin met skin, when a gaze lingered, as hazardous, inappropriate. I didn't know how to identify a father-daughter relationship that was safe. There was always, in every touch, the potential for treachery, for transgression, for taboo. It confused me why people around me couldn't see it too.

I had recurring nightmares about my father. They took place in hotel rooms, like the ones we stayed in in Europe while he was shooting movies. We were in a bed together and he started touching me. I pretended to be asleep and I didn't stop him. Sometimes in the dream I murmured "Daddy." I used a term I had never used to remind him of who he was while he was doing what he was doing. In the nightmare I began to get turned on, often orgasming into wakefulness to then be slammed with a soaking shame. It took me days to recover from those nightmares.

I couldn't figure out why this was happening, why I was feeling and doing all these things. I wondered if it had something to do with my mother's abuse. Had I inherited it somehow? Had those words in her journals infected me? It was hard to know what had happened to me. My father had given me words and ideas, ones that did not belong in a father's mouth or the mind of a daughter. He had treated parenthood as a reckless experiment. But compared to my mother's nightmarish memories, my own experiences paled in comparison. I was also beginning to feel at home in this place I occupied with my father, and, sitting on the floor of a Berlin apartment, tempting him with this powdered Eucharist, I tried to keep us there.

I returned to New York at the end of August and had to move apartments because I had been kicked out of mine for smoking too much. I was alone again. 134 Charles Street was gone. Gregory was gone. My mother was at her cottage in the Hamptons, while the building she had bought in Brooklyn was being renovated. I would call her and try to keep her on the phone.

I called her once when I knew she was in Brooklyn, visiting the construction site.

"Do you want to spend some time with me?" I asked.

"Is there something wrong?" she asked.

"No, I just want to hang out with you. Don't you want to hang out with me?"

"I'm going back to Amagansett," she said, as if she had an important appointment, which she did not.

"But you don't have to," I said. "If you wanted to, you could hang out with me."

There was a long silence.

"I have to go out to Amagansett," she said. We hung up and I cried.

Dr. Sarini had recently put me on Zoloft. The other medications were all doing something: adding sweat, flesh, bottomless hunger, trembling alertness. The Zoloft combined with the Adderall made my mind and body vibrate. I could not be still. During the day, I cleaned my apartment for hours, organizing and reorganizing its contents, arranging and rearranging the furniture. At night, I got dressed up in clothes that were too tight for me, now plush from meds and mood swings, and went out alone to my favorite bars. At Marie's Crisis—a show-tunes bar in the West Village—I met George. George was gay, effusive with his compliments, and eager to party. I took him to the Beatrice Inn, the exclusive lounge frequented by celebrities, downtown socialites, and the offspring of Middle Eastern royalty. "Private party tonight," they'd say if they didn't want you in there. After talking excitedly at each other until three in the morning, George and I went back to my apartment and passed out in my bed. Over the next two weeks, he would come over (from where, I didn't know), tell me to try on outfits and jewelry for him, and we'd topple out into the night. Then pieces of jewelry went missing and he stopped coming around. I came across a photo on George's Facebook page of him wearing a necklace of mine. Alone again, my mind gnawing on this betrayal by a man I didn't realize I didn't know, I called my father in Germany. I talked to him about George stealing from me, large gulps of air punctuating my sentences as I kept forgetting to breathe. My father must have noticed something in my voice, because he begged for time off from his desperately needed acting job and booked a flight to New York, arriving three days later. I was excited to see him and we had a nice few days. We read each other our writing and he cooked me dinner. He built me a bookshelf. The third evening, while I was in bed watching a TV show on my laptop, he lay next to me and put his arm around me. All the breath went out of my body and I froze. I stared at the screen and felt my mouth go dry. He commented on the show and I managed to make a gurgling sound of agreement. When he finally released me from this septic cuddle, I felt dizzy and weak.

The next evening, I started texting George. Did he know the punishment for grand larceny? I asked. I drank beer after beer and sent text after text. I declared to my father, also many beers in, that we needed to go to the police and report George. At the police station, I held out a printout of the Facebook photo of George and my jewelry and explained to a police officer that this guy had stolen from me, jabbing my finger at George's two-dimensional neck, making the paper buckle and thwack. My father tried to interrupt. I could smell the alcohol on his breath, but not the boozy steam that puffed from my own mouth. I felt my father's tall frame vibrating at a high frequency as I stood there, oblivious to my own shivers of derangement.

Back at my apartment my father told me I should just drop it. "Drop it, drop it," he repeated. But I could not. This was all that mattered. I was enraged he couldn't see that. I felt hollowed out, my thoughts, sharp and stinging, spraying themselves across my mind like fire-hosed acid. I screamed at him to get out of my apartment. He grabbed my only set of keys and stormed out. When I tried to call his cell phone, it rang uselessly from my kitchen counter. I felt trapped. My heart smacked against my rib cage, my thoughts thrashed at my brain. I grabbed one of my orange pill bottles and swallowed five Klonopin. I grabbed another brown glass beer bottle and drained it. The door opened and shut and my father was in my living room again. I ran into the bathroom and locked the door behind me. I dismantled a razor blade, wedged myself between the closet and the washing machine, and began slicing up my left forearm. My father banged on the door, begging me to open it.

"You love the drama," I screamed. "You love this," I said as I did snow angels on the bathroom floor, bleeding.

He begged me to open the door.

"You'll just make me go to the hospital," I said.

"No. I won't. I promise. Just open the door," he said.

My father called my mother in Amagansett. My mother called my friend Leah, who came over. When she arrived, I unlocked the bathroom door and came out. She helped me wash and dress the wounds and gave me a croissant to eat, to fill my stomach and absorb the pills. I went to sleep in my bedroom, Leah watching me breathe, and my father went to sleep on the couch. He returned to Germany two days later and called when he landed to check on me. My mother never mentioned what had happened that night.

It was spring, and the weather was turning. The days got warmer and then hotter, mirroring the escalating temperature of my mind. Alone in my apartment, I turned my attention to my body. I discovered a rash on my thigh. I interpreted that ruddy patch as a hazard symbol, warning me of something—but of what? I had long feared I was susceptible to HIV. Memories of my mother's friends who'd died of AIDS flooded me. I scanned my body for any abnormal sensations. But being in a body always felt strange to me. I examined my tongue. Did it look whiter than usual? Were these signs of thrush? I peered into the toilet to examine my stool. Was this normal stool? I turned to WebMD. The more symptoms I put in, or the less related they were, the more likely it seemed that I had HIV or multiple sclerosis. I hadn't been tested since all the unprotected sex I'd had with Gregory, and I became convinced I had HIV. I made an emergency appointment with my gynecologist.

"What brings you here today?" she asked.

"I don't want to show it to you," I said, sitting on the exam room table, sweating and trembling.

"Why not?"

"I'm scared it's HIV and I'm scared for you to tell me it is."

"Just show me."

I lifted up my skirt.

"That is a sweat rash," she said. "Because it's hot outside. It'll go away in a few days. If you want you can put some Cortisone on it."

I demanded an HIV test, but when the results came back negative, I was convinced that the infection was not detectable yet, an invisible threat known only to me. And if I didn't have HIV, I knew there must be something else wrong with me. I went to my GP and told him I felt like there were electric currents pulsing in my head, did he know what that meant? No, he didn't. I went to a proctologist, a dermatologist. They found nothing. Monitoring my body consumed me. Any illness I contracted, I knew, would be insidious, tricky, stealthy. It could be anything. It could be anywhere. My body seemed porous and susceptible and liable to turn against me at any moment.

Two weeks later, the imaginary illness spread from my body to other machines. I became convinced I had been hacked and that my computer communications were being monitored. I stared for hours at the computer logs, watching in real time as the computer told itself in its own language what it was doing. The numbers and abbreviations meant nothing to me but I knew they were detailing every breach, every malign intrusion, which would become clear if only I knew the language. I printed out the system logs, convinced that somehow as the logs moved between their digital form and the printed page, the truth had been intercepted and destroyed. Somewhere, invisibly, wirelessly, in the air around me, fatal distortions were occurring. I sent myself emails written to "them" because I knew they were monitoring my email. They were changing the order and content of my text messages, too. I held my breath and choked back tears of terror as I updated my Facebook status to: "I HAVE BEEN HACKED. DON'T BELIEVE ANYTHING THAT IS WRITTEN ON HERE" or googled how to change my social security number. This preoccupation with infection, with the permeability of borders, with the mutiny of mundane machines—my body, the devices I used to live—took over my life.

I tried to get help. I called AppleCare and explained the invasions I was enduring.

"You should buy chicken wire and surround your house with it," said the AppleCare specialist.

"But I live in an apartment," I said.

"It's just as effective if you put the chicken wire all around the inside of your apartment," he said.

I scribbled these suggestions down in my notebook.

"There's also a special paint you can put on the walls that will make the signal bounce off of them," he told me.

I thanked him and hung up. As I googled "paint to protect against hacking" I realized the AppleCare specialist had been mocking me, and then realized the call must have been intercepted by the culprits.

I went to Tekserve, the computer-repair store. It was a hot summer day, and I arrived with giant sweat stains under my arms and a glistening face.

"My family has been hacked," I told the man at the desk. "The FBI is helping my mom but I just want to make sure my stuff is okay too." I calculated that these embellishments to my story would legitimize me.

"Look for a virus," I said.

"There's nothing here," the guy said, after quickly scanning my external hard drives.

I went back a week later.

"It's FBI girl," said one of the employees, smiling.

"Yep, that's me," I said, smiling back, flattered he remembered me.

I did in fact call the FBI. I spoke to someone who told me to slow down because I was sounding crazy.

"Why would anyone want to do this to you?" he asked.

"I don't know but don't you think that proves that I'm not crazy? If I were crazy, I'd be making up reasons why. So admitting I don't know shows I'm not crazy."

With every passing week, the incursions got worse, and I was called upon to invent new ways of protecting myself. One morning in July I woke up to find that the doorknob on my front door was sagging. I called the police, and soon two officers arrived. It was the afternoon and I was in a vintage pink slip with crescents of yesterday's makeup under my eyes.

"Can you still lock it?" asked one of the police officers.

I closed the door and twisted the lock and it locked. I opened the door.

"Okay, well, was anything taken?" he asked.

"Um, not really. I don't think," I said.

"Well then we can only report this as damage to property since the door can still lock and nothing was taken."

"Well, stuff has been messed around with recently," I said. "Pages were ripped out of my notebook."

The police officers looked at each other. One of them shrugged and said, "I'm sorry, miss, but we can only report this as damage to property."

There was something about a doorknob's being taken apart just enough while still being functional that unnerved me. This was a statement, loud and insolent and mysterious. Were they mocking me? Telling me they could get in if they wanted to? To thwart the invasions, I stacked my dining table chairs in front of the door and snaked ribbons of vintage lace through the legs. If the lace was broken, I'd know that someone had tried to get in. It didn't occur to me that the lace was irrelevant, that the chairs would clatter if someone tried to enter. But these were no ordinary intruders. They were cunning, I knew, and I needed to be smarter and sneakier and more creative than they were in order to defeat them. I didn't realize then that I was the intruder—mastermind of both barricade and breach.

By late summer I was convinced I was being chloroformed and gang-raped in my sleep. Going to sleep was like willfully drowning myself, holding myself under with booze and Klonopin until I could pass out, until my ceaseless vigilance could be momentarily submerged. When

I woke up I inspected my underwear for signs of sexual assault. Any discharge on my underwear and they went into a Ziploc bag and were stored in what would later be labeled my "manic box."

In my "manic box" was:

Ziploc bags full of physical evidence I had collected and labeled. The evidence included: flakes of plaster, strands of hair, lint, sediment from my fire escape and balcony, loose screws, a used Band-Aid, cigarette butts, a torn six of clubs playing card, a dismantled bicycle bell.

hundreds of pages of printouts of computer systems logs

two laptops, dismantled and put back together with tape

an external hard drive containing hundreds of photographs and screenshots of: "possible associates"; rooftops of buildings; all the graffiti on any surface within a three-block radius of my apartment, which I had collected and studied in an attempt to detect a pattern; suspicious cars and vans parked near my apartment; text messages that I did not recall sending or receiving, which I believed to have been altered remotely so as to skew events.

a notebook with: the license plate numbers of cars parked around my apartment, dates and times of phone calls received and made, the letters of people's names and Facebook posts arranged into anagrams that would reveal their secret communiqués.

envelopes labeled "dubious info" containing receipts (taxi, deli, bar), business cards, paper phone-number tabs ripped from a suspicious-looking guitar-lesson advertisement, all found within a one-block radius of my apartment

A soggy receipt in the gutter held secrets. A flyer for a production of *The Phantom of the Opera* was a message, a coded threat. I'd walk around and around my block, scouring the concrete for new evidence, updating my catalog of license plate numbers. But every time I meticulously archived the rotten flower petal, the broken hair tie, the new combination of letters and numbers, I became more disoriented.

Everything I encountered glowed with a radioactive menace. Everyone I encountered took on tremendous significance. They were all connected. Anyone could be one of them. The taxis I got into had been waiting for me. The men who asked for my number on the street were monitoring me. Something had been set into motion, a vast machine that knew where I was, knew what I was doing, could match my mounting fear with more menace. The more embattled I felt, the bigger and stronger and faster the enemy machine became.

By late August I knew I was being constantly monitored. Eyes and ears were on every part of me every second, in a drenching scrutiny. I was listening to one of my favorite childhood audiobooks. In between the narrator's sentences I heard, "Yo, D, what up?" come through the speakers. I realized they had bugged my apartment and I had tapped into the frequency they were using to communicate. I unscrewed all the light fixtures and peered into the wiring in the ceiling. I unscrewed all the outlets and pried around inside them with a screwdriver. I continued to look and examine, searching for proof. I tried to dismantle an old iPod, but the sleek design would not yield its insides. While I was trying to shove the edge of a knife in between the flush seams I heard people outside my door. I ran outside and followed two young men out of the building.

"Were you just inside that apartment building?"

"Um, yeah."

"What were you doing in there?"

"What?"

"Do you know how to open these things?" I asked as I tried to force a fingernail under the track pad of the iPod.

"I want whatever you're on," said one of the guys and they laughed and walked away. I retreated back into my apartment and took my afternoon dose of Adderall.

I bought a camera disguised as a desk fan and spent hours watching the footage. I convinced my mother to pay for people to sweep my apartment for bugs. Two men arrived with machines in black boxes.

"But what if they know that you're here and they've turned off whatever they're using to surveil me so your machines can't pick it up?" I asked.

"That's not how it works," I was told.

My mother sat on the sofa, silent. Her silence and her rare presence confirmed to me that I was right to be so diligent about my safety. Maybe it was because she was familiar with unbelievable stories. She had, after all, been used in a murderous sex cult.

"There's nothing here," said the de-buggers.

I convinced her to hire a forensic computer analyst to look at my computer.

"I can't see anything wrong with this except for these weird things you did to it. What is 'in a sieve they went to sea'?" he asked.

To throw people off my scent I had renamed my computer in settings after a poem my Scottish middle school librarian had read to us.

"There's nothing here," said the forensic computer analyst.

No one could identify the threat so I was forced to live a daily life constantly under siege by something only detectable by me. I had to eat and communicate and sleep and shop and sit on the subway and answer the phone all while the surge of adrenaline threatened to shred my veins. There was a hot, granular quality to my thoughts. The blood thrumming in my ears was hot white noise. Sweat continually covered my brow and darkened my underarms. My speech was breathless and speedy. When I was not at home I could barely breathe or concentrate. When I was outside, my mind spun with images of them prowling inside my apartment, going through my things, embellishing their elaborate methods of surveillance and torment. After a while I couldn't take it and I'd stop whatever I was doing, make an excuse, and run home. One day I fell up the stairs as I sprinted toward my apartment. I entered on my hands and knees. There was no one there. I hadn't caught them. So I just decided not to leave.

I managed to send my Columbia advisor an email saying I would not be able to return to school in the fast-approaching fall, and she sent me the paperwork for a leave of absence, freeing me up to build my entire life around this threat.

I ordered American Spirit cigarettes from the corner deli and Duraflame logs to keep the fire burning even through the sweltering days because it made me feel less alone. I ordered food from FreshDirect. I bought two industrial-sized garbage cans so I wouldn't have to take out the trash often. The garbage sat inside the giant bins in the middle of my living room and festered. I stopped washing dishes. I ate cereal out of Tupperware with a ladle. I ate spaghetti from a vase with tongs. I used an old bowl of split pea soup as an ashtray. My appetite faded completely and I ate only sliced turkey and carrots, and only when my body absolutely demanded it. I barely slept. I was cutting every day and then switched to burning, giving myself two deep partial-thickness burns, causing nerve damage that would last for years.

One day Effie came over. She saw the cuts and burns on my arms and the dark circles under my eyes, smelled the rotting trash, and asked me what was going on. I told her all about the break-ins and the rapes and the surveillance. She spent the night and left before I woke up, leaving the door unlocked behind her because she didn't have a key, which convinced me she was in on it. I texted her: "I'm onto you. I know what you're doing. You're working with them."

"What are you talking about???" she texted back.

No one in my life could be trusted. When friends called, I'd make them confirm their identity through a series of questions, and when satisfied, would launch into the latest update of my persecution. Eventually they stopped picking up my calls. As people fell from my life, I agonized over who was doing this to me. Who had had access to me? Who had been in my most intimate spaces? Was Gregory the culprit? I hadn't heard from him in months. Was he the mastermind of my torment? Maybe everything I'd ever believed or felt had been a lie. Maybe this—this invasion, this war—was the only true thing in my life.

At night, I crouched at the windows, scanning the other buildings and examining each dark silhouette. Overwhelmed by all the eyes that could be watching, I taped spare bedsheets and towels across the windows. The only connection I had to the world was the swathes of sky let in by the skylights in the ceiling. The sky was a living force as the apartment bulged with heat from the sun.

In September, my mother got me a kitten. I named him Bracket. One morning, while in my bedroom examining my mattress with a flashlight—picking up strands of hair and placing them into a Ziploc bag—I heard noises out in the living room. I held my breath, terrified. Bracket was in the bedroom with me, and I reasoned that they wouldn't hurt an animal so I cracked the door open and pushed him out into the other room. I thought the presence of the cat might chase them away. I also felt if I sent him out into the room he would transmit the information to me. Part of me wanted to see them and confront them. Part of me was scared for my life. Perhaps some deep part of me knew there was nothing there and that would be more terrifying than anything else.

I waited in the bedroom as I heard them leave. I could hear very distinctly the sound of multiple footfalls going down stairs. I opened the door. The apartment was empty except for Bracket standing on the dining table. I ran to a drawer and grabbed the largest knife I could find. It was early still, and my eyes were dry and stinging from lack of sleep. I sat on the sofa and gripped the knife with both hands, trying to remember to breathe. As I sat there, I saw myself. For a brief moment of clarity I saw how far things had gone, sitting on the sofa with a knife surrounded by my refuse, and I saw that I could not find a way back or a way out. I cried.

I had an appointment scheduled with my psychopharmacologist and two hours before, the buzzer rang. It was my mother's assistant, sent by her to bring me to the doctor. I sat in Dr. Sarini's office jiggling my leg, talking rapidly of break-ins and rapes and surveillance. After listening for a while, Dr. Sarini said, "You have to choose. Either you take these new medications I'm going to prescribe or I'm calling an ambulance right now. I've sent people far less symptomatic than you to the psych ward."

"I'll take the pills," I said.

I started taking Depakote, Trileptal, and Zyprexa—two mood stabilizers and a heavy-hitting antipsychotic—in addition to all my other pills, including the Adderall. My mother came to visit me one week after I went on the new medications. She slept in my bedroom and I slept on the sofa. I had been instructed by Dr. Sarini to double the dose of Trileptal that morning. I took the two pills and went back to sleep for forty-five minutes. My mother was preparing to leave when I awoke. I sat up and walked into my bedroom, where she was packing. I stood in the doorway. She turned and looked at me and asked, "What are you doing?" My arms and legs were jerking like marionette limbs on strings.

"I don't know," I said. "I'm not doing this on purpose."

I made my way back to the sofa and lay down. My eyes were rolling back in my head and my tongue began to move uncontrollably in my mouth.

"Call the doctor," I managed to say, gesturing to my cell phone.

"It sounds like an overdose," Dr. Sarini said. "There's not much you can do. She just has to ride it out."

My mother brought me a garbage can and I threw up in it. She filled a glass with water and put it to my lips but my mouth and tongue were contorting too much for me to drink from the glass. She crouched next to me as I writhed on the sofa.

Hours later, when I had regained control of my body, my mother left.

Dr. Sarini maintained that I should stay on the new medications—and the old ones, including the Adderall. The new pills didn't take away the paranoia, they merely blurred it. I felt heavy and deadened, the bonfire in my brain now cold, heavy ashes. My hair started to fall out, clogging the drain, snaking around my fingers. I collected the hair every day and stored it in a large envelope, more evidence of wrongs committed. I developed cystic acne, painful and hot. I spent long stretches in front of the mirror squeezing pimples until my chin was smeared with blood. I gained forty pounds. My hands felt weak, dead at the tips of my arms. Glasses of water fell from my grasp and crashed to the floor. It didn't occur to me that it was the medication doing all this to me. I thought it was just my stupid body.

Nanny took care of me in my medicated haze. She was the only person I saw. Nanny, now eighty-three, would travel to Chelsea from Tribeca, climb the steep staircase, balancing on her cane, and stay with me. At night, she rubbed my eyelids to help me get to sleep, as she had done when I was little. We shared the only laugh I can remember in those twelve months. We were trying to put together a laundry hamper, but the components had been mislabeled. We spent a fruitless hour trying to make the parts fit, dissolving in laughter each time we failed. From time to time I would point out evidence of the torment being inflicted on me, and she would nod and agree that, yes, that vase had been moved. Yes, maybe that van had been parked there too long. Even in my delusion, she would never leave me alone.

I had been seeing my therapist throughout what I was told was a manic episode, and I had grown frustrated with her. She seemed not to believe me. I wanted solutions, and she just wanted to talk. I needed to figure out how to protect myself, and she wanted me to reflect. I would have barely any memory of our sessions over the year I was manic. But I would have the beautifully worded case study she would write about me. When she eventually revealed the case study to me a year after my manic episode, I felt betrayed. The woman I had been confiding in had been studying me, turning me into a beautiful, terrifying object lesson. She gave me the dramatic pseudonym of "Juliet," a *theatrical name*, which, she explained, *expresses an aspect of the complex narcissistic and perverse elements in her parent's obsessions with her, obsessions, to be sure, also accompanied by neglect*. I was reduced to a story, and not even my story was my own.

In the case study, she wondered: *How much did the delusions mask Juliet's rage and wish to deplete the mother? . . . How much was she the designated enactment of the father's wishes and envies in this regard? . . . How much did {these invasions} replicate the psychic and sexual invasions of the father? . . . Who did what to whom?*

Who did what to whom? It was a question that had haunted my family. What had happened to my mother? What exactly had my father done to me? How many of my symptoms were the result of the American psychiatric complex invading my body and my mind?

7.

Dr. Sarini recommended a treatment center in Florida where he sent many of his patients, and I agreed to go. I was twenty-five. While most of my peers were getting their master's degrees, getting married, and progressing in their careers, I was being admitted to my latest treatment center.

This time, I wanted to get better. The last year had scared me. And I was tired.

The night before I left for the treatment center, I called my father.

"If you get better—" he started to say.

"If?" I screamed. "If? Why would you say that?"

"I don't know if you'll survive," he said. "I hope that you will but I can't predict the future."

I was ravenously angry.

"What am I supposed to say?" he said.

"You're supposed to lie to me," I screamed.

When I arrived, the center's psychopharmacologist took me off the Depakote, Trileptal, Zyprexa, Klonopin, and Adderall, but put me on another stimulant called Vyvanse, which functioned like Adderall. Forty minutes after I took my morning dose I was chain-smoking on the porch, telling stories about my childhood and sweating through my shirt. Then I would be told by counselors that I talked too much and could we figure out what to do about my sweating problem? Beyond the huge words and complicated metaphors I continued to use, I also gesticulated wildly to a point beyond mere animation, possessed by a crazed and indecipherable sign language. My therapist, Diane, told me to sit on my hands, but then I just swiveled my neck back and forth, as if a current were flowing through me. I wanted to take advantage of this place. I knew that I was lucky to have another chance, and I wanted to get well. I wanted to be calm and receptive and thoughtful, but the medication wouldn't let me.

There were strict rules at the treatment center. We had to keep our bungalows meticulously clean—no water spots on the mirror, no dirty laundry in the hamper. We had to be on time—if we were late to group therapy, we were barred from the room. We had jobs—writing down the messages left on the one communal telephone, walking the treatment center dog, Sophie (who was on antidepressants herself). There were strict regulations surrounding our interactions—sexes were kept separate, and if we developed a close relationship with a roommate, they'd reassign us. If we failed to follow the rules or fulfill our responsibilities, there were consequences—they'd confiscate our TV, revoke our day passes to leave the property. Patients were encouraged to tell on each other, and the daily Community Meeting was a forum where we voiced inexpert opinions on the behavioral, personality—even physical—traits of our peers, and were celebrated for it. One such Community Meeting focused on telling Albert, a near nonverbal schizophrenic who made no eye contact, that he smelled. Albert sat silently in his folding chair staring at the floor as patient and counselor alike told him how gross he was, asking him questions—How often did he shower? Did he know personal hygiene was an important part of getting and staying healthy? Did he own deodorant?—he did not have the words or neurochemistry to answer. After the meeting, Albert continued to smell bad but the community had done its job. A special meeting was called to address the "issue" of me and my friend Dean—a young trans guy with soft features that twitched occasionally from the tardive dyskinesia he had developed from his antipsychotics. We were close, considering getting even closer, and when we weren't smoking cigarettes on my porch, we were watching TV in my bungalow, my head in his lap. Two patients, who would watch us through the window, told the counselors something was going on between us. At the meeting, patients and counselors demanded to know the nature of our feelings for each other and if anything physical had happened. Some were confused about whether Dean was "a lesbian or a straight guy," demanding he explain "what" he was. After forty-five minutes, Dean was begging, out loud, for it to end. That night, he came into my bathroom and lifted his shirt, revealing the seven gaping slashes he had wrought on his chest. I hugged him, trying to keep our chests from touching.

I was placed in trauma group. I didn't request it but my New York therapist, Dr. Hart, had informed my therapist at the center, Diane, about my father, and it was determined that I should be in trauma group. I had to fill out a Trauma Form—a chart where I had to list all the moments when I had felt violated, that had given me "trauma," how I had felt about it then, and how I felt about it now. There was only enough space for cursory answers. My tiny letters snaked around the page until I ran out of room, so details had to be forfeited. Once a week, four of us sat in a circle in Diane's dim office with the door locked. The type of therapy we did was called Chair Work. When it was my turn, I sat in a chair in the middle of the room. Diane got up, grabbed another chair, and placed it so close to me that it touched my knees. This would be where I put my father. I pushed back in my chair. I felt uncomfortable; I told Diane I was afraid. She told me to decide how far back the chair needed to be for me to feel comfortable. I motioned to her to push it away, again and again, until it reached the opposite wall. Diane told me to decide how my father would be sitting in the chair. Did he need handcuffs or did I need bodyguards? I chose two bodyguards and I told her that he needed to be tied to the chair. There needed to be a plank that his head could be tied to so that he couldn't thrust his entire body forward. Diane told me to pick a "me" at a specific age and place her next to my chair. I picked seven-year-old "me." Seven-year-old me was wearing a striped shirt and had a bad haircut. I liked her. Diane told me to look at her and say: "I wasn't there to protect you then but I am here to protect you now. I won't let anything bad happen to you ever again."

I repeated the lines to seven-year-old me.

Diane told me to pick an incident and tell my father about how it had made me feel and what it had done to me. She went to her desk to look for my trauma form, but she couldn't find it.

"It's okay," she said. "We can do this without it. It just said something about touching your dad's penis, right?"

I twisted around in my chair.

"No," I said, the word long and stringy with surprise.

"So pick another one and let's start," said Diane.

She told me to close my eyes and tell my father about the incident I had selected. I recited the story of my father making me lick the tears from his eyes.

"You used me to fill yourself up," I screamed at the chair with my eyes closed.

I listed every incident I had written on my trauma form—from the tale of a toe in a cunt to a Lolita on a horse to a pimp in sunglasses.

I felt the other patients watching me. I felt cuddled by their raptness. My skin grew hot and tears slipped from my scrunched-up eyes. Diane whispered to me to give my father back his shame. This was the script we were given in trauma group. Every session of Chair Work ended with our giving the perpetrator back their shame. The idea was that they were shameless and we, the victims, held their shame for them.

"I give you back your shame," I yelled.

"Again," said Diane.

"I give you back your shame."

Diane asked me if she could put her hand on my back. I allowed it. The confident tenderness of her touch ruptured something inside me, my snot and tears the fluids of this strange paroxysm. I looked around the room and saw the other patients staring at me with love in their eyes. They called me brave and amazing. One patient declared that my father was a monster. I felt giddy and incandescent, covered in the glitter of their admiration. Diane asked if she could give me a hug. I sank into her enormous fake breasts, which were draped in angora and saturated in perfume. Falling into her fragrant bosom while my peers chanted their support, I felt caught in the frenzy of religious fervor—a preacher laying hands on me as I spoke in tongues, ejecting Satan from me, filling me with a faith that would save me as long as I never questioned it.

Diane had an assuredness that unnerved and sedated me. Her memory was bad and she often confused the details of her patients, but she was unwavering. She took a shred of story and stitched and padded until it became something plush and inviting I could hug to myself, ambiguity plumping up into shapely certainty. I told her of the night in Hamburg when I was eight years old and my father had been reading to me in bed. I went to the bathroom and saw spots of blood on my days of the week underwear. When I showed it to him he said,

"You must have broken your hymen." I didn't remember anything else except that I had learned how to ride a bike that day. Under Diane's care, I started to believe my mind was resisting me, that something more had probably happened that I was blocking out. Any dark pockets of non-memory were significant and sinister. Not remembering couldn't mean that nothing had happened but rather too much had happened. Diane later told me that she moved very slowly, intentionally taking her time getting me to say, "I was molested." When I named my father a molester, I was told I was strong, brave, and special. I was a survivor. That felt good.

The language in trauma group was fairytale-like—"icky," "monster," "survive," "persevere," "overcome." I was ready to commit fully to my character, to the story of the molested girl who had overcome her monster. Diane told me never to speak to or see my father again, so I put him on the list of people who weren't allowed to have their calls put through to me or have any information released to them. She told me no good could ever come from someone so evil. The simplicity felt thirst-quenching. I was ready to consume great quantities of this new solution until I felt completely myself. In my previous therapy, words had been soft and pliable. Now they were hard and inflexible. Once you called someone something, that's what they were, that's what they had always been, and that's what they would be forever. I loved stories and now I had one almost like my mother's, both with monsters whose shadows had been enlarged by therapists. I would later tell that story, embellished by Diane, to anyone who would listen. In doctor's offices or dark bars, I would announce my father as the monster I was taught to believe he was. It was my new identity.

I pictured my mother in another dim room confiding in Dr. Bernard all her hang-ups—her pain during sex, her promiscuity, her difficulty talking about feelings, her drinking, that time she had walked in on her father fucking a family friend. She laid them out like colors on an artist's palette as Dr. Bernard dipped the tip of her expertise in, creating images of such enormity and vividness that they crowded everything and everyone else out. I pictured her and Dr. Bernard shaping the amorphous clay of her fears into the forms of Bertie and Russell and "Monkey Boy." My mother was a brilliant artist, and she must have applied that same ambition and rigor to her psychotherapy. It reminded me of how she described surviving Yale: "I was terrified my first semester, but then I just started building huge stretchers that interfered with the people working near me." To deal with her fear, she created enormous, intrusive structures—a canvas or a memory—so large and so overwhelming they interfered with the people living near her.

Dr. Bernard was either a perpetrator or a victim herself. Either she had believed just as strongly in the myths she and my mother were telling together, or she was the ruthless mastermind of a nonconsensual scientific experiment. I would encounter Dr. Bernard's name again, years later, when I watched the documentary *Three Identical Strangers.* It told the story of identical triplets separated at birth who reunited and discovered that they had been victims of a disturbing scientific experiment that involved dividing triplets and twins into different socioeconomic households, withholding any information that the children had siblings, and documenting what happened. The doctors behind the study were Dr. Viola Bernard and Dr. Peter Neubauer—my mother and father's therapists, respectively. Finally here was proof that the people tasked with my parents' care, the people responsible for shaping their lives and, ultimately, mine, were real-life villains.

Now here I was, sitting in a therapist's office, sweating and squirming from prescribed medication as a therapist misinterpreted my trauma form, made up stories, and told me what words to call myself.

Parts of what Diane said were true. My father had transgressed. He had said things that shouldn't have been said. He had been derelict in his parenting in a way that had lasting effects. But did that mean the only way forward was to disavow him, to cut him out of my life as my mother had? Burn it all down and never think about it again, as she'd done with her journals? He had been the parent who asked how I was, the one who had tried to intervene in the treatment that was making me worse. Was silence the only way forward, the only path of healing? I had been told to do many things by doctors. I had been told to take the pills that roiled my brain, and I had done it. And now I'd slug down this story like the obedient patient I was, not questioning if I could be something, or someone, more.

Toward the end of my five-month stay, my mother came for family weekend. The patients and their parents sat in chairs in a circle as Blake, the family therapist, facilitated the session. Each family, when it was their turn, sat in chairs in the center. When it was our turn, I stood up and removed one of the designated "parent" chairs. My mother sat in the remaining one, and I sat in the one across from her.

"You're the only one here who only needs one seat for your parent," Blake said. "How did that make you feel, to take one away?"

"Normal," I said. "Fine."

I talked about my father and the "sexual abuse."

"She's an accomplice, right?" I asked Blake.

Blake nodded.

I was angry at my mother.

"You're an accomplice," I said to her.

Her reactions were barely discernible, her face waxy and stiff with bewilderment. I started to cry.

"My heart is breaking, I just want to hug her," said one of the patients.

"Me too," said my mother.

"So do it!" yelled one of the parents.

The audience was rooting for me. They were protecting me. My mother got up, walked over to me, and placed her arms limply around my shoulders. She stood there for a few seconds and returned to her chair. The hug had not given me what she'd intended, it had given me something else. It had given me its shortcoming, which was far more useful to me.

"Honestly that just felt so awkward," I announced. "I'm so not used to physical affection from you that it just reminds me of how uncomfortable it is." I was glad the hug had been hollow. After all, what was I without my mother's disinterest?

8.

After leaving the treatment center in July 2010, I moved into a studio apartment with no air conditioning in Delray Beach, Florida. I got a job at the Boys & Girls Club and continued seeing Diane. I loved working with the kids and I loved having somewhere to be every day, but I tingled with restlessness. I didn't know how to drive, my friends from the treatment center moved away and moved on, and I'd get uncomfortably drunk on my own. The one person I wanted to talk to was Gregory. I had no idea if he was still alive. I decided to call him, and, with each ring, I pictured a different dire scenario—frozen on a park bench, living under a bridge, long dead and buried. When I heard his voice, I felt a scratching in my chest, something trying to get out and fly to him, and an involuntary smile spread across my face. I pretended I had called by accident, embarrassed about something, although I wasn't clear what. When I'd last spoken to him, he'd barely made sense, ending his sentences with the remark: "Don't you know I don't make any sense? Don't you know I don't know what I'm saying?" Now, his voice sounded clear, his words distinct, not bending and sliding in his mouth like they did when he was drunk. He sounded calm and measured. He told me he was three months sober. He described the final days of his alcoholism and how MusiCares, the not-for-profit organization of the National Academy of Recording Arts and Sciences that helped working musicians get sober, had agreed to pay for one last rehab in Nashville, which is where he was now living. I told him about my treatment center, about Diane, about how everything made sense now that I knew my father was a monster and that I would never speak to him again. We talked late into the night.

"I'm still in love with you," I said.

"I'm still in love with you too," he said.

I scooped ice cream into a bowl in the kitchen, illuminated by the light from the refrigerator, and smiled into the phone. That electric feeling between us had not been dampened, not by my year of near-lethal madness, not by his unsuccessful suicide-by-substance. We said good night and talked every day after that.

After four months in Florida, I decided to go back to school, re-enrolled at Columbia University, quit my job, flew back to New York, and moved in with my mother in her new house in Brooklyn.

The address was 315 Vanderbilt Avenue. It had been a building for the Candy and Confectioners Union, and then a preschool. Like 134 Charles Street, it was not initially designed to be a residence. My mother's bedroom looked out onto a garden through an entire wall of glass. Her bathtub was in the middle of the room, right behind her bed, and the toilet was similarly exposed in the corner. There were two floors of studios and no guest room—only a room for Nanny. I moved into the storage room, which had no door and no furniture. I tipped boxes on their sides to create shelves for my clothes. I was back in a house with no locks, and now, no doors. The bathroom closest to my room didn't have a shower, and Nanny's was outfitted with an uncomfortable geriatric walk-in tub, so I bathed in my mother's bathtub in the center of her bedroom. I rubbed soap under my armpits as I gazed out the wall of windows onto the eight-foot boulder my mother had imported from the Hamptons, listening to her smoker's cough erupt from her as she lay on her bed next to me. I was back living with my mother, bathing next to her in a glass room, boundaries porous as ever.

Some days, I would sit in her studio with her as she worked. She was working on a massive piece that was more than 158 feet long, even bigger than *Rhapsody.* She couldn't come up with a title so she asked me to help her. She explained what the piece was about and its relationship to *Rhapsody* and another piece called *Song*. I stared at the rows of square metal plates with colorful dots in varying sizes, black and white squiggles, monochromatic house silhouettes, that wrapped around the walls.

"Recitative," I said. "The part of an opera closer to ordinary speech that advances the plot."

She loved it. She named it *Recitative.*

And in that moment we were joined. She had needed a word and I had had the right one.

Nanny was eighty-six and retired. She had decided to tie her life to my mother's instead of moving back to England to be near her sister, Thelma. When my mother and Nanny moved into the Brooklyn house, Nanny's life shrank. When we lived on Charles Street she knew everyone in the neighborhood. Nanny's best friend, Helen, lived just three blocks away on Bleecker Street and they had tea every week. She would walk the dog and chat with the couple who owned the laundromat next door and loved to gossip. In Brooklyn, she knew no one and had no responsibilities, but she tried to keep a strict routine. She fed the cat at 5:30 a.m. and then prepared breakfast and brought it to my mother, balancing on a cane and pushing a metal cart. She then lay on her bed watching the news or just staring out the window, waiting for my mother to need something. I would sit in her room, drinking wine, and listen to her talk about her past, telling the same stories over and over and over again, while my mother's anxious dog barked all day.

I was under Dr. Sarini's care again too, and he reintroduced the Adderall and Klonopin and steadily increased the number and doses of medications I was on. I had re-enrolled at Columbia to finish my degree but I was having trouble getting to class. I'd watch TV all day, skip class, and drink with my mother at night. When it was time to complete an assignment, I'd panic and sit frozen in front of my laptop, eyes fixed on a TV show. My sizzling anxiety was the only thing that got me out of the house, but not anywhere I needed to go. It sent me walking the Manhattan and Brooklyn bridges at night, even in the middle of a snowstorm. I walked for hours, waiting for the sear of panic to dissipate. At night, I'd lie in bed and talk to Gregory on the phone. He talked to me about his recovery, about how losing everything had changed his life for the better, and how his desperation had been a gift. He was working the twelve steps of Alcoholics Anonymous, and it was having a profound effect on him. His pursuit of specialness, he explained, had destroyed him, and now, through the humble execution of small, repeated gestures, and a commitment to something other than himself, he was rebuilding his life, repairing relationships, and he was happy. He used words like *acceptance*, *service*, *humility*, and *surrender*, and I thought of how different they sounded from the words I had been given to heal. He told me about the singles he was producing out of a motorcycle repair shop, the artists he was collaborating with, the first song he had written sober. Then, some nights, sitting on the porch of the halfway house he was living in, he'd lower his voice to a whisper and we'd have phone sex.

My therapist, Dr. Hart, whom I had also started seeing again, told me she'd rather see me back in a mental institution than living with my mother in New York. I left her office and called Gregory.

"Can I come live with you?" I asked.

He said he had to talk to his sponsor. He was apprehensive about making any big decisions only one year into his recovery.

"You're two sick people," his father said, when Gregory asked his advice. "How can two sick people take care of each other?"

I took another leave of absence from school and in April 2011, Gregory found us a house to rent in Nashville and arrived in a U-Haul truck he had driven straight from Nashville to pick me and my stuff up.

I loved the little yellow house Gregory had chosen for us, and we spent weeks scouring vintage shops for weird furniture to furnish it with. We planted vegetables in the backyard. In a nearby graveyard, Gregory taught me how to drive in his boat-sized 1986 Mercedes with no power steering. He took me to a Beatles laser light show at the planetarium, an amateur circus by the Cumberland River, and a honky-tonk lesson at the local American legion. For my twenty-sixth birthday, he stuffed a piñata with twenty six pieces of paper, each with something he loved about me written on them: "I love your 'why' questions. I love the way you sleep talk. I love your gift. I love your upspeak. I love the way you read me like you wrote me." We adopted a cat. We built puzzles and listened to audiobooks.

Underneath all these moments still bounced my medications, the amphetamine altitudes and depressant depressions leaving me unable to find secure footing, and the hulk of my new identity—molested survivor repressing memories—heaved beneath the delicate skin of my new life. During the day, Gregory would record artists in the motorcycle repair shop and I'd chain-smoke cigarettes and binge watch *Law & Order: SVU*. Then he'd head to an AA meeting and I'd drink two bottles of wine in my attic office. He'd come home and find me curled in a closet, drunk and weeping about what my father may or may not have done to me.

"What am I not remembering?" I wailed. "What else did he do?"

I knew from my mother and from Diane that there could always be more, something below the surface that could come up and swallow a whole life whole. Since I had been warned not to have any contact with my father, I punished myself for missing him.

The walls of my office were covered with sticky notes, like I was a crazed detective, of questions and theories about my family. I gathered all my hospital bracelets that I had kept over the years and put them, as if they were an award, in a frame on my desk, where I sat every day trying to write. I was working on a collection of short stories about every time I'd ever brought myself or someone else to a hospital, these interventions the only important things I had ever done, crisis after crisis the heartbeat of my life. I wrote a story about seducing my father into sleeping with me. At the moment of penetration, I asked him what he was doing, and described his face as it collapsed with shame. I wrote and wrote, reliving those moments of chaos and inventing new ones, from the safety of my desk, just as my mother had relived her memories, in all their ferocity and falsity, in oil on canvas. I was—with my cigarettes and my wine and my search for answers—closer to my mother than I had ever been.

There was a difference, though. I had a partner who was kind and patient and devoted to me. And I wanted to be a good partner. But it was hard to focus on someone else when I was so preoccupied with myself. The amphetamines and the alcohol didn't help. I'd start drinking and then I'd start fights, cornering Gregory in the living room moaning, "You hate me, don't you" as he quietly tried to slip by me and hide in the bedroom. Sometimes he'd beg me not to drink, sometimes he'd yell, but he'd inevitably hold my hair back when I puked and make sure the water glass on my bedside table was full. It didn't occur to me that being around me was not only dangerous for his sobriety, but utterly unpleasant. One night I went out with a friend and called Gregory very drunk, just to say hi. He told me he had had enough, that he couldn't be around me when I was drunk, and that he was going to sleep at the motorcycle repair shop. I got my friend to drive us to a gas station, where I purchased a three-foot-tall greeting card, writing out shakily with a Sharpie: *Sorry I'm a wreck. I love you*. I surprised him with it at the motorcycle shop, where he was asleep on the front office floor. I thought for sure this toddler-sized trinket with a dramatic inscription would fix everything, but it only made him more upset.

Still, Gregory was patient and saw something in me he didn't want to give up on. As he made us dinner the next night, I sat at the dining table complaining about my anxiety, my emptiness, how I didn't know who I was or what had happened.

"That's everyday, normal existence," Gregory said as he chopped garlic. "Anxiety and not knowing who I am is the baseline, I just improvise on top of that."

"So what do you do about it?" I asked.

"I try to take care of other people so I don't have to think about myself, about whether or not I know who I am. How much ginger do I chop?"

"A tablespoon," I said. "But you at least have a center. You know who you are. Your identity is solid."

"Are you kidding?" he said. "I feel like a child's drawing version of myself most of the time. I'm just pretending to be the kind of person I want to be."

As I chopped the onions, I thought about how Gregory was the strongest person I knew. I thought about how he metabolized shame and regret and turned them into fuel for his unrelenting considerateness. He was kind and gentle in a way I had never experienced before, and he thought of the people he loved constantly, in the same compulsive way I thought about my own mind. I watched Gregory as he carried out his love for me, as he paid attention to my words and asked me questions, as he anticipated my needs, my desires showing up in his actions and the objects they manipulated—a glass of water, a sweater when it was cold, a favorite song to wake up to—like inadvertent mind control. He could predict what would send me spinning, what my mind would fixate on, and would help me try to stay in the present. He had an irrepressible optimism that was directly proportional to how nihilistic he knew he could be, and I watched him take care of himself, nurture his recovery and nurture me, put one foot in front of the other despite the "swirling depths of despair," as he called them, that spun beneath our feet. As I wiped onion-induced tears from my eyes, I tried to imagine the churning slowing, the vortex decelerating, the void slowly filling. I couldn't yet picture what that life would look like, but for the first time I didn't have to live it alone.

I got a call from Nancy, one of my mother's studio assistants. My mother, now seventy, was living on Coca-Cola and potato chips and wouldn't get out of bed.

"I really think you should come here. She's not well," said Nancy.

I arrived at my mother's house at around seven at night. Gregory had stayed in Nashville to work. Her bedroom was dark. I stood in the doorway and said softly, "Mom, Mom, I'm here." She sat up, crossing her legs under her. She blinked.

"Am I upstairs or downstairs?" she asked.

"You're downstairs," I said.

"But am I in Charles Street?"

"No, you're in Brooklyn," I said. Anxiety gripped my guts and squeezed.

"I don't think I know where I am," she said.

"Well, you're right here in your bedroom on the first floor in Brooklyn on Vanderbilt Avenue. That's your garden out those windows, and your studio is in the next room. Upstairs is the kitchen, and Nanny lives here too."

"Is it daytime or nighttime?"

"It's nighttime. I get confused too when I wake up in the middle of the night. Try and go back to sleep," I said.

Over the next few days, I observed my mother's behavior. Something was very wrong. She accused me of taking a raincoat that was hanging in the closet right in front of her. She'd ask me questions over and over again, and, when I told her she'd already asked me, didn't she remember? she'd pretend she hadn't been paying attention the first time or just wanted clarification. But there was something in her sentences, a tell that belied her claims: the pause right before her justification told me that she was as confused and unnerved as I was. I went over to my aunt and uncle's apartment.

"Something's wrong with her," I said. "She can't remember things."

I told them what I had noticed. They told me nothing was wrong.

"That's just Jennifer being Jennifer," my aunt said.

What appeared as symptoms happened to resemble my mother's defining traits. Her whole life, she would forget things she didn't want to remember. The act of forgetfulness liberated her from responsibility, from discomfort, from having to interact with other people on anything but her own terms. That's how it had always been. But now it was different.

I ignored my mother's excuses, I ignored my aunt and uncle, and for the first time I listened to my own intuition. I took my mother to her GP, who referred her to a neurologist.

"Does it look like I have something just terribly wrong with me?" she asked the neurologist.

"I've only just met you," he said.

"Well then would you want me to have something terrible?" she joked. I laughed. It was something I would say to a doctor.

"Now why would I want that?" said the doctor. He didn't get it.

"Oh, I don't know," said my mother. I felt protective of her. I could see her weakness, her fear, and I could see her using repartee to fight against it.

"Spell *world* backwards," said the doctor.

"Dr. Roseman was doing this the other day," she said.

"How about you spell *world* backwards. I don't want a story," said the doctor. I was getting angry. Why wouldn't he want a story? Wasn't the fact that she remembered and could tell this precise story an indication of the thing he was trying to figure out? That the world, backward or forward, still lived inside of her?

"Well, it's *world* and backwards. Same way as frontwards except backwards," she said. I was impressed with this answer, proud, as if she were my precocious child. I felt like I too were meeting her for the first time. As if this bizarre setup had allowed me access to her as a real person, a person who made weird jokes at the worst possible times. I was starting to realize how terrified she must be.

She had to draw a clock and draw shapes. She had to write the sentence: "Today is a rainy Tuesday in December." She had to list all the animals she could think of: "dog, cat, beetle—or is that an insect?—elephant, tiger, water buffalo, snake, silverfish." She had to name a piece of furniture, a fruit. He gave her three words to remember later: *apple*, *table*, *penny*. She had to touch her left ear with her right thumb.

"Stick it to my left thumb?" she asked, pausing with her hand in the air, her thumb sticking out.

The doctor repeated the instructions, and she raised her other hand, thumb out.

She had to count backward from a hundred by sevens, which I would never have been able to do even on my best day. She made it to eight-six.

Who was president? Bush. (It was Obama.) What month? The beginning of winter.

Her deficits flew at me like arrows.

The doctor asked her how many nickels were in a dollar thirty-five. She paused. We all waited in silence, watching as the numbers wouldn't come, the answers stayed obscured.

"That's . . . so depressing," she said, to herself, to the numbers and dates and presidents and clock hands that refused to materialize for her.

The doctor was silent.

"How many did you ask for?" she said.

"How many nickels in a dollar thirty-five," he repeated.

I watched my mother.

"How about how many nickels in thirty-five cents?" the doctor said.

"Six?" said my mother. "Seven? Six?" The doctor just stood there.

"This is truly horrible and scary," she said.

I was frantically going through multiplication tables in my head.

"How about in a dollar?" said the doctor.

"Twenty," said my mother.

"In a dollar thirty-five?"

"Twenty plus . . . I don't know." She gave up. I wanted to hug her, but I didn't. Hugging her as she sat there alone and scared would have felt like touching a sacred statue, something I was not allowed to interfere with without cosmic consequences.

"What were the three words I asked you to remember?" said the doctor.

She looked around the room as if the words were hiding there, scrawled on the frame of the Gustav Klimt poster, embossed on the white paper that lined the exam table. They were not there. She looked at me. *Apple*, *table*, *penny*, I thought so hard I felt for sure she could see them crammed up behind the glass of my gaze. But I couldn't help her.

She was diagnosed with dementia. Over the next week, I found notes she had written to herself: *What's wrong with me? Suicide thoughts. Run tests for neurology. Went to doctor because I felt drugged. Memory loss. Anxiety. Cold symptoms. Helen McEachrane called. I haven't called her in a long time. Have I been sick a long time? Call all people I still want in my life. Devise systems for everything I have trouble with.*

I found a list:

1) How did I get this way?

2) When did I get this way?

3) What did doctor say?

4) How could it happen so fast?

For the first time, I saw her cry. It was a quiet, tidy cry—just a sheen of wetness in her eyes, the sides of her mouth turned down. She made jerky movements as if trying to throw the emotion and the reality off of her. She began to threaten suicide. While looking for socks in her drawer I found pill bottles, full, stuffed inside a pair of socks.

"Mom, why do you have pills stuffed in a sock?" I asked her.

She was dozing on her bed and her back was turned to me. She did not roll over to look at me.

"I just want to have them in case I decide to off myself," she said as I watched the back of her head.

I knew she wouldn't have the follow-through. She was terrified of death. Even the way she phrased it, "off myself," seemed like something she had heard in a movie and liked the way it sounded.

I returned to Nashville and sat down with Gregory to discuss what we should do.

"We should be near her," I said. "We need to go back."

Gregory was apprehensive. New York had violently ejected him, and the thought of returning scared him. But he would go back for me. We rented an apartment seven blocks away from my mother's house in Brooklyn. I re-enrolled at Columbia.

I decided to major in psychology even though all I cared about was books and writing. After so many years spent analyzing my own deficits, I was convinced all I was qualified to do was think about what could go wrong with a mind. I got a job babysitting two children. On the days I didn't have class or work, I'd visit my mother and Nanny. I'd show up at the house four nights a week with a bottle of wine for me, and a back-up bottle, also for me. My mother would already be a few glasses in and we'd drink and smoke and I'd spend hours regaling her with stories from my past, desperately trying to entertain her, generate the conversation she no longer could. I'd ask her questions and when she couldn't answer them I'd answer them myself.

"What's the craziest sex thing you've ever done?" I asked.

"I don't know," she said. "What's the craziest sex thing you've ever done?"

"I had sex with someone while driving down a highway at night," I said.

"What?" she screamed and laughed.

I told her about the time I'd slept with a family friend she knew.

"How was it?" she asked. I described it in graphic detail and she choked on her wine, laughing.

Sometimes she'd share with me what was going on inside of her, and I'd listen, rapt, the ashtray between us filling with butts, the bottles of wine emptying.

"Do you ever get an image stuck in your head and you don't know why it got there but you can't get it out?" she said one day.

"Yes," I said.

"Well, I keep seeing these big whirling blades. Ugh."

"Ugh," I said.

"Well, it's okay because I invented a use for them," she said.

"Like what?"

"Well, they slice through sausages."

Each visit she offered another peculiar dispatch from her interior: "I just lie here like an ingot," she said one day. "Like a piece of lead. I'm in twilight all the time."

I looked for clues in her musings, as if, taken together, they would form a portrait of her illness, which maybe we could stash in a closet and it would deteriorate instead of her.

Sometimes she'd be more direct, and those words, without the padding of metaphor, struck me deeply.

"I don't trust anything I believe right now," she said. "I feel like there's a piece missing. I think that piece may be me."

I felt a pressing obligation to collect all the bits of her I had coveted for so long—her humor and her charm and her brilliance. I needed to get to know her before it was too late. I gave her the "Proust Questionnaire." We sat on her bed cross-legged, with our ankles tucked under us, ashing our cigarettes in the seashell she used as an ashtray.

"What is the trait you most deplore in yourself?" I read from the list of questions.

"Self-involvement," she said. I was surprised that she had such casual self-awareness.

"What is the trait you most deplore in others?" I asked.

"Boringness."

"What do you consider the most overrated virtue?"

"Honesty," she said.

"Why?"

"Because people feel compelled to tell everyone everything and there's quite a lot I don't want to know." I was that person she was talking about, an indiscriminate oversharer.

"What is the quality you most like in a woman?" I asked.

"Not talking too much. I don't like anybody to talk too much," she said.

"What or who is the greatest love of your life?" I asked.

"I don't have one," she said. None of us had stuck. Not her first husband whom she had married at twenty-one. Not my father. And not me.

"If you could change one thing about yourself, what would it be?"

"Everything," she said. I looked up from the screen of my laptop where I was typing her answers. This struck me as unusual, an uncharacteristic humility, maybe regret. "Just because it would be something to do," she clarified.

"What do you consider your greatest achievement?" I asked.

"Continuing to do work."

"What is your most treasured possession?"

"Books."

"What is your most marked characteristic?"

"Bluntness."

"What is it that you most dislike?"

"Not getting my way," she said.

"What is your motto?" I asked.

"Just do the work," she said. That was the only advice she had ever given me. Just do the work. I didn't know how much longer she would be able to live by her own motto, or if it was something I could ever live up to. A few months after her diagnosis, she had gotten to work, and made an enormous plate piece simply titled *Dementia*. On each plate she wrote out the word—in cursive, in dots, in all uppercase, in all lowercase. "Dementia" over and over, as if she were trying to use that brutal word to soothe herself, as if, through the force of her work, she could transform calamity into comfort.

"What is your greatest regret?" I asked.

"I don't have any," she said. I wanted to believe this was because she couldn't remember any, and not because she didn't care about the consequences of her actions and inaction. I felt torn between anger, envy, and sadness. She had lived a life of silence and work and gratification, and she regretted none of it. I wanted to force regret on her like a straitjacket, bundling up everything she had lost and everything she was about to lose in an embrace she could not avoid.

I didn't know how long she would still know who I was, or know who she was. I found my copy of the book she had written, *History of the Universe*, and I asked her to write an inscription to me. I told her she couldn't just sign her name, that I wanted her to write something special, just for me. I left the room. I was afraid—afraid she would have no words for me, that the thought of me would leave her as blank as her illness did. After ten minutes, I came back into her room and picked up the book. She had written:

For Alice, you are my universal history.

In the threat of illness was also an opportunity. Through simple acts of caring I would find what had gotten lost between us for so long. She developed an infection in her abdomen—the old site of her hysterectomy surgery had opened up—and the doctor taught me how to unpack and repack the wound. At home, I would help her take off her leggings and roll down the band of her underwear. I stood her in the bathtub, telling her stories, and gently let the water run over the wound, soaping it as carefully as I could. She didn't argue and she didn't complain.

"I don't like this," she said matter-of-factly.

"I think that's good," I said. "I'd be worried if you did."

"I guess that's true." She laughed.

I dried her off and she lay back down on the bed while I gently bandaged the wound.

Her neurologist ordered an EEG, and I had to keep her awake all night long, without caffeine. We sat shoulder-to-shoulder on her bed as we watched the reality show *My Strange Addiction* on my laptop.

"But why?" she screamed as we watched a woman eat drywall.

She covered the screen with her hands, laughing, as another woman stung herself with bees.

"How do you think she does it?" she asked as a woman talked about her love affair with a carnival ride.

We discussed various ways love could be made to a machine as the sun rose.

A few months later I noticed her ankles were swollen so I brought her to the ER, where they told me she was almost in heart failure. Gregory came to meet me there. We sat next to my mother's bed and Gregory distracted her. He was wonderful with her. They had first met years ago at the height of his alcoholism. He had come over to the house and met my mother in the kitchen. We had always kept the butter in our toaster oven to keep the cat from licking it, and when Gregory saw it he said, "Nice to meet you. I love your butter dish. It looks just like a toaster oven."

My mother laughed so loud that I jumped.

He was good at distracting her from uncomfortable situations.

"Look at that shadow," he said pointing at the wall. "Doesn't it look like a dragon?"

"No, it looks more like the dragon's grandfather," my mother said.

"That's so true," he said.

I sat and listened as they talked. Gregory could encourage the best parts of people, their inventiveness and playfulness. I wished I could be like that with my mother. I wished I could meet her where she was instead of always wishing she would finally chase after me. I watched Gregory as he calmed and entertained her, trying to memorize the vocabulary of care he was so fluent in.

I went home and Gregory stayed with her until they found her a permanent bed. She was moved to the ICU because it was the only place they could administer nitroglycerin.

The next morning she called me.

"They tried to make me sleep on the floor," she said.

"I really don't think anyone tried to make you sleep on the floor," I said.

The nurse told me my mother had panicked and ripped out her IV. She'd run around the ICU, screaming, insisting they were trying to attack her.

"It's called ER psychosis," she told me. "It's not uncommon."

I felt connected to her in that moment. I recognized that impulse, remembered that need to flee the confounding forces conspiring against me.

When they moved her to a private room, I slept on a cot next to her bed. A few days into what would be a six-week stay, I was told she had developed an impacted colon. The nurse responsible for manually disimpacting my mother's colon said they were understaffed and asked if I could help her. I agreed without hesitation. I held my mother's hand as the nurse began the process. My mother yelped, screamed, "Stop," and pushed the nurse away.

"Mom, we have to do this or you won't be able to go to the bathroom," I said.

"I don't care," she said.

"You can even die from it," I said.

"Fine, then I'll die," she said.

"Well, first you'll have to stay in this hospital even longer. Is that what you want?" I asked.

"No," she said, the threat of discomfort more terrifying than death.

"Can we try again?" I asked.

"Okay," she said.

The nurse asked me to hold her down. I pushed down on her shoulder and let her grip my wrist. The nurse reinserted her fingers, and I felt my mother's hand hit the side of my head. Then she pulled my hair. Then she sank her teeth into my arm. I didn't know what to do so I laughed.

"Mom, you just bit me!" I said.

"Sorry, sorry, sorry," she said.

"It's okay," I said. "I wouldn't expect any less from you." She gave a weak laugh.

The next day, a nurse requested my help in holding her down as they reinserted her catheter. We had never figured out how to be intimate with one another, but now, as I pinned her down to make her well—my body so close to hers, accepting the hug of her jaws, her panicked yanks—I realized I had, in a circuitous way, finally found myself in my mother's arms.

Meanwhile, Nanny was getting weaker and weaker. She fell and broke her hip while I was visiting her, and I held her hand and stroked her hair as she was hoisted onto the stretcher. In the hospital she suffered the first of two strokes, leaving her with aphasia that made her words roll around in her mouth and her mouth unable to properly eject them. A month later, she suffered sepsis from a bite from Bracket the cat, who was now Nanny's cat, leaving her temporarily paralyzed from the waist down. A month after that, she was diagnosed with heart disease and had to have surgery. She became so thin, her body so slight and stooped, that she was like a punctuation mark moving through space, an ambulatory parenthesis shuffling across the room. I took her to doctors' appointments and Gregory took Bracket to the vet. I filled her pillboxes and washed her feet. Next to my notebooks and flash cards for school were piles of Nanny's bills and insurance forms and bank statements, for which I was now responsible. Next to my class schedule was a list of my mother's and Nanny's doctors' appointments and lists of their constantly multiplying medications.

When I was little, Nanny always seemed to be preparing for something, and the way she prepared was to worry. She kept crumpled-up tissues in the sleeve of her cardigan. She told me to bring an umbrella but then cautioned me to not get it stuck in the subway doors. She warned me against wearing a necklace while I slept in case it strangled me. I thought of the quirks of her care as I tried to manage the logistics of her aging. I thought of her bearing witness as I tried to make her shrinking life bigger. When Gregory and I came over, Nanny talked and talked. Once she had our attention, she didn't want to let it go. She loved Gregory and would come alive when he walked into the room, telling stories and making jokes. He was much better than I was at sitting and listening as she told the same endless stories over and over. She'd continue to talk to us even after we'd left the room, and I had to decide whether to linger at the threshold so she could finish a story with no end, or choose to walk away. She talked to herself more and more frequently. Not just the usual eruptions of frustration or the accidental out-louding of an observation, but whole conversations.

These were the days when Nanny started to cry. I had never seen her cry before and it frightened me.

"I just don't know. Sometimes I get sad," she would say.

As she cried she said, "Damn! Damn!" I tried to imagine how her life felt to her. Was it occurring to her now that nothing was hers? That the things she had accomplished were not measurable by any known standards? She existed in traces, in people. She was the uncredited voice in the back of the heads of all the people she had cared for. She lived in someone else's home, and she was being cared for by someone else's child.

We were both afraid. We were afraid of what my mother's illness meant for both of us. I felt like I had nothing to give Nanny. I couldn't protect her. I couldn't even figure out how to comfort her. I sat there, watching her cry. Sometimes I'd try to tell her how much she meant to me, try to list all the things she had given me, try to lend bulk to her withering life.

"You saved me," I said. "You protected me so well."

She wouldn't look at me. She stared out the window.

"If it weren't for you I'd probably be dead," I said.

She'd respond with a scoff, or the subtlest shake of her head, refusing my words.

That Mother's Day, I bought my mother a box of Jacques Torres chocolates, and I bought Nanny one too, but Nanny's box was smaller. When I presented them with their gifts, Nanny made a joke about being a half-mother, or a less-mother. I felt a pain in my chest. I hadn't wanted to hurt my mother's feelings by suggesting they were both my mothers, even though that's what it felt like. And I hadn't realized that something as simple as the dimensions of two boxes could render so vividly the pain and ambiguity of our unique situation. I felt angry at myself and sad for Nanny. I hadn't wanted to make her feel small, to make her feel less than, but I was scared that if I gave her a gift whose measurements reflected how I really felt, I would end up shrinking my mother down to nothing.

I wanted to connect with Nanny, but, still prescribed uppers and downers, I'd end up sitting in her room, scrolling on my phone, counting the minutes before I could leave. I'd come home exhausted and sad and angry, and Gregory would cook us dinner and quiz me for my Spanish test. Many nights, I'd drink until I puked and start fights with Gregory when he returned from his AA meeting. I felt scrambled, so many feelings happening at the same time, and under the constant whisking of the Adderall, the sloshing of the benzos. I was so anxious and on so much amphetamine that I'd moan myself to sleep, while Gregory rubbed my back to try to help me calm down. It still didn't occur to me that I could get off the medications. They seemed not like a separate part of me that could be safely excised, but part of the essential network of who and how I was—just as critical and inextricable as my veins or nerves. Dr. Sarini had told me I'd need to be on medication for the rest of my life, and I believed him. I'd take my morning pills and want to start fights with my aunt or my mother's assistant, writing long, rambling emails or texts, which I read to Gregory before hitting send. He'd tell me to wait. He'd beg me to give it twenty-four hours and see how I felt. Be patient. I'd send the emails or texts anyway, oblivious to the damage I was causing. I didn't realize how much energy it took for him to try to haul me back from the powerful amphetamine pull toward discord, time and time again. I tried to fight the current of my volatility by showing up for my mother and Nanny. I tried to take cues from Gregory—his attentiveness, his patience—straining to resist those spinning eddies of lability. When he noticed I was particularly far away—dissociating or trying to keep up with the torrent of anxious thoughts—he would extend his hand for me to shake and say, "Hello, nice to meet you in this moment." There'd be a pause as I returned to myself and then I'd smile and clasp his hand, pumping it up and down, his hand the only tether that could keep me here.

That winter, we got married in my mother's garden, in the beautiful aftermath of a blizzard. I found an eighty-six-year-old humanist minister online who claimed to be "weatherproof." I carried a bouquet of plastic flowers I had played dress-up with when I was five years old. My mother and Nanny were the only witnesses, and we signed the marriage license on top of color charts in the downstairs studio.

I was suddenly living a life where things were happening that weren't just in, or about, my own mind. For the first time I had to stop constantly thinking about what was wrong with me and pay attention to what was wrong with everyone else. I was unused to being needed, and I craved and resented it. As I crouched on the floor washing Nanny's feet, I felt pulled in two directions. I wanted to give her more than just a foot bath, and I also didn't even want to give her this foot bath. I ran my soapy hands over her gnarled feet, trying to press into her the care and love I knew existed in me, to bathe her like she had bathed me. But I felt so many other things besides care and love. Anger pinched at me. Guilt shouldered in and I was pummeled slowly by its great, muscled form. A dazzling sorrow, cold and clear, drenched me. I was fighting, constantly, the invisible bodies of anger, fear, and sadness as they blocked my way, pounced onto my back, skittered around in my stomach, splashed me stunned. I couldn't connect to Nanny the way I wanted to because I couldn't reach her through the horde.

The details of my mother's decline vexed me too. A lifelong smoker, she had a gruesome smoker's cough, which would overtake her especially when she laughed. Making her laugh was one of the things I liked doing the most, but she would start coughing uncontrollably and then vomit. When it didn't bring her to regurgitation, her laugh gave her illness away. She laughed at stories I told her or TV shows, but there would be too much of the laugh, too loud and too often, as if she were doing it just in case it was a moment when a normal person was supposed to laugh. Clichés started to take over her language. She would say "keep your fingers crossed" or "just relax and take it easy" or "well, that's something to think about"—phrases nonspecific enough to sound like an appropriate response to almost anything. In each infuriating banality, I heard the grinding of her forgetting, the slow work of the disease. She developed an infuriating naiveté. She pretended to not know or be able to figure things out. When I told her exercise was good for her, she said, "Really?" When I told her smoking was bad for her, she said, "Really?" When I told her humans needed to drink water or eat vegetables or take showers or brush their teeth or not eat bacon every single day she said, "Really? Why?" I could never tell if she really didn't know or understand, or if this was some childish game she liked to play to try and get out of an activity or keep pace with a conversation. So much of what she did made me angry. Inside this anger I missed the mother I no longer had. I missed the mother I never had. I missed the mother I couldn't have. I hated that woman who couldn't remember anything, the woman who was turning back into a child. I hated the woman who still felt like a child, who couldn't tell that all of this anger was an endless ocean of sadness.

And yet, as her illness progressed, I noticed an unexpected change in her. She became tender, curious. She liked to lie in bed smoking cigarettes and drinking coffee, but wanted to be involved with everything that was happening outside her door. The kitchen of her cottage in Amagansett was directly outside her bedroom, and at the slightest noise, she'd say: "Hello? What are you doing?" I would explain to her that I was pouring a glass of water or going to pee. She would laugh and say a long and loopy "Oh . . ." Any comment I made to someone else and "What are you talking about?" would come bounding from the other room. Then I'd explain about the dry cleaning, or the dog's visit to the vet, or about how maybe this bread was stale. Gregory made a game out of her endless questions. When he was in the other room and she asked, "What are you doing?" he said, "I'm putting roller skates on the dog," as he poured a glass of water. She laughed until she coughed.

"Well, how does he like it?" she asked.

"Well, he's not as good at it as the cat, but he's working on it."

Every time I came over, she'd ask me how I was and was not shy to tell me she missed me. Whenever I had to leave she'd throw her arms around my neck, clutch at my hair like an infant, and tell me she didn't want me to go. "Stay, please." When I struggled with something, she said, "How can I help?" and even though she no longer could, her inquisitiveness felt nuclear, decimating—a simple question able to raze thirty years of distance. My sordid, tumultuous history wasn't relevant any longer. It only mattered that I showed up. After years of begging for her attention, she was finally interested in me. I was the only person she wanted to spend time with. She could also finally name feelings. It no longer occurred to her to avoid emotions. She would say something made her sad instead of just getting another glass of white wine. There was a heartbreaking joy in seeing her able to make that tiny admission. She also seemed content without the excesses that had marbled her life. She was no longer a person amplified by fame, swollen from money, or made tiny and shrunken from avoiding feelings. When everything that had defined her for so long disappeared—her constant need to work, the memories of ritualized sexual abuse, even her desire for alcohol—I was able to see what had stuck. And what had stuck was me.

For my birthday that year, Gregory and I went over to my mother's house. Gregory put a box in front of me, and I unwrapped it at the dining room table. In the box was a stack of index cards with descriptions, in my mother's handwriting, of me. I sat at the table and flipped through them. "Alice likes cats," I read aloud. "Alice has brown hair. Alice can swim. Alice is romantic. Alice is smart. Alice has courage. Alice is a wife. Alice is fun. Alice cares. Alice is thoughtful. Alice is a Democrat. Alice is pretty. Alice takes a ride. Alice lives in New York. Alice is concerned. Alice is real funny. Alice creates. Alice is groovy. Alice demands. Alice is a Greek Goddess. Alice brushes her teeth. Alice can be daunting. Alice is a daughter. Alice is human." It had been Gregory's idea. He had gone over to her house a week before my birthday and asked her to describe me. I was silent. I was stunned. I held in my hands a miracle—my mother, Gregory, and myself. I held my past and I held my future. Gregory knew me. He knew my fears—of being forgotten, of having never been known. It seemed my mother knew me too. Gregory had given me what I had always wanted: words to describe who I was, from the woman who didn't like to talk, the woman who thought she was the only person in the world. I framed those notes and put them on my wall: proof we had all been here, three humbled humans, telling each other we existed.

9.

I was practicing the ballet of small, repeated gestures that made up my life with Gregory. I was early for every class, my performance earning superlatives from my professors. I made the dean's list. Gregory was recording bands. He encouraged me to write, and we wrote songs together.

My mother sold her Brooklyn house and moved out to Amagansett, which was too small to accommodate both her and Nanny. My aunt and uncle took over the management of my mother's care. She now had caretakers looking after her and was happy living by the beach. Gregory and I decided that we would move back to Nashville after I graduated that year and agreed that we couldn't leave Nanny, now eighty-nine, behind.

"I can't let Nanny's biggest fear come true," I said. But mostly I didn't want my fears to come true. I didn't want to picture me without Nanny.

"We'll take her with us," said Gregory.

The next day, we told Nanny we wanted to move to Nashville and that we wanted her to come with us. She started to smile and her eyes filled with tears.

"I'll have to learn a Southern accent," she said, smiling wide. "Yeehaw."

Nanny needed a place to stay until I graduated and we could make the move, so Gregory and I moved her and Bracket to a nursing home four blocks away from our new apartment on the Upper West Side. We helped her settle into her room, unpacking boxes and coaxing the cat out from under the unfamiliar bed. We brought Nanny down to the dining room, where residents were required to eat dinner. I helped her into a chair at a table with three male residents. I kissed the top of her head and said goodbye. We paused in the doorway and watched her. I was nervous the others wouldn't welcome her, that she would get her feelings hurt. But as I watched, Nanny started laughing. She leaned forward and said something to the gentleman next to her, who leaned forward to receive her words. She laughed again.

Every day she had new stories to tell—about her occupational therapy, about walkers being stolen, about her speech therapist. She told me, laughing, the story of a fellow resident who had called her into his room to ask for her help in taking his pants off. Because of her aphasia, we sometimes couldn't understand her words, but her joy was loud and clear. She made me a bracelet in occupational therapy and presented it to me proudly. She was excited to move to Nashville with us, and started talking about the future more than she did the past.

On November 12, 2015, seven months before we were scheduled to move to Nashville, six months before I would finally graduate, I was at a friend's house on the Upper East Side having dinner. Halfway through the dinner, my phone rang. It was Gregory telling me the nursing home had called him. Nanny had fallen and was on her way to the hospital.

I pushed my plate away, grabbed my coat, took the elevator downstairs, and flagged a cab. As I slid through the dark I felt like an explorer, a cartographer of the moment. Was this the moment when Nanny's end appeared, the bottomless drop-off I hadn't been expecting, but maybe should have been? I had imagined it so many times, what it would look like, what it would feel like, but I had never imagined it would be so still and silent. The sound had dropped out of everything and an anesthetic inertia filled me as I wove through Central Park in the dark. As we pulled up to the hospital and I paid and thanked the driver, as I announced my arrival to a woman behind a desk, my words felt independent of me.

"Hi, sorry, I think my grandmother is here," I said.

"What's her name?"

"Oh, sorry," I said, and spelled out her name.

I apologized again to the woman when she told me Nanny hadn't arrived yet. And then suddenly Gregory and I were hugging in the empty waiting room with the *Law & Order: SVU* theme song playing in the background. We were directed to a room in the ER and as we approached it I saw Nanny through the doorway. She was lying on a gurney with a blanket up to her neck. She was pale and a vicious purple bump the size of a baseball protruded from her forehead. A plastic tube extruded from her mouth, the stalk of an exotic plant, as if the injury had made her something more than herself, something rare and strange. Through my shock, I could not see a badly injured woman, I could only see indestructible Nanny and her powers of survival.

Two doctors approached us and told us she had hit her head and was being taken for scans. It would be helpful, they said, if we had the power of attorney forms. Gregory went back to our apartment to get the papers. I sat and waited.

Two doctors appeared and led me into another room. One began to speak but I interrupted.

"Should I sit down first?" I asked.

"Yes."

"So it's not good," said one of the doctors. "Her brain moved three centimeters from the impact, and she has a brain bleed that looks like it's been there for a while. The neurologist will be calling you very soon to decide what you want to do."

They walked away. I sat staring at my hands. A few minutes later, a nurse told me that the neurologist was on the phone.

"I'm so sorry you're going through this," the neurologist said.

"Thank you. What's the prognosis?"

"Well, that partially depends on what you can tell me about your grandmother. She's your grandmother, correct?"

"Sure. What do you mean?"

"What I need to know is what kind of life would be worth living for her? What would she consider a good quality of life?"

"If she couldn't speak or feed herself she wouldn't want to live," I said. I was surprised at how quickly I had answered. This was the biggest decision I had ever had to make, deciding what life meant for someone else. But in this moment, I realized I knew Nanny.

"Well, that answers a lot for me. In this case, the best we can hope for, with surgery going perfectly, is that she would need to be on the tube for the rest of her life."

The cry leaped out of me before I even notice it had formed.

"Okay. Thank you," I said, shaking as I put the phone back in the receiver.

When I returned to the waiting room Gregory was there with the forms. I told him what the doctor had said and he began to cry. We gripped each other tightly.

They wheeled Nanny back from the scans and into a small room and I squeezed into the space beside the bed. Her left eye was shocked open, the pupil unfocused and unmoving. One of the doctors appeared in the threshold of the room.

"I'm so sorry that it wasn't good news," he said. "You have some decisions to make."

"If she'll never have the tube out I think there's really only one option," I said.

"Right," he said.

My eyes landed on his name tag, which announced him as Dr. Doctor.

"Your last name is Doctor?"

"Yes, yes it is," he said. He smiled a tiny smile, which he then quickly wiped from his face. Tonight I didn't care about the story this would make, the unbelievable detail of a doctor named Dr. Doctor.

I went outside to call Nanny's sister, Thelma, in England. I knew the news would be conveyed just by the ring at such an hour, by it being my voice on the phone. There could be no other reason I was calling. I told Thelma what had happened and that there was no hope for recovery. My voice wobbled. Thelma's voice, usually high-pitched and girlish, now was clotted and rough as she repeated, "Oh, oh, Alice." We said goodbye.

I called my aunt Julie.

"If you want to say goodbye we are at Mount Sinai on 113th Street. You should come now if you want."

Julie brought us satsuma oranges, which we ate as we watched the beeping machines.

"Could she really not pull through?" Julie asked. "It seemed like she squeezed my hand just now. She can't see through that eye? Squeeze my hand if you can hear me," she said to Nanny.

I felt angry at her hope. Of course she couldn't pull through because that was not how this story went. We had entered into the one where she didn't make it. There wasn't any plot twist here.

The doctor asked, "Are you ready?"

"Yes," I said.

The doctor removed the tube. Buttons were pressed and the hiss that had been in the background went away. Nanny stopped breathing. Minutes passed and my blood rushed to my ears and my heart clanked. Then, with the sound of something heavy being dragged along the ground, she took air into her lungs again. We watched Nanny breathe. And then we watched her not breathe. It went on and on. Violent stillness and silence and then violent movement and sound as she ripped air into her. I held her hands in mine and I spoke to her.

"Thank you for everything you did. You saved me. You protected me. I promise I will be okay. Gregory will keep me safe. I will look after Bracket. You were so strong and so brave. You kept everything together. You kept me together. I love you so much. Everything will be okay. It's okay."

I repeated myself over and over. "Thank you." "It will be okay." "You saved me." I talked and talked. Everything I had ever wanted to say to her surged through me. I kissed her forehead. I said goodbye. We left.

She lived for seven days. Then one evening, during dinner, my phone rang. Nanny was dead.

She was Nanny. But her name was Eileen Denys Maynard, and she died.

Gregory went over to the nursing home to clear out her things so I didn't have to. He wept the whole time he folded her wool sweaters and long pleated skirts into cardboard boxes, placing the little lavender sachets she used to keep them smelling fresh on top of the clothes. In storage, she had boxes of photographs, stacks of Playbills, bins full of blank postcards and old calendars. Later, when we went through my mother's storage for our move to Nashville, we found many more boxes of Nanny's. She had also kept everything of mine. She had packed up all my childhood clothes, all my passports, all my toys, all my books, all my drawings and French tests and book reports, the creatures I had made out of old osso buco bones, the bear she had stitched for me, the mat she had sewed for my preschool nap time. She had protected my past. And I kept everything of hers. I kept all her clothes—the long wool skirts, the sweaters from Scotland, the white linen aprons from governess school. I kept all her photographs, all the souvenirs she had saved from the Concorde—a crystal ashtray, a Walker fountain pen with the airline's logo on it. Among her things, I found a photograph of the two of us in a hammock. I was a baby asleep on her chest, as she rested her chin on my head. I recognized the feeling of packing myself into her, tucking myself between her arms, under her chin. I recognized the feeling of tracing the cuticles of her fingernails. I also found all the notebooks she had kept detailing her experiences with my family, all her frustrations with my parents and her fervid desire to protect me, to help me be understood, laid out in her tiny script, her dyslexic words. As I read her notebooks, read her story, our story, I was learning all the ways language and love lived inside of me—as infection, as weapon, as heartbeat, as cure.

III / Someone

1.

In May 2016, three months before I turned thirty-one, I finally graduated. My mother, my aunt, and Gregory attended. It was exhilarating to get attention for something that didn't involve me hurting myself. We ate coconut cake and laughed. My mother's studio manager gave me a stack of books by Joan Didion. I wanted to do more things that made people happy for me, that made them feel good to be around me.

A month later, Gregory and I moved back to Nashville. I got a job at the Boys & Girls Club and started work on a memoir. Gregory recorded artists and wrote songs. Every month, we hosted charades nights with all our friends. We planted a garden and fought squirrels. I found two kittens in a hollow tree, so we had four rescue cats. Gregory's parents moved to Nashville from Pennsylvania to be near us. We had never been thought of as the reliable ones, the ones worth tying a life to, and suddenly his parents were trusting us to pick out a house for them, sight unseen. I found a new psychiatrist and decided to wean off my medications, Adderall first. It scared me how effortless it was to go off it, and how much better I felt. My heart stopped crashing around in my chest, my leg didn't slip off my other leg on a sweat slick, my jaw loosened. I could hear and notice what was going on around me, and inside of me. I wasn't on edge all the time. I had fewer arguments, I asked more questions, I was more patient. People started treating me differently. I had always been the friend that people shared their darkest secrets with, but now I was the friend who could be relied on. With the guidance of my psychiatrist, I started tapering off the other medications. I wanted to see who I was underneath all the pills, what parts of me—feelings and thoughts and sensations—suspended in the chemical permafrost, would emerge and proliferate. The last medication to go was the Klonopin, the highly addictive anti-anxiety medication I had been prescribed for almost fifteen years. Research had just come out that prolonged use of Klonopin was associated with a greater risk for dementia, and I was still on a high dose. The withdrawal from Klonopin was notoriously difficult and could be lethal. I called it the Murphy's Law of withdrawal: anything that could go wrong went wrong. There was diarrhea and flatulence, there were hand tremors, there was skin crawling, there were temperature fluctuations, there were appetite changes, there were cold sweats, there were chills, there was insomnia, there was nausea, there were headaches, there were heart palpitations, there was forgetting, there was a lack of focus. I developed a tic where I twirled my hair constantly—while I was talking to people, while I was driving, even lying down in bed. I wore a shower cap around the house all day so I couldn't get at my hair. I felt an invisible hand choking me—strong fingers wrapped around my throat as I went about my day. But I wanted to know who was on the other side of this drug, and I used my dissociation, also made worse by the withdrawal, as a tool, treating each new symptom as a curiosity, a discovery to be examined and cataloged.

After spending months tapering off Klonopin, I was medication-free for the first time since I was sixteen. I felt better than I ever had. I felt streaked with joy, beams of sunlight painting over the gray of my brain. I sat on my front steps and stared at a tree and felt completely overwhelmed by the idea that I was able to sit on the steps of my house and look at it. Gratitude replaced the discontent I had been scratching at all these years. Along with joy, I felt rinsed with sadness, clear and fluent. Gregory and I invented the "Safety Cry," where every Sunday we picked an uplifting but cry-inducing film so we could cry together. It had been hard to cry on Klonopin, and I now discovered that I loved crying. It had a lingering narcotic effect that left me drained and sated at the same time. I had always been afraid of being alone, being quiet with my own mind, and now I welcomed it. I took long drives by myself, delighting in my autonomy, only possible because I felt I was becoming a person, separate from everyone else, brimming with myself. The medications had blunted my orgasms but now they were so intense I would often burst out laughing in the middle or scream, "What the fuck is this?" or leak tears from my eyes. One lasted five minutes. No longer needing to mediate the effects of prescription speed, I was able to stop drinking, which made everything even better. The constant feeling of wrongness, of being in the wrong place—whether that place was a house, a country, or my own body—was replaced by a sense of arrival, of landing.

After four months without Klonopin or alcohol, I was in a state of bliss, a bliss that I could safely pry away from pathology. I wasn't manic, I was well, and well felt so foreign and so fantastic that it registered as euphoria. I looked at things with a swelling, oozing love that I would have previously only attributed to drug trips depicted in movies where a character licks a tree or cries at their own arm hair. My self-loathing had dissolved. I stood in a yoga class, staring at myself in the mirrored wall, and was overcome by the realization that I loved myself. I loved Gregory even more than before, which I hadn't thought possible. I was getting the first natural sleep I had gotten in twenty years. I liked my job. I was volunteering at Planned Parenthood and the Nashville Adult Literacy Council. I had deep friendships and was rekindling important ones from my past. By our second year in Nashville, I had finished the memoir I had been working on. By the third year, I had signed with a top literary agency in New York City. My life had heaved and sloughed off an obsolete version of itself, revealing something fresh and new, tender with possibility.

In early June 2019, I was having menstrual cramps. I was curious about holistic treatments, and my GP had recommended CBD oil for everything and anything. I did research all day and read only glowing reviews about the safety and benefits of CBD. I drove to my local organic market and bought a bottle of the most potent formulation. I had researched dosage but the consensus was that it didn't really matter because nothing bad could ever happen with CBD oil. The worst that could happen, I'd read in the *New York Times*, was that you'd sit on your couch with a bag of chips and zone out.

I took the first dose of 60 mg when Gregory and I went to his parents' house for dinner and a movie. Halfway into the movie I felt twitchy, my eyes felt gritty, sandpapery, but it was subtle. After the movie we went home and got in bed. I had read that the correct dose for sleep was 160 mg, so I took two more droppers full and went to sleep.

I woke up around 1 a.m. As I slipped into consciousness, I realized I was gone. I realized, too, that there was nothing doing the realizing. I couldn't locate myself anywhere. My "I" had vanished. There was a feeling of a heavy, slick rope slipping through my fingers, fast, and then I became the rope, I was the thing sliding away, fast.

I groaned and squirmed on the bed, trying to lock something into place, trying to hold any part of myself down. I was cartwheeling through a roaring emptiness. I was on the verge of blacking out, but panic withheld that merciful unconsciousness from me. My heart was slinging around in my chest, a bowl of gelatin on a high-speed train. A booming heat overcame me. I ripped off my nightgown and flailed my legs trying to fan myself into coolness. I crawled off the bed and opened the linen closet on my hands and knees. I reached my arms inside and dragged out all my old pill bottles—pills I kept in case of emergency. There had to be something in there that would make this stop. I was shaking and couldn't hold the bottles in my hands so I knelt on the floor with them spread around me and tried to see the labels and read the words, but the numbers and letters disintegrated and lost all meaning.

"What's wrong, what's going on?" Gregory, now awake, was standing over me. I gurgled a few times before I could speak over the frantic galloping of my heart. I didn't know where the words came from or how they took on sound. "Something's wrong," was all I could manage. I started tearing at the pill bottles. I screamed and screamed as I tried to bring a palmful of pills to my mouth. Gregory knocked the pills out of my hand, wrapped me in his arms, and managed to pin me to the bed. Still screaming, I tried to wrestle away from him, twisting beneath him. I needed to get away. I needed to get away from what was happening inside my mind. I was witnessing something I wasn't supposed to. The experience was too big for me, it didn't fit inside me, and I blew apart. I screamed and screamed, at a life I knew was ending, a life that had just begun in so many ways, the life I had always wanted. I knew I was dying.

"I love you," I said to Gregory, my face pressed into the bed. "I'm sorry."

I went completely limp. I could feel him drag me up from the bed. Floating above my body, I saw a mass of heavy nothing spiked with limbs that dangled, flopping in Gregory's arms, a coil of something that was unwinding itself, losing its shape, slipping away.

"You're okay, you're okay," he said over and over as he struggled to lift me up and hold me against his body.

Somewhere inside the emptiness, I saw the glowing marble of the life I had finally achieved. A voice—my voice—told Gregory to get me under the shower. He dragged me to the bathroom, turned on the shower, and put me under the spray of water. I told him to make it as cold as possible. I sat under the freezing torrent until my body was wracked with shivers. My breath came faster and deeper and for a moment I started to feel like I was finding my footing. The cold hooked itself into my mind, dragging its bucking, sliding form back to me, back to my contracting muscles, my wildly beating heart. For a brief moment, I felt nudged toward wholeness again. I told Gregory to make me slowly warm, and he turned the water temperature gradually hotter. The moment my body stopped shivering, though, the connection was lost, and I returned to the terror of spinning through blankness. I motioned for him to crank it back to freezing until I could shiver again. We continued like this for three hours. Gregory had given me three Klonopin and we were both waiting for me to pass out. I begged for more medication, but he refused. After an hour of shivering and warming, I couldn't get cold enough and started to panic. Gregory packed my body with Ziploc bags full of ice and I finally began to shiver again. I became afraid of what would happen when the hot water ran out and we would have to turn the shower off. I knew I would disintegrate completely and be gone. Gregory found a recording of shower sounds on YouTube and cranked the volume up as he slowly turned the tap off. He collected all the blankets and towels we had in the house and piled them on top of me. I lay in the bathtub, Gregory sitting on the toilet watching over me, until the meds knocked me out.

Over the next four days, I could barely eat or drink. The sensation of food, even water, inside my body felt like something terrible was being done to me. My body would get cold and then hot. Nausea sloshed over me. My limbs tingled and my hands shook. In my chest was a nest of fat, writhing worms, my heartbeat frantic beyond rhythmicity, terrorized out of cadence.

On day five, I went to an emergency appointment with my psychiatrist who diagnosed me with panic disorder and PTSD. She put me on propranolol, a blood pressure medication to help with the physical symptoms of panic; Klonopin; and Seroquel, the sedating antipsychotic I had been on before, to knock me out at night. The panic and dissociation were debilitating, exhausting, and took up every inch of my body, all my attention, and every second of my life. According to the *DSM*, dissociation is *a disruption, interruption, and/or discontinuity of the normal, subjective integration of behavior, memory, identity, consciousness, emotion, perception, body representation, and motor control*. There is nothing it does not touch.

I was preoccupied with where my thoughts came from and how they were still being generated without me here. Everything familiar—Gregory's face, my purring cats, the angles of my home, the gestures of my body—became terrifying and strange. When I lay in my bed, extending my arm to take a sip of water from the glass on my bedside table or throwing an arm over my head, I flashed back to all the gestures I had made as I tried to twist myself back into my body. When Gregory wrapped me in his arms at night, I remembered the weight of him on top of me as I had screamed and squirmed beneath him. Gregory's face terrified me. We were so close and spent so much time together that he normally felt like an extension of me. And since I had become unrecognizable to myself, the sensation of looking at his face was horrifying and surreal. It was the same with my own face. I couldn't unlock or lock into place that it was me, my face. Every time I accidentally caught sight of it, brushing my teeth or if I forgot to keep my gaze down at my hands—equally unrecognizable as mine—I felt that nauseating drop that preceded a plunge into blank panic. I was not real, yet I was conscious. Nothing was actually happening, besides the mundane movements of living, yet every moment was stranger and more terrifying than it had ever been. I woke every morning with dread sticking to me like sand. I constantly scanned my body and the world for potential hazards. At any moment I could tip and fall into the endless emptiness. My body told me I was under assault, and the assailant was my own mind. I didn't know how to avoid the trigger if the trigger was consciousness. My days were spent scheming ways to survive the moment, assessing each second for its surreality and unlivableness. I knew that with dissociation, the more I questioned it—wondered at the origin of my words or inspected the joists of reality—the worse it would get. I worried, too, that even if I returned to some kind of normal connection to reality, to myself, I would not be able to recognize it. I was afraid I had seen too much, glimpsed the secret mechanisms behind everything I was and everything there was, and I would never again be able to accept the simple, solid, absolute state of existing I had recently enjoyed. All I wanted was to return to myself. Just at the moment when I had become a person, someone I recognized, I became the most nothing I had ever been.

Words were the only thing that tethered me to some splinter of myself. I sat under a tree in my backyard and wrote about every single detail of every moment. It calmed me, but I knew I couldn't write forever and I didn't know what would happen when I stopped. An enormous wave was about to crash over me, tug me under, and send me spinning, and writing froze it at its cresting. I wrote gratitude lists. I wrote lists of likes and dislikes, trying to remind myself of who I had been. I wrote down what had happened to me, trying to prove that I was a person something had happened to. Technically, barely anything had happened. I had been asleep and had woken up and somewhere in between I had been stolen. Dissociation and PTSD were psychological responses to traumatic events, but I was traumatized not by an external event that my mind was trying to escape, but by the experience of my mind escaping itself. The event was the response, the response was the event. And words, their powers of differentiation, were all I had to name the before and the after, to announce the thing that had destroyed me, and, I hoped, to declare the thing that would save me.

I listened to the audiobooks that had filled my mind as a child. I started thinking in the third person again, as I had done when I was little. The only way I could bear to look at my reflection in the mirror, as I washed my unfamiliar face or my alien hands, was to narrate what I was doing in my head: "She is brushing her teeth," "The water is warm." But this desperate reliance on words stretched their functioning dangerously. There were terrifying moments when words started to become disarranged and then dismembered. I would be listening to an audiobook and suddenly wouldn't be sure I understood the words. I would be reading a book and the words would become the black, inert lines that they in fact were, my mind no longer able to elevate them into meaning.

Two months later I was still nowhere to be found. In this splintered state I needed older touchstones. I needed to go back to the beginning. Back to what had built me. Maybe then I could figure out how to be the architect of my renovation, build a bulwark against a mind that kept tearing itself down. I went to visit my mother, searching for something she could not give me. I sat across from her in the Amagansett living room, watching her eyes floating in the white static of her mind, as I floated in my blankness behind my eyes. Nanny was dead. There was only one person left: my father.

After three decades, after all the courtroom allegations, after Diane's confident assessment, after reading the statistics that 99 percent of all cutters, 99 percent of all bed wetters, and 99 percent of all dissociaters had been sexually abused, after years of being an ocean away from him, my father was as unreal to me as I was to myself, as towering a villain as my dissociation. I decided I would confront my father. I would tell him my story, ask him his, and write it all down.

Gregory and I took long walks around the neighborhood and talked about my rescue plan.

"I need to go there and find out what really happened," I said.

"What if things go wrong and it's not safe? This could make you much, much worse," he said.

"How could I be worse? I'm already nothing. I'm not here. I'm gone."

Gregory was silent.

"I can't keep going like this. I don't want to have to kill myself. I need to do something drastic," I said.

"Okay, then let's do it. But I think you should have strict rules. Don't just go into this unprepared," he said.

I called Diane, my therapist and trauma counselor from Florida, and told her I was going to see my father and confront him about our past.

"You're fucking crazy," she said. "You'll never get what you're looking for. You're trying to play a game he's been playing much longer than you, and he's way better at it."

I realized it might be a terrible idea. But there were no pills that could fix me. There was no more money for another fancy mental institution, no time for ten more years of introspection. I needed to find my own way out.

I emailed my father and asked him if we could Skype. I wrote about my dissociative break. I still felt I could tell him anything—that had not changed. He wrote back and we set a time and date to talk. I had not seen him since my manic episode eight years earlier. As his image filled my screen, I was filled with a mix of hope and fear. He was framed in a tight close-up, his face behind a scrim of cigarette smoke.

"Hello? Can you see me?" he said.

My body struggled between a melting relief and a rigid apprehension. I stared at his face, which had aged in a way that surprised me. For a moment, I forgot I was in this moment too, as if I were watching him on TV.

"I can see you," I said.

We exchanged no pleasantries, and I launched into the story of what had brought me back to him.

"Usually with dissociation," he said after I had finished, "there's some sort of core trauma, and I can't figure out what yours is."

I paused. I felt my body go hot.

"I have an answer for that if you want it," I said.

"What is it?" he asked.

"Well, I've actually been thinking about this for a while. I think it would be interesting to have a conversation, a dialogue between a person who has lived the consequences of trauma however you define it and the person who contributed to that experience of trauma." My opacity sheathed me. I knew I needed to slide the truth out of its ornate casing and let the blade fall however it may, but I didn't know how to ask my father why he had invited me into sexuality. Why he had said all the things he had said. I didn't know how to tell him he was part of the reason I split off from myself.

"I think with trauma there is sometimes a temptation to try and find one singular event that caused a massive upheaval. But it can be more than that. It can be an accumulation of small-seeming violations that can last a lifetime," I said.

"You're absolutely right. You're absolutely right," he said. "Trauma does not need to be one event. It can be a context, a situation, which is lasting. That's very insightful, what you say, and that is true."

I had forgotten how good it felt to be affirmed by him, even if he didn't understand fully what he was affirming. He always overdid his concurrence and it had always made me feel special.

"You did a lot of things that really damaged me. There are things you did and said that had lasting effects," I said.

"Well I should go into therapy with you," he said. "You should be my therapist."

"Well . . . I could come to Paris and we could sit down and talk about the last thirty years," I said.

He agreed, clearly not realizing what he was agreeing to. I was scared but I was also far enough away from myself that I felt like nothing could get me. My dissociation, for how much it tormented me, presented an opportunity. And I would take it.

2.

Gregory and I departed Nashville for Paris in October 2019. I had always loved airports. There were rules, and I knew them. It felt good to obey, to move swiftly, to be efficient and ready for anything. When I was little, flying across the Atlantic Ocean twice a year, I learned the names of the flight attendants on each flight and took Polaroid pictures with them. I craved the over-salted, semi-frozen airplane food. Now, twelve years since I had last been in Paris with my father, I held my passport open, and recited my name to the TSA agent. I had both passports with me, the blue and the burgundy, the American and the German, and I studied each one, the same name, the same face, different versions of me that had lived in such different worlds. Gregory was beside me. I was making this trip with someone who, despite how insubstantial I felt, was full of me—full of my love and of love for me. We didn't know what awaited us, but I was propelled by the desperation my dissociation had ignited, and I had beside me the person even it could not drive away.

As we approached the Paris apartment in a taxi, I saw my father waiting outside. I was afraid of how I would feel when we embraced. When he hugged me I laughed out loud, something old and automatic. I didn't know if feeling happy to see him was bad. We were greeted inside the lobby by the concierge, who had lived in the building for forty years. She recognized me and gave me a big hug. The elevator smelled exactly the same as I remembered. It was made of lacquered oak and rectangular panes of glass and was extremely tiny. I used to race it, sprinting up the winding, carpeted stairs as the elevator glided alongside and then above me, its dark, shining bulk ascending like a sea monster, window-eyes glinting and cables trailing like tentacles. The apartment was so full of light, so familiar. My father had left on my bed the hippopotamus stuffed animal I had had as a child. I jammed my face into its fraying flank, trying to dive back into the oldest parts of myself, the parts I hoped still existed. I stood on the terrace with Gregory and scanned the zinc roofs and blue sky for the thing that would bring me back. As I walked through the thresholds of my childhood—the lobby, the elevator, the huge metal front door—I waited for the walls of myself to stack back up, the doors to settle back under their lintels, the triangle of roof to drop back over my head. I announced all the things I remembered to Gregory, pointing out the tin ornaments my mother had painted, the sharp edge of the fireplace where I had split my lip open as a toddler, my voice getting louder and louder as it tried to carry over the abyss and reach me. I had wanted the force of this place, the powerful fist of nostalgia, to punch me back into existence. But as I exhausted the memorabilia and memories, I realized it would take more than this to return home.

My father's partner of fifteen years, Colombe, prepared a delicious meal of lamb chops and caramelized endives. I had first met Colombe when she had come with my father to visit me for my twenty-first birthday. She was a beautiful, intense, fiercely intelligent woman with a mane of coarse curls who had been the editor in chief of French *Vogue*. I had liked her instantly, and had been confused about how such formidable women could be so duped by my father. Over dinner, Gregory told them his story of recovery from drugs and alcohol. He told the whole story, not leaving out any details. They were impressed and moved. While Colombe and my father chain-smoked and we spread cheese on little boiled potatoes, I read aloud from question cards I had brought with me.

"What annoying behavior of yours do you blame your mother for?" I read.

"Falling in love with critical women," said my father.

"What lie do you keep telling yourself?" I read.

"Probably the one I'm not aware of," said Gregory, and we all laughed.

"That's intelligent, that's subtle," said my father.

"What's the funniest thing your inner child wants?" I read.

"A hug," said my father.

"I want gigantic shoes that I can bounce really high up and down with," said Gregory.

We laughed.

I hadn't realized how much I wanted Gregory to know my father, to be known by him. I was surprised at the lively ease of the evening, but I was wary of it too.

After dinner, my head was spinning from exhaustion. I lay down and closed my eyes and immediately felt unsafe, all the parts of my mind becoming loose, too loose, threatening to wobble apart as I moved from consciousness into sleep. I felt a bolt of nausea in my gut and my skin got hot. Oh fuck, it was happening again. My heart started to throb and the avalanche of dissociative panic threatened to bury me. I took a Klonopin and a Seroquel, grabbed my pillow, and made my way to the bathroom, in case I needed to put myself in the shower again. I spread a towel on the tile floor and lay down next to the bathtub. My stomach churned as I waited, hoping for my medication to sneak past the panic and ambush me into unconsciousness. Suddenly, the door burst open and Gregory raced to the toilet. Instantly, my stomach cramped. When Gregory was done, I sank onto the toilet, ecstatic with relief. This was food poisoning, not my mind breaking down again. I was here and I was safe.

THE NEXT DAY, I took Gregory to the Jardin du Luxembourg, where Nanny and I had spent so much time together. We ate waffles with powdered sugar, which I'd loved as a child. We watched the carousel turn. We listened to the tock of boules hitting as white puffs of smoke rose from the cigars of the old Frenchmen who came every day to play. We smelled the shit from the ponies who lifted their tails and made their deposits as they swayed along the paths, children on their backs. Two bright-green parakeets wound in and out of the horse chestnut trees. As I surveyed the idyllic scene, I felt in danger; my chest twitched with anxious heartbeats, rivulets of sweat trickled from pits to wrists. As a group of elderly Parisians practiced tai chi nearby, Gregory and I went over the rules of the impending confrontation with my father, discussing contingency plans for if he got drunk, if he got angry, if things got out of control.

My father and I had decided to begin our "therapy sessions" the following day. I unpacked all the journals, spanning twenty years, I had brought with me and stacked them on the dining table next to his pile of notebooks, spanning fifty years. At the appointed time, we sat down, facing each other across the table.

Gregory stood next to the table and addressed us.

"You both need to follow the rules," he said. "First of all, there is no alcohol consumption allowed during these sessions." I looked at my father. We had come up with that rule for him. The last time I had seen him, he had been drinking seven beers a night. He noticed us both looking at him and said, "Yes, yes okay."

"One person gets to talk for up to half an hour without interruption, with the exception of questions for clarification," continued Gregory. "Then the other person gets to respond without interruption. If it gets too heated or too difficult, either person can walk away at any time. Just say, 'I need a break,' and take a pause. If you can't follow the format and can't resist interrupting, I'll be in the other room and if I hear yelling I'll come in and encourage a break."

I thought about the temper and impatience I had inherited from my father, the litigious style of arguing I had learned from him. I hoped we'd be able to follow these rules. It helped to know Gregory was in the next room, listening to the rise and fall of our voices, monitoring for signs of distress.

"Sometimes Alice and I will have what I call 'friend talks,'" said Gregory. "We take anything personal out of it and she'll tell me something about me that she doesn't like and I'll listen as if I'm just a good friend of hers. And sometimes I've done that and I've said, 'He sounds like a real asshole.' It validates her reality and it helps take the potency out of how upset she is with me so I can listen to it without being reactively defensive."

"Yes, yes. That's very wise," my father said. He had the demeanor of an eager, impatient student, his pen poised for note-taking, his shoulders thrust back.

"Any amendments can be made to these rules as you go," said Gregory. "Are you ready?"

"Yes, I'm ready," said my father. "I don't know what I'm ready for, but I'm ready."

"Good luck," Gregory said and left the room.

I pressed record on my phone and placed it on the table between us. My father lit a cigarette. I watched his cheeks cave in as he inhaled.

We each had a notebook open before us, and we uncapped our pens. I pulled ten yellowed pages from a folder and laid them on the table between us. It was the final divorce judgment.

"I wanted to give you a chance to tell your side of the story," I said.

He read the papers, the cylinder of ash on his cigarette lengthening. He sighed.

"I remember how it started," he said. "Jennifer came up to me one day and said that since New York is not a no-fault state she had to have a reason to divorce me. There are three reasons which constitute fault in a marriage. One is adultery, one is abandonment, and the third is physical violence. Since I had not abandoned Jennifer but she had abandoned me, that didn't work. I had committed adultery with the Spanish actress, and I had always admitted that, but since Jennifer and I had sex after, it counted as forgiven. So that didn't work. And the third one, physical cruelty—I never raised a finger to her. She was desperate. I didn't want a divorce. I spoke to a friend who was a lawyer and I said, 'There are no grounds for divorce,' and he looked at me and said, 'That's what lawyers are for. We invent them.'"

I wrote those last three words down in my notebook and underlined "invent."

"They came up with this idea of inappropriateness. They accused me of having an 'unduly stimulating' relationship with you," he said, quoting from the files. "I was an extremely interactive father. That was our defense. It was probably very stimulating for you, but not only sexually. I taught you languages, we talked philosophy, we invented stories, we played Scrabble. In the course of the trial they said that I was a very interactive mother—ah you see!" He laughed at his Freudian slip. "A very interactive father. And that Jennifer was an aloof mother. Some perceived me as being too close to you for a parent. And I was devastated by the way that was used against me instead of in my favor. My whole behavior during that time in the first, let's say, four years of your life, was determined by two things. One was that for the first six months of your life, Jennifer and you had very little physical contact because she had contracted an infection in the hospital and was in excruciating pain and couldn't hold you or breastfeed you. The second was that you were allergic to formula and cow's milk. The only thing you could keep inside you was goat's milk. And I went to get it every morning at a little shop on the corner. In the first years of your life I was mothering you very much."

I pictured him filling up empty spaces—filling me with the milk I couldn't get from anywhere else, filling the space between me and my convalescing mother, and now, filling the gaps my mother's silence and her forgetting had left behind. Circumstances had made him the final authority on our history. I stared at the waveform on my phone as it recorded the peaks and valleys of his rendition. I was wary of him and the pages that were his to fill. My chest got hot, thudding as he stapled these facts onto the blank spots of my story. I didn't know what I wanted from him, what I needed him to say.

"I also felt I needed to protect you from Jennifer," he continued.

"From what?" I asked.

"From her damage and from her aloofness. That's what I wanted to do all along since you were born," he said.

"Protect me?" I said. "It says in these files that you were against therapy for me. Did you think I shouldn't be in therapy?"

"I was afraid for you and for me. During the trial, I was specifically against the court-ordered forensic psychiatrists. I remember a scene that terrified me. When I met with one of the forensic psychiatrists she asked, 'Do you take showers with your daughter?' I said, 'No.' 'But you did? Until what age?' she asked. I said, 'Four.' And she said, 'Did you ever have an erection when you were taking a shower with her?' and I said, 'No.' She looked at me and said, 'How do you know that Alice wasn't aroused?' And then I remember in my mind saying, 'I didn't check whether her clitoris was hard.'" He scoffed. "I thought it was disgusting. These were the moments when I said, 'What world am I living in?' That's when this term of inappropriateness really started to be discussed. Would I be able to hold a child back who was about to cross the street at a red light—or was it inappropriate? I was against forensic psychiatrists because I had the feeling that therapy was not there to help you, it was there to prove their case. Over years of this trial every single problem you had was monocausally attributed to me. I really thought that they would brainwash you. And you were getting worse. And then you told me Dr. Shore had hit you."

He read through the pages. "Wait," he said. "It says here: 'When the question of therapy for Alice was raised, Dr. Neubauer recommended that they see Dr. Shore.' Yes, this is interesting. I must have raised the question of therapy for you, in my sessions with Dr. Neubauer. It was I who brought you to therapy in the first place." He threw the papers down on the table. "You stayed in treatment with Dr. Shore for a year and you were in an even worse state by the end. And not only because of how I behaved. It was the whole atmosphere. Which was lies and wars and exaggerations and defensive behavior on my part. Poor child.

"And no one ever proposed a session with you, me, and Jennifer," he continued. "No one ever had the idea during this whole fucking trial when you were gliding into mental illness, when I was on the verge of suicide, when Jennifer was dealing with her abuse, nobody ever thought to bring the three of us under supervision in a therapeutic session."

"It allowed Mom to disappear even more," I said.

"Yes!" He clapped his hands together as if trapping the realization in midair.

"Because she's nowhere here," I said.

"Nowhere!" He sighed. "My god. This makes me angry."

I studied his face. He looked more sad than angry.

"Basically if I had agreed to Jennifer's terms, if I had not fought it, I would have probably had the initial visitation schedule. The outcome would have been the same but without destroying your mental health." He banged the table hard. "Fucking idiot I am," he said in a violent whisper. I saw him see his past, remote and yet so close. I felt sorry for him. He seemed smaller and weaker than I remembered. I thought of Diane's dim room, where I told her that bodyguards would need to tie him to a chair for me to be able to confront him. But now, as we sat across from each other, I didn't feel threatened.

We broke for the day, and I went to the kitchen to pour another cup of coffee.

"More coffee? After so much coffee?" my father exclaimed.

"It's half decaf," I said.

I opened a kitchen cabinet and took out a rose-flavored loukoum candy, the size of a die, I had bought earlier and bit into it.

"You're eating that already? In the middle of the day?" he asked, a disproportionate disgust fattening his words.

"Yes," I said, suddenly unsure of myself.

"Let's go for a walk," Gregory suggested.

We decided to walk to Montmartre, a two-hour trek. I got some roasted red peppers and couscous from the refrigerator.

"You're eating now?" my father asked.

"Yes, we're going on a four-hour walk," I said.

"Yes, because people eat before a four-hour walk," he said, an ugly glaze of sarcasm stippling his words.

"Yes, they do," I said.

I mentioned to Gregory I wanted to buy a mille-feuille at the bakery because it had been years since I'd had one and I wanted him to try it.

"Another pastry?" interrupted my father.

"I haven't had one in years," I said, my voice becoming high-pitched.

My father walked onto the terrace and lit a cigarette. Gregory followed him. I watched them from the dining table. Gregory told him I had grown a lot since he knew me a decade ago. He said I was healthier than either of them, that I was a kind and loving and caring person who was trying really hard. My father listened intently, nodding his head. Then he got up and left the apartment, striding by me in silence. Fifteen minutes later, as I was putting on my shoes in the bedroom, the top of his head appeared near the bottom of the bedroom doorway. Then the rest of his prostrate body emerged. He was crawling on his hands and knees with a pink box held aloft with one hand.

"Mea culpa, mea culpa," he chanted.

He had bought me three pastries from the bakery across the street.

"You should be able to eat whatever you want. I'm sorry."

I laughed. This was an apology true to who he was—the funny, creative, intense man who had always been able to make life so colorful and so confusing. The swiftness with which he had heard and processed information, decided he was wrong, thought of a creative way to demonstrate his fault, and executed it with such panache moved me.

The next day we reconvened at the table with our notebooks.

"I'm not just here to talk about the allegations from the trial," I said, pretending to write something down so I didn't have to look him in the eye. "You did and said things that had lasting effects on me. That made me feel violated. I have them written down here."

I turned to a bookmarked page in my notebook. I read the list to him. I watched him as he heard me describe licking the tears from his eyes, hearing compliments about my ass or tales of my mother's cunt, being appraised by a pimp, being cast as lovers in incest cinema. He stared into the distance. I didn't know how he would react. I didn't know if he would be angry, if he would simply deny that any of this had happened, if he would call me crazy and accuse me of inventing things. His face flickered with clarity and, I thought, pain, like the sun slipping in and out from behind fast-moving clouds.

"Do you remember any of this?" I asked.

"Some of them I have a vague memory of. Some of them I don't," he said.

"Do you remember telling me I had a great ass? That was your favorite compliment for me."

"No, it was probably the most inappropriate compliment but I made many compliments about you," he said. He paused for a moment. "It was the way I inappropriately joked with you. I think it was also a way of starting to distance myself from you, to let you have distance and see you more as an adult. I don't know, I'm just thinking."

"Your attempt to see me more as an adult? Do you equate adultness with sexuality?" I asked.

"With, with words which, well . . ." He fell silent again. "It was not sexually connotated. It was as if I said, 'You have a nice nose.'"

"There's a difference between a nose and an ass," I said.

"Freud would say not," he said. "It was a comment. You have a great ass, Alice." He shook his head. His voice dropped lower and quieter. "You don't say that to your daughter, absolutely true."

He read the next incident from my notebook.

"'Lick the tears from my eyes,'" he read. "My god, I have a vague memory now that you mention that. Wait—" he started flipping through the stack of notebooks, dating back to the eighties. "Yes," he said, and read an excerpt from his notes: "'Alice licked my face on the way back from Lübeck. Then she licks my face while I'm napping and says, 'That's my way of kissing.' If you said that when you were four, right, July 10, 1989, maybe it was one of these rituals between us." Watching him comb through his stockpile of stories, I felt outmatched. He had written, dated proof of who little Alice had been and what she had done and said. I reminded myself that he did not own little Alice, she lived in me too.

"I don't remember that," I said. "But you asked me to lick the tears from your eyes. It doesn't matter if I licked your face three years before."

"You were also in a situation where you saw your father crying," he said. "You were probably doing it out of concern and compassion for me at that moment. I really tried to hide my despair from you, I really did. I had nowhere to turn with my despair and my helplessness. I felt existentially threatened. I had to let go constantly when I was going away. When we were together, I was very interactive with you. We did many things together. And I loved it, and you were very responsive because you were very precocious. I became a child myself in a way. I might have considered you my partner more than is appropriate. The connotations were not sexual. I never ever, ever, ever had any erotic fantasies concerning you. I made you my accomplice. It was a little transgressive probably, doing that with your child."

"To what end?" I asked.

"To be your pal. You were my only friend. It also had to do with the fact that I was losing your mother. I was losing Jennifer in two senses—because of my affair with the Spanish actress and because Jennifer was losing herself after she discovered she had been abused. And that's when all her fears started that I would abuse you. She would come into the room totally drunk when I was telling you a good-night story and try to drag me out of the room. My family was breaking up. Jennifer's fear that I would molest you was a driving element."

"But it wasn't just Mom's fears. You actually said and did things that were damaging. You told me you stuck your toe up Mom's cunt, you told me fathers secretly want to sleep with their daughters, you told me we should do an onscreen sex scene," I said.

"I think I said that every daughter secretly wants to sleep with her father, which is the Electra Complex," he said.

"Is that any better?" I asked.

"I never had any erotic fantasies about you. Never. Never. Never." He sighed. "Verbally, I'm very inappropriate. I totally agree. I'm just trying to understand how I felt when I said these things. I always had problems with limits. Right before I met your mother, I had spent ten years as the protégé of Gilles Deleuze. I was an anarchist. We were all for revolution. It was a revolution that included sexuality. I was a revolutionary in my fucking stupid young mind and I was in love with Deleuze because he took me into his group. We saw ourselves as a team of secret provocateurs, which is maybe how I treated you too. It was my desire to be different with my children, a childish revolt against the way I perceived America's puritanism. The way I treated you didn't have to do with sexuality, it had to do with affirming my special kind of being different." His last sentence rang in me like a tuning fork. I had been trying to lilt myself into that lofty register of specialness my whole life. I had used my brokenness as a way of setting myself apart. I knew what it meant to scramble to fill gaps in a self. I had done it with cuts and burns, with medications, with diagnoses, and finally, with words. He had done it with me. I was torn between recognition and repulsion.

"I understand that need for uniqueness," I said. "But the way you were different with me had to do with sex, or was at least very sexual. And it wasn't just words. You arranged naked photos of me to be taken while I was, as you said, 'still a Lolita.'"

"Did I really use the word 'Lolita'?" he asked. "I don't remember that."

"I remember it very clearly because I was about to turn eighteen."

"The big scandal of *Lolita*," he said, "was not that an older man fell in love with a young girl, it was the idea that the young girl seduced him. That it was sexually exciting for her, too." I noticed a change in his voice, a tone suited for arguing a dissertation. We had entered into abstraction; this was not about me anymore.

"Can a thirteen-year-old girl seduce an older man? Does she have enough agency in that context?" I asked.

"That was the revolutionary, scandalous idea of the book," he said. "Have you read Freud's theories on infantile sexuality? In those essays he describes babies masturbating, the idea that children can have sexual fantasies and sexualized behavior. That book almost got him shot when it came out, but it was a great discovery, which still today in America is not accepted because they have taught a very puritanical version of Freud. You must not forget, I might have enhanced your own Oedipal fantasies. I remember a conversation we had when you were sixteen where I said, 'Alice, I'm not attracted to you,' and you were very insulted."

I felt a rush of anger. It sounded too generic, placing the blame on the latent or overt sexual fantasies of a girl. I was offended and unnerved by the cliché. I didn't remember this conversation but I could easily imagine it.

"That may very well be true," I said, my words flinty and sharp. "But they were enhanced because of how you behaved. If your daughter asks you to take naked photos of her, you say no. It was up to you to say no."

"I'm not defending my behavior," he said. "I'm just trying to explain. You could be very persuasive, very demanding. I don't remember the term 'Lolita' and if I said it, it was not because I as an older man wanted to see my seventeen-year-old daughter naked; it was because you insisted that before your eighteenth birthday you wanted to do something transgressive. And I think that gave me the idea, which was based on Kleist's play *Penthesilea*, about the queen of the Amazons. She was always the woman I was most fascinated with. Not because she was sixteen but because she was the first successful woman warrior. We both developed the screenplay together. You were not a passive participant in this and in my point of view not a victim either.

It clearly went too far. And I was shocked myself when I saw the photographs. I was shocked about the scandalous aspect of it. And at the same time I found them great."

"This was my life," I said. "Not a play or a psychoanalytical theory or philosophical treatise. My life." I was angry and in my anger I felt clearer, more solid.

He was silent. He lit another cigarette and rubbed his brow. He read the lines of my list over and over again. I watched his eyes move back and forth across the page, the muscles of his face contract and release.

"That photographer who did the Lolita photos was one of your many friends who came onto me when I was a teenager. Do you remember all your friends we hung out with at bars and clubs? The ones who were always kissing and groping me? Tim and Karl and Johann?"

"I had no idea they were kissing and groping you," he said, his face twisted with disgust.

"It felt to me like you were encouraging those relationships," I said.

"No. I was not encouraging them," he said. "I was proud of you and I wanted to show you off. You had grown to be a radiant, intelligent, beautiful, articulate teenager, and I was proud of you. I tried so hard to pull you out of those nightclubs."

"But you brought me there in the first place," I said.

"I thought, okay, she's seventeen. Fuck it, she's old enough to take care of herself. And you wanted to go there!" He raised his voice. "We had been to clubs before. We had been going out. You were a wild young adult." This was true. I had been wild. That summer was just the beginning of the reckless choices I would make. Where did my recklessness begin and his transgression end? At what age did the mantle of accountability fall across my shoulders? I struggled to hold on to the mass of my convictions, the dimensions of my lived experience. I focused on the anger that was rising inside me, hot and bright.

"That wild young adult was your child! Not your girlfriend, not your wingman," I yelled.

"I tried to drag you out of there by your hair. You laughed at me and hid under a table!"

"Of course I didn't want to leave! I was a teenager! You can't obliterate all the rules and then expect me to follow them when it suits you."

The room echoed with my words. I braced myself for his retaliation, but there was only silence. My father looked down at his hands. Gregory appeared in the doorway. I waved him away, and he backed out of the room.

My father, his voice soft and low, said, "I was a mess. Bettina had left me and taken Elena to Venice. I had lost my second child. I was hundreds of thousands of dollars in debt. I was drinking. I was a total fucking mess for years. And I had no one. I had no one to turn to."

He put his hand on my list, as if suddenly aware of how real it was.

"I shouldn't have said or done any of these things period, period, period. There's no excuse," he said. "I'm totally shocked and ashamed."

Silence collected around us. He offered no more excuses, no more justifications. He let his shame rest between us, an offering.

"The big tragedy about all this is that I was in a desperate symbiosis with you and I let things happen," he said. "It was—I wouldn't say sick—but it's making your daughter share your own intimacy. That is crossing a line. It was out of pure desperation. I didn't have anybody else to share my despair with. That was . . . I don't like the word *inappropriate*. It was inconsiderate and selfish because I thought more of my own pain, of my own despair, than I thought of the effect it had on you."

I wasn't sure how to proceed. His vulnerability was so appealing, so comforting. But I also wanted to challenge it.

"It did have a huge effect. Why didn't you help me when I got sick? I remember thinking you were interested in the drama of it, and I remember your anger when you came to my apartment when I was first going manic," I said.

"I was unstable myself, and it took me time to realize you weren't well," he said. "You were always exuberant and hyper and then when I realized this was something more, I tried to accompany you. To accompany you and to find solutions for your manic and paranoid demands. I had no experience in this and you had screamed at me to get out. That was the third time someone I loved was yelling at me to get the fuck out. I was scared and overwhelmed and I acted not like I should have."

"You did have experience . . . with Till," I said.

"I should have brought him to a hospital," he said, and repeated it twice. "But you can't force another person." There existed in him pain of which I was not the center, pain that wasn't about me.

"And when I saw you suffering in the same way as my brother," he continued, "I thought, what can I do? What can I do? I saw my child going crazy. And what do you do? Sit down and say, 'Let's have a cup of tea'? No idea. No idea. No idea."

It had not occurred to me that he had come not to gawk at my despair, but because I had needed him, that it would have been difficult for him to come all the way to New York, in the middle of a desperately needed job.

"I was constantly afraid that you would kill yourself," he said. "I was, for eight years, waking up every morning at four o'clock, afraid I would get the phone call telling me you were dead. I didn't know who would call me. I was even afraid no one would call me."

"That must have been awful," I said. As I watched those years play out on my father's face, I felt a breathless, terrifying awareness. I imagined him in this apartment, wondering if his child was alive or dead, wondering if the woman he had loved would even acknowledge him enough to let him know. I saw the ways he had been inflated and shrunk down, at once too huge to be human and too insignificant to inspire compassion. Now, our exchange was rescaling him, changing his dimensions until we both fit inside the same story.

We decided to take a break and Gregory, my father, and I went to Montparnasse Cemetery, where Jean-Paul Sartre and Simone de Beauvoir were buried. My father kept asking strangers where Sartre's grave was. His words were apologetic and conciliatory but his body, tall and thin and vibrating, communicated a frenzied urgency that caused the strangers to take a step back. This intensity was so familiar; I recognized myself in it. Like he had always done since I was little, he walked far, far ahead, unaware of the distance accumulating between us. I remembered, as a child, watching his back as he left me a block and a half behind. But this time, I was not alone. I held hands with Gregory. I watched as my father got smaller and smaller, and I laughed.

When we arrived home, my father ran into the other room and then called for me. On the floor were two large portraits, drawings done by my father decades ago, one of my mother and one of him. They were beautiful. He had captured my mother as she put on makeup, making the exact same face I had seen her make my entire life when I watched her getting ready to go out—her eyes wide and her mouth open and round as if she were saying 'oh.' The drawing was dominated by rich reds punctuated by the intense turquoise of her wide eyes. This was an intimate, vulnerable moment. I felt joined to my father, realizing that we both housed the same memory of my mother. In his self-portrait, rendered only in grays and blacks, he stood staring at the viewer with a cigarette burning in his hand. His eyes were penetrating yet detached. This moment was intimate, but it was not vulnerable.

As we looked down at the portraits, I said, "The story I came to believe after trauma group was that the abuse was more physical when

I was little and then you were strategically changing your approach the older I got and the more aware I became. To me it was like you were the most intelligent predator I had ever seen."

"Oh my God. Can you say that again?" He ran across the room to get his notebook. I followed him and sat down next to him, repeating what I had said as he wrote.

"That's what they taught me in trauma group," I said. "The early years were more physical, and then, as I got older, it got dangerous for you to say words to me or do things to me, because you'd get caught, so you started living vicariously through your friends." He wrote furiously in his notebook. "That's what I thought until recently. Until this trip. Does that make sense?"

"It makes . . ." He paused and stared down at what he had written. "Horrifying sense. Because if any of that were true then I would really have to kill myself." He fell silent.

"I've had nightmares for years where you are raping me in a hotel room," I said, scraping the last, most secret dregs of his influence out of me. "I'll have a nightmare about a sexual encounter with you and wake up orgasming. I have deep shame because of that."

He put his face in his hands, trying to contain the tears that had come. I had never seen him cry like this. An intimate, discreet cry that was not meant to be seen by others.

"I'm so sorry," he said through his hands. "I'm terribly sorry. Can you forgive me?"

"I'm sorry it took this long for us to . . ."

"Talk about it," he said. "Thank you for having the courage to come here. Thank you."

He stared at his notebook, his shoulders shaking.

I felt my own body letting go, the fear and suspicion I had harbored for so long falling from me. I was proud of us. The way we exchanged words had been partially responsible for all the bad, but it had made up the good as well. It was only because we were willing to say anything to each other that we could say everything we needed to.

"'To me you were the most intelligent predator I had ever seen,'" he read aloud, my words echoing back to me.

"Are you flattered?" I asked, the teasing tone an offering, the beginnings of forgiveness.

"At least it's a superlative," he said weakly. We laughed and closed our notebooks.

3.

Oh FUCK!" my father said, standing in the middle of the airport. "I forgot my passport and my credit card and my identification."

Gregory, my father, and I were flying from Paris to Hamburg. It was the first time I had traveled with my father in twelve years. Airports were a nexus of all the things that set him off: lines, rules, waiting. Going to a supermarket with him was like walking a tightrope between two buildings. Being at an airport was like defusing a bomb. He patted himself down muttering, "Fuck, fuck, fuck," and unzipped the little pouch strapped around his waist. He swung into action, finding the very first person in a uniform and telling them the unfortunate turn of events. The uniformed man had his bland work-patience face on, but when he understood what my father was saying—that he did not have the one essential thing needed to travel and wanted to travel anyway—his eyes sharpened and his mouth went rigid. He could not help him. There was nothing he could do.

We speed-walked to the information desk and my father explained the situation. No ID. No credit card. No passport.

"I'm sorry, sir, you will not be able to travel without identification," said the man behind the counter.

"Can't you just google me?" my father asked.

When they told him, like speaking to a child, that one could not fly on an airplane without identification, it simply couldn't happen, his remaining composure unraveled. He threw his arms around a large column near the counter and thrust himself backwards and forwards on it. His trench coat flapped behind his body as he threw himself around. From far away, it would have looked like the climax of a dance performance. I kept repeating his name, but he didn't hear me. He was not allowed to fly.

He was distraught, his rage and desperation giving way to sorrow. He apologized to us over and over.

We decided that Gregory and I would take our scheduled flight and he would take a later one. I tried to comfort him.

"This is how it's meant to be," I said. "Just think, now you'll be able to arrive home to *both* your daughters for the first time in twelve years."

His face brightened.

"I love that," he said. "You're absolutely right."

It felt good being able to comfort him.

Gregory and I flew to Hamburg, leaving my father behind.

When we pulled up to my father's apartment in the taxi, Elena was waiting for us, leaning her tall body against the building. When she noticed the taxi she ran to open the door for me, and we shared a hug that rocked us back and forth. Her excitement was pure and conspicuous and it felt good. I had not seen her in twelve years. Three years ago, at nineteen, she had been runner-up on the reality TV show *Germany's Next Topmodel* and had parlayed that exposure into a successful career as a model and Instagram influencer. I was unsure where I stood with her. She had told me once that I was her role model. At fourteen she had gotten some shady guy to give her a tattoo on the inside of her lower lip and she had chosen the letter "A" for "Alice." I had been both worried and touched. I had tried, as best I could, to nurture our relationship, despite the distance and my struggles. But it was difficult to keep in touch. We Skyped maybe once a year. She was traveling the world modeling and influencing, and I was going through things I didn't think she could understand.

We entered the Hamburg apartment where I had spent so much of my youth. The walls were covered in sentences and phrases and drawings and quotes and newspaper clippings that residents and visitors had scrawled or glued over the years, cave paintings that told the history of this place and its people. There was a framed black-and-white photo of an advertisement my father had done for VH1. He was shirtless, holding a burning newspaper. There was a quote above his head that read, "NO MORE I LOVE YOU'S—A RESOLUTION I'VE BROKEN AGAIN AND AGAIN," a reference to the Annie Lennox song. I used to read it over and over, thinking the quote the most beautiful sentence I had ever read. There was a newspaper clipping about my father kicking his girlfriend Sonia out, and replacing her with a pet rat. I located my contributions. There was a clay rendering of my father's head that I had made in middle school hanging on the wall. There was a transcription of a children's song about spiders in bathtubs my father, my toddler sister, and I would sing together loudly through the streets. There was a quote about hating George W. Bush. I still existed here, even though I had been away for so long. I felt a shudder of grief, reading these epitaphs of the person I had been, then a surge of warmth, that my traces on these walls, these lives, persisted and were valued.

Other people had added their marks to the walls, and I saw how much time, how much shared experience, had passed me by. An enormous poster of my sister hung on the living room wall. Envy growled inside me as I calculated the wall space we each occupied, the success she had encountered being the daughter of my father, the darkness and the failures I had gleaned from that parentage. I thought of the decade I had stayed away. In 2013, two years after I had gotten out of the treatment center, I received an email from my father. When I saw his name in my inbox, I stiffened. What trick was he trying to pull now? I opened it and read that Oma, after having suffered two strokes, "adamantly wanted to die" and that my father would help her. It had always been Oma's wish to die in my father's arms, and he was tasked with preparing the lethal medications. My aunt Mareike, my father, and Opa would be gathering the next evening to say goodbye as my father helped her pass. I called my grandparent's number at 6 a.m. the next morning. It was the first time I had dialed the number in years. Should I explain my absence? Should I apologize? Opa picked up. Should I tell him how much I'd missed him? Should I tell him how sorry I was, for his wife who was about to die, for staying away?

"You sound much younger," I said.

He didn't say anything and passed the phone to my father who put the phone to Oma's ear. I hadn't spoken German in twelve years, and I struggled with my words as I shared memories of my time in Lübeck with her. I paused and then told her I was engaged. I assumed my father was listening, and had hesitated to share the news because I was trying to follow Diane's rules and keep him from me, but I wanted to let Oma know that I was loved. I told her I loved her and said goodbye. Two years later, Mareike developed bladder cancer and asked my father to help her die too. I never went to see her. I was too angry, too afraid to risk exposure to my father's malignancy. Opa got more decrepit and eventually asked my father to help him die as well. I never spoke to him before he died. The last thing I ever said to him was that he sounded younger.

I stayed away until it was too late, until there was almost no one left. And I had not for one moment considered my father's pain. It had fallen to him to lovingly help end the lives of his entire remaining original family, and I had thought only of how this might be an attempt to manipulate me, a "game," as Diane had put it.

I had never explained to my sister why I hadn't come. I kept track of her life and her life with my father via the Internet. A simple scroll revealed how well she had turned out, successful and autonomous and liked at the age when I was accelerating my deterioration, and the pure-love connection she got to enjoy with a mother who had always focused all attention and energy on her and a father who had not said and become too many things to her. They were profiled in a magazine article that had the line "Between us there are no secrets" emblazoned above their laughing heads. I took a screenshot of that article and sneaked looks at it, fuming. I hated them in those moments. I felt used and left behind. In my silence and absence, I was protecting him, and being left with nothing. I felt jealous of what they had, and sometimes I made myself feel better by imagining that my father had not found her as irresistible as me. He had not chosen to recruit her as a partner so I must be the special one. I saw these ruminations for the petty, confused distortions they were but they still felt real. I was angry. I was angry at Diane for her stories, angry at my sister for not needing me in hers, angry at myself for needing to believe in one so badly. But really, I was heartbroken.

My father texted that he was in a taxi on the way to the apartment. We went outside to greet him when his taxi arrived.

Gregory, my father, Elena, and I all sat in the living room. After a few minutes of pleasantries, my father described what we had been doing for the past week.

"The reason Alice didn't come for all those years was because she thought I was a pedophile," he said to my sister.

I watched my sister's face. It was still and serious. She started to say something about how these were just rumors, stories Jennifer had invented.

"No," said my father. "I'm not a pedophile but I behaved very badly."

Elena was silent. She nodded her head. "It's good that you're both doing this," she said.

As I heard my father make this naked admission and my sister receive it without resistance, I felt held. My father had stuck up for me, confirmed my reality, invited my sister into it too, and she had accepted the invitation. I saw clearly the traces of the live-wire luck that had been sparking through my entire life, that had led me to the love hidden in the heart of our failings and misfortunes.

We walked to a nearby restaurant. I walked arm in arm with my father, and Elena walked with Gregory a few steps behind.

She confided in him that she had been nervous about this reunion.

"We were scared to come here, too," said Gregory. "But you should know that what happened between them was the beginning of something really special. A lot of healing has taken place."

"That makes me really happy," she said.

As I talked to Elena, my father and Gregory talked. My father asked him about our lives together, about his continued recovery. He asked his advice about how he could get along better with me.

"You don't always need to respond," I overheard Gregory say. "Sometimes silence is the best response."

The next day, Gregory, my father, and I rented a car to go to Lübeck to visit the cemetery where my grandparents and Till were buried. My father brought a bucket and brushes to clean the graves, just as Oma had done years ago. After an hour of scrubbing at the gravestones and pulling weeds, we got back in the car and drove to my favorite places in Lübeck. We ate potato pancakes at the Kartoffel

Keller, where everything on the menu was made out of potatoes. We posed in front of the stained-glass windows of the Marienkirche, which depicted the Totentanz, where people danced in a line as Death summoned them to their demise. We walked through rows and rows of marzipan pigs and marzipan potatoes and whole marzipan towns at the Niederegger, the large stone building where marzipan had been invented. At the end of the day, we visited my favorite building in Lübeck—the Holstentor, with its torture chamber. I remembered feeling, as a child, that this was a room that could hold the volume of my roiling imagination, even the murkiest, most disgusting sediment that bubbled up. Now in my thirties, I ran my hands over the spiked roller that was part of the machine that stretched the victim's body, and peered inside the torture barrel at the spikes that would pierce a man's torso as he was enclosed in it. It felt much smaller, much less menacing. I noticed that there were no spikes inside the barrel. My young imagination had filled them in. The thumbscrews were behind glass and looked tiny and innocuous. The chastity belt looked like it could easily be broken out of. A harmless crudeness had replaced the powerful sense of barbarity and transgression.

I bought a mug in the gift shop and we left. Outside the Holstentor, a man approached my father for an autograph. "Bitte, bitte," he pleaded as my father loped away.

"Nein, nein," said my father.

At first I chided him. "Why not just give him an autograph?" Because he didn't want to, because it was his time, because they always wanted to talk, because he didn't want to. I saw my father's own struggle to free himself of his story, distance himself from the person other people thought he was—a celebrity or a pedophile. I watched the fan pursue my father and saw a tired man who wanted to get away from his past. And I understood. I had the choice to leave behind the things that had pursued and defined me for so long. I could choose to stop defining my father, too.

WE FLEW BACK TO PARIS, and Gregory left for Nashville. I stayed behind to spend more time with my father and my sister, who had come to Paris to spend a few days with me. Elena and I went to the Palais de Tokyo. I took her to a drag show, and we marveled at the muscular drag queens singing Serge Gainsbourg through cigarette-plugged mouths, drifting en pointe across the stage.

As we walked through Paris, I stole glances at her profile. When I saw her face, a face I had known so well from infancy to middle school, I saw a record of the time I had been away, a record of my failings as a sister. I had been a regular presence in her life until she turned twelve and then I had vanished. Any pain she might have experienced on the other side of these years had never occurred to me until now. I had left her, a little girl who loved her sister, and disappeared with no explanation. I wanted to know this human being who had gone on without me, had accumulated her own hurts and disappointments, one of which might be me.

"I'm sorry I wasn't there for you," I said. "I'm sorry I didn't tell you what was happening. I wanted to protect Dad for you. I wanted to protect the image you had of him, to make sure I didn't project all my stuff onto your relationship with him."

"That's very brave and kind," she said.

To my surprise, I started to cry. Elena put her arm around me.

"I'm sorry we lost so much time," I said.

We continued to walk, my body wedged into hers, maneuvering through the streets, dodging passersby.

"I'm sorry I wasn't there," I said again. "Can you forgive me?"

"I think you need to forgive yourself," Elena said. "I'm not angry. When I was little I saw Dad suffering because of everything that was going on with you, and I was maybe angry at you for making him feel bad because I associated you with his suffering. But I'm not angry now."

She caressed my arm with one finger, and that small gesture felt like an agreement, a reassurance that I hadn't lost her.

The next day, Elena left for Hamburg and my father and I were alone together. Those last days in Paris we laughed a lot. We walked to the Musée D'Orsay and my father told me stories about Paris, its buildings and history. At dinner he had me write down all the German verbs I could think of that started with "ver" and pointed out the ones with multiple meanings. It reminded me of the stories and word games of my childhood. We watched one of his favorite movies, *Lawrence of Arabia*, on a daybed mattress on the floor. We sat close, watching the epic tale unfold on the tiny screen of his laptop, straining to hear the dialogue through the crappy speakers. I was aware of how neutered the space between us had become. It no longer coursed with nauseating electricity. When our shoulders accidentally touched, or when he squeezed my arm to indicate the imminence of a really good scene, I didn't shrink from the contact. I invited it. At thirty-four, I experienced for the first time his uncovetous touch—a hand that demanded nothing of my body, my personhood. Whenever I had watched my sister casually brush the hair away from my father's face, or walk arm in arm with him down the street, I felt I was watching something impossible and unattainable. And now I could access it too.

I was learning things about my father. I had forgotten he was a good cook. I had forgotten how funny he could be. I watched him tend to his plants on the terrace and saw in him a tenderness I had overlooked. I found myself tabulating all the signs of his aging. He was losing his hearing in one ear. I counted the dark spots that had formed on his arms, watched him as he changed shirts, as if I could fortify his rail-thin body with my gaze. I felt my heart unfolding, a novel hurt that

I finally understood as love deferred. One afternoon, I spontaneously patted his head while we were watching TV. I smiled to myself as I felt the temperature inside me fail to rise, as the cadence inside my chest chugged out an unremarkable ode, as my body told me there was finally nothing more to this story.

4.

My mother's disembodied voice came from the other room. She wanted a cigarette and she wanted to tell me that the local news anchor was wearing too much makeup. My mother was dying but didn't know it.

Two years after the trip to Europe, my father had been diagnosed with cancer. I told him I'd come look after him as he underwent radiation, and Gregory and I booked a flight to Paris. One month after that, shortly before we were scheduled to leave for Europe, my mother was diagnosed with acute myeloid leukemia and given two weeks to live. Gregory and I flew to New York and took the bus out to Amagansett.

We brought my mother to a hematologist to confirm the diagnosis. He was late in seeing us, and Gregory and I did our best to keep her distracted. I played her Rufus Wainwright's "Poses," and Gregory showed her funny animal videos. I paced the exam room and read strange Yahoo questions aloud to her (*How do you unbake a cake? Why does my arm shake and turn bright red when I'm eating dirt?*).

The doctor examined her and then spoke to us privately, without her in the room. He confirmed the diagnosis and told us to ask the receptionist for information about hospice care.

I approached the reception desk.

"I need the number for hospice," I said, my voice breaking.

"So she won't be coming to her appointment on August ninth?" she asked.

"No, she's dying. I need the number for hospice," I said.

"So you need to cancel the appointment?"

"I guess, yeah."

The receptionist wrote a number on a piece of paper and I folded it and refolded it before putting it in my pocket. On the way back home, my mother lay across the backseat with her head in my lap. In a small voice, she asked if she could hold my hand. I felt fear and awe at this gentleness. I opened my hand to receive hers. Her hand felt like silverware wrapped in a warm silk napkin, her bones slippery under her thin, hot skin.

"Am I squeezing you too hard?" she asked.

"You can squeeze me as hard as you want," I said.

I turned my face toward the window and felt the feelings crowd my throat until it throbbed, tears bottlenecking behind my eyeballs. I could not cry right now, in front of my mother. Gregory, who was driving, snaked his left hand between the door and the seat to hold my free hand.

Rufus Wainwright's "Poses" played again.

"Now who is this?" my mother asked, though I'd answered the same question just before.

"Rufus Wainwright," I said.

"He's sort of fabulous, isn't he?" she'd say.

There was a pause and we listened to the song.

"Now what does he look like?" she asked.

I pulled up a photo of him as a young man, as he was when he'd recorded the album.

"Hideous brooch," she said.

We arrived home and while my mother slept, I broke the news to my aunt and uncle and the two caregivers. When she woke up, I was relieved to hear her ask for a cigarette, but she didn't want to eat. I tried to tempt her with potato chips, bacon, Chinese food. All her favorites. Finally I bought six pints of fancy ice cream at the farmer's market. I stood over her bed and spooned ice cream into her mouth, reading aloud the copy on the back of the container that described how the Earl Grey ice cream was made.

Gregory came in to give her the pills she had been taking for years.

"What are these?" she asked.

"They're the medication to turn you into a mermaid," he said.

"Again?" she quipped.

I lay in bed next to her and showed her the photograph my editor had sent me of the book jacket. I'd finished my book months earlier and had sold it to a publisher. I had only told a handful of people. I told my mother the good news over and over. She was in ecstatic disbelief every time. I angled my iPad toward her and zoomed in on the book jacket.

"Fabulous," she said.

I told her about my impostor syndrome, about my fears for the future.

"I'm so scared," I said.

"Don't be scared."

"Why not?"

"Because what's the point?"

I realized I would not only miss my mother, I would miss Jennifer Bartlett. All I'd ever wanted was to sit with the great artist and brilliant thinker and discuss my work, but that was no longer who she was. I would not be her peer, but I could be the daughter whose hand she wanted to hold.

A few days later, hospice came to have me sign paperwork and give us the medications my mother would need. They presented me with a box of morphine and a box of lorazepam, and syringes to squirt the medications under her tongue. They gave me a pamphlet that described exactly what dying would look and sound like. I slipped it into a folder without looking at it.

I had ordered her a hospital bed and we moved her into the living room while the bed was being set up. She moaned and yelled. To distract her I googled Marlon Brando photos on my phone and showed her the one with the most bulging biceps. Every so often I'd put the photo in front of her face and she'd stop moaning.

"He's fabulous," she'd say.

"What do you like about him?" I'd ask.

"Everything," she'd say.

Soon she'd begin to moan again.

"Why am I sitting here?" she'd ask.

"Want to see a photo of Marlon Brando?"

"Sure," she'd say, her voice weak.

I'd show her the picture on my phone.

"Oh, he's fabulous," she'd say, her voice stronger.

"What do you like about him?"

"His lips. His hair. His eyes. His neck."

It went on like this until the bed was finished.

We moved her back into her room, and I sat next to her, writing as she dozed.

"What are you doing?" she asked.

"I'm writing," I said.

"Oh, good."

My aunt Julie arrived later that day. I was in my mother's room reading *David Copperfield* aloud to her. I left the room so they could be alone. I heard them laughing. My mother had a good day, asking for cigarettes, listening to music, drinking a smoothie, laughing. That night, things turned quickly. She moaned and asked what was wrong with her.

"You have a fever," I told her.

I stood to re-wet the compress I was holding to her forehead.

"Don't leave," she said.

I lay down next to her.

I wanted to hold her, to take her in my arms and squeeze her tightly. But I didn't move.

"Do you want to hold my hand?" I asked.

"Yes," she said.

I held her hand.

I couldn't help myself. "I love you very much," I said.

She scrunched up her face and in a voice gravelly with contempt said, "Why?"

I didn't know what to say. I had thought I could sneak in, get at the soft place, but it was still bulwarked.

She squirmed in the bed.

"Is there somewhere I can go?" she asked.

I could sense her panic.

"Do you want to go to the beach?" I asked.

"Yes," she said, her eyes closed.

"Do you want to go swimming in the ocean?"

She had always loved the ocean.

"Yes," she said.

"Is the water calm or wavy?"

"Calm," she responded.

"Is it dark blue or can you see to the bottom?"

"I can see to the bottom."

I asked her how far out she was going to swim.

"As far as I can go," she said.

"Do you want someone to swim with you?"

"No," she said.

"You like being alone, don't you?" I said.

"Yes."

"Are you going to swim back to shore?"

"No," she said.

"What are you going to do out there alone in the ocean?"

"Stay there and have a really nice time," she said.

Two days later she died.

AFTER THE HOSPICE NURSE ARRIVED and made the pronouncement, my aunt and I washed my mother's body. We put her in a hot-pink Shamask dress, and I doused her in the requisite high dose of Fracas perfume. I lifted her cooling wrist to my nose and smelled the fragrance on her skin one last time.

The weather forecast that day had been for an isolated tornado, which was the best description of Jennifer Bartlett I'd ever heard. The meteorological isolated tornado never happened, I could only assume because the departure of my mother, my very own isolated tornado, left no air for it.

All day the next day, I kept thinking I heard my mother calling me. I kept hearing "Alice" from the other room. Or maybe it was "Alice!" Or maybe it was "Alice?"

A disembodied voice that was now only in my head.

A week later, we spread her ashes in the ocean. I chartered a sailboat and my aunt, uncle, twin cousins, Gregory, and I boarded the water taxi to bring us to *The Starlight*. The weather was gray and rainy, but the captain and crew were kind and we shared our food with them. When we reached a nature preserve, we dropped anchor. Miles Davis's *Sketches of Spain* played through a Bluetooth speaker as we poured a bottle of white wine into the sea. The moment the booze hit the water, the clouds split open, the gaudy guts of a shamelessly showy sunset spilling across the horizon. A thick, golden light spread over our faces, which were all turned toward the sun's extravagant sinking. It looked exactly like an endless, excessive oil painting. It looked, in its extreme, bragging beauty, almost insolent. I recognized it. Gregory, tears and light in his eyes, said: "Jennifer looks good up there." We laughed. I stripped down to my swimsuit and I lowered myself into the Atlantic. I swam out, holding my mother's ashes aloft. We were as far out as we could go. I didn't want to leave her, but she needed to be alone.

Acknowledgments

Thank you to Vincent Katz and Bob Holman, whose temperatures rose from the long-form fever dream this book originally was and who believed in its communicability. Thank you to Jan Hashey, Peter Schlesinger, and Eric Boman, who were, one after the other, the critical components in the Rube Goldberg machine that slingshotted this book from that land of dreams and sickness into reality. Thank you to David Plante for your early guidance and enthusiasm. Thank you to Jane Rosenman for the gift of "warm and direct" and of chronology. Thank you to Julian Lethbridge for your support and friendship. Thank you to my chosen family, who have stuck with me through everything written here and more: Leah Aron, Oliver Barry, Kate Biggart, Jacob Bills, Erica Blinn, Bracket the Cat, Nancy Brooks Brody, Paula Cooper, Madison Cox, Jessica Craig-Martin, Thelma Denyer, Jamie Diamond, Amelia Edelman, Sophie Ellsberg, Caitlin Evanson, Ilian Georgiev, Daisy Holman, Trinity James, Adèle Jancovici, Molly Josephs, Effie Kammer, Joan LiPuma, Jessica Losch, Julie Manheimer, Ricky Manne, Julián Mesri, Kristine Michelsen-Correa, Rachel Eve Moulton, J.P. Nocera, Gavin O'Neill, Jessica Pearson, Eduard Riddle, Ivy Shapiro, Kevin

Smith, Amanda Stone, Anna Della Subin, Tiffany Taalman, Aaron Lee Tasjan, and Emily West.

Thank you to Nicole Dewey, Cindy Spiegel, Andy Tan-Delli Cicchi, Nora Tomas, Liza Wachter, and Alexis Hurley.

Thank you to Strick & Williams for the impossibly perfect cover.

Thank you to Kimberly Witherspoon and Maria Whelan at Inkwell Management for seeing what you saw and seeing it through. I adore you both.

Thank you to my publisher, Spiegel & Grau, for giving me a professional and creative home.

Thank you to my editor and friend, Julie Grau. You put my life between two glossy covers and my dream into my hands. To steal your words (after you've made mine so much better): Some people just feel necessary.

Thank you to Colombe Pringle for your steadfast care of the Carrières.

Thank you to my in-laws, Gary and Patricia Lattimer, for defying every in-law cliché and for believing in me and offering so much support.

Thank you to Julie, Takaaki, Max, and Julia Matsumoto for being the family I would also choose and for all the laughter.

Thank you to my sister, Elena Carrière, for your open mind and open heart.

Thank you to Eileen Denys Maynard, "Nanny," for your love, sacrifice, and diligent note-taking.

Thank you to my mother and father. Thank you for everything you did right and everything you did wrong.

And finally, thank you to Gregory Lattimer, who healed me and who knew all along.

About the Author

Alice Carrière is a graduate of Columbia University. She lives in Nashville, Tennessee, and Amagansett, New York. This is her first book.

War Over Kosovo

War Over Kosovo

Politics and Strategy in a Global Age

Edited by
Andrew J. Bacevich and Eliot A. Cohen

COLUMBIA UNIVERSITY PRESS NEW YORK

COLUMBIA UNIVERSITY PRESS
Publishers Since 1893
New York Chichester, West Sussex

Library of Congress Cataloging-in-Publication Data

War over Kosovo : politics and strategy in a global age /
edited by Andrew J. Bacevich and Eliot A. Cohen.
p. cm.
Includes bibliographical references and index.
ISBN 0-231-12482-1 (cloth : alk. paper) — ISBN 0-231-12483-X
(pbk. : alk. paper)
1. Kosovo (Serbia)—History—Civil War, 1998– 2. United States—Military policy. I. Bacevich, A.J. II. Cohen, Eliot A.

DR2087 .W37 2001
949.7103—dc21 2001042269

∞

Casebound editions of Columbia University Press books
are printed on permanent and durable acid-free paper.
Printed in the United States of America

c 10 9 8 7 6 5 4 3 2 1
p 10 9 8 7 6 5 4 3 2 1

Contents

Acknowledgments *vii*

Introduction Andrew J. Bacevich and Eliot A. Cohen *ix*

Contributors *xv*

1. Operation Allied Force: "The Most Precise Application of Air Power in History" *William M. Arkin* 1
2. Kosovo and the New American Way of War *Eliot A. Cohen* 38
3. First War of the Global Era: Kosovo and U.S. Grand Strategy *James Kurth* 63
4. Hubris and Nemesis: Kosovo and the Pattern of Western Military Ascendancy and Defeat *Anatol Lieven* 97
5. Kosovo and the Moral Burdens of Power *Alberto R. Coll* 124
6. Neglected Trinity: Kosovo and the Crisis in U.S. Civil-Military Relations *Andrew J. Bacevich* 155
7. Revolution Deferred: Kosovo and the Transformation of War *Michael G. Vickers* 189

Index 211

To Owen Harries

Acknowledgments

This volume was made possible by a generous grant from the Smith Richardson Foundation. The editors would like to thank the trustees and governors of the Foundation and especially Dr. Marin Strmecki, vice president and director of programs.

We would also like to thank James Warren, our editor at Columbia University Press, for taking this project on. We are grateful to Nicholas Frankovich and Plaegian Alexander of the Press for seeing it efficiently through to completion. Philip Saltz prepared the index for which we are likewise grateful.

Finally the publication of this book coincides with the retirement of Owen Harries as founding editor of *The National Interest*. Any periodical necessarily represents an expression of its editor's tastes, temperament, and values. With *The National Interest* during the sixteen years of Owen's tenure this has been acutely the case. Not only bearing the stamp of Owen's own personality—cultured, elegant, intellectually courageous, and sparkling with wit and insight—his journal has also reflected a mind that values integrity, candor, clear thought, and well-crafted prose. Owen is a great editor and remains a great friend and we affectionately dedicate this book to him.

Introduction: Strange Little War

Andrew J. Bacevich and Eliot A. Cohen

Why Kosovo?

The Kosovo war was, for the conventional military historian, small beer. The vast preponderance of forces tilted entirely to one side: The U.S. defense budget was fifteen times the size of Serbia's entire gross national product, and that figure didn't even include the budgets of America's NATO allies. Yet despite Slobodon Milosevic's eventual capitulation and despite the extraordinary absence of combat casualties on the allied side, the unexpectedly protracted two-and-a-half month bombing campaign left a sour aftertaste. Although NATO's air attacks on the whole had been remarkably precise, they had resulted in hundreds of unintended casualties in Serbia and had accidentally turned a wing of China's embassy in downtown Belgrade into rubble, unleashing a furor in Beijing and creating enormous embarrassment for Washington. As initially advertised, Operation Allied Force was supposed to be short and sweet. As those expectations faded, evidence of wrangling, recriminations, and finger pointing within the alliance and between civilian and military leaders became increasingly difficult to conceal. Meanwhile, NATO's abject failure (or inability) to put an end to the displacement and massacre of large (if disputed) numbers of ethnic Albanian Kosovars made a mockery of the campaign's grand moral justification, leaving the United States and its allies fending off accusations of gross miscalculation, callousness, or outright bad faith. Finally, there was the unsavory aftermath of victory itself: Two years after the conflict, Kosovo is neither democratic nor prosperous, its border neither well-defined nor peaceful. That the conclusion of NATO's first significant war found the Supreme Allied Commander Europe, General Wesley Clark, ending his tenure not with a victory parade, but with an unceremonious summons to leave his position early seemed somehow oddly appropriate. Clark's humiliating removal (to make room for a loyal lieutenant of the secretary of defense) was just one more reminder that from start to finish, this war—launched by former antiwar activists and draft evaders against a Balkan thug who seemed a throwback to a vintage "B movie"—had been at least slightly bizarre. Why, then, should we care about the war over Kosovo?

In different ways, the authors of this work reply, "because it has important things to tell us about the way developed countries will wage war in years to come." Far more than the Persian Gulf War of 1991, which had showcased much of the technology on display in Kosovo, Operation Allied Force exposed the limits of the military capabilities that the United States and its allies had developed to wage the Cold War. Whereas the Gulf War lent itself to neat, if misleading and indeed specious lessons learned, Kosovo stands as an uncomfortable warning about even the lopsidedly successful use of force. No amount of self-congratulation or spin in Brussels or Washington could mask the war's discomforts and anomalies, the bickering and mistakes of its leaders, their lapses and misjudgments.

A New Era of Warfare?

Every century, it seems, has its typical form of large scale war: The eighteenth century had its cabinet wars fought with cruel politeness for districts of Europe and swathes of North America; the nineteenth century its mass wars for the creation and exaltation of nation states; the twentieth century its total wars, unlimited in the ambitions that inspired them and the carnage they produced. The twentieth century's last great conflict, the Cold War, had the potential to devastate the planet in one global spasm between two vast blocks of nations armed and prepared for war on the largest scale. Small wars have always existed as a kind of counterpoint to the main event—colonial skirmishing, imperial policing, and eventually revolutionary war as well. These wars shaped, and were in turn shaped by, the larger conflicts for which they were often precursors, interludes, or sequels. For a brief moment of time after the fall of the Berlin Wall and the collapse of the Soviet Union—the events of 1989–91 that marked the real end of the twentieth century—it seemed as if both large and small wars might become obsolete.

Unfortunately, however, events soon proved that peace was not, after all, at hand. The Cold War's gratifying denouement yielded not reconciliation but heightened violence and new fears. The Gulf War did not end substantial international conflict. Epidemics of internal conflicts plagued nations in Europe, Africa, Asia, and Latin America. "Ethnic cleansing" became a seemingly commonplace phrase, while at the other end of the spectrum of conflict India and Pakistan engaged in nuclear posturing, and evidence grew that weapons of mass destruction were becoming increasingly available to the developing world. A rising military power, China periodically flexed its muscles, threatening Taiwan and asserting its claim to various small islands in the western Pacific. Exploiting the openness that is the defining characteristic of globalization, other problems commanded attention: narco-trafficking, international organized crime, and a new breed of cyber-anarchists. Incidents of terrorism occurred with sufficient frequency to persuade many observers that it posed the most insidious and perhaps the most dangerous threat of all.

The international community and major powers such as the United States responded to these developments with an odd combination of boldness and hesitation, at times acting with singular determination, as in the Persian Gulf in 1990, at other times doing next to nothing, as in Rwanda in 1994. When the international community did act—usually but not always with the United States in the van—the results were mixed.

The new century began, in any event, as an era of intense military activity. No nation manifested this more clearly than the United States, the world's sole military superpower. In the 1990s, to an extent that was never the case during the Cold War, the use of force by the United States became routine. Throughout his two terms in the White House, Bill Clinton, the first post–Cold War president, employed American military power more often, in more places, and for more varied purposes than any of his predecessors. For the United States, the military history of the 1990s is, first of all, a story of unprecedented—and, given Clinton's personal background, unexpected—activism.

To be sure, in comparison with any of the "real" armed conflicts of the twentieth century—the World Wars, Korea, Vietnam, or even the Persian

Gulf—Kosovo ranks as a puny event, more on a par with an exercise in old-fashioned gunboat diplomacy than an actual war. Western publics, the American chief among them, have seemingly endorsed this view. A year after the last allied bomb fell on Belgrade the war had all but vanished from public consciousness. Operation Allied Force faded into the ranks of myriad other military actions of the 1990s—cruise missile strikes, bombing campaigns, and armed interventions—that briefly qualified as newsworthy and then were quickly forgotten. Yet in many respects, this strange little war, not the much larger and more spectacular conflict with which the 1990s began, holds the key to understanding that decade—and with it, the emerging security challenges of the twenty-first century.

The Persian Gulf War, which sealed the end of twentieth-century warfare, was supposed to have settled things, an expectation vividly captured in President George Bush's exclamation that the United States had at long last "kicked the Vietnam syndrome." But Americans persuaded themselves—and much of the rest of the world—that victory in the Gulf had resolved more than simply a reluctance to use force carried over from Vietnam. The war put to rest nagging doubts about the basic competence of American arms. It seemingly affirmed the effectiveness of an approach to warfare—to include a preference for employing "overwhelming force"—that the Pentagon had developed and refined over the previous fifteen years. Operation Desert Storm demonstrated the capacity of U.S. forces to integrate and employ cutting edge technology. It set an ostensibly powerful precedent for how the United States would put its vast military power to service on behalf of American diplomacy in the aftermath of the Cold War. It demonstrated beyond the shadow of a doubt that the experiment with an All Volunteer Force had succeeded: The nation embraced "the troops" as the finest that America had to offer. The U.S. military emerged from the war as the embodiment of American greatness. By no means least of all, the war healed the cleavage that since Vietnam had existed between soldiers and civilians and had bred an especially acute antagonism between the officer corps and civilian elites.

In fact, as events would soon make clear, Operation Desert Storm left unsettled more than it had resolved. By the end of 1992, evidence that the Persian Gulf War was less than advertised had already become irrefutable. The victorious commander in chief George Bush had been dismissed from office; the putative loser, Saddam Hussein, remained in power in Baghdad, as he does even today, unbowed and defiant. To replace Bush, Americans had elected a president who brought with him all of the Vietnam-induced divisiveness that Desert Storm had supposedly laid to rest. Even before Bill Clinton became commander in chief, the services were already embroiled in the first of a never-ending series of embarrassing scandals—the Navy's Tailhook fiasco. Meanwhile, a variety of arduous new commitments—large-scale humanitarian interventions into northern Iraq and Somalia, for example—were making short work of expectations that the chief raison d'être of the post–Cold War military would be to fight and quickly win the occasional conventional war.

Reflections on a One-Sided War

The inspiration for this small collection of essays stems from our conviction that Kosovo provides a made-to-order opportunity to assess the implications of the changing international security environment, especially for the United States and its military, in the decade since Operation Desert Storm. This seemingly trivial Balkan war offers an invaluable window through which to gain perspective on the evolving military history of the new century, and with it the Age of Globalization, particularly as it pertains to the United States.

What follows is not a comprehensive narrative of the war as such: This is a task that others will undertake, and in some measure already have.[1] Rather, our intent is to place the war for Kosovo into a broader context. Contributors offer commentary from a variety of perspectives. William Arkin provides a concise account and critical analysis of the air campaign itself. He describes an operation in which the technology worked remarkably well, but in which the high command was internally divided, blundering, and in many ways unprepared for fighting a war in an age of instantaneous sharing of information around the world. Eliot Cohen sees Operation Allied Force as an event bringing into focus a new American approach to war, one that marks a radical break from past practice that originated in the nineteenth century. The difficulty, in his view, lies in the lag between American doctrine and institutions, on the one hand, and the new realities on the other. James Kurth assesses the conflict as an expression of a U.S. grand strategy that since the end of the Cold War has become ever grander. He sees in it, however, recklessly bad strategy, which ignores the interests of potential rivals such as China and Russia and therefore invites future complications. His pessimism finds an echo in Anatol Lieven, who situates NATO's neo-imperial disciplining of the Serbs within the larger tradition of Western military imperialism. At the tactical and operational levels, Lieven argues, Western military superiority is more apparent than real, and he turns to the Russian experience in Chechnya to illuminate his point. Alberto R. Coll explores the troubling moral questions raised by NATO's bombing campaign, both in terms of what the use of force accomplished and what it failed to do. Andrew Bacevich uses the war as a point of departure for reflecting on the evolving and increasingly problematic relationship between soldiers and American society. Finally, Michael Vickers uses Operation Allied Force to assess the American response to the ongoing "Revolution in Military Affairs." Contrary to those who saw in Kosovo a demonstration of new technological capabilities, Vickers is struck by the increasing age of the American arsenal and the unwillingness of those who design and employ that arsenal to break out of a Cold War mold.

Although as editors we confess to feeling at best ambivalent and at worst discouraged about most of the trends that Kosovo has revealed, we do not pretend that the essays that follow present a unified view of the war. When it comes to particulars, our contributors differ among themselves. They may not agree with one another that the war should have been fought at all; they may bring to their analyses different degrees of pessimism about the long-term prospects of conventional military power in a world of low-intensity war. What we all share in common, however, is a conviction that NATO's strange little war against Yugoslavia merits something more than self-congratulation or instant oblivion. As they enter a decade that will prove no less unpredictable than that just passed, the United States and its allies would do well to heed the cautionary tale that emerges from the war over Kosovo.

Note

1. See Ivo H. Daalder and Michael E. O'Hanlon, *Winning Ugly: NATO's War to Save Kosovo* (Washington, D.C.: Brookings Institution, 2000) for a straightforward narrative account of the war.

Contributors

William M. Arkin is a defense expert, independent writer, and consultant. He is a columnist for the Web edition of the *Washington Post* and for the *Bulletin of the Atomic Scientists* and serves as a military analyst for MSNBC. Mr. Arkin consults for Human Rights Watch, the largest human rights organization in the United States, and the Natural Resources Defense Council.

Andrew J. Bacevich is professor of international relations at Boston University, where he also serves as director of the university's Center for International Relations. His most recent book, written with Eliot A. Cohen and Michael Eisenstadt, is *Knives, Tanks, and Missiles: Israel's Security Revolution* (1998).

Eliot A. Cohen is professor of strategic studies at the Paul H. Nitze School of Advanced International Studies of the Johns Hopkins University and is the founding director of the Center for Strategic Education there. In addition to publishing several books related to strategy and military affairs, he serves as military book review editor of *Foreign Affairs* and is a contributing editor with *The New Republic.*

Alberto R. Coll is dean of the Center for Naval Warfare Studies at the United States Naval War College. He is the author of two books and numerous articles on the relationship of morality to statecraft and grand strategy, has served on the advisory board of *Ethics and International Affairs*, and was a principal deputy assistant secretary of defense in the first Bush Administration.

James Kurth is Claude Smith Professor of Political Science at Swarthmore College. Professor Kurth is the author of more than sixty essays and the editor of two volumes relating to international politics and defense and foreign policy, including a series of articles in *The National Interest* examining the interactions between the global economy, postmodern society, culture, and American grand strategy.

Anatol Lieven is senior associate for foreign and security policy in the Russia and Eurasia Center of the Carnegie Endowment for International Peace in Washington. He served previously as correspondent for *The Times* (London) and covered the conflicts in Afghanistan, the southern Caucasus, and Chechnya. His latest book, *Ukraine and Russia: A Fraternal Rivalry*, was published in 1999 by the United States Institute of Peace.

Michael G. Vickers is director of strategic studies for the Center for Strategic and Budgetary Assessments, a Washington-based think tank specializing in military strategy, the defense budget, and the emerging revolution in military affairs (RMA). A former U.S. Army Special Forces officer and CIA operations officer with extensive operational experience, he has published extensively on matters relating to military technology and the RMA.

War Over Kosovo

1 Operation Allied Force: "The Most Precise Application of Air Power in History"

William M. Arkin

At two in the afternoon Washington time, 8:00 P.M. local time on March 24, 1999, the North Atlantic Treaty Organization (NATO) initiated offensive military operations against Yugoslavia. Thirteen (of 19) NATO members committed aircraft, and eight put their planes in action to bomb a sovereign nation that had attacked neither any alliance members nor its neighbors.[1]

Operation Allied Force came after more than a year's effort by the six-nation Contact Group (including Russia) to find a negotiated solution to stop Serbian human-rights violations in Kosovo, one of four jurisdictions of the Federal Republic of Yugoslavia (FRY).[2] In 1998, systematic violence against ethnic Kosovar Albanians erupted, and by the fall an estimated 250,000 Albanians had been driven from their homes by Yugoslav military and paramilitary forces. Intelligence agencies predicted that tens of thousands were threatened by approaching winter weather. The situation prompted the United Nations Security Council to adopt resolution 1199 (UNSCR 1199) on September 23, calling for a cease-fire and the return home of refugees and the internally displaced.[3]

Throughout the crisis, NATO had prepared and refined military options to amplify the diplomatic process. "Activation warnings" for two different air operations were issued the day after the Security Council passed UNSCR 1199. One operation was known as the Flexible Anvil "Limited Air Response" and the other as the Allied Force "Phased Air Campaign."[4] Flexible Anvil, relying predominantly on cruise missiles, "was designed as a quick-strike, limited-duration operation, primarily to be used in response to a specific event."[5]

Richard Holbrooke, the Clinton administration's chief Balkan troubleshooter, departed for Belgrade on October 5 to meet with Yugoslav President Slobodan Milosevic. To demonstrate allied resolve, NATO on October 13 issued a higher activation "order," threatening air action. In the face of this threat, Milosevic seemingly gave way. He agreed to reduce Serbian security forces in Kosovo and to permit international verification missions in and over the province. The North Atlantic Council (NAC) agreed to a "pause" in its threats, and in late October it suspended execution permission for air operations.[6]

After a brief period when conditions in Kosovo seemingly stabilized, attacks against ethnic Albanians resumed. On January 15, 1999, a massacre of 45 civilians allegedly occurred in the village of Racak. The Contact Group called on both sides to end the cycle of violence, summoning representatives of the Belgrade government and Kosovar Albanians to Rambouillet, France, for direct discussions on how to end the violence in Kosovo. On January 30, the NAC authorized NATO Secretary General Javier Solana to commence air strikes against Yugoslav targets if an agreement was not reached.

But the Rambouillet talks ended unsuccessfully on March 19, and NATO began preparations to initiate bombing. Days before the talks broke down, Belgrade launched "Operation Horseshoe," its methodical campaign of ethnic cleansing—Yugoslav troops and 300 tanks were massing in and around Kosovo.[7] Holbrooke once again flew to Belgrade on March 22 in a last-ditch effort to bring Milosevic to terms. That same day, the NAC authorized Solana, subject to further consultations, to ready a broader range of air options.[8] NATO planned initially to conduct a two-day demonstration strike hitting targets throughout Yugoslavia "in an attempt to convince Milosevic to withdraw his forces and cease hostilities." Two escalating response options would back up the 48-hour plan: the first, a response to continued Yugoslav acts in Kosovo, and the second, a response to aggression against NATO.[9]

Many in the NATO leadership and member governments remained hopeful that a show of force would compel Milosevic to yield. "There was that abiding belief . . . that the campaign will last two nights and that after two nights, Mr. Milosevic would be compelled to come to the table," said one senior U.S. general.[10] After the fact, U.S. officials claimed that they had cautioned allied leaders not to initiate strikes unless they were willing to escalate and go all the way. But there is no evidence that the principal players—Solana, Holbrooke, and General Wesley Clark, the Supreme Allied Commander Europe (SACEUR), in particular—questioned expectations that limited strikes would succeed in coercing Milosevic.[11]

This chapter describes the 78-day air war that ensued—from its diffident beginning on March 24 until its abrupt conclusion on June 10. The focus is on the military dimensions of Operation Allied Force: the conduct and the evolution of the bombing campaign that became in the eyes of its proponents "the most precise application of air power in history."

The Plan

Every military operation begins with a plan, and Operation Allied Force began life as NATO OPLAN 10601. The official history says that preparation of 10601 began in response to a NATO directive in June 1998. In reality General Wesley Clark, who was both SACEUR and commander in chief (CINC) of United States European Command, directed General John Jumper, commanding U.S. Air Forces in Europe, to begin developing options for an air war a month before, in May. In other words, U.S. planning for what would become Operation Allied Force began prior to and proceeded separately from the planning effort within NATO. This penchant for "U.S. only" planning reflected Washington's greater propensity to use force, an assertion of American prerogatives as the dominant partner in the North Atlantic community, and the complicated relationship of Clark, as the theater CINC, with his air-warfare subordinates. As part of the American effort to portray the U.S. role as "supporting [and] not leading" the NATO effort, attempts were made to portray the separate track as existing only to the very limited extent that operational security demanded it.[12] But even as the conflict began, separate NATO and "U.S. only" tracks continued, with alliance members denied the details of U.S. cruise-missile strikes and operations by B-2 and F-117 stealth aircraft.

Between the summer of 1998 and March 1999, NATO and U.S. planners examined an assortment of alternatives, from the limited air response to a robust "U.S. only" option called Nimble Lion, and even to "forced entry" ground campaigns. Planners found themselves responding to General Clark's ever changing "commander's intent," which provided guidance on what targets would or would not be hit in Yugoslavia. First Clark asked for a plan that would focus on five key radio-relay nodes, then for an unlimited campaign, then for strikes limited to below the 44 degree north longitude, then for a campaign employing cruise missiles only, then for one executed exclusively by U.S. and British forces. Throughout, however, certain key requirements remained fixed: Minimize collateral damage, avoid any friendly losses, and preserve the Yugoslav civil infrastructure.[13]

According to General Clark, shifting military priorities reflected an absence of political consensus. "There simply was no consensus on the part of the nations to lay in place the full array of military options," he would later testify.[14] In some ways, then, from the very beginning the prospect of escalation was implicit in any "plan." Alliance members who were determined to use force were willing to sacrifice military realism to secure political unity, believing that, once military action had begun, NATO would have no choice but to expand operations as conditions required. Should a mere show of force be unsuccessful, doubting parties would be lobbied to agree to do more.

By the time Allied Force commenced, NATO had gone through more than 40 iterations of the air-campaign plan. The version actually initiated on March 24 included three combat phases. Phase 1 would establish air superiority over Kosovo and degrade command and control throughout Yugoslavia. Phase 2 would attack military targets in Kosovo and those Yugoslav forces providing reinforcement into Kosovo south of 44 degrees north latitude. Phase 3 would expand air operations against a wide range of military and security-force targets throughout Yugoslavia, including the capital city Belgrade. If Phase 1 did not force the Serbian leadership to accede, Phase 2 and 3 would up the ante.[15]

Within each phase, significant disagreements existed inside both the U.S. and NATO militaries with regard to strategy and priorities. Those engaged in Nimble Lion planning wrestled with a host of constraints: targets within Montenegro were restricted, and critical command and control nodes—particularly telephone exchanges—remained off limits due to concerns about collateral damage, as did electrical-power generating plants and television transmitters. One effect of the restrictions was to preclude a concentrated effort in the initial 48 hours to neutralize Yugoslav air defenses. The ostensible priority at the outset of hostilities would be to establish air supremacy, but the constraints actually worked against that goal.

Looking beyond the 48-hour bombing "demonstration," General Clark and his air-warfare commander, U.S. Air Force Lieutenant General Michael Short, disagreed fundamentally about the proper design of an extended campaign. Should it concentrate on "strategic" targets in Yugoslavia or on "tactical" targets throughout Kosovo? Short believed that "Body bags coming home from Kosovo didn't bother Milosevic, and it didn't bother the leadership elite."[16] Taking Desert Storm's 1991 strikes on Iraq as his model, he argued for delivering a powerful strategic blow against the Serb leadership in Belgrade. "I believe[d] the way to stop ethnic cleansing was to go at the leadership . . . and put a dagger in that heart as rapidly and as decisively as possible," he told Congress after the war.[17]

Clark, applying what Vice Admiral Daniel J. Murphy, commander of NATO naval forces, called "a ground commander's perspective," had other ideas.[18] He wanted Yugoslav forces to bear the brunt of NATO's attacks. His focus was not only the perpetrators of ethnic cleansing on the ground in Kosovo, but also special police and paramilitary forces throughout Yugoslavia.

Among army officers, a belief that wars are ultimately decided on the ground is an article of faith. But if Clark was affected by service bias, other matters also weighed heavily on his thinking. He, and not General Short, was directly responsible for translating political guidance into operational plans. He, not his air commander, appreciated how fragile and tentative was the consensus within the alliance in support of any military action. If commanders became too insistent in demanding a more aggressive approach to using force, they would undermine that consensus and—without a shot having been fired—hand Slobodan Milosevic a victory.

Thus, from his vantage point in Belgium, Clark concluded that his political masters would never agree to opening the war with a Desert Storm–style all-out air assault on Belgrade. Advocating only the most modest bombing campaign enabled Clark to reassure those alliance members hoping that Milosevic might yet have a rapid change of mind. Doing so also seemed to signal that NATO's military chiefs saw no need even to consider mounting a ground invasion, a prospect that several members of the alliance were unwilling to countenance even as a theoretical possibility.

In short, NATO began the war without having achieved any consensus on what the alliance would do if the hostilities extended beyond 48 hours. Although the very fact that it was a "phased" campaign implied the possibility of escalation, the alliance had postponed any decision on what that escalation would entail. Clark and his civilian masters would play it by ear: if Milosevic did not quickly cave in during Phase 1, there would be opportunity to escalate and accommodate alternative approaches.

In practice, this was an invitation to do a little of everything. As General Henry Shelton, chairman of the Joint Chiefs of Staff, said three weeks into the war, the idea was to "gain and maintain air superiority, to put pressure on the Serb leadership by attacking those fielded forces in Kosovo, as well as other leadership and high-priority targets throughout the country, and then to degrade the Serb military capabilities to conduct offensive operations."[19] "Demonstrate, deter, damage, degrade," read other articulations of military objectives.[20] The four "Ds" permitted commanders and politicians alike to extend the bombing beyond Phase 1 with some semblance of purposefulness without committing themselves to having an immediate effect on the ground in Kosovo. To publics that had endorsed NATO's military action with the expectation that bombing would stop the Yugoslav military in its tracks—even Clark in a moment of candor said that his mission "was to halt or disrupt a systematic campaign of ethnic cleansing"—the four "Ds" seemed vague to the point of being devoid of meaning.[21] It is no wonder that the Defense Department would say that the objectives of Operation Allied Force had to be "refined" as the war proceeded.[22]

The plan actually executed on March 24, accommodating the differing notions of air power entertained by both Clark and Short, included both a "strategic attack line" and "a tactical line of operation." The former concentrated on Serb air defenses, command and control, forces of the Yugoslav army, and Ministry of Interior, along with the infrastructure, supply routes, and resources that sustained those forces. The tactical line of operation focused on those Serb forces actually deployed in Kosovo and southern Serbia.[23] Altogether there were eight fixed target groups: airfields and air-defense missile sites and facilities comprising the Integrated Air Defense System (IADS); leadership (or "counter-regime" targets as they were officially called); command, control, communications, computers, and intelligence (C4I); ground forces along with ammunition/military storage and border posts; electrical power; petroleum; lines of communications; and military industry. A ninth "crony" target set was unofficially added in early May, encompassing facilities judged to be of personal, financial, or psychological importance to Milosevic and his associates.[24]

Once the haggling among allies—across civil-military lines, and between services—reached a conclusion, preparations took on the assembly-line atmosphere now standard in any high-intensity air war. As planners moved from the general to the specific, they produced a list of more than 600 prospective targets, with a subset of "approved" targets. Gaining actual approval to strike a target entailed a host of considerations:

> Is this a legitimate target [under international law]? How does it relate to our military goals? What role does it play in our opponent's system of operations and how will it affect him if it is destroyed? Can we constrain our intended damage to this target only? What is the likelihood of unintended damage and how can we minimize unintended damage by changing the time of day or the physical direction of the attack?[25]

Actual sorties were then choreographed in a way that would minimize collateral damage, avoid friendly losses, and preserve Yugoslavia's infrastructure. Reflecting these constraints, among the targets excluded from attack at the outset of the war were headquarters and ministries in "downtown" Belgrade, the electrical-power system, the telephone system, civilian television and radio, non-air-defense targets in Montenegro, dual-purpose industry, and anything that posed the risk of substantial civilian casualties.[26]

Phase 1 would open with strikes mostly against early-warning, air-defense, and military-command and control elements; and ground-force installations, particularly special police and other armed "counter-terrorism" and palace-guard organizations.[27] Follow-on targets, including ground units and supporting installations, were intended to isolate and immobilize Yugoslav forces. The hope, according to General Shelton, was to limit the ability of Yugoslav forces "to move both horizontally [and] laterally on the battlefield" by damaging the road and bridge network and denying units in the field access to the petroleum supplies essential to the operation of mechanized forces.[28]

But most of this was mere window dressing. The *real* plan rested on a single unstated assumption: As soon as Milosevic saw that NATO meant business, he would sue for terms.

Phase 1

Operation Allied Force actually began with U.S. and British air- and sea-launched cruise-missile attacks, followed by a pair of B-2 stealth bombers,

F-117 stealth fighters, and two waves of additional strike aircraft from the United States, Britain, France, Canada, Spain, and Germany. It was the first combat use of the long-range stealth bomber, which flew exhausting missions from the United States to deliver, also for the first time, satellite-guided bombs, released from altitudes of 40,000 feet. In all, during the first night of the war there were four separate waves, with a total of 214 U.S. and 130 allied aircraft. Those attackers dropped just over 100 laser-guided bombs, and launched 27 conventional air-launched cruise missiles (CALCMs), Tomahawk sea-launched cruise missiles, high-speed antiradiation missiles (HARMs), and 8 air-to-air missiles. Compared to the Gulf War, the scope of the effort was modest in the extreme.[29]

By 6:00 A.M. on March 25, NATO reported that it had hit 53 targets.[30] According to the alliance, early-warning radar and air-defense headquarters, command posts, and communications centers had received particular attention, though a couple of industrial and oil targets were also struck. About 20 percent of the targets were Yugoslav army and paramilitary barracks, headquarters, and ammunition depots.

From the very outset, President Bill Clinton made it clear that American ground troops would not be committed to the fight.[31] "What we have indicated to the Congress and to the country is that this is an air operation," Secretary of Defense William Cohen said at his first press conference.[32] Indeed, there would be no need for ground troops because the operation was expected to conclude in short order. Appearing on PBS's *Newshour* the first night, Secretary of State Madeleine Albright breezily announced the administration's expectations. "I don't see this as a long-term operation," she predicted.[33]

Yet the same night, General Shelton gave reporters a different message, indicating that Operation Allied Force would "continue until such time as we achieve our objectives." The campaign, he said, was not "time-phased." As to the precise definition of those objectives, the Pentagon was less clear. "We are determined to discourage and deter [Milosevic] from continuing waging his assault against the Kosovar people," Shelton said. "We are doing that in a way that will send a message." "We would like very much for Mr. Milosevic to stop his slaughter of innocent people," added Secretary Cohen. "In the event he fails to do so, we will continue to damage his capability of waging that in the future."[34]

News reports from Yugoslavia March 25 indicated that, far from stopping the slaughter, Serb forces in Kosovo were actually intensifying their ethnic cleansing.[35] "Operations by the Serbs in Kosovo have continued," acknowledged National Security Adviser Samuel R. ("Sandy") Berger. "I think that pattern has continued and, if anything, has somewhat increased."[36]

President Clinton may have stated that NATO's goal was "to protect thousands of innocent people in Kosovo from a mounting military offensive,"[37] and Secretary-General Solana may have claimed that "we are doing our best to stop the killing which is taking place at this very moment in Kosovo,"[38] but the fact is that Phase 1 was never intended to physically prevent Yugoslav forces from continuing their offensive in Kosovo. To the extent that Phase 1 air operations had anything to do with Yugoslav forces in the field, they were designed simply to deter those forces, not to destroy them. In an interview on CNN on March 26, General Clark said, "It was *always* understood from the outset that there was no way we were going to stop these paramilitary forces who were going in there and murdering civilians in these villages."[39]

Having justified its attack on Yugoslavia as necessary to halt a campaign of ethnic cleansing, NATO found itself conducting air operations largely irrelevant to that purpose. Moreover, Clark and his commanders faced the unwelcome prospect of conducting a military campaign of indeterminate length, with political restrictions on their use of air power, and a seemingly irrevocable prohibition on the use of ground forces. "We are going to systematically and progressively attack, disrupt, degrade, devastate and ultimately destroy these forces and their facilities and support," General Clark asserted on March 25, "unless President Milosevic complies with the demands of the international community. In that respect the operation will be as long and difficult as President Milosevic requires it to be."[40] It was a bold statement indeed, but it contained more than a smidgen of bluff. Unfortunately for Clark, others—not least of all Clinton, Albright, and Cohen—had given Milosevic enough hints to enable him to see through that bluff.

Critics of Allied Force found fault with more than just its operational flaws. Diplomatically, the harshest criticism of NATO came from Russia and China, who demanded an immediate end to bombing. President Boris Yeltsin suspended cooperation with NATO, warning that Moscow reserved the right to take "adequate measures" if the conflict worsened. But within NATO and in the United States, many wondered whether or not the gradualist approach and the preclusion of ground troops had merely emboldened Milosevic's forces. "These bombs are not going to do the job," Senator John McCain told the *New York Times*, reflecting a commonly stated complaint.

"It's almost pathetic. . . . You'd have to drop the bridges and turn off the lights in Belgrade to have even a remote chance of changing Milosevic's mind. What you'll get is all the old Vietnam stuff—bombing pauses, escalation, negotiations, trouble."[41]

Meanwhile, the Yugoslav people reacted to bombing by blaming NATO, not Milosevic, for their predicament. NATO's restraint may actually have encouraged a resurgence of Serb nationalism and popular defiance. As one U.S. Air Force study noted, in the early stages of the war, life in Belgrade went on virtually as normal: "Buses ran, shops were open, and people went to cafes and restaurants. . . . The Yugoslav people felt they could carry on with their lives since they were not being harmed."[42] Serb solidarity and determination may have encouraged Milosevic to believe that he could wait NATO out—that the allied consensus would weaken or that international pressure would force an end to the bombing without obliging him to make any concessions. "What we saw was a solidification of the [Yugoslav] political will," says Jumper.[43]

Phase 2

Given Belgrade's refusal to play by the 48-hour script and with the first of a massive tide of Kosovar Albanian refugees arriving in neighboring countries, the NAC decided on March 27 to escalate the air campaign to Phase 2. At his departure for Camp David on March 28, President Clinton in a statement at the White House said: "I strongly support Secretary General Solana's decision yesterday to move to a new phase in our planned air campaign, with a broader range of targets including air defenses, military and security targets, and forces in the field." The key reference that indicated a change in emphasis was Clinton's mention of forces in the field. Its hopes for a prompt resolution of the crisis now dashed, NATO, in the words of British Defense Minister George Robertson, had "agreed that the range of targets for our air strikes should be broadened and the attacks intensified to focus increasingly on the forces involved in the repression."[44]

With the beginning of Phase 2, the disagreements between Generals Clark and Short over the proper use of air power became more pronounced. Escalation had not removed the restrictions on targets that Short classified as "strategic," including "downtown" Belgrade, the electrical-power grid, and civilian communications facilities. Even certain air defenses could not be attacked to Short's satisfaction due to continuing concerns about collateral damage. On the other hand, the promise to go after the perpetrators of repression turned out to be less than advertised, Short arguing that pursuing mobile forces in the field would put his pilots at risk. Although Clark wanted to intensify the attacks on Serb units in Kosovo, he was hamstrung by his own insistence that there be no allied losses. In effect, he was unable to persuade his own subordinate to carry out his intended purpose. In the end, attacking Serb forces in Kosovo meant bombing fixed facilities such as garrisons and headquarters buildings, most of them probably empty.

With elusive air defenses still surviving in Kosovo, and Yugoslav forces dispersing, Phase 2 had little effect. Strikes against air defenses and infrastructure, Shelton said in an artfully phrased admission of how little was being achieved, continued to "set the conditions for moving on up to the forces in the field."[45] Given the continued refusal even to consider the introduction of NATO ground forces, claims that Serb ground forces had now become the real focus of attention served only to undermine further the campaign's credibility. There was little prospect that air power alone could physically stopping ethnic cleansing, conducted by small, scattered groups in villages throughout the province. From the perspective of allied pilots, attacking forces in Kosovo translated into hunting down and hitting individual vehicles—with negligible effect on the progress of Operation Horseshoe. Secretary Cohen would later claim that the attacks proceeded according to plan, creating the conditions that shifted the "balance of power" toward the Kosovo Liberation Army (KLA). NATO, he said after the war, had been "creating the possibility that the military efforts of the Kosovar Albanians, which were likely to grow in intensity as a result of Milosevic's atrocities in Kosovo, might be a more credible challenge to Serb armed forces."[46] But that is patent nonsense. In claiming that its Phase 2 efforts constituted a serious effort to stop ethnic cleansing by killing its perpetrators, NATO (and by extension the Clinton administration) was being either stupid or disingenuous.

With the shift to Phase 2, disagreement mounted within NATO as to who had the authority to approve additional targets. "There was some . . . confusion in terms of how this is going to operate, in terms of whether or not individual members had to approve or disapprove [targets]," Cohen admitted.[47] "Entire classes of targets were delegated for approval by NATO's military commanders," he said, and were subject to a variety of rules, as well as to an ultimate veto exercised initially by the United States and Great Britain.[48] The widening circle of approved targets did not, however, include "highly sensitive" categories such as the power grid or downtown Belgrade.

Yugoslav civilian casualties also proved an increasing irritant within NATO. Minimizing civilian casualties had always figured prominently in the planning and targeting process. Every target was "looked at in terms of [its] military significance in relation to the collateral damage or the unintended consequences that might be there," General Shelton said. "Then every precaution [was] made [sic] . . . so that collateral damage is avoided."[49] Assessments were performed by feeding prospective targets into several databases to determine whether any facilities off-limits to targeting . . . such as embassies, hospitals or places of worship—were nearby.[50] Using the blast radius of weapons and nearby population density, military planners used a four-tiered grading system to project civilian deaths and injuries likely to result from hitting a particular target. For "sensitive targets" these estimates were distributed directly to President Clinton, French President Jacques Chirac, and Prime Minister Tony Blair, who approved or canceled attacks, restricted the weapons employed, or modified the timing.[51]

Though the impression given by Yugoslav propaganda and a critical press might have suggested otherwise, civilian casualties in the opening days of the war were in fact kept extremely low. One reason was that the bombing effort itself was not all that intense.[52] And 100 percent of NATO weapons expended were precision-guided.[53] Between March 24 and 29, all weapons delivered were guided; only on the fifth day of the war did U.S. forces employ their first "dumb" bomb; only on the sixth day was the first cluster bomb employed. Severe restrictions requiring pilots to positively identify intended targets and to avoid possible civilian damage led to many mission terminations. Poor weather canceled entire waves.[54]

Bad weather or not, tension among key alliance members increased even more when Solana decided on his own volition on March 31 to further escalate the air campaign to Phase 2a (or 2-plus). As a result, on April 3, NATO conducted its first air strike against targets in central Belgrade, attacking the headquarters buildings of the Serbian and Federal Ministries of Interior. The French government protested, and after Presidents Chirac and Clinton consulted with one another they agreed that henceforth France would be informed in advance of any targets that carried a high risk of civilian casualties, as well as of planned attacks against the electrical grid, telephone system, or downtown Belgrade. Chirac specifically asked to review any targets in Montenegro.[55]

As infrastructure attacks expanded during the first week of April, NATO pilots were still wrestling with the daunting and complex problem of figuring out how to get at Yugoslav mobile forces. From experience during exercises and during the Gulf War, pilots and targeters knew that they had a "steep learning curve" to climb. Mountainous terrain, a well-dispersed foe who operated in small contingents and was well-armed with air defense weapons, the Serb tactic of hiding in villages or of using Kosovar Albanian refugees as human shields—all of these complicated the task. "It took all the technology we had to be able to track these guys, learn who they are, learn their habits, be able to predict what they're going to do next," said Jumper.[56]

Operation Allied Force had now lasted well beyond the 48 hours that many speculated would suffice to coerce Milosevic. As the war came increasingly to look like a protracted enterprise, the best that NATO spokesmen and leaders could say was that Milosevic was paying the price for his brutality. They vowed that the alliance would persist.

When Milosevic met with Russian Prime Minister Yevgeni Primakov in Belgrade on March 30, the Yugoslav leader offered a partial withdrawal of his forces from Kosovo if NATO would stop its air strikes, an offer NATO firmly rejected. Was air power indeed having an effect? Or was this just Milosevic's effort to create fissures within the alliance? Regardless, barely a week of bombing had occurred, and the alliance found itself increasingly on the defensive. "I think right now it is difficult to say that we have prevented one act of brutality," acknowledged Pentagon spokesman Kenneth Bacon, stating the obvious on the same day Milosevic met with Primakov. In an interview for CBS-TV, President Clinton pleaded with the American people to "have a little resolve here, to stay with your leaders, to give us a chance to really see this thing through. This air campaign is not a 30-second ad."[57]

Milosevic's War

Milosevic could not defeat NATO militarily. Though Russia was perceived as being in Yugoslavia's corner diplomatically, neither Russia nor China were willing to intervene to save Yugoslavia on the battlefield or in the Security Council. Milosevic's best bet was to erode NATO's political consensus. A combination of resolve, shooting down aircraft, taking prisoners, destabilizing Macedonia and Albania with refugees, and playing on civilian casualties and the image of Yugoslavia as unjust victim just might undermine the fragile public support for Allied Force within NATO. If Milosevic could frustrate NATO's expectations that it could win through air power alone, he might be able to force the alliance to consider the use of ground troops, which almost assuredly would divide the alliance.

In Kosovo, Yugoslav military planners calculated that they could defeat the KLA and expel (or kill) the Kosovar Albanian population in some five to seven days from the onset of hostilities. Some 40,000 Serbian troops were already in Kosovo, manning 859 tanks and 672 armored vehicles, supported by 1,163 artillery pieces.[58] Based on what they had observed in Operation Deliberate Force, NATO's two-week air campaign in Bosnia in 1995, Yugoslav commanders anticipated a demonstration attack and felt confident that they could sufficiently disperse and hide forces to neutralize NATO's air advantage. When bombing began, Yugoslavia did not aggressively challenge NATO aircraft. Fire control radars were not extensively used, negating NATO's electronic dominance. Mobile SA-6 SAM's and shorter-range antiaircraft artillery and man-portable air defense systems, of which there were many, moved frequently.[59]

Though Yugoslavia initially husbanded its high-altitude missiles and kept its radars "quiet" to thwart NATO's antiradiation missiles, General Short minimized the risk that these SAMs posed to his aircraft by requiring pilots to remain above 15,000 feet in altitude and by flying larger "packages" of strike aircraft accompanied by dedicated jammers and air-defense-suppression fighters. In this way, Short largely frustrated Milosevic's desire to shoot down NATO planes. But this came at a price: flying at high altitude made it even more difficult for NATO to positively identify and attack mobile ground forces.[60]

Even without radar, Yugoslavia fired 845 SAMs, mostly mobile SA-6s, during the course of the war.[61] Although Yugoslav air defenses managed to shoot down only two manned aircraft, by their very survival they contributed to another purpose useful to Milosevic, namely to increase the likelihood of NATO pilots making mistakes. In a sense, civilians paid twice for NATO's determination to avoid its own casualties: First, NATO's reluctance not to "get down in the weeds" and attack the perpetrators of ethnic cleansing facilitated the success of Operation Horseshoe; and second, bombing conducted from higher altitude (at least in the first month of so) reduced the accuracy of NATO pilots, increasing the likelihood of civilian casualties.

"We are taking all possible measures to minimize collateral damage or damage to innocent civilians or nearby property that is not associated with the target," General Clark stressed in his first press conference.[62] Yugoslavia was ready from the outset, using the Internet, state-run media, and an energetic and supportive Serb expatriate community to challenge this claim, charging that NATO was intentionally targeting civilians and civilian facilities. When it came to waging "information war," Belgrade seized the initiative, issuing a barrage of reports, dominating the news media, and sowing dissension within NATO.[63] As soon as the first day's air strikes occurred, Yugoslav Foreign Minister Zivadin Jovanovic was complaining that many civilians had already been killed.[64]

In fact there were no civilian casualties on the first night. Indeed, a week into the war, only a single civilian had been killed in all of NATO's attacks.[65] Yet Clark had to devote a good part of his day to reassuring allied militaries and governments on issues of civilian collateral damage. Despite what was happening on the ground, NATO was always on the defensive and never did succeed in putting Yugoslav's claims into perspective. By April 14, when as many as 73 civilians were killed on the road between Djakovica and Decane when pilots confused tractors pulling farm wagons with military vehicles, Belgrade had succeeded in conveying the impression that this was a regular occurrence.

To protect their own forces on the ground and confound targeting, Serb units intentionally operated among civilian refugees, in villages, and near prohibited targets such as churches.[66] When aircraft did start to go after ground elements in Kosovo, Yugoslavia also made use of a variety of camouflage, concealment, and deception efforts to fool NATO, employing a mix of low- and high-tech decoys.[67] The NATO rule, according to Short, was that "we had to put eyes on target every time we were going to strike a tank or an artillery piece."[68] Before the 15,000-feet restriction was lifted for certain attacks in Kosovo, that requirement, combined with poor weather, meant that far fewer attacks were actually undertaken than were attempted. Still, once attacks on mobile forces in Kosovo got underway around day thirteen, Yugoslav forces were forced to modify their operations.[69] According to Admiral Murphy, "We took away the roads, we took away the day time, . . . we forced them to hide under trees and inside barns."[70] But making life difficult for the Serb forces was not the same as rendering them ineffective.

In late April, just prior to the upcoming Washington NATO summit, General Clark received permission from Solana to begin quietly assessing possible ground options.[71] Within NATO there was still no political consensus to go forward with serious planning for a ground war. Yet the senior military staff at SHAPE headquarters was reportedly telling Clark, "If you want to induce the Serbs to leave Kosovo, you are going to have to use ground forces to do it." Clark also had two ulterior motives for wanting to initiate ground war planning. First, he wanted to shore up his support among American generals, particularly among skeptics in the Joint Chiefs of Staff and in the U.S. Army who were critical of his handling of the war thus far.[72] Second, he wanted to acquire leverage that he could use to expand the air campaign well beyond the parameters permitted by Phase 2. "One of the reasons we were successful in getting the go-ahead to go downtown," he would later testify, "was because it was an alternative to ground troops."[73]

Two weeks into what would become an eleven-week campaign, NATO leaders were insisting that they had always said that the campaign would be "difficult and time consuming."[74] The forces made available to Clark were increasing several fold. By week two, the number of aircraft had reached almost 600, an increase of almost one-third from March 24. Fourteen NATO members committed themselves to providing an additional 500 aircraft.[75] NATO also launched wide-ranging diplomatic efforts to convince Milosevic to pull back his military before bombing destroyed his country. This included, most centrally, enlisting Russia as a partner in the search for a diplomatic agreement. On the day of the Djakovica-Decane incident, the worst case of civilian deaths so far in the war, Yeltsin named former Prime Minister Vladimir Chernomyrdin as his presidential envoy on Kosovo. A week later, Yeltsin stated that Moscow "cannot break with leading world powers" over Kosovo, signaling the narrow limits of Russian support for Belgrade.

The Beginning of the End

The NATO Washington Summit starting on April 23 gave Milosevic his last chance to shatter the political consensus. Leaders and parliamentarians in Italy, Germany, and Greece had all at different times called for bombing pauses. Although the summit suggested the prospect of high drama, alliance leaders merely reconfirmed their commitment to the war and agreed to escalate the air campaign even further. Two decisions in particular were key: electricity and industrial infrastructure were added to the list of authorized targets, and attacks would henceforth occur on a round-the-clock basis.[76] Significantly, Phase 3 would not formally be requested, a move that would have required the NAC to certify a formal "consensus." Instead NATO leaders took the shortcut of authorizing Solana to decide on behalf of the NAC. Clark still had to "request specific additions to target categories," particularly those with "high political connotations."[77] The "U.S. only" targeting circle expanded slightly to include British planners and intelligence experts who would help identify likely targets amongst the personal property and businesses of Milosevic and his cronies.

NATO had already employed economic and political means—sanctions, tightened travel restrictions, frozen financial holdings—to foster "anxiety and discontent within Belgrade's power circles."[78] The United States had also undertaken "Operation Matrix," a covert operation that included harassing and pressuring Milosevic insiders by faxing and calling them on their cell phones.[79] Attacks on factories associated with Milosevic and his associates were used as threats to foment discontent in the inner circle and amongst the Serbian elite. Knocking out electrical power would begin to put pressure on the civilian population as a whole. "We were trying to find additional targets," said Deputy Secretary of Defense John Hamre. "We had hoped that the air campaign would have brought the Milosevic government to a realization that this was a losing cause earlier. . . . it went longer than we thought."[80] Explaining his rationale for attacking targets that just a month before had been considered illegitimate, Clark suggested that "Economic dislocations that are bound to affect the electricity and heating are going to charge up the opposition and bring greater pressure against [Milosevic]."[81]

As the air war proceeded into May, the tempo of attacks increased markedly, as did the resulting damage to the military and civilian infrastructure of Yugoslavia. At the same time, the KLA, which earlier had suffered a string of defeats at the hands of Yugoslav forces, began to regroup. There were signs that military defections and dissent amongst Yugoslav conscripts and reservists were mounting. For the first time since the war had begun, a number of mayors in Serbia were now speaking out against Milosevic. And families of service members were beginning to protest openly—not against NATO but against the regime.[82] NATO also announced on April 24 that, as a result of attacks on fixed SA-2 and SA-3 sites, it had formally achieved air superiority in the mid to high altitudes. General Short revised the applicable rules of engagement to allow certain aircraft to drop to lower altitudes. Attacks on Serb mobile forces in Kosovo finally started to show results.

By the beginning of May, NATO had conducted around 12,000 sorties, 3,500 of which were strikes on some 230 individual fixed targets. Yugoslavia's two oil refineries in Novi Sad and Pancevo were put out of action and sixteen oil storage depots were bombed. NATO aircraft hit a total of 31 fixed communication sites, including nineteen relays between Belgrade and the south. More than twenty road and rail bridges were damaged or destroyed (five over the Danube river in the north). About 20 percent of Yugoslavia's ammunition storage depots was assessed as significantly damaged, and 20 percent of army and paramilitary barracks had also been attacked.

Despite the declaration of air superiority, attacks on Yugoslav air defenses and airfields continued to absorb some 30 to 35 percent of the daily sorties in May. Although Yugoslav aircraft were shot down every time they challenged NATO in the skies, General Short insisted on the time-consuming (and smart-weapons-intensive) effort to destroy planes on the ground by attacking hardened aircraft shelters on Yugoslav air bases. Some 71 shelters were struck by early May with 40 listed as destroyed.

Even during Phase 3 continuing political constraints meant that outside of Kosovo itself Short did not have enough targets to attack. NATO's main effort continued to be against supporting infrastructure and supply lines, more bridges and transmitters, barracks and far-afield storage depots. Although NATO did hit some targets in downtown Belgrade, attacks there continued to be controversial, and targeters managed to get political approval to hit only three Yugoslav telephone exchanges, one in Pristina, Kosovo's largest city. Beginning on May 2, the post-summit emphasis on industry and the psychological targets added electrical distribution to the target list, a change that the alliance trumpeted as a sign that the campaign was coming into its own. "The fact that the lights went out across 70 percent of the country, I think, shows that NATO has its finger on the light switch in Yugoslavia now, and we can turn the power off whenever we need to and whenever we want to," NATO spokesman Jamie Shea said on May 3. By mid-May, 85 percent of Serbia was without power.

Each day in May set a new record in terms of the number of NATO's strikes, with some attacks now originating from NATO air bases in Hungary and Turkey. The number of attacks on Yugoslav forces in and around Kosovo steadily increased, with AC-130U gunships and B-52 bombers loaded with "dumb" bombs entering the fray for the first time. Yugoslav forces in Kosovo remained dispersed, able to operate only in small groups. But if that tactic enabled Serb units to evade the full brunt of NATO's air effort, it also inhibited their efforts to eliminate the KLA. Indeed, from its sanctuaries in Albania, Montenegro, and Macedonia, the KLA was finding a second wind.

Yugoslavia Withdraws

Yet as the air offensive entered Phase 3, the spectacle of public events and controversies eclipsed the campaign itself. The Reverend Jesse Jackson traveled to Belgrade to free three U.S. Army prisoners captured on the Macedonian border. The media reported that NATO was running short of cruise missiles and other guided weapons. The glacial deployment of U.S. Army attack helicopters to Albania and General Clark's inability to bring them into the war provoked both wonderment and sharp criticism. Mounting evidence of civilian collateral damage provoked continuing calls for bombing pauses from various NATO countries, suggesting that allied unity was becoming increasingly precarious. Criticism of the conduct of the war from prominent military historians and commentators, among them retired Army Colonel Harry Summers and John Keegan, mounted. Perhaps worst of all, a targeting error resulted in NATO's bombing of the Chinese embassy. All the while, the action that really counted progressed behind the scenes. Deputy Secretary of State Strobe Talbott, Russian special envoy Chernomyrdin, and Finnish President Martti Ahtisaari, representing the European Union, were engaged in intense negotiations with the Yugoslavs that looked for a way to end the war.

From inside Yugoslavia, independent press reports of civilian protest and speculation regarding growing dissatisfaction with Milosevic's leadership increased. Although NATO admitted that despite its best efforts fresh reserve troops and units were still entering Kosovo to augment the Yugoslav 3rd Army, it also claimed that the reinforcements were a sign of its own success—the additions were needed to replace combat casualties and exhausted troops. On May 20, President Clinton himself reported that "Each day, we hear reports of desertions in the Serbian army, dissension in Belgrade, unrest in Serbian communities."

Toward the end of May, with the support of American intelligence and Albanian artillery, the KLA mounted a counteroffensive. "This is the beginning of a new phase of aggression, the so-called land operation," Major General Vladimir Lazarevic, commander of the Yugoslav Pristina Corps, said.[83] Regardless of the ferocious debate inside NATO about the need for a ground war, Belgrade saw threatening signs that suggested NATO preparations for just that contingency.

When the International Criminal Tribunal for the Former Yugoslavia on May 27 indicted Milosevic for war crimes, time for the Serb dictator was running out. Despite an early shoot-down of a coveted F-117 stealth fighter, Yugoslavia had never been able to inflict any notable damage or any casualties on NATO. Despite collateral damage and the enormous discord over the mistaken bombing of the Chinese embassy, NATO remained united. Opposition to Belgrade within the international community as a whole, now including Russia, actually solidified as the war dragged on. Russia had actively joined NATO in pressing Milosevic to submit. And finally, the street parties in Belgrade had ended: After weeks of isolation and bombing, Serbs were exhausted. There were indeed increasing signs of popular unrest and dissatisfaction—Milosevic himself was potentially threatened by his own people.

As the air war peaked in intensity the last week of May, Yugoslavia began hinting that it would accept the set of principles proposed by the so-called Group of Eight. By implication, Belgrade was signaling a new willingness to withdraw all of its forces from Kosovo and to accept the deployment of an international peacekeeping contingent "with NATO at its core." On June 3, Belgrade formally accepted proposals drawn up and presented by Chernomyrdin and Ahtisaari, paving the way for NATO peacekeepers to occupy the province.

No one could say with certainty why Milosevic had capitulated when he did. U.S. officials were convinced that once NATO and Russia spoke with one voice the Serb dictator Milosevic concluded he had no other options.[84] "It's very difficult to say why tyrants give way because they have their own particular way of behaving," President Chirac said in an interview at the end of the war:

> But I think there were at least two things: the total isolation in which he found himself; he had, without any doubt, banked on Russia's direct or indirect support . . . and also on a split between the democracies, reputed to be weak, particularly the European democracies. . . . Secondly, his power . . . rested on a military and police system which has been considerably weakened by the air strikes to which he's been subjected. . . . So the very foundation of his power has, in a way, been degraded at both the technical and psychological levels, to the point when, as has been said, it was difficult for him to hold out any more.[85]

One very big question was the extent to which the bombing itself had contributed to Milosevic's decision. Was this indeed the first war won by air power alone?

The Score

On June 9, Operation Allied Force came to a close, 78 days after it had begun. In all, the alliance had flown a total of 38,004 sorties, of which 10,484 involved strikes on "strategic" and "tactical" targets while another 3,100 were suppression of air-defense missions.[86] By the end of the war, 829 aircraft from fourteen countries were available for tasking. Strike, electronic-warfare, reconnaissance, refueling, and support aircraft flew from some 47 locations in Europe and the United States.[87]

NATO had expended 28,236 weapons.[88] U.S. and British surface ships and submarines had fired some 218 Tomahawk sea-launched cruise missiles while B-52 bombers launched another 90 conventional air-launched cruise missiles (CALCMs).[89] A total of some 12,000 tons of munitions were expended.[90] Though the raw numbers suggest that an average of 362 weapons were dropped per day, 70 percent or more of the bombs were dropped in the war's final three weeks, meaning that, for the first eight weeks of the war, bombs delivered per day were closer to 150 in number. If the air war was having limited effect in the early days, more than weather and collateral damage constraints were to blame.

The United States was far and away the dominant player. The U.S. Air Force delivered 21,120 weapons (or 75 percent of the total). Including U.S. Navy and Marine Corps aircraft and missiles, weapons delivered by the United States numbered 23,506 (or 83 percent of the total).[91] A mere 22 heavy bombers—five B-1s, six B-2s, and eleven B-52s—delivered close to 12,000 weapons (constituting some 2,400 tons).[92] U.S. and allied planes were flying roughly equal numbers of strike missions at the end of the war,[93] but the vast majority of weapons were being dropped by U.S. aircraft. Notably, two-thirds of the U.S. strikes occurred at night.

By war's end, about 35 percent of all the weapons employed were precision-guided munitions (PGMs), more than three times the percentage expended in the 1991 Desert Storm campaign. In the early weeks of Operation Allied Force, "smart" weapons constituted more than 90 percent of the ordnance employed. By mid- to late-May, only 10 to 20 percent of the weapons dropped were guided. The United States delivered 6,728 PGMs, including the first combat use of the satellite-guided Joint Direct Attack Munition (JDAM) delivered by the B-2. The Joint Standoff Weapon, a long-range cluster bomb, was also used for the first time, being expended in small numbers by the U.S. Navy. JDAM, CALCM, and selected Tomahawk missiles were satellite-guided and therefore impervious to weather. Poor weather adversely affected the operation of all other guided weapons (with the exception of antiradiation missiles).

In all, according to the Defense Department, NATO attacked more than 900 targets, 421 of them fixed installations.[94] Of these, half were military facilities. Of the 421 fixed targets attacked, 232 were "destroyed" or sustained severe damage. Another 135 targets sustained "moderate" or "light" damage, and 51 sustained no damage (see Table 1.1). A total of some 9,815 "aim points" were designated at targets of all types, and 58 percent of these aim points were successfully struck with PGMs.[95] The extensive targeting of ground-force installations focused on paramilitary units and on paramilitary and army barracks, depots, and headquarters. NATO assessed that it had destroyed approximately 111,500 metric tons of Serb ammunition and military equipment. Although installations were bombed throughout the country, the majority of the targets were in Kosovo and in the southern portion of Serbia.

In total, some five hundred Yugoslav civilians were killed in incidents of collateral damage, and some nine hundred were injured.[96] Clark professed that NATO had "no estimate . . . whatsoever" of Yugoslav military deaths,[97] though some NATO sources were claiming 5,000 to 10,000 Yugoslav military casualties at the end of the war.[98] After the fact, Belgrade would report that 240 soldiers and 147 "policemen" were killed by NATO bombs.[99]

NATO attacked Yugoslavia's air defenses throughout the country, but never with sufficient intensity (or design) to neutralize the entire air-defense system. Key nodes in the command and control of the system remained intact at the end of the war. Although the Pentagon stated that two-thirds of the long-range SA-2/3 missile force and a "significant" quantity of mobile SA-6's were destroyed,[100] postwar studies found only three of eighty SA-6 launchers destroyed.[101] In all, Yugoslavia fired 845 SAMs, downing two NATO aircraft and 25 unmanned aerial vehicles.[102] A total of 1,200 Navy and Marine Corps EA-6B sorties were flown in support of air defense suppression, and U.S. and NATO aircraft fired 743 HARM missiles and expended 1,479 towed decoys. Air Force Chief of Staff General Michael Ryan boasted that Yugoslavia's eight airfields "were closed and much of their air defense infrastructure was destroyed."[103] Yugoslavia's air force sustained considerable damage, with shoot-downs or bombing destroying 121 aircraft and helicopters.[104]

TABLE 1.1 Operation Allied Force Targets and Assessed Damage

		Level of Damage				
Category	Total	Destroyed	Severe	Moderate	Light	None
Infrastructure						
Counter-regime	7	1	1	3	2	0
Electrical Power	19	6	0	0	9	4
POL	30	13	10	7	0	0
C4I	88	31	6	18	9	23
Bridges and railroads	68	39	8	2	6	12
Military industry	17	4	5	4	1	3
Military Forces						
Ground forces facilities	106	23	35	31	16	0
Border posts	18	5	3	5	3	2
Airfields	8	0	5	3	0	0
Air Defenses						
Integrated air defense system	28	12	4	6	4	2
SAM sites and facilities	32	15	6	5	1	5
Total	421	149	83	84	51	51

C4I: Command, control, communications, computers, and intelligence; POL: Petroleum, oil, and lubricants; SAM: Surface-to-air missiles.

Note: C4I counter-regime (leadership) categories include numerous strictly military headuarters, command posts, and communications facilities.

SOURCE: U.S. Air Force, Air War Over Serbia (AWOS) Study Group; data obtained by author.

Attacks on leadership and command and control included two of Milosevic's residences, a number of ministries and army headquarters, and a half-dozen underground command centers serving the government, military, and air-defense system. More than 30 percent of military and civilian relay networks were damaged, and the Pentagon rated national command, control, and communications (C3) capabilities in a "degraded status" by war's end. Though long-range transmitters were extensively hit, the telephone and cell-phone systems otherwise remained largely intact. Telephone communications had been a major target in the Gulf War, but remained largely off-limits due to collateral-damage concerns and allied investments.[105] Forty-five percent of TV broadcast capability was declared "non-functional," and by the end of the war radio broadcasts were limited to urban areas only.[106] Two major state broadcast houses were bombed, one in Belgrade and the other in Novi Sad, the attack in Belgrade killing 16 civilians.[107]

NATO reduced Yugoslavia's capacity to manufacture ammunition by two-thirds, eliminated its oil refining capacity at Pancevo and Novi Sad, and destroyed more than 40 percent of its military fuel supplies. Seventy percent of road bridges and 50 percent of rail bridges attacked throughout Serbia and Kosovo were damaged or destroyed.

Contrary to Yugoslav propaganda, NATO did not bomb water installations, dams, or pharmaceutical plants, and there were no attacks on food storage or other targets immediately affecting the survival of the civilian population. Electrical-transformer stations and power lines were attacked, first with new so-called "soft bombs" to short-circuit electrical distribution, and then later with laser-guided bombs. But electrical generation remained off-limits in an attempt to minimize the long-term effect of bombing on the civilian population.[108] Although by Phase 3 NATO was eager to pressure the civilian population, NATO legal officers intervened to keep many prospective targets off-limits. In some instances, legal review was compromised by inadequate intelligence, resulting in a number of steam-powered central-heating plants in urban areas being destroyed.

Although a "crony" targeting plan was developed in late April, only two targets associated specifically with this objective ended up being attacked. Nor is there any evidence that covert action associated with the crony strategy influenced Milosevic in his final decisions to agree to the Group of Eight principles.[109] As the war entered June, new targets had been approved for attack in the event that Milosevic rejected the Chernomyrdin and Ahtisaari proposal. These included the Yugoslav telephone system.[110]

While 3,000 to 5,000 weapons fell on "strategic" targets in Serbia and Montenegro, the great majority of NATO weapons were dropped in Kosovo, the majority of those against mobile forces. The effectiveness of NATO attacks on Yugoslavia's military and paramilitary in and around Kosovo has proven to be the most controversial aspect of Allied Force. Shortly after the cease-fire, NATO announced that about 47,000 Yugoslav troops and nearly 800 tanks, armored personnel carriers, and artillery guns had left Kosovo. That such a robust force should have survived to retire in good order immediately ignited controversy as to whether NATO during the war had been inflating its claims of what it had destroyed. General Clark told Congress in July that 110 tanks, 210 armored vehicles, and 449 artillery and mortar tubes had been hit.[111] For its part, Yugoslav propaganda was claiming that NATO had hit nearly 500 decoys but only 50 tanks.[112] Numerous articles in the Western media speculated that as little as one-tenth of NATO's damage claims against Yugoslav forces were actually true.

After a three-month assessment of missions flown against Yugoslav forces, Clark in September 1999 released slightly revised figures. A thorough survey by the Kosovo Strike Assessment evaluated some three thousand strike missions flown against mobile targets. In 1,955 of these strikes, pilots dropped weapons, and reported that they had hit 181 tanks, 317 armored vehicles, 600 other military vehicles, and 857 artillery guns and mortars. In the end, this study concluded that NATO aircraft had hit 93 tanks, 153 armored vehicles, 339 military vehicles, and 389 artillery pieces and mortars.[113]

After the war, yet another study group, the Allied Force Munitions Effectiveness Assessment Team (MEAT), visited Kosovo, inspecting 234 locations where mission reports stated that something had been hit. The team found evidence of bombing in 191 locations, but very little evidence of damaged or destroyed equipment. Although Clark claimed in September that the strike assessment had validated more than half of the reports as "successful strikes," the MEAT team could neither verify the mission reports filed by the pilots themselves nor find much evidence of equipment having been removed. On the other hand, the MEAT team did find a significant amount of damaged and destroyed equipment at locations *unrelated* to pilot mission reports.[114] Although the possibility that the Yugoslav army had removed the hundreds of missing vehicles during the war and their withdrawal could not be completely discounted, NATO failed to produce hard intelligence or evidence to substantiate its claim to have dealt the Serb forces in Kosovo a serious physical blow.

Who Shot John?

"NATO accomplished its mission and achieved all of its strategic, operational, and tactical goals in the face of an extremely complex set of challenges." So the Defense Department reported to Congress in October 1999.[115] The dust had hardly settled before competing postwar arguments were being made about which NATO actions "won" the war: Was it strikes in Kosovo and the looming "threat" of a ground war, as General Clark asserted, or was it infrastructure attacks on civilian morale targets such as electricity, media, and leadership, a thesis preferred by air-power advocates?

In truth, we may never know what drove Slobodan Milosevic to finally accede to NATO's demands. But given that Belgrade's strategy hinged on the belief that it could out-wait NATO, the very fact that the bombing continued and that the alliance hung together was probably more important than whether a particular target or group of targets had received a knockout blow. In the end, the phased air campaign that few actually expected to go beyond a couple of days had escalated and accelerated "according to plan." The target list had expanded as more aircraft became available and as NATO's political leaders shed their squeamishness. And the commanders organizing the missions and the pilots flying them proved sufficiently flexible and discriminative to accommodate themselves to the changing political climate in which they labored. But to see in Operation Allied Force the validation of any theory about warfare or doctrine would be sheer nonsense.

Speaking at the International Institute for Strategic Studies in London on the war's first anniversary, Lord Robertson, British Minister of Defense during Allied Force and Solana's successor as NATO Secretary-General, insisted that the alliance had been "absolutely right" to go to war, to act when and how it did. "It may not surprise you that I am saying this," he said, "but frankly, it surprises me that I have to keep repeating it."[116] Yet if NATO and U.S. officials sounded defensive about their victory, one reason was that criticism of Operation Allied Force, both during and after the war, was by no means limited to the usual quarters. Even people usually identified as air-warfare partisans disassociated themselves from NATO's war, complaining about the political and military constraints and about their inability to pursue some optimal air warfare strategy.

Among those complaining the loudest was Clark's own air commander. General Short believed that the conduct of Allied Force had been flawed from the outset. "I'd have gone for the head of the snake on the first night," he told Congress in October. "I'd have turned the lights out . . . dropped the bridges across the Danube . . . hit five or six political-military headquarters in downtown Belgrade." If Short had had his way, "Milosevic and his cronies would have woken up the first morning asking what the hell was going on."[117]

The conventional retort to General Short is that such an idealized air strategy was politically unacceptable. Still, even though Allied Force did not produce the instant gratification promised by Short's scenario, as the campaign progressed the weight of effort did slowly shift to broader "strategic" and infrastructure targets, allowing the Air Force to claim ultimate vindication. To General Ryan, the Air Force Chief of Staff, it was abundantly clear that Milosevic had capitulated because air power brought the war home to Serbia. "The lights went out, the water went off, the petroleum production ceased, the bridges were down, communications were down, the economics of the country were slowly falling apart, and I think he came to the realization that in a strategic sense, he wasn't prepared to continue this."[118] The "strategic center of gravity," Ryan said, "was in and around Belgrade[, the focus of] . . . support for Milosevic and his repressive regime."[119]

Ryan insists that no Air Force officer ever "believed that air power could stop directly the door-to-door infantry thuggery that was driving the Kosovars from their homes. Nor could air power directly stop the slaughter and war crimes that were taking place in isolated villages."[120] Similarly, Air Force General Joseph Ralston, vice chairman of the Joint Chiefs of Staff during the war (and Clark's replacement after the war), rejected the notion that airmen should be held accountable for NATO's failure to knock out Serb ground forces in Kosovo. Those forces were beside the point. "The tank, which was an irrelevant item in the context of ethnic cleansing, became the symbol of Serbian ground forces. How many tanks did you kill today? All of a sudden, this became the measure of merit although it had nothing to do with reality."[121]

In fact, once the 48-hour demonstration attack failed, NATO's assigned task became one of stopping in their tracks the Yugoslav forces perpetrating ethnic cleansing. That is what NATO publics expected, what NATO political leaders promised, and what Clark as the senior military commander vowed to accomplish. Short and other Air Force officers may have believed that the best way to stop ethnic cleansing was indirectly, by mounting a strategic bombing offensive. But both prior to and during the war, they failed to convince Clark or political authorities in Washington and Europe that such an approach was the optimum way to achieve NATO's objectives.

Throughout Operation Allied Force, NATO demonstrated an almost obsessive concern for civilian casualties and damage. It employed a greater percentage of smart weapons than in any other conflict in history. Civilian "micro-management" approached levels not seen since the Vietnam War. Enormous efforts were made, largely successful, to minimize short- and long-term civilian effects. When mistakes did occur in the 78 days of bombing, changes in operational procedures, weapons selection, and limits on targeting were implemented almost immediately. In this sense, the NATO war does merit Secretary of Defense Cohen's description of it as "the most precise application of air power in history," but it was superb technical display concealing a legion of political, military, intelligence, and leadership miscues.

On the political level, leaders failed to take the measure of Slobodan Milosevic despite years of wrangling and negotiations with the Serb dictator. War with Yugoslavia was not Desert Storm, where the coalition was largely in the dark with regard to Iraqi society and Saddam Hussein's intentions. Holbrooke, Albright, Solana, Clark, and others knew the Yugoslav leader intimately. Clark in particular took pride in being a student of Milosevic. Yet at the top, a bizarre confidence in the prospects of a mere demonstration attack prevailed. NATO and the United States had misread their adversary.

On the strategic level, political leaders failed to articulate clear objectives, greatly complicating the efforts of military planners to relate means to ends in a realistic manner. Despite ex post facto claims that alliance leaders had never placed their confidence in the demonstration attack, there was in fact no serious planning for alternative contingencies. No consensus on a proper strategy existed—this despite the luxury of having a "U.S. only" channel where contingency planning could have proceeded without the need to take allied sensitivities into account.

Within the high command, General Clark, the misnamed Supreme Commander, was unable to get his subordinate, General Short, to follow orders, and then he failed to relieve Short when he refused to do so. The Defense Department and Air Force leadership, despite their knowledge of the debilitating tensions between Generals Short and Clark, failed to intervene and resolve them.

The Air Force (and air power advocates generally) clearly failed to educate political leaders, the media, or the public with regard to air power's actual potential and limitations in a setting like Yugoslavia. The end result, regardless of one's devotion to a "tactical" or "strategic" solution in Kosovo, was that the Air Force propagated an exaggerated sense of the ease with which attacks would occur, of the effects of even accurate weapons, of damage potential, and of the ability to properly "read" the opponent.

Most crucially, the Air Force also failed to understand and convey the reality of how long it would take (and what it would take) to coerce Milosevic. There may indeed have been an optimal air-power-only plan for winning in 1999, but the Air Force as an institution failed to produce that plan, and certainly failed to make a convincing case to NATO and Washington decision makers that hitting Yugoslavia hard from the outset might actually shorten the war without entailing unreasonable risk of civilian casualties and friendly losses.

Notes

1. The participating nations were Belgium, Canada, Denmark, France, Germany, Italy, the Netherlands, Norway, Portugal, Spain, Turkey, the United Kingdom, and the United States. Aircraft from the United States, the United Kingdom, France, Canada, and Spain conducted bombing on the first night. Long-range cruise missiles were fired by the United States and Britain.
2. The FRY consists of Montenegro and Serbia, which is made up of Serbia itself, the autonomous province of Vojvodina, and Kosovo.
3. The earlier UNSCR 1160 adopted in March 1998 condemned the excessive use of force by Yugoslav forces in Kosovo and established an embargo against the FRY.
4. DOD, Kosovo/Operation Allied Force After-Action Report, 30 January 2000, pp. A2, 21; discussions with USAFE planners.
5. DOD/JCS, Joint Statement on the Kosovo After Action Review, 14 October 1999.
6. DOD, Kosovo/Operation Allied Force After-Action Report, 30 January 2000, p. A4.
7. James B. Steinberg, "A Perfect Polemic: Blind to Reality on Kosovo," *Foreign Affairs* (November-December 1999): 128.

8. DOD, Kosovo/Operation Allied Force After-Action Report, 30 January 2000, pp. 2, A7.
9. Ibid., p. 23.
10. Gen. John P. Jumper, U.S. Air Forces in Europe, presentation at The Eaker Institute for Aerospace Concepts, Operation Allied Force: Strategy, Execution, Implications Colloquy, 16 August 1999.
11. The U.S. Department of Defense contends that it "made clear to our allied counterparts that Operation Allied Force could well take weeks or months to succeed"; DOD/JCS, Joint Statement on the Kosovo After Action Review, 14 October 1999.
12. USAFE Briefing, "Integration of Aerospace Power in Operational Planning, or Doctrinal Implications of our Kosovo Planning Exercise," December 1999.
13. Testimony of General Wesley Clark before Senate Armed Services Committee Hearing on Lessons Learned from Military Operations and Relief Efforts in Kosovo (21 October 1999); Dana Priest, "Bombing By Committee: France Balked at NATO Targets," *Washington Post*, 20 September 1999, p. A1.
14. U.S. Congress, Senate Armed Services Committee, Hearing on the Situation in Kosovo, Testimony of General Wesley Clark, SACEUR, 1 July 1999.
15. Dana Priest, "Tensions Grew with Divide over Strategy," *Washington Post*, 21 September 1999, p. A1.
16. John A. Tirpak, "Short's View of the Air Campaign," *Air Force Magazine*, September 1999, pp. 43–47; Dana Priest, "Tensions Grew with Divide over Strategy," *Washington Post*, 21 September 1999, p. A16.
17. Testimony before Senate Armed Services Committee Hearing on Lessons Learned from Military Operations and Relief Efforts in Kosovo, 21 October 1999.
18. Dana Priest, "Tensions Grew with Divide over Strategy," *Washington Post*, 21 September 1999, p. A16.
19. Hearing of the Senate Armed Services Committee, Lessons Learned from Military Operations and Relief Efforts in Kosovo, 14 October 1999.
20. The official military objective was later stated as: "Demonstrate the seriousness of NATO's opposition to Belgrade's aggression. . . . deter Milosevic from continuing and escalating his attacks on helpless civilians and create conditions to reverse his ethnic cleansing; and damage Serbia's capacity to wage war . . . or spread the war to neighbors by diminishing or degrading its ability to wage military operations DOD." Kosovo/Operation Allied Force After-Action Report, 30 January 2000, p. 7.

    On the first night of Allied Force, Secretary Cohen stated: "The military objective of our action is to deter further action against the Kosovars and to diminish the ability of the Yugoslav army to continue those attacks if necessary"; DOD News Briefing, Wednesday, January 24, 1999.

NATO listed its political objective in a statement issued at the Extraordinary Meeting of the North Atlantic Council held on April 12, 1999 (reaffirmed on April 23 at the Washington Summit). They included:

> a verifiable stop to all military action and the immediate ending of violence and repression;
> the withdrawal from Kosovo of Serb military, police and paramilitary forces;
> the stationing in Kosovo of an international military presence;
> the unconditional and safe return of all refugees and displaced persons and unhindered access to them by humanitarian aid organizations; and
> the establishment of a political framework agreement for Kosovo on the basis of the Rambouillet Accords, in conformity with international law and the Charter of the United Nations.

21. General Wesley Clark, Remarks to the American Enterprise Institute regarding military action in Yugoslavia, 31 August 1999. This position is consistent with Gen. Clark's attitude before the war as well.
22. DOD, Kosovo/Operation Allied Force After-Action Report, 30 January 2000, p. 7.
23. Special Department of Defense Press Briefing with General Wesley Clark, Supreme Allied Commander, Europe, Topic: Kosovo Strike Assessment Also Participating: Airmen and Analysts from Operation Allied Force and Post-strike Assessment Work, Brussels, Belgium, 16 September 1999.
24. William M. Arkin, "Smart War, Dumb Targeting?" *The Bulletin of the Atomic Scientists* (May-June 2000): 46–53.
25. Statement of the Honorable John J. Hamre Deputy Secretary of Defense Before the House Permanent Select Committee on Intelligence, 22 July 1999.
26. DOD/JCS, Joint Statement on the Kosovo After Action Review, 14 October 1999; Testimony of Secretary Cohen, Hearing of the Senate Armed Services Committee, Lessons Learned from Military Operations and Relief Efforts in Kosovo, 14 October 1999; see also testimony of General Shelton to the House Armed Services Committee, 14 April 1999.
27. Such attacks emulated Iraqi attacks in December 1998 against Saddam Hussein's "special" Republican Guard and Presidential security forces; see William M. Arkin, "The Difference Was in the Details," *Washington Post*, 17 January 1999, p. B1.

28. Hearing of the Senate Armed Services Committee, Lessons Learned from Military Operations and Relief Efforts in Kosovo, 14 October 1999.
29. On the first day of Desert Storm, 2,388 coalition sorties were flown, with more than 1,000 strikes, 400 against Iraqi ground forces.
30. Dana Priest, "Tensions Grew with Divide over Strategy," *The Washington Post*, 21 September 1999, p. A1.
31. "I do not intend to put our troops in Kosovo to fight a war," President Clinton declared in his March 24 address to the nation; Statement by the President to the Nation, the Oval Office, 24 March 1999.
32. DOD News Briefing, Wednesday, January 24, 1999. Secretary of Defense William S. Cohen and CJCS Gen. Shelton. "Others in the administration reiterated the no ground force pledge. Secretary of State Madeleine Albright said on March 24: "I think that NATO had some contingency planning for this, but this is not our plan to use ground forces." Transcript, Interview of Secretary of State Madeleine K. Albright on *Newshour with Jim Lehrer*, PBS, 24 March 1999. National Security Advisor Samnuel R. Berger made the same point on March 25: "We do not have, as the President indicated, an intention to put ground forces in Kosovo in a combat situation"; Transcript, Press Briefing by National Security Advisor Sandy Berger, 25 March 1999.
33. Transcript, Interview of Secretary of State Madeleine K. Albright on *Newshour with Jim Lehrer*, PBS, 24 March 1999.
34. DOD News Briefing, Wednesday, March 24, 1999.
35. Transcript, NATO Press Conference, Secretary General Dr. Javier Solana and SACEUR General Wesley Clark, 25 March 1999.
36. Transcript, Press Briefing by National Security Advisor Sandy Berger, 25 March 1999.
37. Statement by the President to the Nation, the Oval Office, 24 March 1999.
38. Transcript, NATO Press Conference, Secretary General Dr. Javier Solana and SACEUR General Wesley Clark, 25 March 1999.
39. Emphasis added.
40. Transcript, NATO Press Conference, Secretary General Dr. Javier Solana and SACEUR General Wesley Clark, 25 March 1999.
41. Quoted in R. W. Apple Jr., "Conflict in the Balkans: News Analysis, A Fresh Set of U.S. Goals," *New York Times*, 25 March 1999, p. A1.
42. Air Force Doctrine Center, "Operation Allied Force: An Initial Doctrinal Assessment," (December 1999).
43. Presentation at The Eaker Institute for Aerospace Concepts, Operation Allied Force: Strategy, Execution, Implications Colloquy, 16 August 1999.
44. Transcript of briefing, Defense Minister George Robertson and the Chief of Staff, General Guthrie, London, 28 March 1999.

45. Testimony of General Henry Shelton to the House Armed Services Committee, 14 April 1999.
46. Hearing of the Senate Armed Services Committee, Lessons Learned from Military Operations and Relief Efforts in Kosovo, 14 October 1999. See also DOD/JCS, Joint Statement on the Kosovo After Action Review, 14 October 1999.
47. Testimony of the Honorable William S. Cohen to the House Armed Services Committee, 14 April 1999.
48. Hearing of the Senate Armed Services Committee, Lessons Learned from Military Operations and Relief Efforts in Kosovo, 14 October 1999.
49. Testimony of General Henry Shelton to the House Armed Services Committee, 14 April 1999.
50. Director of Central Intelligence Statement on the Belgrade Chinese Embassy Bombing, House Permanent Select Committee on Intelligence, Open Hearing, 21 July 1999.
51. Dana Priest, "Bombing By Committee: France Balked at NATO Targets," *Washington Post*, 20 September 1999, p. A1. See also U.S. Congress, House Permanent Select Committee on Intelligence, Hearing on the Bombing of the Chinese Embassy, 21 July 1999.
52. By the end of the first week, reportedly only some 90 attacks against 70 targets had been carried out. The majority of targets—16 radar and early warning sites, 18 surface-to-air missile sites, 12 other air defense facilities, and eight airfields—were associated with air defenses and the establishment of air superiority.
53. Secretary of Defense William S. Cohen, Remarks as Delivered to the International Institute for Strategic Studies Hotel del Coronado, San Diego, Calif., 9 September 1999.
54. Weather would continue to be a problem throughout the war. Only 21 of 78 days were 50 percent or better cloud-free; in Kosovo, NATO operated under conditions in which there was at least 50 percent cloud cover more than 70 percent of the time. The Air Force says 16 percent of all strike sorties were lost due to weather. DOD/JCS, Joint Statement on the Kosovo After Action Review, 14 October 1999. Also, U.S. Air Force, "Air War Over Serbia," hereinafter cited as AWOS. This Pentagon study has not been declassified or released. The author has had extensive discussions with the AWOS study team and has reviewed AWOS documents and draft materials.
55. Dana Priest, "Bombing By Committee: France Balked at NATO Targets," *Washington Post*, 20 September 1999, p. A1.
56. Hearing of the House Armed Services Committee on Support of Operation Allied Force, 26 October 1999.
57. Transcript, Interview of the President by Dan Rather, CBS, The Cabinet Room, 31 March 1999.

58. AWOS data obtained by the author.
59. Yugoslavia's long-range air defenses, according to the U.S. Air Force AWOS, were made up of three SA-2 systems, 16 SA-3s, and 80 SA-6s. It had 130 SA-9s, and 404 air defense artillery guns (ZSU-57-2 and M53/59). Man-portable SAM systems (SA-7/14/16) numbered 10,000 plus.
60. Testimony before Senate Armed Services Committee Hearing on Lessons Learned from Military Operations and Relief Efforts in Kosovo, 21 October 1999; DOD/JCS, Joint Statement on the Kosovo After Action Review, 14 October 1999.
61. AWOS data obtained by the author. Yugoslavia fired 188 SA-3s, 477 SA-6s, 124 man-portable SAMs, and 56 unknown SAMs.
62. Transcript, NATO Press Conference, Secretary General Dr. Javier Solana and SACEUR General Wesley Clark, 25 March 1999.
63. William M. Arkin, "NATO Info Strategy Bombs," washingtonpost.com, 26 April 1999 (http://www.washingtonpost.com/wp-srv/national/dotmil/arkin042699.htm).
64. Yugoslavia, Ministry of Foreign Affairs (MFA) Daily Dispatch, 26 March 1999.
65. Human Rights Watch, "Civilian Deaths in the NATO Air Campaign," February 2000.
66. DOD/JCS, Joint Statement on the Kosovo After Action Review, 14 October 1999.
67. Statement of Lieutenant General Marvin R. Esmond, Deputy Chief of Staff Air and Space Operations, United States Air Force, 19 October 1999.
68. Testimony before Senate Armed Services Committee Hearing on Lessons Learned from Military Operations and Relief Efforts in Kosovo, 21 October 1999.
69. The Defense Department says this "limited the Serb ground forces' combat effectiveness" and "and made them ineffective as a tactical maneuver force"; DOD/JCS, Joint Statement on the Kosovo After Action Review, 14 October 1999.
70. Hearing of the House Armed Services Committee on Support of Operation Allied Force, 26 October 1999.
71. U.S. Congress, Senate Armed Services Committee, Hearing on the Situation in Kosovo, General Wesley Clark, SACEUR, testifying, 1 July 1999.
72. Dana Priest, "A Decisive Battle That Never War," *Washington Post*, 19 September 1999, p. A1.
73. Testimony before Senate Armed Services Committee Hearing on Lessons Learned from Military Operations and Relief Efforts in Kosovo, 21 Oct 1999.
74. Statement of Secretary of Defense William S. Cohen, Brussels, 7 April 1999.
75. This included combat aircraft from Belgium, Denmark, France, Germany, Italy, The Netherlands, Norway, Portugal, Spain, Turkey, the United Kingdom, and the United States.

76. Secretary of Defense William S. Cohen, Remarks as Delivered to the International Institute for Strategic Studies, Hotel del Coronado, San Diego, Calif., 9 September 1999.
77. U.S. Congress, Senate Armed Services Committee, Hearing on the Situation in Kosovo, General Wesley Clark, SACEUR, testifying, 1 July 1999; DOD/JCS, Joint Statement on the Kosovo After Action Review, 14 October 1999; Dana Priest, "Bombing By Committee: France Balked at NATO Targets," *Washington Post*, 20 September 1999, p. A1.
78. DOD/JCS, Joint Statement on the Kosovo After Action Review, 14 October 1999. See also speech by National Security Adviser Samuel R. Berger at the Council on Foreign Relations, Washington, D.C., 26 July 1999.
79. William M. Arkin, "Ask Not for Whom the Phone Rings," washingtonpost.com, 11 October 1999 (http://www.washingtonpost.com/wp-srv/national/dotmil/arkin101199.htm).
80. U.S. Congress, House Permanent Select Committee on Intelligence, Hearing on the Bombing of the Chinese Embassy, 21 July 1999.
81. Testimony before Senate Armed Services Committee Hearing on Lessons Learned from Military Operations and Relief Efforts in Kosovo, 21 October 1999.
82. DOD/JCS, Joint Statement on the Kosovo After Action Review, 14 October 1999.
83. Dana Priest, "A Decisive Battle That Never Was," *Washington Post*, 19 September 1999, p. A1.
84. Speech by National Security Adviser Samuel R. Berger at the Council on Foreign Relations, Washington, D.C., 26 July 1999; U.S. Congress, Senate Armed Services Committee, Hearing on the Situation in Kosovo, General Wesley Clark, SACEUR, testifying, 1 July 1999.
85. Television interview given by M. Jacques Chirac, President of the Republic, to TF1, Paris, 10 June 1999.
86. UK Ministry of Defense, Kosovo: An Account of the Crisis, A Paper by Lord Robertson of Port Ellen, September 1999.
87. Hearing of the House Armed Services Committee on Support of Operation Allied Force, 26 October 1999.
88. AWOS data provided to the author.
89. AWOS data provided to the author; DOD, Kosovo/Operation Allied Force After-Action Report, 31 January 2000, p. 92.
90. This is based on the delivery of some five thousand 2,000-lb.-class weapons, five thousand 1,000-lb. weapons, seventeen thousand 500-lb. weapons, and one thousand sub-500-lb. weapons of all types, including cruise missiles, JDAMs, guided and unguided bombs, cluster bombs, HARMs, etc.
91. AWOS data provided to the author.

92. AWOS data provided to the author. No more than two B-2s were in the theater at any one time. See also William M. Arkin, "In Praise of Heavy Bombers," *The Bulletin of the Atomic Scientists* (July-August 1999): 80.
93. Testimony of William Cohen, Secretary of Defense, to the Senate Armed Services Committee, on Operations in Kosovo, 20 July 1999. The allies were able to conduct 47 percent of the strike sorties, but provided only about 29 percent of the overall support sorties.
94. Statement of the Honorable John J. Hamre, Deputy Secretary of Defense, before the House Permanent Select Committee on Intelligence, 22 July 1999.
95. AWOS data provided to the author (excludes Tomahawk cruise missile).
96. Human Rights Watch, "Civilian Deaths in the NATO Air Campaign," February 2000. On 29 August 2000, the Serbian Public Prosecutor brought charges against NATO for Yugoslav attacks, stating that 504 civilians had been killed and 913 injured, 454 of them seriously.
97. Special Department of Defense Press Briefing with General Wesley Clark, Supreme Allied Commander, Europe, Topic: Kosovo Strike Assessment Also Participating: Airmen and Analysts from Operation Allied Force and Post-strike Assessment Work, Brussels, Belgium, 16 September 1999.
98. Nick Cook, "War of Extremes," *Jane's Defence Weekly*, 7 July 1999.
99. Agence France Press (Belgrade), "Belgrade to Try Clinton, Blair for NATO 'warcrimes,'" 29 August 2000.
100. Nick Cook, "War of Extremes," *Jane's Defence Weekly*, 7 July 1999.
101. AWOS data provided to the author.
102. AWOS data provided to the author.
103. General Michael E. Ryan, Chief of Staff, United States Air Force, Remarks at the AFA National Convention,14 September 1999.
104. This included 14 MiG-29s, 24 MiG-21s, 23 Galebs, 22 Super Galebs, 2 Oraos, 7 Curls, 15 helicopters, and 14 "other."
105. William M. Arkin, "Ask Not for Whom the Phone Rings," washingtonpost.com, 11 October 1999 (http://www.washingtonpost.com/wp-srv/national/dotmil/arkin 101199.htm).
106. Testimony of William Cohen, Secretary of Defense, to the Senate Armed Services Committee, on Operations in Kosovo, 20 July 1999; U.S. Congress, House Armed Services Committee, Subcommittee on Military Procurement, Hearing on the Performance of the B-2 bomber in Kosovo, testimony of Lieutenant General Marvin R. Esmond, Deputy Chief of Staff for Air and Space Operations, Department of the Air Force, 30 June 1999.
107. Human Rights Watch, "Civilian Deaths in the NATO Air Campaign," February 2000.
108. William M. Arkin, "Yugoslavia Unplugged," washingtonpost.com, 10 May 1999 (http://www.washingtonpost.com/wp-srv/national/dotmil/arkin051099.htm).

109. William M. Arkin, "Smart War, Dumb Targeting?" *The Bulletin of the Atomic Scientists*, (May-June 2000): 46–53.
110. William M. Arkin, "Ask Not for Whom the Phone Rings," washingtonpost.com, 11 October 1999 (http://www.washingtonpost.com/wp-srv/national/dotmil/arkin 101199.htm).
111. U.S. Congress, Senate Armed Services Committee, Hearing on the Situation in Kosovo, General Wesley Clark, SACEUR, testifying, 1 July 1999.
112. *Aviation Week & Space Technology*, 26 July 1999, p. 68.
113. Special Department of Defense Press Briefing with General Wesley Clark, Supreme Allied Commander, Europe, Topic: Kosovo Strike Assessment Also Participating: Airmen and Analysts from Operation Allied Force and Post-Strike Assessment Work, Brussels, Belgium, 16 September 1999.
114. In all, the MEAT found 26 tanks and self-propelled artillery guns on the ground, 30 armored vehicles and air defense guns, and eight artillery pieces. They also found 136 destroyed or damage military vehicles. The MEAT expected to find tanks at 64 geographic locations, but only physically found 14 tanks.
115. DOD/JCS, Joint Statement on the Kosovo After Action Review, 14 October 1999.
116. Dinner Speech by Lord Robertson, NATO Secretary General, International Institute for Strategic Studies, Arundel House, London, 22 March 2000.
117. Testimony before Senate Armed Services Committee Hearing on Lessons Learned from Military Operations and Relief Efforts in Kosovo, 21 October 1999.
118. "Reconstitution Efforts Won't Impact Readiness," Air Force Policy Letter Digest, August 1999.
119. General Michael E. Ryan, Chief of Staff, United States Air Force, Remarks at the AFA National Convention,14 September 1999.
120. General Michael E. Ryan, Chief of Staff, United States Air Force, Remarks at the AFA National Convention,14 September 1999.
121. Dana Priest, "Tensions Grew With Divide Over Strategy," *Washington Post*, 21 September 1999, p. A16.

2 Kosovo and the New American Way of War

Eliot A. Cohen

The Kosovo war marks a departure from the traditional American way of war. From a style of warfare that has been since the middle of the nineteenth century direct, simple, and overwhelming, the United States has turned to a style of conflict that is quite different, and to which it has not yet completely adapted. The Kosovo war did not by itself force that change; the conflict did, however, crystallize it.

The Old American Way of War

"Facing the Arithmetic"

By the end of 1862, little had gone well for the Union. After dramatic successes in the first half of the year, the Confederacy had launched counteroffensives that first hurled the Army of the Potomac off the peninsular approaches to Richmond, scattered a newly assembled army at the approaches to Washington, and invaded Maryland, scooping up over 12,000 prisoners at Harper's Ferry along the way. In the West, Confederate General Braxton Bragg had nearly succeeded in wresting Kentucky from the Union. Although driven back to Tennessee, Bragg remained a looming menace to Northern gains there. Back in Washington, Union finances were in shambles, the Emancipation Proclamation was a sham, and the November elections had gone against the Republican Party. The gentle, melancholic man in the White House grieved over the death of a favorite son earlier in the year, and many friends who had fallen in combat since.

To cap it all off, the Army of the Potomac, under its fumbling new commander—the third in four months—had just failed spectacularly at Fredericksburg, Virginia. On December 13, General Ambrose Burnside had launched an assault on a naturally strong ridge, fronted by half a mile of open field swept by Confederate rifle and artillery fire. During fighting that lasted from dawn until the early afternoon, some 12,500 men had fallen as casualties, many of the wounded dying of exposure on the open fields. Robert E. Lee's Army of Northern Virginia had suffered perhaps a third as many casualties.

How did the grieving President react? According to a secretary, William Stoddard, Lincoln remarked a few days later that:

> if the same battle were to be fought over again, every day, through a week of days, with the same relative results, the army under Lee would be wiped out to its last man, the Army of the Potomac would still be a mighty host, the war would be over, the Confederacy gone, and peace would be won. . . . No general yet found can face the arithmetic, but the end of the war will be at hand when he shall be discovered.[1]

After Fredericksburg, as he had after so many other defeats and disappointments, Abraham Lincoln would continue his search for the general who "understood the arithmetic." When Lincoln finally found him in the person of Ulysses S. Grant, he placed Grant in charge of all his armies and backed him unflinchingly. "Grant is the first general I've had," he said approvingly. When Grant presided over his own bloody fiascoes such as the battle of Cold Harbor in June 1864—an ill-conceived assault every bit as bungled as Fredericksburg, costing perhaps 7,000 casualties in the space of an hour—Lincoln uttered not a word of protest.

Lincoln is one of the fathers of the modern "American Way of War."[2] If the long and brutal conflict of 1861–1865 provides the most vivid expression of that approach to waging war, subsequent conflicts are replete with reminders that the convictions manifested by the likes of Lincoln and Grant lived on after Appomattox. It echoes, for example, in the speech given by Lieutenant General Leslie McNair on the eve of America's first large European operation during World War II, the TORCH landings in North Africa:

> Our soldiers must have the fighting spirit. If you call that hating our enemies, then we must hate with every fiber of our being. We must lust for battle; our object in life must be to kill; we must scheme and plan night and day to kill. There need be no pangs of conscience, for our enemies have lighted the way to faster, surer, and crueler killing; they are past masters. . . . Since killing is the object of our efforts, the sooner we get in the killing mood, the better and more skillful we shall be when the real test comes.[3]

McNair's call for his fellow citizens to get into a killing mood serves as a useful reminder: The bloodlust that Americans have come to associate with George S. Patton was by no means unique to Patton himself. In World War II, it permeated a generation of officers schooled in the traditions of Grant and William T. Sherman, many of whose members in 1918 had experienced killing in close quarters on the Western Front.

A quarter of a century later, the American way of war was alive and well in Vietnam, finding expression in a thinly fictionalized account of the war by Josiah Bunting, a Vietnam veteran who was then teaching at West Point:

> [Colonel] Manley could build a battle, could 'orchestrate forces' better than any commander in Vietnam. His casualties were quite heavy—indeed, a cynical reporter once called him a 'butcher'—but his body-count for two months running had been the highest for a unit its size in the whole combat theater. It was gratifying to the General to have such a commander working for him.[4]

Even in the Persian Gulf War of 1990–1991, viewed as the antithesis of Vietnam and the incubator of so much that was novel or even revolutionary, the classic American way of war found expression. Surely, when Chairman of the Joint Chiefs of Staff General Colin Powell declared that the American objective in Kuwait was "to cut off the [Iraqi] army and kill it," Lincoln would have approved. Here—seemingly—was another general who did not flinch when confronting the arithmetic of battle.

Aggressiveness, Decision, Maximum Effort, Bright Lines

Four qualities distinguish the old American way of war. The first is extreme aggressiveness, at all levels of conflict, from the tactical (the conduct of individual fights) to the operational (the orchestration of battles in time and space) to the strategic (the planning out of campaigns to achieve the objectives of war). Whether fighting Indians on the Western frontier, Spaniards in Cuba, Germans in the Argonne or Normandy, a compulsion to seize the first available opportunity to close with and destroy the enemy characterizes the preferred American approach to warfare. (One of the very first moves in the American Revolution—fought nominally to defend against George III's repression—was a lunge to grab Quebec.)

American military heroes are the bold, the dashing, the audacious—whether they are Stonewall Jackson evading and then striking multiple Union armies attempting to trap him in the Shenandoah Valley in 1862, or Jimmy Doolittle attacking Tokyo with a handful of bombers in 1942. The quintessential American military leaders are those eager to attack: Ulysses S. Grant, pushing into the Wilderness in 1864 and declaring himself determined to "fight it out on this line if it takes all summer," or John J. Pershing who insisted that a vast American army would end World War I by undertaking offensives that European powers had given up as suicidal. Admiral Ernest King's insistence upon a quick riposte at Guadalcanal in response to Japan's devastating offensives in 1942, or General Marshall's desire to invade France in 1943, or the aspirations of General Hap Arnold to win the war through strategic bombing—all manifest the urgent determination to take the fight to the enemy that is the essence of the traditional American way of war.

Nor did this aggressiveness manifest itself only in the realm of strategy. The American armed forces have, in the twentieth century at least, favored offensive tactics. In between the world wars the Marine Corps sedulously cultivated the art of amphibious assault written off as impossibly bloody by the British veterans of Gallipoli. "Search and destroy," not pacification, dominated the American military style in Vietnam, and more than a few Air Force generals still believe that a less restrained use of air power might have brought that war to a different conclusion. The residual desire to carry the war to the enemy in the old way—to "go downtown" as fighter pilots like to put it, appeared in Kosovo as well, as frustrated Air Force generals made clear repeatedly. But such yearnings had by then become vestigial and, more importantly, operationally irrelevant.

Closely coupled to American aggressiveness at the outset of war has been the quest for decisive battle, the clash of arms that could clinch a decision. This search for the engagement that would finish the war has obsessed American generals from Robert E. Lee hoping to bring the Union to its knees at Gettysburg to Douglas MacArthur attempting to conclude the Korean conflict with a decisive lunge to the Yalu River.

Colonel Harry Summers began a short study of the Vietnam war with a telling anecdote that captured the American military's discomfort with the Indochina war. "You never beat us in a single battle," he recalled telling a North Vietnamese counterpart during the final armistice negotiations. "That's true," the Vietnamese colonel replied, after a moment's thought. "That's also irrelevant." That brief exchange captures the frustration and outrage that American officers felt when fighting a war in which undoubted, and hard-won tactical victories, measured by ground taken and casualties inflicted, did not translate into strategic success. Virtuosity in grand tactics—the big battle, rather than the campaign, much less strategy—has obsessed generations of American officers who pore over Lee's brilliant flanking maneuver at Chancellorsville, convinced that it will yield profound insights into the art of generalship despite the fact that Lee's victory came at an unaffordable cost in casualties and produced no lasting gains. Similarly, in the decades before World War II, the quest for the decisive engagement obsessed U.S. Navy war planners who could not imagine that a war with Japan might be decided not by a super-Jutland of the massed fleets in the Philippine Sea, but by attrition.

The third characteristic of the American way of war, again tied to the previous two, is discomfort with ambiguous objectives, constricted resources, and political constraints. The revulsion of the American military from the Vietnam experience represented not only its reaction to that war, but a sense that somehow the rules for successful warfighting had been violated at their core. In November 1984, Secretary of Defense Caspar Weinberger—expressing that revulsion on behalf of the officers who had fought the Vietnam war—articulated preconditions for the use of force, henceforth to become canonical within the defense establishment. The "Weinberger doctrine" consisted of six principles:

1) The United States should not commit forces to combat overseas unless the particular engagement or occasion is deemed vital to our national interest or that of our allies. That emphatically does not mean that we should declare beforehand, as we did with Korea in 1950, that a particular area is outside our strategic perimeter.
2) If we decide it is necessary to put combat troops into a given situation, we should do so wholeheartedly and with the clear intention of winning. If we are unwilling to commit the forces or resources

necessary to achieve our objectives, we should not commit them at all. Of course, if the particular situation requires only limited force to win our objectives, then we should not hesitate to commit forces sized accordingly. When Hitler broke treaties and remilitarized the Rhineland, small combat forces then could perhaps have prevented the holocaust of World War II.

3) If we do decide to commit forces to combat overseas, we should have clearly defined political and military objectives. And we should know precisely how our forces can accomplish those clearly defined objectives. And we should have and send the forces needed to do just that. As Clausewitz wrote, "No one starts a war—or rather, no one in his senses ought to do so—without first being clear in his mind what he intends to achieve by that war, and how he intends to conduct it." War may be different today than in Clausewitz's time, but the need for well-defined objectives and a consistent strategy is still essential. If we determine that a combat mission has become necessary for our vital national interests, then we must send forces capable to do the job and not assign a combat mission to a force configured for peacekeeping.
4) The relationship between our objectives and the forces we have committed—their size, composition, and disposition—must be continually reassessed and adjusted if necessary. Conditions and objectives invariably change during the course of a conflict. When they do change, then our combat requirements must also change. We must continuously keep as a beacon light before us the following basic questions: Is this conflict in our national interest? Does our national interest require us to fight, to use force of arms? If the answers are "yes," then we must win. If the answers are "no," then we should not be in combat.
5) Before the United States commits combat forces abroad, there must be some reasonable assurance that we will have the support of the American people and their elected representatives in Congress. This support cannot be achieved unless we are candid in making clear the threats we face; the support cannot be sustained without continuing and close consultation. We cannot fight a battle with Congress at home while asking our troops to win a war overseas or, as in the case of Vietnam, in effect asking our troops not to win, but just to be there.
6) The commitment of U.S. forces to combat should be a last resort.[5]

Setting an impossible standard of purity and simplicity, the Weinberger rules did not survive long in practice. But they did represent an ideal to which succeeding political and military leaders pledged allegiance. Officers imbibed them at war colleges, and though criticized sharply by some—including Secretary of State George Shultz—they continued to exercise an influence well after Weinberger had departed office. Even in the late 1990s a retired four star general would recall: "As a young officer, I literally carried a copy of that for 10 years with me in my briefcase because I thought it was so important, and it had such a dramatic effect on me when I read it, to think, 'Holy mackerel, it's really as simple as this.' I said, 'Finally, there's a realization about what a military can and cannot do for a democracy.'"[6]

The Bush administration during the Persian Gulf crisis of 1990–91 prided itself on having conducted the war in a way that adhered to the Weinberger doctrine. The administration insisted that in going to war with Iraq it did so in pursuit of four well-defined objectives. In reality, they were anything but well-defined. Only one of the avowed American objectives during the Gulf War (driving the Iraqi army out of Kuwait) could be fairly described as straightforward. The others were far more ambiguous than advertised. The first, ensuring the security of American citizens, had been rendered nugatory by Saddam Hussein's release of American hostages. The restoration of the legitimate government of Kuwait depended on one's definition of legitimacy, and the last, "ensuring the security and stability of the Persian Gulf," offered ample room for confusion and misinterpretation. What mattered, however, was to convey the *impression* that ambiguity had been banished from the planning and conduct of war. At about this same time, the term "exit strategy"—having in hand a plan to extricate oneself from a messy military commitment even prior to launching that commitment—became a popular term of art in the defense establishment.[7]

Finally, the traditional American way of war has rested on a similarly clear-cut understanding of civil-military relations, in which the tasks of soldiers and politicians are discrete and well understood. Two overarching principles define a proper civil-military relationship. The first is a prohibition on civilian "interference" in military operations. The second is the obligation of apolitical officers to dutifully execute the policies laid down by the political leadership. In short, the tradition of civil-military relations draws a bright line to separate the realm of the soldier from that of the politician. This tradition goes back to the Civil War, or rather to the reaction of regular officers to that war, evidenced most notably by Major General Emory Upton's posthumously published study *The Military Policy of the United States*.[8] A brilliant (and definitely offense-minded) tactician, Upton scorned the incompetence of civilian notables turned generals, the indiscipline of hastily raised volunteer units, and the meddling of politicians, as he understood it. His book crystallized an orthodox disdain for citizen-soldiers and interfering statesmen that has lasted for well over a century.

Here too, the American way of war has been framed by an understanding of the Vietnam and Gulf wars as morality tales of how wars should not, and should be conducted. The former, in the telling that retains wide credibility with most military and many civilian leaders, is a sorry tale of President Lyndon Johnson personally selecting bombing targets. The latter, in contrast, is portrayed as an exemplary case study in civil-military effectiveness, with primary credit given to President George Bush as a commander in chief who provided broad overall guidance and ample resources, and then allowed his field commanders to fight the war as they saw fit.

As described here, the old American way of war is, of course, something of a caricature. In practice, it has never commanded universal support among American political and military leaders. Rarely in actual practice has the United States been able fully to live up to it. (This was true even of the Persian Gulf War, the claims of Bush administration veterans notwithstanding). The traditional American way of war stands more as a statement of ideal conditions than real circumstances—what war ought to be more than what it has actually been.

The Kosovo war did not represent a conscious abandonment of this tradition, which in the Pentagon and within policy circles remains even today the conventional wisdom. But the war did illustrate the extent to which modern conditions had rendered that tradition inadequate and, indeed, obsolete. Furthermore, Kosovo demonstrates the extent to which the circumstances of the post–Cold War era have obliged American military and civilian leaders to extemporize an approach to war that differs radically from past practice—even as they trumpet their fealty to the approved lessons of Vietnam and the Persian Gulf. Indeed, the continuing influence of those two conflicts on American thinking about war, the former seeming to violate all the precepts of the old way of war, the latter affirming them, constitutes a barrier that conceals from view the emergence of this new way of war. Among civilians and soldiers alike, the old doctrines—now hardened into prejudices—remain intact. Unable or unwilling to grasp the extent to which actual practice—not just in Kosovo—has already superseded the traditional

American way of war, they cannot even begin to assess the implications, military and otherwise, of the tradition that is emerging to replace it.

The New American Way of War: From Weinberger's Rules to the "Beauty of Coalitions"

During the Cold War Americans told themselves that their country should wage war for concrete, vital interests—a conviction codified as Weinberger's first principle. Such too seemed to be the lesson of Vietnam, when America's leaders threw away lives, apparently, in pursuit of intangibles. The result ever since has been a tendency on the part of political leaders to define the purposes of American military action as being overwhelmingly large, to inflate the significance of the object pursued and the clarity with which that object has been defined.

Yet in Kosovo, as in other 1990s U.S. military interventions such as in Somalia or in Haiti, vital American interests were never at stake. To be sure, President Bill Clinton, in his first address to the nation on the Kosovo conflict, said the opposite. He insisted that the United States and its allies were obliged to "act to prevent a wider war; to diffuse a powder keg at the heart of Europe that has exploded twice before in this century with catastrophic results."[9] Despite President Clinton's references to World War I originating in the Balkans—a prime example of the inflation of strategic purposes—the likelihood that Serb repression in Kosovo would somehow trigger a great power confrontation between Russia and the West was minimal. If anything, the reverse was true: NATO's intervention in the war was likely to precipitate friction with the shrunken remnants of the Soviet empire.

Administration rhetoric also emphasized a moral imperative for U.S. and NATO action, finding in Serb actions parallels with the crimes perpetrated by Nazi Germany. But the suffering of the Kosovar Albanians, if awful enough, did not match the agony of Rwanda during the spring of 1994, which the Clinton administration had largely ignored. Serb forces in Kosovo sought to expel the province's ethnic Albanian inhabitants, not to exterminate them, and the atrocities, although substantial, did not rise to the level of genocide. Just as the remnant of Yugoslavia in 1999 was not the Balkan powder keg of 1914, so too Slobodan Milosevic was not Adolf Hitler.

Why then did the U.S. and its allies intervene? The administration's actual motivation for war in Kosovo seems to have stemmed from a number of lesser concerns, all of them legitimate, but none of them qualifying even remotely as "vital interests." One objective was the desire to forestall the second- and third-order consequences of another Yugoslav war, for example, the destabilization of Macedonia and its absorption by Greece, possibly triggering a conflict with Turkey. A second objective was to maintain the cohesiveness of NATO, a self-referential objective (taking an alliance to war in order to preserve the alliance with which one might at some point wish to go to war). Finally, humanitarian concerns no doubt played a role in motivating the United States to intervene. Ending the suffering of Kosovar Albanians would testify to the unacceptability of such behavior, particularly in other parts of Europe but also beyond.

None of these purposes could be considered objectionable; by the same token, however, none qualify as self-evidently vital, much less meriting President Clinton's assertion that the objectives envisaged included "A future in which leaders cannot keep, gain or increase their power by teaching their young people to hate or kill others simply because of their faith or heritage. A future in which young Americans who set out . . . to serve our country will not have to fight in yet another major European conflict."[10] Yet in their ambitious reach these lofty goals mirror the equally hazy or remote interests that motivated the United States to use force in a variety of contexts since the Cold War. The Bush and Clinton administrations alike lavished these operations—the invasions of Panama and Haiti, for example, or the deployments to Somalia as well as the periodic (now all but continuous) military operations against Iraq—with a rhetorical justification well beyond the limited and prudent calculations that brought them about. The December 1989 intervention in Panama, for example, became a crusade to "defend democracy in Panama" and combat drug trafficking;[11] the standoff with Iraq became a decisive test of world order.

Conceivably, the politicians who compared the Balkan crisis of 1999 to the Balkan crisis of 1914 were deceiving not only their publics, but to some extent themselves, about the actual stakes for which they had gone to war. To most members of the public since the Vietnam War, the notion of using force to overawe opponents, to demonstrate commitment, to send signals, and in general to create an international climate of deference to American wishes (or at least fear of American displeasure) has been anathema. The political leader willing to confess publicly that he or she was putting American soldiers at risk merely to defend such discredited concepts as "credibility" or "reputation" would be brave to the point of foolhardiness. Yet in virtually every instance in which the United States employed military power in the 1990s such considerations in all likelihood provided the deeper rationale leading to the use of force. "The reputation of power is power," wrote Thomas Hobbes in *Leviathan*. For no state is this more true than an imperial state—a state like the United States since the end of the Cold War.

Long unwilling to admit the implications of their position of global dominance, Americans have tended to think of power as something like a checking account—draw it down with trivial expenditures and the balance will be inadequate for the larger emergencies of national security. It would be no less plausible, however, to think of power as a muscle, its strength maintained and enhanced through exercise. Such, at least, appears to have become the implicit, and perhaps the unconscious doctrine of U.S. foreign policy.

In this the United States does not differ from any other great imperial power, seeking to sustain its position by periodically employing military power to remind friend and foe alike of its capacity and willingness to exert its power. Like the imperial powers of bygone years, the United States throughout the first decade of the post–Cold War era has used force for purposes that are not merely less than vital, but indirect. The hazard posed by an ethnically cleansed Kosovo on Balkan stability is a good example of not a secondary but a *tertiary* interest: The United States went to war over Kosovo—a place of almost no intrinsic value—less to correct Serb misbehavior there, than to preclude adverse consequences elsewhere, for example, a general deterioration in the relations of the Balkan states that could ultimately pit Greece against Turkey and, hence, undermine NATO. In a similar vein, British nineteenth-century statesmen embroiled their soldiers in the Sudan—a place of little intrinsic value—to protect Egypt, which was essential to protect the Suez Canal, which was crucial to defending the sea lanes to South Asia, which enabled Great Britain to secure the real prize, India.

Both logics—that of reputation, and that of second-order interest—smack of the sort of calculus that led to Vietnam, and hence cannot be introduced into public discourse about strategy. Ambiguity and nuanced political objectives have acquired an equally ill repute. Of all the supposed lessons of Vietnam, none has received wider endorsement than an insistence on defining "precise and achievable objectives." Fuzzy purposes and open-ended commitments helped doom the U.S. effort in Vietnam, and hence the language of American strategy now pointedly employs terms like "end states" and "exit strategies," which are viewed as essential to the conduct of war.

In truth, during the various U.S. military interventions of the past decade, an absence of clarity and precision has been the rule, not the exception. Nearing the end of his term in office, George Bush dispatched U.S. forces to Somalia on a limited humanitarian aid mission scheduled to conclude by Bush's last day in office on January 20, 1993. In fact, Operation Restore Hope was nowhere near completion on that date and soon thereafter metamorphosed into a bloody—and ultimately unsuccessful—vendetta against a local warlord. Efforts to impose precision, to include pre-announced exit dates, on the U.S.–led intervention in Bosnia met similar failure. Secretary of Defense William Perry vowed, on November 30, 1995 that American forces would be out of Bosnia within a year of their arrival.[12] Speaking for the uniformed military, General John Shalikashvili, chairman of the Joint Chiefs of Staff, offered public assurances that the U.S. could and would adhere to such a deadline. Both would eat crow a year later, when the U.S. military commitment to Bosnia was extended and eventually became all but permanent.

These lapses from the sort of clarity mandated by the Weinberger doctrine may reflect muddiness of thought on the part of political and military leaders. They reflect as well, however, the intrinsic uncertainties of strategy itself. To the extent that the old American way of war accepted Clausewitz's iron dictum that war is an extension of politics by other means, it did so by limiting politics to the setting of larger objectives that victory in battle would secure. Once those objectives were defined, Americans preferred to keep politics as far apart from war as possible.

Yet in defining the relationship between war and politics so narrowly, Americans misconstrued Clausewitz, whose actual intent was to argue that politics suffuses war. Viewing war in this light, the objectives for which any conflict is fought must of necessity be adjusted in accordance with political exigency, changing moods and preoccupations, shifting constellations of domestic and international political forces, and the consequences of success or failure on the battlefield.

American leaders insist otherwise. During the Kosovo war, for example, the scramble for an unambiguous statement of political purpose led to an absurd formulation of allied objectives. Thus, when President Clinton explained to the nation the purpose of American-led air strikes he declared:

> Our strikes have three objectives: First, to demonstrate the seriousness of NATO's opposition to aggression and its support for peace. Second,

> to deter President Milosevic from continuing and escalating his attacks on helpless civilians by imposing a price for those attacks. And, third, if necessary, to damage Serbia's capacity to wage war against Kosovo in the future by seriously diminishing its military capabilities.[13]

At almost the same time, the Secretary General of NATO (who claimed that it was he who had actually ordered the bombing) indicated that the purpose of Operation Allied Force was to "prevent more human suffering and more repression and violence against the civilian population of Kosovo."[14] Both leaders indicated—as did their subordinates—that Serb acceptance of the proposed Rambouillet accord would cause the war to cease.[15]

Thus, the ostensible purpose for which the American-led alliance fought was the deal proposed at Rambouillet: the creation of an autonomous (not independent) Kosovo, composed of an Albanian majority and a Serb minority living together, under continued Yugoslav sovereignty. Yet the solvent of violence—both Serb repression and NATO's bombing—made the erection of such intricate structures all but impossible. A vengeful Albanian population would accept neither long-term affiliation with Yugoslavia, nor the presence of Serb neighbors who had, in many cases, cooperated in their expulsion from their homes. In Kosovo, the quest for simplicity, clarity, and finality in war objectives led, by the beginning of a new century, not to a genuine settlement imposed by arms but only to a precarious and violent truce.

America's allies often think of the United States as a lone gunslinger; American statesmen sometimes think of themselves the same way—as Henry Kissinger, to his later regret, once confessed to Italian journalist Oriana Fallaci. American defense planning assumes that the United States will wage its wars on its own—at least such are the assumptions embedded in the doctrine of "two major theater wars," which shapes American force structure. American politicians and soldiers prepare for wars in which the United States confronts its opponents alone. Critics, both domestic and overseas, deride the United States for its lack of understanding of foreign cultures and its blithe assumption that the psychology of other peoples differs in no material way from that of the American heartland. There is some justice in all this, but the purely unilateral way of war died in the United States a long time ago. The change did not occur all at once. Since 1917 the United States had always fought as a member of a coalition, but until Kosovo in most cases it did so while insisting upon maximum freedom of action. In World War I the United States was careful to identify itself as an Associated, not an Allied Power, and it strove to keep its forces independent from those of France and Great Britain. In World War II, it attempted, insofar as possible, to exclude its allies from participation in the Pacific save in a completely subordinate role. (Europe, where the U.S. was a latecomer to the war, was admittedly a different situation). In Korea, Vietnam, and the Gulf, the United States thoroughly dominated its allies, who had very little say in the broader direction of the war. The United States today goes to war leading coalitions into battle, and over the space of a century it has made itself a remarkably adroit leader of multinational military enterprises.

Kosovo marked a departure, though, in that here, to an even greater extent than in the Gulf War, the maintenance of a coalition became something of an object in itself. In Operation Allied Force, for the first time, coalitional concerns intruded upon the strategy and operational concepts of the war. Thus, in a Pentagon briefing Major General Charles Wald responded to a question about NATO's 18 other members:

> They all have a vote on everything. They can vote on whether we start this or not. They can vote on whether we continue. They can vote on everything. That's the strength and probably the weakness a little bit of what we have going on here. But the beauty of the fact is we're a coalition. This is not one nation against Serbia. Therefore, as 19 nations we all have an equal vote, so I won't talk on specific targeting, but the fact of the matter is this is 19 nations going against Serbia together. We're not the only ones that vote. Everybody votes.[16]

In fact, one might say that American strategy now has a coalitional habit. When General Wald continued—"I will tell you that as we go down this campaign, the mission that's been given to General Clark has been given by 19 nations to execute. That's who we answer to."—he spoke with an air of irritated but unquestioning acceptance.[17] Politicians and military planners alike are uncomfortable with the prospect of going to war without allies. On occasion they provide some military support that the United States requires—basing, peacekeeping, a few military specialties like minesweeping, or a greater tolerance for risk and loss (particularly true of the British, and to some extent the French). By and large, however, the quest for coalition partners stems primarily from a desire for political legitimacy abroad and at home. This yearning stems as well from years of institutionalized coalition building and operations—NATO may have outlived its original purpose of sheltering Europe from a Soviet onslaught, but for half a century now it has taught American officers to work with foreign militaries. What is customary has become desirable; to this extent, the decades of mobilization during the Cold War had the effect on the American military mind that a hot war would. It created an instinct to work with allies, whether or not doing so was strictly necessary or even beneficial. The coalitional impulse received further reinforcement from the desire to legitimize the use of force. A multinational operation allows Americans and others to pretend that, say, keeping Iraq down is not a constabulary act of American imperial will, but a mere discharge of the mandate of the United Nations. Hypocrisy, perhaps, but humbug has its place in the conduct of foreign policy.

The coalitional habit extends well beyond a mere wish to have troops of other nations side by side with Americans. It includes a fine web of procedures and protocols that allows military organizations to work harmoniously with one another; a prime example of this is the air tasking order that specifies not only which targets aircraft will attack but such mundane matters as radio frequencies, tanker rendezvous points, and the like. American units have developed experience in sharing intelligence with not entirely trustworthy friends, in attaching liaison units to unfamiliar armies, in conducting maritime operations with multinational flotillas. The spread of English as the world's *lingua franca*, and the enormous number of foreign officers who have studied in the United States (and American officers who have served for extended periods abroad) facilitates America's coalitional habit.

Coalition leadership comes, of course, with a price. Some times this is no more than the dollar cost of providing logistical support and equipment; at others, as in Kosovo, it is the wearing irritation of coping with allies who usually wish to hold the United States back from waging war in its preferred style. (Kosovo was unusual in this one respect, however: One ally, Great Britain, actually preferred a more aggressive course, to include the early use of ground forces if air power did not drive the Serbs out.) But the benefits, to this point at any rate, far outweigh the costs, so much so that the United States may lose the willingness to consider (although not, in all likelihood, the physical ability to conduct) operations in the face of universal disapproval. On the other hand, the Kosovo war, in which allies as reluctant as Greece nonetheless took part, suggests that the United States will never lack for partners. After all, states join alliances out of mutual interest, but among lesser partners that interest may well include a desire to constrain a leader as much as to assist in achieving a common purpose.

Operational Style: Air Power and the Long March to 73 Easting

Since the early days of World War II, air power has commanded a central place in the American way of war. Still, until the Persian Gulf War, a deep and abiding skepticism about the utility of air power as an independent instrument permeated the United States Army, and through it the defense establishment. The Air Force, of course, disagreed. But the Navy was divided, seeing air power as a powerful but far from decisive tool of military action, and the Marine Corps, self-sufficient unto itself, played little role in national debates over the proper role of air power. The Army, however, which provided many of the chairmen of the Joint Chiefs of Staff and theater commanders in Europe, the Persian Gulf, and Latin America, had the last word—and the last word was to be wary of the extravagant claims of air advocates. Moreover, such Army prejudices exercised a more subtle influence on strategic thought through civilian leaders such as Weinberger whose own military service had been with the Army.

After Operation Desert Storm, however, and despite the continuing skepticism of General Colin Powell, the extraordinarily influential chairman of the Joint Chiefs of Staff, civilian elites came to see air power as the ideal vehicle for deriving political utility from U.S. military dominance in a unipolar world. The apparent contribution of air power to the triumph over Iraq, and its subsequent application—however inelegant—in Bosnia, Serbia, and Kosovo persuaded many that air weapons employed independently offered the ideal tool for the sorts of military problems facing the United States in the 1990s, and the new century beyond. As a result, in the first decade of the post–Cold War era, air power became the weapon of choice for American statecraft.

Two technological developments (reinforced by formidable tactical expertise) account for this development. The first is the routinization of precision. American warplanes can now deliver ordnance with something approaching pinpoint accuracy as a matter of course. "Dumb" (i.e. unguided) munitions still remain in the U.S. military inventory, but the norm in all four services is to employ bombs or missiles guided by any of a number of means—homing on laser reflections or infra-red signatures, electro-optical guidance, or through use of Global Positioning System navigation. To be sure, bombs still go awry, and the friction and fog inherent in war means that—as in the bombing of the Chinese embassy in Belgrade—the wrong target will occasionally get hit. But by any historical standard the technological advance in weapons accuracy has been immense: after centuries of warfare in which the vast majority of ordnance expended hit nothing except unoccupied land or sea, today most weapons actually hit their intended targets.

The second advance is no less critical, but more subtle. It is the ability to employ weapons against an adversary without suffering losses, except very rarely and indeed almost by accident. Hardware, organization, and skill enable American forces first to locate, identify, and accurately characterize enemy defenses and then to avoid, neutralize, or destroy them. This means that in many cases, and certainly against fixed targets, American air power can operate with near impunity. By and large, American politicians and commanders can realistically plan for the punishment of smaller opponents without anticipating the loss of pilots or expensive aircraft.

The combination of precision and virtual invulnerability makes air power overwhelmingly attractive for medium scale applications of force (as in the Balkans) and for more routine forms of policing (as in Iraq). In practice, the American high command can titrate the amount of violence it wishes to apply to a potential opponent. As it demonstrated in Kosovo (and continues to demonstrate in the no-fly zones over Iraq), the United States can conduct combat operations over a period of months, even with some civilian casualties on the other side, without arousing a furor of opposition at home.

Air power offers precision and impunity—and, one might add, the appearance of control. Unlike ground forces committed to combat, air forces can cease operations within hours or minutes. Unlike ground forces, air forces can decrease, increase, or redirect the amount of violence they deliver on comparatively short notice. Air operations against third-rate opponents such as Yugoslavia or Iraq offer the peculiar prospect of war without real combat interaction. Opponents may counterpunch in some asymmetric fashion—by speeding up ethnic cleansing as the Serbs did in Kosovo or by firing off a few missiles as Saddam Hussein did in 1991. But "surprises" of this type are still very different from the shock of close combat. The inability of NATO warplanes to stop Slobodan Milosevic's Operation Horseshoe in Kosovo may have been an embarrassment; but the bloody punishment that Mohammed Farah Aidid's militiamen administered to American Rangers in Mogadishu in 1993 was a military defeat that led directly to policy failure. The preference for aerial warfare seems a way to bypass the hazards of ground combat: in Kosovo, in fact, the American government went out of its way to deny itself that option. Thus, the attractiveness of the scalpel seems to rule out the military equivalent of bone saws; but scalpels are not a solution to every surgical problem.

As has often been noted, precision air warfare is not without its drawbacks. Formidable though it appears, it actually exercises a relatively narrow range of military effects. Fielded forces can reduce their vulnerability by "hugging" the civilian population or by taking cover in forests and urban areas. More importantly, as precision becomes technically possible, it quickly becomes politically imperative; accidents as an inevitable byproduct of war become less acceptable. Public opinion abroad and at home, diplomatic reactions by foreign governments (allied, neutral, and hostile alike) are all less forgiving.

Reliance on air power (albeit a radically different kind of air power than the bludgeon of World War II strategic bombing) represents some elements of continuity with the old American way of war. The same cannot be said of changed American attitude toward ground combat. Here too, a combination of training and technology have produced what is, from one point of view, tremendous increases in military effectiveness. The demoralized, ill-disciplined semiconscript force of the late Vietnam era has given way to an all-volunteer, and highly professionalized Army and Marine Corps.[18] The long march from Hamburger Hill to 73 Easting—the former the scene of a notorious battle in the A Shau valley that cost 450 Americans killed or wounded, the latter a notable victory over Iraqi forces in 1991, won without friendly casualties—has provided the United States with exceptionally effective ground combat forces.

Assuming, that is, that Americans are willing to use them. Kosovo suggests just how hesitant the U.S. officials have become in that regard. The agonizing deliberations over the deployment of Task Force Hawk—fewer than two dozen Army helicopters, guarded and muffled by nearly 5,000 men and women—showed that politicians and generals alike found it increasingly difficult even to conceive of ground forces participating in a limited ground war. In contrast to modern air war, ground combat is more likely to mean casualties, except in some extraordinary circumstances—the Kuwait theater of operations in 1990–91, for example, offered a uniquely favorable situation for the heavily armored forces the United States deployed there. But casualties, even in numbers that are minute by any historical standard, have seemingly become unacceptable. When, as occurred earlier in the Yugoslavia intervention, U.S. commanders tell their troops that the first mission is force protection, this represents a fundamental change in American attitudes to ground warfare.

Why this shift in attitudes has occurred is uncertain.[19] Military leaders attribute casualty sensitivity to a public that is unwilling to face up to the realities of war. But survey data among military and civilian elites suggest otherwise. It appears, in fact, that the American military has become more sensitive to casualties than civilians. This stands to reason: in the absence of conscription, the public seems to regard America's servicemen and women much as they view police and firefighters—as people who deserve honor for the risks they run, but who have volunteered to put themselves in a position to do so. The roots of the present-day aversion to casualties are probably several. They may include a deep-seated reaction to the trauma of Vietnam, in two ways: a mistrust of military adventures launched for murky or merely limited political purposes, and a professional disgust at the squandering of human life. Casualty sensitivity may go deeper yet, being the military manifestation of broader trends in civil society. In a world that no longer accepts, with a fatalistic shrug, the notion of accidents and bad luck, in which, for example, corporations find themselves held accountable for the lung cancer that afflicts smokers who have chosen their habit, tolerance for combat losses has declined precipitously. It is not only that the stakes of war appear to be (and are) low; it is that the hazards of war—once a common phrase—no longer evoke the philosophical resignation they once did.

It is no coincidence that one slang for getting killed in Vietnam was "getting wasted." War is nothing if not waste on a hideous scale. But a society, including its military, which is fundamentally unwilling to accept the idea of waste has accepted a peculiar notion of war. And, for the moment, that is exactly what the United States has done.

The New Proconsuls

In 1986 the United States overhauled its system of defense organization. The Goldwater-Nichols Department of Defense reorganization act of that year continued trends evident in defense legislation going back to 1947. Since the end of World War II, the influence of the services on the conduct of military operations has diminished, with power moving to the Chairman of the Joint Chiefs of Staff (and the Joint Staff which now reports to him alone) and to the theater Commanders in Chief, or CINCs. Although it would only become apparent years after the fact, the Goldwater-Nichols Act had the further unanticipated consequence of draining power from the Office of the Secretary of Defense as well, increasing military authority at the expense of civilian control.

General Wesley Clark, Supreme Allied Commander Europe (SACEUR) and commander in chief of European Command (CINCEUCOM), dominated decision-making during the Kosovo conflict. Precisely, he served as the focal point for strategic decision-making, even if, in retrospect, cross-cutting pressures from NATO members limited his autonomy. Clark's was the dominating personality, even if he endured more than his share of frustration in gaining the decisions he wished. In some ways he represented a throwback to an eighteenth-century style of warfare. Clark carried much of the burden of negotiating with the multiple governments that contributed forces to the coalition battle. Indeed, one of the peculiarities of the Kosovo conflict lay in the deference that the United States showed to allied leaders. Despite providing more than three-quarters of the effective force—that is, those elements that delivered precision guided weapons, coordinated and controlled air operations, and assessed their effects—the United States yielded to a style of collective decision-making that soldiers found agonizingly slow. What seems *not* to have occurred was shaping of alliance strategy and action by political and military authorities in Washington—the kind of central control exercised during World War II by Roosevelt and his chiefs of staff. Not only did the President and the Secretary of Defense seem remarkably detached from the conduct of operations; their statutory advisers, the Joint Chiefs of Staff, contributed little to the planning and conduct of the war. Indeed, their first meeting with the President occurred the day the Milosevic regime announced its intention to withdraw from Kosovo.

The rise of the CINC reflected, no doubt, the effect of personality. Clark, a brilliant, politically sophisticated, and assertive soldier, exercised perhaps disproportionate, or at least unusual control over a foreign policy establishment at home that had sent American forces off to limited engagements before, but evinced little stomach for war leadership. But Clark's dominant role reflected as well the bureaucratic consequences of Goldwater-Nichols, which, in reducing the role of the service chiefs had left political leaders with but two channels of military advice—the CINC overseas, and the Joint Chiefs of Staff chairman at home. The latter, General Henry Shelton, seems to have been a cautious and not terribly forceful bureaucratic player, thus reversing the pattern of the Gulf War, when a dominant chairman, General Colin Powell, controlled all communications between the CINC, General Norman Schwarzkopf, and civil authority.

What seems, in all events, to have dropped out of the civilian-military dialogue was a presentation of different options and a debate among military authorities about the best course of action, conducted in the presence, and for the ultimate benefit of, civilian leadership. Indeed, implicit in the Goldwater-Nichols legislation was the view that such debates produced confusion or tawdry bargaining, a questionable interpretation of the historical record.

Beyond this military centralization, however, lay a further more pervasive and subtle development, the rise of the CINC as imperial proconsul. Gone are the days when senior generals and admirals think of themselves as the mere executors of policy rather than its formulators. Clark's record in pushing for operations against Milosevic, and his dominance of the intra-Allied debate is mirrored in other theaters of the world. America's Asian security policy bears the clear imprint of the views of the commander in chief of the Pacific Command (CINCPAC). American drugs and security policy in Latin America likewise reflects the influence of the commander in chief of Southern Command (CINCSOUTH)—and (during the Clinton Administration) of the retired four-star general who is the "czar" of White House counter-narcotics policies. American generals and admirals, having experienced a half-century of the Cold War, have become more than comfortable with a strong role in setting policy, negotiating deals, and even setting the objectives for which force should be used. Admiral Leighton ("Snuffy") Smith, the NATO commander during operation DELIBERATE FORCE in 1995 summarized his view of civil-military relations this way:

> I said this publicly a number of times. In Western militaries, the military follow the guidance of their political leaders, their authorized and rightful political leaders, okay? 'If you want me to go after the war criminals—and I do not think that's a good idea right now—if you want me to go after them, give me the order, get the hell out of my way, and stand by for the consequences.'[20]

Within ten days of the beginning of the war in Kosovo, a senior officer told the *Washington Post* that "I don't think anybody felt like there had been a compelling argument made that all of this was in our national interest"—as if that were for the military itself to decide.[21]

The development of a military that no longer sees sharp lines between the making of policy and its execution, between a necessary literacy in political matters and the arts of manipulating government to do what it believes desirable, is a troubling development. It has occurred, in part, because civilian leaders have in large measure abdicated responsibility for shaping the course and conclusion of military operations. When General Norman Schwarzkopf went to negotiate an end to the Gulf War he did so without the benefit of instructions or guidance from his civilian superiors, who seem to have delegated to him and to Chairman of the Joint Chiefs of Staff, General Colin Powell, the final decision on how to end the Gulf War. In this, as in other cases, the differences between the first Bush and the Clinton administrations, often proclaimed by members of both administrations, are more apparent than real.

Beyond Kosovo

To be sure, no way of war is a fixed thing. Under the right set of circumstances leaders and their society may accept very different styles of conflict. But barring some cataclysmic event—a twenty-first-century Pearl Harbor—it seems likely that the American way of war will prevail for some time to come. Given that prospect, three large consequences follow.

First, the United States now operates with a kind of cognitive dissonance with respect to force structure and doctrine. Its soldiers, sailors, airmen and marines live the new American way of war. Their arms, their training, their doctrine, and their fundamental beliefs about war bear the imprint of the old one. Adapting the legacy of the old way of war to meet the imperative of the new one has proven a daunting challenge. The new American way of war demanded by the new responsibilities undertaken by U.S. soldiers requires something other than an old Cold War–era force—fewer armored brigades and more B-2 bombers; the abandonment of military jargon about "end states" and "exit strategies;" the development of organizations dedicated to peacemaking and other "Operations Other Than War"; and the recruitment of personnel whose primary interest lies in such activities rather than becoming "warriors." None of these changes will come easily.

Secondly, the United States must face up to the vulnerabilities inherent in its new way of war. First and foremost among them is casualty sensitivity, but those potential vulnerabilities also include increasing deference to allied opinion and an unwillingness even to contemplate serious land operations. These problems are societal and political in nature, but they may respond, at least to some degree, to technological and organizational solutions. The more advances in military technology allow the United States to wield effective, and above all sustained military power without exposing itself to losses, the better. One piece of good news in the Kosovo war was America's ability to conduct relatively modest operations over a prolonged period. From a traditional point of view such an operational style has little to recommend it; but if political circumstances require chronic, incremental, and highly constrained military operations, better to execute them well than badly.

Finally, the American leaders, civilian and military alike, must consider whether the current balance in civil-military relations is the right one. The narrowing of channels of military advice may have had the effect of undermining real civilian control. To regain freedom of maneuver civilians may find it useful to pit their chief military adviser—the Chairman of the Joint Chiefs of Staff—against the theater CINC. Another alternative would be an effort to reinvigorate the Joint Chiefs of Staff as a collective body offering advice. In any event, civilian leaders must re-establish the clear lines between making policy and executing it, strongly advocating courses of action and attempting to influence them. Conceivably, such an effort to re-assert civilian supremacy may produce uncomfortable confrontations, and perhaps a few dismissals or resignations—if so, however, the price is worth it.

These challenges for the American way of supreme command are compounded by the peculiar difficulty Americans now have in speaking frankly about war. The old way of war may have been brutal, but at least it was honest. It is symbolic, perhaps, of a larger change in how the countries of the West now think about conflict that Secretary General Javier Solana could declare, while announcing the bombing of Serbia: "Let me be clear: NATO is not waging war against Yugoslavia."[22] Some amount of disingenuousness characterizes most war. But there is something more than usually disheartening in the quibbles, evasions, and semantic contortions that pervaded the Kosovo operation—in which war was not war, in which an absence of results signified progress, and in which an utterly implausible objective was declared a precise and achievable "end state." Perhaps Western leaders, including Americans, have concluded that waging war is a subject that no longer merits serious consideration. If so, they are making a grave mistake.

The end of the Cold War transformed America's role in the world. Prior to World War II the United States was but one of several Great Powers. By the end of that conflict it had become the undisputed leader of a grand coalition. Today, it views itself, in the possibly unfortunate phrase of Secretary of State Madeleine Albright, as "the indispensable nation," or, as others might term it, "the global hegemon." American power pervades the international system. Civil war in Rwanda, border disputes in the Levant, jousting over coastal waters in the South China Sea—all engage American interests, and ultimately, American power. These inescapable interests and commitments occur in a radically changed international environment, in which the bipolar conflict of the Cold War has irretrievably collapsed, and in which the United States, because of the strength of its economy and culture, bestrides the world. The strangely successful Kosovo war—the bloodless victory that left the winners disconcerted and discontented—marked another milestone in an era that has evoked a new way of war. Like all others, that approach to war will last for a duration of time—years or decades—that its practitioners cannot hope to know.

Any way of war has its strengths and its weaknesses; all ultimately succumb to altered political circumstances and changing techniques and technology. For the moment, devising an open formulation of the new American way of war, perfecting its methods, clarifying its assumptions, and recognizing its limits—while accepting the likelihood that it too, will, at some point, prove inadequate—will be challenge enough.

Notes

1. Don E. Fehrenbacher and Virginia Fehrenbacher, eds., *Recollected Works of Abraham Lincoln* (Stanford, Calif.: Stanford University Press, 1996), p. 426.
2. For the classic description of the "American Way of War," see Russell Weigley's book of that name (Bloomington: Indiana University Press, 1973).
3. E. J. Kahn, *McNair, Educator of an Army, by Chief Warrant Officer E. J. Kahn, Jr.* (Washington, D.C.: The Infantry Journal, 1945), p. 8.
4. Josiah Bunting, *The Lionheads: A Novel* (New York: Braziller, 1972), p. 56.
5. Caspar Weinberger, National Press Club, 28 November 1984, reprinted in *Defense* (January 1985): 1–11. Also at: http://www.amsc.belvoir.army.mil/ecampus/gpc/prework/strategy/use.htm
6. General Howell Estes Jr., in "Give War a Chance," Program 1715 of *Frontline*, PBS, 11 May 1999. Transcript at http://www.pbs.org/wgbh/pages/frontline/shows/military/etc/script.html
7. See Gideon Rose, "The Exit Strategy Delusion," *Foreign Affairs* 78, no. 1 (January-February 1998).
8. Emory Upton, *The Military Policy of the United States* (1904; reprint, New York: Greenwood, 1968). See also a commentary by this author, "Making Do

With Less, or Coping with Upton's Ghost," Strategic Studies Institute monograph (Carlisle Barracks, Pa.: U.S. Army War College, 1995).

9. Statement by the President to the Nation, 24 March 1999. http://www.pub.whitehouse.gov/uri-res/I2R?urn:pdi://oma.eop.gov.us/1999/3/25/1.text.1
10. Remarks by the President at the Commencement of the United States Air Force Academy, 2 June 1999. http://www.pub.whitehouse.gov/uri-res/I2R?urn:pdi://oma.eop.gov.us/1999/6/4/7.text
11. President George W. Bush, Address to the Nation Announcing United States Military Action in Panama, 20 December 1989. http://bushlibrary.tamu.edu/papers/1989/89122000.html.
12. David E. Johnson, "Wielding the Terrible Swift Sword: The American Military Paradigm and Civil-Military Relations," (Cambridge, Mass.: Harvard University Olin Insitute for Strategic Studies, 1996); http://data.fas.harvard.edu/cfia/olin/pubs/no7.htm
13. Statement by the President on Kosovo, 24 March 1999. http://www.pub.whitehouse.gov/uri-res/I2R?urn:pdi://oma.eop.gov.us/1999/3/24/5.text.1
14. Press Statement, Dr. Javier Solana, Secretary General of NATO, 23 March 1999. http://www.nato.int/docu/pr/1999/p99-040e.htm
15. See, for example, Secretary of State Madeleine K. Albright's interview on *Face the Nation*, CBS, 28 March 1999; http://secretary.state.gov/www/statements/1999/990328.html
16. DOD News Briefing, 19 April 1999. http://www.defenselink.mil/news/Apr1999/t04191999_t0419asd.html
17. Ibid.
18. There is an important distinction. When, as in the case of the Marine Corps, the bulk of infantry consists of troops serving only one term of enlistment, the term "professional" must be qualified. But that is an extreme case, and as recruitment becomes more difficult the armed services have turned their attention to the need to retain personnel in lieu of bringing more in.
19. For a good overview of this issue, see Eric V. Larson, *Casualties and Consensus: The Historical Role of Casualties in Domestic Support for U.S. Military Operations* (Santa Monica, Calif.: RAND, 1996).
20. "Give War a Chance," Program 1715 of *Frontline*, PBS, 11 May 1999.
21. Bradley Graham, "Joint Chiefs Doubted Air Strategy," *Washington Post*, 5 April 1999, p. A1.
22. Secretary General Solana, press statement, 23 March 1999.

3 First War of the Global Era: Kosovo and U.S. Grand Strategy

James Kurth

NATO's war for Kosovo has been widely seen as the first example of a new kind of armed conflict, the prototype for a twenty-first century way of war. Indeed, observers have touted the war as first of its kind in at least four different ways. To begin with, Kosovo was ostensibly the first truly humanitarian war, fought not for national interests as traditionally defined but for the furtherance of human rights alone. Second, Kosovo was the first real war undertaken by the NATO alliance, fought with the full authorization and participation of NATO members acting as an organization. Third, in the estimation of many well-informed analysts, the war for Kosovo provides the first real example of victory achieved through air power alone, a war won without having to engage in ground combat operations. And finally, the war was the first case of a completely bloodless victory, a war in which NATO prevailed without suffering a single combat casualty. Any one of these unique features would assure the Kosovo War a distinctive place in the annals of military history. The conjunction of the four should make that place truly extraordinary.

As we will see, all of these claims about the Kosovo War are true, but they are also incomplete. They could therefore be misleading both about the causes of the war and about its implications for future conflicts. To understand these causes and consequences, we will need to examine the war in the context of the grand, or national, strategy of the United States. For the Kosovo War was, inter alia, an outgrowth of a new grand strategy that the United States has developed in the aftermath of the Cold War.

Among the Kosovo War's distinctions, it was the first American war of the global era.

The United States and Grand Strategy

It is often thought that grand strategy—a concept that historically was most articulated by the centralized nation-states of Europe—cannot really apply to the United States, with its free-wheeling democracy, fragmented political system, and disorderly decision-making process. Alexis de Tocqueville, writing in the 1830s, was the first of a long line of distinguished analysts to argue that democracies, particularly pluralistic ones like the United States, are incapable of adhering to coherent and consistent foreign policies.[1] They are, in short, incapable of adhering to anything remotely resembling a genuine grand strategy.

In practice, however, diplomatic historians (as well as foreign adversaries) have discerned a good deal of coherence and consistency in U.S. policy, sustained over long periods of time. These periods include much of the nineteenth century (when the grand strategy was defined by continental expansion and the Monroe Doctrine); the first three decades of the twentieth century (when it emphasized commercial expansion and U.S. leadership in the world balance-of-power system); and the Cold War (when it comprised containment, nuclear deterrence, and the promotion of an open international economy). The "new" grand strategy of each successive period builds on the strategy it supercedes, revising and expanding it to fit the altered realities and opportunities created by American victories in successive wars. In a sense, there has been a single U.S. grand strategy, continuing, developing, and evolving for over two centuries.[2]

U.S. grand strategy has always included both security objectives and economic objectives, as well as particular approaches to achieving these ends at particular times. During the Cold War, for example, the United States emphasized military containment and free trade.[3] During the same period, the U.S. also supported the development of rather sophisticated international institutions with which to achieve its security and its economic objectives. These included international security organizations, such as the North Atlantic Treaty Organization (NATO) and the Organization of American States (OAS), and international economic organizations, such as the International Monetary Fund (IMF), the World Bank, and the General Agreement on Tariffs and Trade (GATT). The U.S. also developed a rather sophisticated ideology, one that gained wide international appeal and comprised both political and economic ideals. This was liberal internationalism, whose political ideal was liberal democracy and whose economic ideal was free markets. All of these features were elements of U.S. grand strategy during the Cold War.[4]

After the collapse of the Soviet Union and the end of the Cold War, the United States modified and expanded elements from its earlier grand strategies and used them as the basis for a revised grand strategy. The result reflected not only new realities and opportunities created by the American victory in the Cold War; it also reflected particular transformations that had developed during the last decade or so of the Cold War. Indeed, U.S. grand strategy at the beginning of the twenty-first century is the product of six new realities that characterize the contemporary United States and its role in the world. Two of these new realities pertain primarily to the international security system, two to the global economic system, and two to the American social system. Several of these converged to bring about the Kosovo War.

The New Realities and the Global Era

With regard to the international security system, the most obvious new reality is that the United States now finds itself the sole superpower. But although it is the greatest power, the U.S. is not the only power. Since its power, although formidable, is not great enough that it can act alone in world affairs, the United States must lead and cooperate with other states to achieve its own purposes.

This points directly to the second new reality about the international security system, namely, the enhanced American reliance on selected international organizations as vehicles to legitimize U.S. grand strategy. As we have seen, the United States has a long tradition of using international organizations through which to exercise leadership and gain cooperation. Now that the United States is the sole superpower, one whose leadership can readily be interpreted by other states as domination, the imperative of working through international organizations—even if only as a cloak for de facto unilateral action—has become even more pronounced. Among security organizations, NATO clearly is seen by U.S. policymakers as the most useful for these purposes.

The new security realities are the result most obviously of the American victory over the Soviet Union in the Cold War. The new economic and social realities result from particular developments that began even before the Cold War ended and that developed within the United States itself, coming to maturity in the 1990s.

Any nation's grand strategy must take into account that nation's economic and social conditions. U.S. grand strategy during the Cold War era—a strategy whose core elements consisted of containment, nuclear deterrence, and the promotion of an open international economy—reflected particular economic and social realities that existed during most of that time. The economic realities were American industrial power and American leadership in the international economy. The social realities were the ordering of Americans into large, hierarchical organizations—a distinctive feature of what has been termed "modern society"—and the existence of a basic national consensus around an ideology of liberal internationalism.

Today, more than ten years after the end of the Cold War, economic and social conditions are radically different. The American economic reality no longer centers on industrial power, and the American social reality no longer adheres to classic liberalism. Four great economic and social transformations have displaced the old reality. These transformations have been most pronounced in the United States, but their impact has been global in scope. Indeed, they have brought about a whole new era that can best be identified as "the global era." These transformations have had a corresponding effect on American grand strategy, which U.S. policymakers have redesigned to fit their conception of the global era. The Kosovo War was among the first fruits of that revised strategy.[5]

The Four Great Transformations and Liberal Globalism

The four transformations giving birth to the global era are the following: the emergence of a global economy, replacing what had been merely an international economy; the development of an information economy, replacing what had been the industrial economy; the development of the postmodern society, replacing what had been modernity; and the decline of the nation-state, superseded in some countries (particularly the United

States, Canada, and Western Europe) by a multicultural society along with a new form of liberalism.[6]

The current era has been given different names. Three of the more common ones—the "global era," the "information era," and the "postmodern era"—testify to the prominence and defining power of the first three of the transformations. The fierce debates about multiculturalism in American society testify to the prominence of the fourth.

Although the consequences of these four transformations are truly global, they have developed more in some countries than in others. Among the major powers, they have advanced most within the United States and Britain, somewhat less so in Germany and Japan, and still less in Russia, China, and India. Indeed, the *uneven* advance of these global transformations, combined with the U.S. leadership in promoting them, probably will produce even greater international misunderstandings and conflicts in the future than will the simple transformations themselves. Within the United States itself, these transformations have made America a very different country from what it was as recently as the Cold War. These transformations have also accentuated the ways that the United States differs from the other major powers.

The four transformations have had major consequences for American ideas, ideology, and even identity. For example, the development of *the global economy* has increased the freedom and mobility of business enterprises and weakened the constraints of governments. The global economy has thus reinforced the traditional American idea of free markets. But it also has promoted a newer and broader idea, that of the open society.

Similarly, the emergence of an *information economy* that has displaced the industrial economy has increased individual choice and devalued conventional hierarchies. The information economy has thus reinforced the traditional American idea of liberal democracy—but it too has promoted the newer and broader idea of the open society.

The global economy and the information economy are therefore two powerful forces whose ideological bias favors openness. But the ideology of the open society implies, indeed advocates, the limitation of state sovereignty and the weakening of the nation-state. This is particularly the case in regard to state-imposed barriers or regulations concerning the free movement of goods, capital, migrants, and information across national borders. This ideology of the open society, which most American political, economic, and intellectual elites now endorse, represents a fundamental challenge to traditional conceptions of international relations, still held by policymakers in many states, including Russia and China.

The development of *the postmodern society* has eroded the great pillars of modern society—government bureaucracies, military services, and business corporations—and the attitudes of deference, duty, and loyalty that often went with them. In their place, the postmodern society has promoted the two interrelated ideas of expressive individualism and universal human rights. Together, they form a new ideology in which individual rights are universal, universal rights are individual, and such rights are fundamental, even absolute. Conversely, the nation-state does not bestow rights, and the nation-state has no rights.

The development of a multiracial or *multicultural society* celebrates the idea of cultural diversity. Like the postmodern society, the multicultural society also promotes the idea of human rights. Although it might seem that a multiplicity of cultural groups would lead logically to an emphasis on the rights of the community, in practice it has led instead to an emphasis on the rights of the individual. Like the ideology of the open society, the ideology of human rights also points toward the limitation of state sovereignty and the decline of the nation-state. This is particularly the case in regard to international institutions overruling national governments in order to enforce human rights.

Traditional American ideology advocated liberal democracy and free markets. In foreign affairs, this ideology translated into liberal internationalism, and its most prominent proponents were Presidents Woodrow Wilson and Franklin Roosevelt. Because of the four great transformations, the 1990s saw a revival of this traditional ideology and, indeed, its expansion with a more explicit emphasis on promoting human rights and the open society. This modified version of liberal internationalism is more accurately termed "liberal globalism"; its most prominent proponents have been President Bill Clinton and Secretary of State Madeleine Albright.

The new American ideology of human rights and the open society—liberal globalism—in turn has provided the justification, and sometimes a compulsion, for a new kind of U.S. military interventionism. This has been humanitarian intervention, as in Somalia, Haiti, and then Bosnia. The U.S.-led war against Serbia over Kosovo represented the culmination of this trend toward humanitarian intervention. Vaclav Havel and others have described the Kosovo War as an altogether new kind of conflict, one in which the objectives are not traditional national interests but instead universal human rights.[7] These observers saw the Kosovo War as the first purely humanitarian war and, on that score, gave it their approval. But, as we shall see, this is not the whole story; Kosovo was also the first war fought in response to the new U.S. grand strategy of the global era.

The Grand Strategy of the Global Era

The new U.S. grand strategy of the global era reflects the changing realities that we have described. The elements of Cold War–era grand strategy have undergone their own transformation to become the elements of the new grand strategy. In most cases, this transformation has involved expansion, in regard to both the scope of objectives and the particular means employed to achieve these objectives.

The American interest in promoting an open international economy has expanded into support for an open global economy, even an open global society. U.S. grand strategy aims ultimately to eliminate all economic or social borders everywhere in the world. Borders separating nation-states would become about as significant as the borders separating the fifty states of the Union. The preferred means of achieving this open international order have expanded correspondingly. Support for free trade has given way to all-out advocacy of globalization.

The policy of containing the communist great powers, particularly the Soviet Union and China, has also expanded, this despite the Soviet Union itself having disappeared. The United States still pursues a de facto policy of containing (or more subtly of managing) Russia and China. To this has been added a policy of containing or managing several lesser powers that no longer have strong alliance ties with Russia or China. These are the usual suspects: Iran, Iraq, Libya, North Korea, Cuba, and occasionally Syria. These states are nationalist in their identities, authoritarian in their regimes, statist in their economies, and anti-American in their public rhetoric. They represent the antithesis of the American ideology of liberal globalism. The United States has often classified such states as rogues.[8] The military strategy employed to implement the policy of containment has likewise expanded. Whereas during the Cold War that strategy centered on nuclear deterrence, of late it has shifted to one that, while not abandoning nuclear deterrence, emphasizes conventional capabilities to deter, but also to retaliate against and punish by employing precision weapons.

The enlarged ambitions and objectives of liberal globalism have also encouraged the United States to expand its use of international organizations to achieve American security and economic objectives. In regard to security organizations, the United States has expanded the functions of the United Nations, the Organization for Security and Cooperation in Europe (OSCE), and NATO, particularly concerning peace-enforcement (no longer just peacekeeping) operations undertaken in the name of human rights and humanitarian intervention. In regard to economic organizations, the U.S. has broadened the functions of the IMF and the World Bank. It has led the campaign to transform the GATT into a fully-parallel economic institution, the World Trade Organization (WTO). Consistent with the so-called "Washington Consensus," this troika of economic institutions presses relentlessly to break-down national borders and supplant state enterprises, all in the name of the global economy and the open society.

Opposition to the U.S. Grand Strategy: Losers and Winners

Within a few years after the end of the Cold War, all the elements of the new U.S. grand strategy for the global era were in place. But by the mid-1990s, that strategy was already beginning to produce a backlash.

American promotion of the new realities of the global era, the American ideology of liberal globalism, and the consequent new U.S. grand strategy together are revolutionizing human affairs. This revolution is one of the most profound in human history, and it is certainly the most wide-ranging. Indeed, it is the first truly *world* revolution, its reach extending well beyond even the grandest claims of Marxism in its day.

Great revolutions can be expected to generate great opposition. The American-led global revolution has already generated significant opposition among important states. The major sources of opposition are found in three large nuclear powers (Russia, China, and India) and one large religious realm (the Islamic world). Some of this opposition comes from losers in the new global economy, but some, perhaps even most, comes from winners.

The first and most obvious sources of opposition to the American-led global revolution are the *losers* in the new global economy. These include

Russia and, more generally, most countries with an Eastern Orthodox religious tradition. They also include most of the Islamic world.

For a variety of reasons that are related to cultural traditions, Orthodox countries (Russia, Belarus, Ukraine, Moldova, Romania, Bulgaria, and Serbia) have been unsuccessful in making the transition from communism to liberal-democratic and free-market structures adaptable to an open society and a global economy. In contrast, most countries with a Roman Catholic tradition (Poland, Lithuania, the Czech Republic, Slovakia, Hungary, Slovenia, and even Croatia) have made this transition successfully. Largely Protestant nations (Estonia and Latvia) also have been successful. This dichotomy among ex-communist countries—between the more Western and the more Eastern, between the Roman Catholic or Protestant and the Eastern Orthodox—means that the political and economic developments of the 1990s revived and reinforced an ancient historic divide, corresponding to the great schism between Western and Eastern Christianity, even to the ancient division between the Latin and Greek halves of the Roman Empire. This particular cultural divide provided a major illustration of Samuel Huntington's famous argument about "the clash of civilizations."[9]

In their current condition of political and economic weakness, the governments of Russia and the other Orthodox countries cannot mount an effective and sustained opposition to the United States and its promotion of the global economy, the open society, and humanitarian intervention. But among the populations of these countries, there is now substantial resentment of and resistance toward the United States. The Kosovo War against Orthodox Serbia sharpened this resentment and resistance.

In Islamic countries as well, efforts to establish viable and resilient liberal democracies and market economies have failed. Most today are alienated from the American global project. As in the Orthodox world, governments in the Islamic world are neither willing nor able to mount a sustained and effective opposition to that project. But again, within their populations exists widespread resentment and resistance, manifested most obviously in militant organizations based upon Islamic revivalism.[10]

Even among the *winners* in the new global economy, opposition to the American-led global revolution is growing. These winners include China (and more generally many countries with a Confucian cultural tradition) and India.

Most Chinese, both in China itself and overseas, attribute their economic success to their own culture—to "Asian values" and a distinctive approach to the global economy in their own way. The Asian interpretation of the region's economic crisis of 1997–1999 has reinforced this conception. The countries with the most open currency-markets (South Korea, Thailand, and Indonesia) suffered the greatest disruption and decline; those whose currency-markets were most regulated (China and, ironically, Taiwan) experienced little disruption and continued their economic growth.

India's entry into the global economy has been recent, and its benefits for that country have been unevenly distributed. For now, however, India (or at least its vibrant information sector) qualifies as an emerging winner in the global economy. This success has occurred, however, in tandem with growing Hindu nationalism and India's development of a nuclear arsenal.

Thus the opposition to the United States and its global project is quite disparate. Some opponents are politically and economically weak and divided (the Orthodox and Islamic countries). Some are economically strong but still divided among themselves (the Confucian countries). But together, these sources of opposition constitute a vast region, really all of Eurasia and more; resistance to the American global project stretches from Russia and Eastern Europe, through the Middle East, through South Asia, to China and East Asia. This vast region contains four of the great civilizations that Huntington has identified as most likely to clash with the West: "Slavic-Orthodox," Islamic, Hindu, and "Sinic-Confucian." In this region too are four nuclear powers—Russia, Pakistan, India, and China—each seeing itself as the center of its particular civilization.[11]

U.S. leadership in humanitarian intervention, especially in Kosovo, has sharpened the opposition to the American global project. Humanitarian intervention presents a serious and specific threat to the norm of national sovereignty, and most of the opposition states saw the Kosovo War as a prime example of a U.S. grand strategy that aims to impose and enforce globalization. Furthermore, when the circumstances leading to humanitarian intervention in one state seem analogous to circumstances existing elsewhere, that intervention can also suggest a serious and specific threat to states worried that they may be next. This was the case with the Kosovo War, where Russia saw analogies between Kosovo and Chechnya, China saw analogies between Kosovo and Tibet, and India saw analogies between Kosovo and Kashmir.

The Balkans and Grand Strategy

By the late 1990s, the Balkans had become the central theater for implementing the new U.S. grand strategy of the global era. That such a marginalized place should serve such a grand purpose might seem strange, but of course it was not the first time that this poor and violent region has served as the arena for the grand strategies of the great powers.

The Balkans had been the crucible of bloody conflicts on four major occasions in the twentieth century. In the 1910s, the decay of the Ottoman Empire led to the Balkan Wars, and the recently-independent and expansionist Serbia conquered Kosovo at that time. A characteristic tactic in these Balkan Wars, one used by the Serbs against the Albanians in Kosovo, was state-organized massacre of ethnic groups, with the objective of ethnic cleansing. Serbia was an ally of Russia, which protected and promoted it in the international arena. As is well-known, Serb ambitions to acquire Bosnia led to the assassination of Archduke Franz Ferdinand, heir to the throne of Austria-Hungary, and to the outbreak of the First World War.

In the 1930s, tensions within the Kingdom of Yugoslavia (cobbled together by the victorious Allies after the First World War) led to conflict between Serbs and Croats, to German invasion and occupation, and to a sort of civil war between the different ethnic groups of Yugoslavia, within the larger conflict of the Second World War. Once again, a characteristic tactic in this Yugoslav civil war was ethnic massacre, combined with the new tactic of guerrilla warfare. The most successful guerrillas were the Communists, many of them Serbs who were supported by the Soviet Union. A new Yugoslav federation ruled by the Communist Josef Broz Tito was the result.

In the late 1940s, the decay of the British Empire led to a civil war in Greece, pitting conservatives against Communists. Communist Yugoslavia supported the guerrilla insurrection of Greek Communists until 1948, when Marshal Tito broke with Stalin. However, the United States thought that the Soviet Union itself was providing the principal support for the guerrillas, and this perception formed the basis for the Truman Doctrine in 1947 and for a sharper definition of the emerging Cold War.

Finally, the decay of Communist Yugoslavia in the 1980s after Tito's death led to a new civil war in the 1990s between the different ethnic groups of that country. As at the time of the Balkan Wars of the 1910s, the Serbs once again conquered the territories of other groups, employed state-organized massacres with the objective of ethnic cleansing, and enjoyed broad Russian support. This latest round of ethnic conflict in Yugoslavia, involving Orthodox Serbs, Catholic Croats, and Muslim Bosnians and Albanians, seemed a prototype of a new kind of larger world conflict, the "clash of civilizations."

This periodic centrality of the Balkans in great power conflicts in part results from the region's ambiguous geographical position between Europe and the Middle East. Indeed, observers have differed over whether the Balkans are in or out of Europe or in or out of the Middle East.

The Balkan people themselves have commonly perceived themselves as being part of Europe, as have many Americans. In the last decade, the U.S. State Department has often referred to the region as South-Eastern Europe, a term which implies that the Balkans are important to the security of Europe and (since Europe is manifestly important to the United States) also important to that of the United States. Conversely, the Balkans have also been seen as lying beyond Europe, part of a vaguely-defined East. This view is common among many Europeans. During the first half of the twentieth century, the Balkans were often referred to as part of "the Near East."

In any event, whether the Balkans are in Europe or merely near it, the region also exists in proximity to the Middle East, and thus to the vast U.S. economic interests in the oil of that region and to the important U.S. political interests in the security of Israel. For more than two decades, the United States has believed that Iraq and Iran posed a threat to these important interests. In the 1990s, these two nations numbered among those rogue states accused of developing weapons of mass destruction that would pose a serious threat to U.S. national security. This threat from the Middle East exercised an important influence on the way that the Clinton administration came to conceive of new purposes for NATO and to perceive the conflicts in the former Yugoslavia.

Reinventing NATO's Strategic Concept

Prior to the 1990s, when the Soviet Union posed the most serious threat to U.S. national interests, NATO offered the primary instrument to contain that threat. With the collapse of the Soviet Union, NATO became a very strange institution, magnificent in its capabilities, deluged with applicants for membership, but without any obvious purpose. Throughout the 1990s, U.S. policymakers wrestled with the problem of reinventing NATO, particularly the redefinition of both its purpose and its membership.

The first step in the redefinition of NATO was "enlargement," the admission to membership of the three Central European states of Poland, Hungary, and the Czech Republic. But this kind of redefinition did not fundamentally change NATO's purpose. Although the Russian threat was greatly diminished, to NATO's three new members—its Eastern flank—that threat still seemed very real. So the enlarged, post–Cold-War NATO, like the smaller Cold War NATO, was still focused on Russia.

At the same time, however, the Clinton administration was developing the conception that U.S. national interests in the Middle East, threatened by rogue states such as Iraq and Iran, could be better protected if NATO's responsibilities included not only new territories within but also beyond Europe. A NATO willing to go "out-of-area" could make itself most useful in the region of the Middle East, important both in regard to "the flow of vital resources" and "the proliferation of NBC weapons and their means of delivery."[12]

Since the formation of NATO in 1949 its purpose and strategy had been elaborated in a formal and authoritative document known as "The Strategic Concept." NATO had adopted the previous version of the Strategic Concept in 1991, just after the end of the Cold War. The Clinton administration sought to redefine and expand the purpose of NATO in an easterly direction by promoting a new Strategic Concept that would focus on new threats and tasks. The goal was to have the alliance formally adopt this new document at the most important and symbolic NATO meeting of all, the 50th Anniversary Summit to be held in Washington in April 1999. The new Strategic Concept would articulate an expanded and expansive redefinition of "security challenges and risks":

> The security of the Alliance remains subject to a wide variety of military and nonmilitary risks which are multidirectional and often difficult to predict. These risks include uncertainty and instability in and around the Euro-Atlantic area and the possibility of regional crises at the periphery of the Alliance, which could evolve rapidly. . . . Some states, including on NATO's periphery and in other regions, sell or acquire or try to acquire NBC weapons and delivery means.

> Any armed attack on the territory of the Allies, from whatever direction, would be covered by Articles 5 and 6 of the Washington Treaty [the central articles in the original NATO treaty of 1949, which specified a direct attack upon members of the Alliance]. However, Alliance security interests can be affected by other risks of a wider nature, including acts of terrorism, sabotage and organized crime, and by the disruption of the flow of vital resources.[13]

Other members of NATO were not as convinced as the United States that the alliance should shoulder out-of-area responsibilities, and particularly in the Middle East. They were also not as convinced that NATO had the military wherewithal to enforce this new purpose. However, the Clinton administration was determined to press forward with its own new strategic concept (and with NATO's new Strategic Concept). For the administration to make its case, it became important to demonstrate the necessity of NATO's out-of-area expansion and to affirm NATO's military capabilities to undertake such operations effectively.

Kosovo as Strategic Testbed

The Balkans—which are both in Europe and out of it and which are the bridge between Europe and the Middle East—were the obvious place to begin the great march of NATO out-of-area and into vital resources. Increasing violence and repression in Kosovo in 1998 provided occasion and opportunity. A NATO war against Serbia would provide the defining or rather redefining moment, one that would redefine NATO's central purpose from the containment and management of Russia to the containment and management of rogue states and that would shift NATO's central theater from Central Europe first to South-Eastern Europe or the Balkans and then to the Middle East. Such a war would demonstrate NATO's new purpose and its new capabilities. Of course, the war would have to be both successful and short (something like the "splendid little war" of a hundred years before, the Spanish-American War of 1898). Indeed, it would have to be so successful and short that it would come to a triumphal end in time for the opening ceremony of the Washington Summit on April 23, 1999.

The Clinton administration had convinced itself that an air war against

Serbia would indeed be both successful and short, that Serbia would yield to NATO demands after only a few days and a few sorties of bombing. This confidence stemmed from the administration's reading of NATO's role in the climactic chapter of the Bosnian civil war in 1995, when limited bombing had seemingly caused the Bosnian Serbs to yield to the demands of the international community. By crediting its own action with ending the Bosnian War, the administration engaged in analysis that was incomplete and self-serving. In truth, the main force that paved the way for a negotiated settlement over Bosnia in 1995 was not the bombing by NATO but an offensive by Croat and Bosnian Muslim armies that threatened to overrun most of the territory held by the Bosnian Serbs.[14] The Bosnian War, like all previous wars, was decided not with an air war alone, but with a land war. But in its enthusiasm to go to war with Serbia over Kosovo, the Clinton administration overlooked all of that.

Reinventing NATO was not the sole purpose that U.S. policymakers had in mind when they decided to go to war with Serbia over Kosovo. More traditional security and economic interests, however, were not among those purposes. By any conventional definition of such interests, the United States had virtually none at stake in Kosovo. Serbia did not obviously threaten aggression against any other state, even Albania. Granted, some observers worried that violence in Kosovo might spill over into neighboring states such as Albania and Macedonia, leading somehow to a wider conflict pitting Greece against Turkey, but this security argument was so indirect (not to say far-fetched) that, by itself, it could hardly provide a rationale for NATO intervention. As for U.S. economic interests in Kosovo, these were nonexistent. It seems clear that the United States did not undertake the Kosovo War in order to achieve any of the traditional security and economic objectives of its grand strategy.

There were, however, ideological and political objectives that a war for Kosovo might serve. As noted above, the new realities of the global economy and the multicultural society have brought into being the new ideology of liberal globalism, with its emphasis on human rights and openness. Liberal globalism has also brought into being a political constituency on behalf of these ideas, located principally within the American media and universities. Some U.S. officials eager for war in Kosovo were responding to this ideology and constituency. But as we shall argue in a later section, humanitarian objectives may be necessary for the United States to go to war in the global era, but they are not sufficient.

Rambouillet and the Pretext for War

The actions of the U.S. diplomats in the Rambouillet negotiations in February and March 1999 strongly indicate that the United States wanted Serbia to reject a political solution to the problem posed by Kosovo. This rejection would then be used to justify a NATO war against Serbia.[15]

The main text of the proposed "Interim Agreement for Peace and Self-Government in Kosovo" consisted of thirty pages of small print and dealt with Kosovo itself.[16] Although it included stipulations that were disputed by the Serbs, the document contained nothing that was particularly unusual or unacceptable by normal diplomatic practice. However, the agreement also included two appendices. Appendix A was a boring list of weapons cantonment sites in Kosovo. Appendix B, entitled "Status of Multi-National Military Implementation Force," was altogether different from what had gone before.

Appendix B authorized NATO forces to have free movement and to conduct military operations anywhere within the Federal Republic of Yugoslavia (FRY) and therefore within Serbia itself. Clause 8 reads:

> NATO personnel shall enjoy, together with their vehicles, vessels, aircraft, and equipment, free and unrestricted passage and unimpeded access throughout the FRY including associated airspace and territorial waters. This shall include, but not be limited to, the right of bivouac, maneuver, billet, and utilization of any areas or facilities as required for support, training, and operations.

Other clauses further amplified the rights of NATO military forces within Serbia.

Appendix B obviously posed a direct threat to the sovereign independence of Serbia, as well as to the practical security of the Milosevic regime. It was predictable that the Serbs would reject it and therefore would have to reject the agreement.[17]

That the Serbs would reject Appendix B was more predictable still, given a particular event in their history. In the Serb understanding of their past, the ultimatum which Austria-Hungary presented to Serbia on July 23, 1914 in the aftermath of the assassination of Franz Ferdinand stands out as a particularly infamous document. Much of that ultimatum contained nothing that was very unusual or unacceptable in normal diplomatic practice, and indeed, the Serbs agreed to accept several burdensome stipulations. However, one clause gave the Austro-Hungarian security officers unimpeded access throughout Serbia for purposes of investigating the assassination.[18] Serbia saw this as a direct threat to its sovereign independence. It also saw it as a deliberate move by Austria-Hungary to provoke Serbia to reject that clause and therefore the ultimatum. That rejection would then be used to justify a declaration of war against Serbia. Despite this understanding of the consequences, Serbia did reject the clause. Thus began the long and terrible chain of events consisting of the Austro-Hungarian declaration of war upon Serbia; Russia's declaration of war upon Austria-Hungary; the invasion and destruction of Serbia; the explosion of the Balkan war into the First World War; and, ultimately, Serbia's resurrection within the new and greater Yugoslavia. The Serbs view their rejection of the Austro-Hungarian ultimatum as being tragic but heroic and ultimately vindicated by history.

In any event, Serbia did reject the Rambouillet Agreement, and NATO led by the United States did go to war over Kosovo on March 24, 1999. Eleven weeks later, when Serbia accepted a new agreement with NATO on Kosovo in order to end the war, that agreement contained no clauses authorizing the movement of NATO forces within Serbia itself. In explaining to the Serbian people why it went to war rather than sign the first agreement and why it had agreed to sign the second, the government of Slobodan Milosevic gave a prominent place to this difference.

The Kosovo War came about as a consequence of the new U.S. grand strategy, and the war itself has had consequences for that strategy. But these consequences are not quite as momentous as has often been argued. To understand what the consequences actually are, we will examine the war as it relates to five strategic issues: humanitarian war, NATO enlargement, victory through air power, U.S. relations with Russia, and U.S. relations with China.

The Kosovo War and Humanitarian War

The Kosovo War has been seen by many as the first humanitarian war, a war fought for the furtherance of human rights alone, rather than for the traditional objectives of national interests. This writer has argued above that the main U.S. purpose in the war was in fact the furtherance of NATO. However, the Kosovo War did achieve clear humanitarian results, such as the end of the Serbian atrocities and the return of the Albanian refugees. In that sense, the war was indeed a humanitarian war.

What are the future prospects for more humanitarian wars, such as the Kosovo War appeared to be? Alas, countries where the potential exists for the state to undertake large-scale massacres of ethnic groups, comparable to the Serb-organized massacre of Albanians in Kosovo in 1999 (as well as of Croats in Croatia in 1991 and of Muslims in Bosnia in 1992–1995) are plentiful. The most obvious current candidates to become victims of state-sponsored massacres in the future are the Kurds in Iraq, Christians in Sudan, and Hutus in Burundi (the obverse of the Tutsis slaughtered in Rwanda in 1994). Indeed, these peoples have been the victims of such massacres in the recent past or are even suffering them at present. There are also the well-known, but disputed, cases of the Chechens in Russia and the Tibetans in China.

Massacres organized by a state and directed against an ethnic group approach the definition of genocide given in the *United Nations Convention on the Prevention and Punishment of the Crime of Genocide*; preventing and punishing them would clearly qualify as humanitarian.[19] And since such massacres are implemented by the organized force of a state, stopping them would normally require a comparable organized force, i.e., one or more other states undertaking a war against the perpetrators. State-organized massacres would thus be the most suitable, and perhaps the only suitable, targets for humanitarian war, following the prototype of the Kosovo War.

The doleful history of state-organized massacre suggests, however, that other states, even when representing "the international community," are not inclined to undertake a purely humanitarian war to stop them. This was true not only of the state-organized massacres that occurred during the Cold War era, but also those occurring after the Cold War ended but before Kosovo.

It is, of course, easy enough to understand why humanitarian war was not a practical option for the international community (such as it was) or for the United States (as its purported leader) during the Cold War. In the bipolar conflict between the United States and the Soviet Union, almost every U.S. military intervention had to be grounded and justified in terms of concrete U.S. national interests related to that great struggle. The United States could not afford to expend military resources on matters totally unrelated to its own interests. During the Cold War, there were many cases of large-scale, state-organized massacres of ethnic groups in response to which the United States did nothing. These cases include the Baltic states in 1949,

Tibet in 1959, Indonesia in 1965, Burundi in 1972, Syria in 1982, and Iraq in 1988.

The removal of constraints that had been imposed by Soviet-American bipolarity, along with the advent of U.S. global hegemony, gave rise to the notion that humanitarian war against state-organized massacres had at last become feasible. The actual experience of the 1990s, however, revealed other reasons why, in most cases, the United States could not be relied upon to wage humanitarian war against massacring states. Sadly, in the 1990s, the actions of the Serb government against the Albanians in Kosovo and earlier against the Croats and the Bosnian Muslims were not especially unique. The decade saw at least four comparable examples where a state representing one ethnic group undertook systematic violence against another ethnic group living within the boundaries of the state. This was the case in Rwanda in 1994 (the Hutu regime against the Tutsis), Burundi from 1993 to the present (the Tutsi regime against the Hutus), Sudan throughout the 1990s (the Islamic regime against the Christians), and Iraq through much of the 1990s (the Iraqi Ba'ath regime against the Kurds).

Each of these four cases had similarities to the conflict between the Serb state and the Kosovar Albanian population and Kosovo Liberation Army (KLA). But with the exception of Iraq, U.S. military intervention in these cases was never seriously considered. And in Iraq the United States's use of military force to protect the Kurds was largely fitful and ineffective. As in Kosovo, in each case no traditional, obvious U.S. national interest was at stake. Unlike Kosovo, though, where a less obvious but significant U.S. national interest was involved (the promotion of NATO, an international institution that was central to U.S. grand strategy), in these other four cases no other U.S. national interest was at stake. For all its rhetoric about human rights and humanitarian intervention, the Clinton administration was actually quite unwilling to undertake any war on *purely* humanitarian grounds, no matter how compelling the situation.

In this regard, the administration was merely responding to political realities within the United States. In truth, the political base for humanitarian intervention is quite narrow. The idea that the United States should undertake military operations—and sustain military casualties—to support human rights or even prevent genocide is one that most segments of the American public and of the American military reject. Only among the professional liberals and liberal professionals who inhabit the worlds of the media and academe does the idea of purely humanitarian intervention find favor. Few members of this liberal elite have actually ever served in the U.S. military; nor are their children likely to do so.

Humanitarian intervention is the consequence of liberal globalism carried to its logical conclusion, in which the United States as the sole superpower, without any "peer competitor" and without apparent constraints, is obliged to "do something" in the face of evil. Humanitarian intervention represents a rejection of that other great tradition of thinking about international relations, realist internationalism, prominent in U.S. foreign policy under the constraining conditions of the Cold War.

Humanitarian intervention also represents a rejection of the "Weinberger-Powell doctrine" governing the use of force. For the U.S. military, the Weinberger-Powell doctrine summed up the "lessons learned" from the failures of the Vietnam War. In the eyes of the doctrine's adherents—especially soldiers themselves, but also their supporters in Congress and the public—the successful Persian Gulf War of 1990–1991 seemingly confirmed the validity of those lessons.

But the Weinberger-Powell doctrine constitutes a huge obstacle to military operations conceived for humanitarian purposes. During the 1990s, this would have important consequences for the politics of military interventionism. First, the narrow political base for humanitarian intervention causes supporters of liberal globalism to avoid seeking approval for such operations from the more conservative Congress, and to justify this avoidance by saying that Congress is isolationist and irrational. Since this avoidance of Congress, composed of the elected representatives of the American people, evades a principal element of the Weinberger-Powell doctrine (public and congressional support as a precondition of military operations), the liberal elite is driven to denigrate the doctrine itself. Second, the narrow political base forces that elite to avoid the use of ground forces in combat operations, and therefore to avoid the use of overwhelming force, because unacceptable casualties would likely result. Since this avoidance of overwhelming force is an evasion of another principal element of the Weinberger-Powell doctrine, the liberal elite is again driven to denigrate the doctrine as wrongheaded and obsolete.

The military consequences are not without irony. Proponents of liberal globalism call for military action in response to humanitarian catastrophe, but political realities place off-limits the sort of action most likely to be effective: the massive and aggressive deployment of ground troops. This leaves only air operations, in particular punitive bombing, as in Bosnia in

1995, in Iraq sporadically after the Gulf War and especially in 1999, and in Serbia in 1999. But as Operation Allied Force suggests, these air operations by themselves may only achieve their political objectives when they expand to the point of hurting civilians, either by killing them "collaterally" or by deliberately targeting their economic necessities, such as electric-power grids and water-supply systems.[20] In the air war against the Serbs, when mere symbolic bombing proved insufficient, moves toward strategic bombing proved necessary. These actions against civilians hardly seem to fit the normal definition of "humanitarian."

As for the future, the United States does not seem likely to undertake a humanitarian war in large areas of the world where it has no traditional or obvious national interests, in particular sub-Saharan Africa and South Asia. Elsewhere, where the United States does have obvious national interests, these interests will likely inhibit U.S. intervention to protect the rights of ethnic minorities, especially when regimes friendly to the United States are doing the abusing. While the United States may well wage a war against a state such as Iraq or Iran for conventional security or economic reasons and then justify that war as being a humanitarian enterprise, this is humanitarianism as fig leaf rather than as actual motive. But such may well be the only role that humanitarian war will play in U.S. grand strategy in the near future.[21]

The Kosovo War and NATO Enlargement

The second way in which the Kosovo War has been seen as a new kind of war lies in it being the first real NATO war, with the full authorization and participation of alliance members acting collectively. This feature of the war is both true and important.

This writer has argued that the major U.S. objective in the Kosovo War was to expand NATO's purpose into regions that had hitherto been "out-of-area." Formal NATO enlargement (the admission of new members, such as Poland, the Czech Republic, and Hungary) was to be supplemented by informal NATO enlargement (imposing order on new areas, such as the Balkans and the Middle East). If Serbia had yielded after a few days of bombing, as the Clinton administration had expected, Operation Allied Force would have demonstrated that similar methods of coercion (NATO-authorized bombing) would work again against similar "rogue" adversaries (Libya, Syria, Iraq) in a similar area (the Middle East).

In some sense, NATO won the Kosovo War as the Clinton administration had originally expected. Bombing by itself, without the use of ground forces and without any American combat casualties, did bring about a Serb surrender. NATO did adopt the new Strategic Concept at the 50th Anniversary Summit, despite the fact that at the time the war was still being waged and its outcome appeared uncertain. However, the bombing campaign took eleven weeks rather than one; it required attacks on civilian targets rather than a limitation to military ones; and it produced disputes among NATO decision-makers that often put the alliance's political consensus at risk. Indeed, in a sense, beyond an agreement to begin bombing, there never was a consensus within NATO: no consensus on how to orchestrate the campaign, no consensus on how to escalate, and no consensus on how long to persist. The lesson that most NATO decision-makers took from Operation Allied Force was not how easy it is to bomb even a weak adversary into submission, but how difficult. The subsequent NATO occupation of Kosovo has also been disappointing due to the reverse ethnic cleansing of the Serbs by the Albanians, as well as continuing violence and corruption among the Albanians themselves. The lesson that most NATO decision-makers have taken from the ongoing occupation is that, however easy it may be to send military forces into a country, getting them out may be another matter altogether. As a result, among the European members of NATO, there has been little triumphalism about its Kosovo victory. Indeed, for the purposes of facilitating future out-of-area operations and informal NATO enlargement, that victory now seems to have been a Pyrrhic one.[22]

The Kosovo War and Air Power

A third way in which the Kosovo War has been seen as a first is as the first-ever fulfillment of the long-sought dream of victory through air power alone. Related to this unique and pioneering feature of the war is the fourth way in which it was a first: The war was the first case of a completely bloodless victory—NATO prevailed without suffering a single combat casualty. These two features of the war most obviously involve U.S. military doctrine and operations. However, they are closely connected to U.S. grand strategy as well.

A military doctrine emphasizing air power has been a crucial part of U.S. grand strategy since the Second World War. During the Cold War, a military doctrine of nuclear deterrence was integral to the grand strategy of containing the Soviet Union. Since the end of the Cold War, a military doctrine of punitive bombing has become integral to the grand strategy of managing rogue states.

In the second half of the twentieth century air power played a role in U.S grand strategy similar to that which naval power played in British grand strategy in the nineteenth century. In each case, the leading world power of the day tried to convert its comparative advantage in industry and technology into a way of war that minimized its military casualties. Britain and the United States have shared a number of qualities during the periods when each was the leading great power. Economically, each has been the leading industrial, technological, and financial power of its time. Politically, each has been a leading liberal democracy, with governments responsive to public opinion expressed in regular elections.

In the industrial era of the nineteenth century, Britain had a comparative advantage, really an absolute one, in capital-intensive industrial products and also in capital-intensive weapons systems, above all in warships. In the industrial era of the twentieth century, America had a similar advantage in capital-intensive industrial products and also in capital-intensive weapons systems, above all in bombers, missiles, and aircraft carriers. Now, in the information age, the United States has acquired a new comparative and absolute advantage, this time involving knowledge-intensive or high-technology products and services and knowledge-intensive and high-technology weapons, above all in surveillance systems, stealth aircraft, and precision munitions. Conversely, when it comes to labor-intensive commercial products and labor-intensive weapons systems, Britain and the United States have been at a comparative disadvantage. In military affairs, this has meant a disadvantage in the fielding of traditional land forces, particularly infantry and artillery.

Britain and the United States have also been the leaders in liberal-democratic politics. In liberal democracy, governments must respond to public opinion. This has not prevented British and American governments from expending great numbers of lives in combat, as the two world wars in the British case and the Civil War and the Second World War in the American case attest. But democracies will endure great sacrifices only when the cause itself is manifestly great (as in those great wars). When the stakes are more modest—as with Britain's nineteenth century colonial wars or U.S. interventions in the Caribbean through much of the twentieth century—democracies expect that operations will be conducted with economy, especially when it comes to the sacrifice of their own troops.

These features of the British economy and political system drove Britain to adopt a particular way of engaging in war. The British way of war comprised a particular trinity, which consisted of naval power, financial power, and diplomatic skill.[23] Whenever possible, Britain deployed these assets within a strategy of grand coalitions. In the obvious sense, this meant a grand coalition of several powers who united to defeat the hegemonic ambitions of some overwhelming European land power. In another sense, however, it meant a grand coalition of comparative advantages, in which Britain provided the bulk of the coalition's naval forces, its financial power bought or supported the land forces of the other powers, and its diplomatic skill kept the coalition in place.

Similar economic and political features seem to be driving the United States to an analogous form of waging coalition warfare. The present-day American way of war comprises its own particular trinity, consisting of air power, technological superiority, and international organizations. In deploying these assets against some rogue power, the United States prefers to act through a grand coalition rather than unilaterally. Furthermore, it organizes that coalition with an eye toward comparative advantage, in which the United States provides air power and a technological edge while persuading its coalition partners to provide land forces (and to sustain any casualties entailed by the operation). The Gulf War and the Kosovo War lent apparent plausibility to this strategy. The Gulf War demonstrated that the United States could fight a land campaign and sustain very few casualties. The Kosovo War demonstrated that it could win a war without any land campaign and without any casualties at all.

Whatever advantages a military strategy based on air power and punitive bombing may offer in the abstract, there are major limitations to its application in practice. The range of states susceptible to such a strategy is quite narrow. On the one hand, a target-state has to have reached a certain level of urban and industrial development so that it has something essential to lose through bombing, and its government must be responsive to popular pressure from the people who feel pain caused by that loss. Although Serbia fit these conditions in the Kosovo War, Iraq during the Gulf War did not. (Despite intense bombing of Baghdad, a land campaign was still necessary to defeat Iraq and to achieve the U.S. war aims.) Nor is it clear that North Vietnam fit them in the Vietnam War. (The actual impact of the U.S. bombing of Hanoi and Haiphong in 1972 remains a matter of debate.) The less advanced the level of political and economic development, the less likely it is that punitive bombing will be effective. It did not work against the guerrillas in South Vietnam, and it would not work against the guerrillas in Colombia.

Conversely, of course, the target-state cannot be so developed that it has acquired its own weapons of mass destruction, and therefore the capacity to deter the United States through mutual assured destruction. It is inconceivable that the United States would employ a Kosovo-type strategy against Russia or China, i.e., the bombing of Moscow or Beijing in expectation of extracting political concessions. Indeed, it is not even clear that it would be able to employ such a strategy against North Korea by bombing Pyongyang.

Excluding potential adversaries who are too developed and those who are not developed enough leaves only about a half-dozen rogue states that are plausible target-states for a doctrine of punitive bombing. These are, again, the usual suspects: Iran, Iraq, Libya, and, at the lower end of development, perhaps Sudan and Afghanistan. As it happens, four of these (Iraq, Libya, Sudan, and Afghanistan) have already been the target at some point of some kind of U.S. punitive bombing, and in no case has the bombing yielded decisive results. In short, the new American way of war displayed in Kosovo may well have at best limited applicability for the future.

From War to War: The Mismatch of Military Strategies

More generally, the military strategies used by the United States in winning one war have rarely fit a later war; strategies that have brought victory in some circumstances have failed to do so in different ones. The U.S. military strategies that won the Second World War against Germany and Japan (the offensive use of mobile armored forces by the Army, carrier task forces by the Navy, and large-scale strategic bombing by the Air Force) were based upon the U.S. advantages in both mass and mobility. However, these strategies soon became obsolescent in the Cold War against the Soviet Union. They were replaced with the military strategy of nuclear deterrence, within the context of the generally static grand strategy of containment. A strategy of mass and mobility was succeeded by a strategy of mass destruction and rigid lines.

The United States did try to apply its World War II strategy of mass and mobility in the early stages of the Korean War. (General MacArthur's invasion at Inchon followed by the break-out from the Pusan Perimeter offers the most conspicuous example). This worked against North Korea, but failed once Communist China intervened in the autumn of 1950. The "new war" against China obliged the United States to develop an alternative military strategy in Korea, that of attrition within the context of a limited war. Although this military strategy could not result in a victory in the World War II sense, it could achieve the objective of preserving South Korea, which adequately served the grand strategy of containment.

In turn, the United States initially tried to apply its Korean War strategy of attrition and limited war to Vietnam. (General Westmoreland's search-and-destroy operations during the period 1965–1968 were the most controversial example). Although not without success (the U.S. and its South Vietnamese allies did destroy much of the Viet Cong at the time of the 1968 Tet Offensive), for the most part, this military strategy failed in the different circumstances of Vietnam.

In the 1980s, the venerable strategies of mass and mobility (especially the latter) that had won the Second World War enjoyed a second coming—updated and modernized with high-technology weapons. In the army and air force this expressed itself as the Air-Land Battle Doctrine and in the navy as the Forward Maritime Strategy, both designed to win a conventional war against the Soviet Union. As it happened, the Soviet Union collapsed a few years later, and these strategies were never implemented as planned. However, after Iraq's invasion of Kuwait in 1990s, the Air-Land Battle Doctrine (along with much of the U.S. Army in Europe) was transported from the north German plain to the vast expanse of the Arabian desert, where it won the Gulf War.

In short order, the U.S. military strategy that won the Gulf War against Iraq became obsolescent. It did not fit the new great challenge for U.S. military operations, the ethnic conflicts of the 1990s, particularly those in Yugoslavia. The Air-Land Battle Doctrine and the massive and mobile armored forces that were suitable for the North German plain and for the Iraqi desert were not suitable for the mountainous terrain of the Balkans. As General Colin Powell put it, in contrasting Iraq with Bosnia, "we do deserts, we don't do mountains."

This record of mismatch between the strategies of one war and the necessities of the next one suggests some caution about the applicability of

Kosovo to future conflicts. The particular military strategy that appeared to win the Kosovo War—precision bombing of civilian targets—is unlikely to fit the particular circumstances of the next war that engages the United States. The potential adversary that most resembles Serbia is probably Iraq, but the United States has already tried a version of the precision bombing strategy there in the past few years, and that strategy has not yet achieved its objectives.

The Kosovo War and the Russian Problem

Russia viewed the U.S.-led NATO war against Serbia as a serious threat, not just to its traditional national interests in the Balkans but also to its neo-traditional cultural identity as an Orthodox country. The war confirmed and sharpened Russian suspicions of the real purposes of the United States and NATO in international politics, suspicions which had already become widespread in Russia in the previous year or so, due to NATO enlargement and the Russian financial crisis of 1998.[24]

Russia has considered the Balkans to be its natural sphere of influence since at least the 1870s. Its victory in the Russo-Turkish war of 1877–1878 resulted in the independence of Serbia and Bulgaria from Turkey. Both became Russian allies. The original Russian alliances with Serbia and with Bulgaria were based upon ties of mutual national interests, Slavic ethnic identity, and Orthodox religious tradition. The Russian alliance with Bulgaria fell victim to the intricate calculations and maneuvers of Balkan politics in the First and Second World Wars, when Bulgaria sided with Germany. However, the Russian alliance with Serbia continued right up until 1948, when Tito's Yugoslavia (containing Serbia) broke with Stalin's Soviet Union. This break in the traditional alliance was relatively brief, since Stalin's successors restored generally good relations with Yugoslavia. When the Soviet Union and Yugoslavia both dissolved in the same year, 1991, their largest constituent nations, Russia and Serbia respectively, were re-established as independent states, and the old alliance between them was also revived.

Similar ethnic and demographic situations reinforce this renewed Russo-Serb alliance. About 25 percent of Russians reside outside the boundaries of Russia, where they lived as minorities in former Soviet republics, especially in the Baltic states, Ukraine, and Kazakhstan. Similarly, about 25 percent of Serbs reside outside the boundaries of Serbia, where they lived as minorities in former Yugoslav republics, especially in Croatia and Bosnia. Conversely, within Russia itself, many non-Russian minorities remain, particularly Caucasian Muslims who comprised a substantial majority of the population in Chechnya. Similarly, within Serbia itself, a substantial number of non-Serbian minorities remain, particularly the Albanian Muslims, who comprise a 90-percent majority in Kosovo. Given these similarities, Russia sees Serbia as a smaller version of itself. In Russian eyes, an attack on Serbia is an attack on Russia, or at least on Russian interests and identity.

These historical and cultural factors help explain Russia's attitudes and behavior during the Kosovo War. The U.S.-led NATO campaign against Serbia directly challenged Russia's conception of its traditional sphere of influence and its neo-traditional Orthodox culture. Not surprisingly, Russia opposed the war throughout its duration, and it voiced this opposition, vociferously if ineffectively, in every international organization where it was a member, most importantly in the UN Security Council. The surprise occupation of the Pristina airport by a small contingent of Russian troops at the war's end—an action seen in the West as reckless, annoying, or just silly—was a desperate Russian attempt to preserve a symbolic presence in its traditional sphere, while NATO's occupation of Kosovo was extinguishing the substance.

During Operation Allied Force itself, it appeared that the war might cause serious and long-term damage to U.S. and NATO relations with Russia. By the time that the war was a year in the past, however, a clearer perspective had emerged. The war largely confirmed and crystallized previous Russian views toward the United States and NATO, ones that already existed even before the bombing of Serbia began; it did not fundamentally alter these views. Russia had already become concerned about the United States dominating international politics as the sole superpower—about "U.S. hegemonism." So too, it had already become concerned about NATO enlargement. Russia saw the Kosovo War as amply demonstrating the validity of these concerns.

Conversely, however, the war did not permanently prevent Russia from re-establishing normal, if wary, relations with the United States and other NATO states on other issues; Vladimir Putin tried to do so soon after he was elected as president. In short, the Kosovo War will become one more difficult chapter in the complex history of relations between Russia and the West since the end of the Cold War, a history composed of both competition and cooperation. Drawing on an analogy from an earlier era, the impact of the

1999 U.S.-led NATO war against Serbia on Russian-American relations will probably be about the same as the impact of the 1968 Soviet-led invasion of Czechoslovakia on Soviet-American relations.

Yet for the United States to think that it could get away with another Kosovo-like war that threatened Russian interests or identity would be a serious error. Russia generally accepted the 1995 U.S.-led military intervention against Serbia in Bosnia. It greatly resented the 1999 U.S.-led war against Serbia in Kosovo. A third such military intervention anytime soon, especially in a country in a traditional Russian sphere of influence (e.g., in the Caucasus or in Central Asia) would very likely produce a fundamental and enduring Russian reaction. Here the historical analogy would be more like the U.S. reaction to the 1979 Soviet invasion of Afghanistan.

The most important consequence of the Kosovo War for Russia involves not its relations with the West but its relations with itself, i.e., its relations with the Russian minorities outside of Russia and with the non-Russian minorities within Russia. Russia can readily interpret the Kosovo War as establishing useful precedents for its own future wars. If the United States and NATO can use military force to protect a repressed minority within another state, then surely Russia could legitimately use military force to protect a repressed minority, particularly a Russian one, within a neighboring state. In the future, Russia could use Kosovo to justify military intervention in such states as Estonia, Latvia, Ukraine, and Kazakhstan, even if the real motive was not the protection of the Russian minority and its safety but the restoration of Russian power. Such a Russian intervention would lack the legitimation bestowed by an international organization, as the U.S. intervention was legitimized by NATO, but it would gain legitimation, at least in Russian eyes, by the fact that Russia was only acting to protect its own people in its own backyard.

Also, if the United States and NATO can bomb cities and civilians, then surely Russia can legitimately do so as well. Indeed, Russia has already done so with the bombing of Grozny during the Chechnya war of 1999–2000, citing NATO's bombing of Belgrade as a precedent. Moreover, the U.S. success in ending Serbian repression of the Albanians in Kosovo obviously did not deter Russia from engaging a few months later in similar repression of the Muslims in Chechnya. Indeed, it may have prompted the Russian action, since Russia was now convinced that a rebellious province eventually could provide the opportunity for a disruptive U.S. involvement of some sort.

The Kosovo War and the Chinese Problem

China also viewed the U.S.-led NATO war against Serbia as a serious threat, even though its stakes in the war were not as obvious as Russia's. China's concerns involved its own version of national interests—Kosovo as possible precedent for U.S. involvement in Taiwan or in Tibet—and its own version of cultural identity—the indignity of having its embassy in Belgrade bombed.

As with Russia, the war confirmed and sharpened Chinese concerns about "U.S. hegemonism." Like Serbia and Russia, China has its own rebellious province (Taiwan) and repressed minority (Tibet), and it was concerned about the precedent that the Kosovo War could set for international and especially U.S. meddling in such cases. This was enough to cause China to join Russia in opposing the war throughout its duration, particularly in the forum of the UN Security Council. However, although the analogy between Kosovo and Taiwan or Tibet may have been potentially relevant in the abstract, it was certainly remote in the concrete details, to say nothing of geographical distance. By itself, this Chinese concern about the precedent of the war would not have had a major impact on Sino-American relations.

The U.S. bombing of the Chinese embassy in Belgrade, however, transformed the war from minor irritant to major issue. From a Chinese perspective, that bombing could only have been deliberate. The Chinese credit the United States (as the United States credits itself) with the highest technology in military intelligence. Since the particular embassy floor that was hit housed a Chinese intelligence unit and since the CIA had selected this particular target, U.S. claims of having bombed the building by accident were simply not plausible. The Chinese were furthered angered by the American refusal to offer a convincing explanation or to punish the responsible officials. The embassy bombing transformed the Kosovo War from being just another chapter in the long history of Balkan wars into being yet another chapter in the long history of Western contempt for China, a dramatic reminder of what the Chinese call "the century of humiliation."

As was the case with Russia, the U.S. success in ending Serbian repression of the Albanians in Kosovo did not deter China, a few months later, from issuing harsher threats against Taiwan and from increasing repression in Tibet. Indeed, it may have prompted these actions, since they served to make a statement that China (unlike the Serbs) could not be intimidated and humiliated.

The Kosovo War and Grand Strategy: The First and the Last

The Kosovo War was the first war that the United States undertook to carry out its grand strategy for the global era. It was fought not for traditional security and economic objectives but for new institutional and ideological ones. It was not fought for the old purpose of defending NATO but for the new purpose of enlarging it. It was not fought for the old ideology of liberal democracy and free markets but for the new ideology of cultural diversity and global society. It was not fought to contain Russia or China but rather as if Russia and China did not even exist. Most importantly, it was not fought with the expectation of it being a serious military ordeal that might entail significant American casualties but as a splendid little war to be won easily by American high technology.

Even in the global era, however, the United States will still have traditional and vital security and economic interests to defend. It will still have to live with other great powers, particularly Russia and China, without driving them into permanent opposition and into being a permanent threat to those vital interests. And it will still need a grand strategy that is based upon these old realities as well as the new ones.

The Kosovo War was the first U.S. war of the global era. But it will not be the last. It should, however, be the last U.S. war fought to enlarge an international organization. It should be the last U.S. war justified as being a purely humanitarian war. It should be the last war fought in disregard of Russia or China. Above all, from the perspective of U.S. grand strategy and the American people that strategy is supposed to serve, the Kosovo War should be the last U.S. war fought with the expectation of victory after a few days of limited bombing and with no American casualties. That is, it should be the last war fought by the United States in the expectation that it won't really be a war at all.

Notes

1. Alexis de Tocqueville, "Conduct of Foreign Affairs by the American Democracy," in *Democracy in America*, vol. 1 (1835; reprint, New York: Vintage Books, 1945), pp. 240–245.
2. James Kurth, "America's Grand Strategy: A Pattern of History," *The National Interest*, no. 43 (Spring 1996): 3–19. Also see Walter A. McDougall, *Promised*

Land, Crusader State: The American Encounter with the World Since 1776 (Boston: Houghton Mifflin, 1997).

3. In this sense, U.S. grand strategy has always been both realist and liberal. Realist theories of international relations focus on international security, while liberal themes focus on the international economy. In practice, however, successful strategies in the real world have combined both, e.g., the British grand strategy in the nineteenth century and the American grand strategy during the Cold War. At its best, the Anglo-American tradition in grand strategy has been *both* realist and liberal. See my "Inside the Cave: the Banality of I.R. Studies," *The National Interest*, 53 (Fall 1998): 29–40.
4. James Kurth, "The American Way of Victory: A Twentieth-Century Trilogy," *The National Interest* 60 (Summer 2000): 5–16.
5. Some analysts might argue that the U.S. bombing of the Bosnian Serbs in 1995 was the first such war. But that bombing was very limited in virtually every respect: the type, number and location of the targets; the number of sorties; and the duration of the bombing. The U.S. bombing helped to end a war, but it did not itself add up to one. On the relationship between globalization and U.S. military operations, see Andrew J. Bacevich, "Policing Utopia: The Military Imperatives of Globalization," *The National Interest*, 56 (Summer 1999): 5–13.
6. I have discussed the four great transformations at greater length in my "Global Trends and American Strategic Traditions," in Pelham G. Boyer and Robert S. Wood, eds., *Strategic Transformation and Naval Power in the 21st Century* (Newport, R.I.: Naval War College Press, 1998), especially pp. 8–18. The following discussion of the transformations and the opposition to them draws from my "American Strategy in the Global Era," *Naval War College Review* 53, no. 1 (Winter 2000), especially pp. 7–16.
7. Vaclav Havel, "Kosovo and the End of the Nation-State," *The New York Review of Books* 46, no. 12 (10 June 1999): 4.
8. The United States has also described Sudan as a rogue state because of its support of terrorism; Sudan is certainly a rogue, even though it is not much of a state. In June 2000, Secretary of State Madeleine Albright announced that the U.S. government was replacing the term "rogue states" with the term "states of concern." The change reflected improvements that were now perceived in the internal politics of Iran and the foreign relations of Libya, North Korea, and Syria. *New York Times*, 20 June 2000, p. A8.
9. Samuel P. Huntington, *The Clash of Civilizations and the Remaking of World Order* (New York: Simon and Schuster, 1997), especially pp. 158–163.
10. One might have thought that the Kosovo War, with the United States fighting on behalf of the Bosnian Muslims, might have softened this Islamic resentment and resistance. It appears, however, that many in the Islamic world view the

Kosovo War as simply more evidence that the United States is determined to impose globalization by force, and the fact that particular Muslim peoples (in Kosovo and earlier in Bosnia) were beneficiaries is merely an accident.

11. Paul Bracken, *Fire in the East: The Rise of Asian Military Power and the Second Nuclear Age* (New York: Harper Collins, 1999).
12. Robert E. Hunter, "Maximizing NATO: A Relevant Alliance Knows How to Reach," *Foreign Affairs* 78, no. 3 (May-June 1999), especially pp. 201–202. Hunter was U.S. Ambassador to NATO from 1993 to 1998. The quoted phrases are used in NATO Office of Information and Press, "The Alliance's Strategic Concept," *NATO Review* 47, no. 2 (Summer 1999): D9.
13. Ibid.
14. Adam Roberts, "NATO's 'Humanitarian War' over Kosovo," *Survival* 4, no. 3 (Autumn 1999), especially pp. 109–112. Also see the account by Richard Holbrooke, *To End a War* (New York: Modern Library, 1999), especially 142–162.
15. Christopher Layne and Benjamin Schwarz, "For The Record," *The National Interest* 57 (Fall 1999): 10–11.
16. U.S. Department of State, "Rambouillet Agreement: Interim Agreement for Peace and Self-Government in Kosovo." http://www.state.gov/www/regions/eur/ksvo_rambouillet_text.html
17. Charles Simic, "Anatomy of a Murderer," *The New York Review of Books* 47, no. 1 (20 January 2000): 29. Simic states about the specific clause 8, "The U.S. introduced, at the last minute, an additional demand."
18. A classic and thorough account of the Austro-Hungarian ultimatum and the Serbian rejection is given by Sidney Bradshaw Fay, *The Origins of the World War*, 2nd ed., vol. 2, chapters 5 and 7 (New York: Macmillan, 1930). The text of the ultimatum is given on pp. 269–273; that of the reply is given on pp. 344–347.
19. The text of the UN Genocide Convention is given in George J. Andreopoulos, *Genocide: Conceptual and Historical Dimensions* (Philadelphia: University of Pennsylvania Press, 1994), pp. 229–233.
20. Roberts, "NATO's 'Humanitarian War' over Kosovo," pp. 114–116. A thorough analysis of the air campaign is given by Daniel L. Byman and Matthew C. Waxman, "Kosovo and the Great Air Power Debate," *International Security* 24, no. 4 (Spring 2000): 5–38.
21. Humanitarian war is analyzed and debated by Charles Krauthammer, "The Short Unhappy Life of Humanitarian War," *The National Interest*, 57 (Fall 1999): 5–15; and Elliott Abrams, "To Fight the Good Fight," *The National Interest* 59 (Spring 2000): 70–77.
22. For an overview of NATO after the war, see United States Institute for Peace, "Transatlantic Relations in the Aftermath of Kosovo," *Special Report* (15 May 2000). The prevailing attitude of NATO members one year after was summed

up by a senior NATO official: "Kosovo was such a resounding success that no one in the Alliance wants to repeat it ever again." *The New York Times* (18 June 2000), "The Week in Review," p. 5.

23. For a comprehensive account of British grand strategy, see Paul Kennedy, *The Rise and Fall of British Naval Mastery* (New York: Scribners, 1976).
24. See the analysis of Russian decision-making on the Kosovo War in Oleg Levitin, "Inside Moscow's Kosovo Muddle," *Survival* 42, no. 1 (Spring 2000): 130–140.

4 Hubris and Nemesis: Kosovo and the Pattern of Western Military Ascendancy and Defeat

Anatol Lieven

A scrimmage in a border station—
A canter down some dark defile.
Two thousand pounds of education
Drops to a ten-rupee jezail . . .

With home-bred hordes the hillsides teem.
The troopships bring us one by one,
At vast expense of time and steam,
To slay Afridis where they run.
"The captives of our bow and spear"
Are cheap, alas! as we are dear
—Rudyard Kipling, Arithmetic on the Frontier

I

NATO's victory in Kosovo in 1999 confirmed proponents of the "Revolution in Military Affairs" in their belief that technological development is bringing about changes in warfare comparable in its implications to the greatest military transformations of recent centuries. They also believe that for decades to come the advantages stemming from this revolution will accrue overwhelmingly to the West and, primarily, to the United States. Above all, Kosovo is taken to prove that aerial bombardment alone can in fact win wars. In the wake of Kosovo, even distinguished military commentators like John Keegan, who were previously skeptical of such claims, have been won over.[1]

This essay will argue that to see Kosovo as the paradigm for war in the first half of the twenty-first century would be a grave mistake. It would, of course, be pleasant to think that all wars could be decided in the West's favor by the use of high-precision weapons from a safe distance, thereby discouraging potential adversaries from confronting the West in the first place. But the success of NATO's air campaign in Kosovo is unlikely to deter those adversaries. Rather, it will persuade those adversaries to confront the West indirectly, using nonstate actors against Western troops on the ground in circumstances that will render the West's technological edge moot.

Rather than ushering in a new paradigm of warfare, NATO's victory in Kosovo represents the further evolution of that technological superiority that has helped Western powers repeatedly to defeat their non-Western opponents and dominate the world over the past five centuries. Yet this long period of Western military dominance has not been without its share of defeats at the hands of ostensibly inferior opponents. On numerous occasions in every age, Western powers have suffered local setbacks so severe as to jeopardize their claim to political preeminence. The reasons for these defeats derive from multiple sources, prominent among them difficult local conditions and overconfidence on the part of Western nations. But looming largest of all is culture.

The operations undertaken by Western powers in places such as the Balkans display more than a passing resemblance to old-fashioned imperial policing, however much that particular term may have fallen out of fashion. Yet in contrast to the imperial policing of the nineteenth and twentieth centuries—the French in Indochina and North Africa, the Americans in the Philippines and the Caribbean, the British in any number of places—these new operations proceed in a more tangled context. Public tolerance for failure or even minor missteps has shrunk. Meanwhile, the risks accompanying intervention are vastly greater. On the one hand, Western publics expect that their militaries will bring these operations to a quick, tidy, and cheap conclusion. On the other hand, the prospect of these "small wars" escalating into something much larger—to include the potential use of weapons of mass destruction by nonstate actors—means that the consequences of miscalculation are potentially disastrous.

In 1879, the British could lose more than 1,500 men in a single hour at

Isandhlwana, shrug it off, and go on to conquer Zululand. In 1993, the loss of 18 American Rangers sufficed to force the United States out of Somalia. But the issue goes beyond the willingness to sustain casualties. Mogadishu—along with Beirut, Grozny and other battlefields—suggests that the locus of political and military struggle is shifting from the mountains and jungles of the past, into the "urban terrain" of Third World cities—conditions unfavorable to the style of warfare preferred by American or Western European forces. Within those cities, the most dangerous enemy is not the general schooled in the conventions of traditional warfare, but the cunning, charismatic irregular who combines in one person the terrorist, ward politician, clan leader, criminal warlord, and gang boss. To defeat such an adversary requires an intimate knowledge of local conditions, exceptionally difficult for the "imperial police" to acquire. It may also demand commanders who themselves manifest the gang leader's mix of flexibility and utter ruthlessness—not qualities nurtured in the officer corps of the typical Western democracy. In the movie *Casablanca*, the character played by Humphrey Bogart taunted a German officer, "Major, there are parts of New York I wouldn't advise you to try and invade." In the decades since, New York may have been (partially) pacified, but Western nations contemplating intervention in quarters disordered by civil war, ethnic conflict, or massive violations of human rights would do well to heed Bogart's warning.

II

Viewed simply as a display of technological superiority, the punishment inflicted on Yugoslavia at the hands of NATO air forces compared to the inability of Yugoslav air defenses to retaliate recalls certain nineteenth-century campaigns. On November 3, 1839, the British frigates HMS *Volage* and HMS *Hyacinth* engaged the Chinese southern fleet off Chuenpi on the Pearl River, in the first major engagement of the First Opium War. The *Volage* and *Hyacinth* were small frigates, mounting only 28 and 18 guns respectively—ships already outclassed for more than 30 years by the modern heavy frigates pioneered by the U.S. and French navies. These two British warships faced 29 large Chinese war-junks under the command of one of China's bravest and most determined officers, Admiral Kuan T'ien-p'ei. Yet within a 45 minutes, the small British force sank four Chinese warships and damaged most of the rest so severely that they escaped only because the

British mercifully ceased fire. In this engagement, hundreds of Chinese were killed; on the British side, a single seaman was wounded.[2]

From the Chinese point of view, disaster had only just begun. The arrival of a British paddle-steamer, HMS *Nemesis*, armed with Congreve rockets, confronted China with a threat to which it could make no effective response whatsoever. On land, too, British regiments equipped with muskets (once again, verging on obsolescence in Europe) repeatedly defeated numerically superior Chinese forces defending some of the most formidable fortifications in the Chinese empire. For example, at the second battle of Chuenpi, on January 7, 1841, the British army killed some 400 Chinese without losing a single soldier.[3]

The First Opium War was perhaps the moment that established European and North American military dominance of non-Western states and societies of the nineteenth and early twentieth centuries. The technological overmatch evident in this conflict presaged other lopsided imperial victories such as Ulundi in 1879, when British regulars killed thousands of Zulus at the cost of ten killed, or Omdurman in 1896, where they imposed a similar loss ration on the followers of the Khalifa Abdullahi.

In contrast to the classic battles of the late imperial age, however, the technological disparity in the war for Kosovo led NATO ultimately to focus allied air power not against the Yugoslav army on the ground in Kosovo but against Serb society. In fact, when the war ended Yugoslav forces withdrew from Kosovo in good order, hardly suggesting an army that had been beaten in the field. Yugoslav military losses amounted to an estimated 500 dead, substantially fewer than NATO propaganda had claimed.[4]

Indubitable, however, is the effect of NATO's bombardment on Yugoslav infrastructure. NATO air forces (or rather American air power, modestly augmented by Europe) demonstrated persuasively that precision air weapons can destroy from a safe distance any large fixed target like a bridge, power station, oil refinery or factory. Given a sufficient stock of cruise missiles and "smart bombs," the United States at minimal cost in American lives can inflict acute damage on the economies of states much more powerful than Yugoslavia.

Any modern organized state, dependent on a modern economy and transport links, will have to take this threat very seriously indeed—just as coastal or riverine Asian states in the nineteenth century were obliged to take seriously the ability of Western squadrons to roam at will, strangling trade, landing raiding parties, and bombarding forts and cities into submission.

III

Yet if the First Opium War signaled the advantages that technology bestowed on the West in the wars for empire, it also included a number of incidents—perhaps less well known—that prefigured later Western vulnerabilities. One of these occurred at the end of May 1841 near Canton. Infuriated by the behavior of British troops who requisitioned food from local Chinese, engaged in occasional acts of rape and looting, and generally displayed a contempt for Chinese culture, thousands of local peasants took up arms intending to expel the British.

Wielding homemade weapons and led by smaller groups of "braves" — local hard men normally engaged in village and clan feuds or in criminal activity—the peasants succeeded in forcing the British troops to withdraw from the countryside into the town of San-yuan-li, their assault aided by an intense thunderstorm that soaked British muskets and ammunition. British losses were modest—one British Indian soldier killed and 15 wounded—but these amounted to more than the Chinese army and fleet succeeded in inflicting in most battles of that war.

The incident was also affected by the moral terms of the First Opium War. On the British side, this was a war that dared not speak its name (and as such highly reminiscent of our own day when Western states rarely acknowledge that in using force they are waging war). For all the Palmerstonian rhetoric about Chinese "barbarism" and "arbitrariness," the British public was painfully aware that this was a war in defense of an indefensible trade, which China morally and legally had every right to ban. In the press and parliament, the military expedition was roundly criticized. That criticism, in effect, constrained the actions of British forces in the field. Proceeding initially with great and uncharacteristic caution, they avoided battles with the Chinese and sought what would now be called a "political solution." At San-yuan-li, British soldiers seem to have hesitated about firing volleys into the crowds of Chinese peasants. By the time the British lost their inhibitions they were already in a precarious situation.

Meanwhile, the undefined character of the conflict, together with the element of genuine spontaneous mass mobilization, allowed Chinese authorities to deny responsibility for the peasant attacks and to continue talking to the British. Indeed, the incident at San-yuan-li may have been a harbinger of the "Taiping" rebellion a few years later. For much to Britain's dismay, the First Opium War so badly shook the prestige of the Manchu state that it became acutely vulnerable to attack by both bitterly anti-Western internal rebels and Britain's European rivals. Very soon, therefore, the British found themselves trying to prop up the regime that they had just defeated.[5]

Barely mentioned in British sources, the affray at San-yuan-li was vastly magnified in later Chinese nationalist and Communist lore as the moment when the masses removed from the palsied hands of the alien Manchu dynasty responsibility for China's defense. Although such propagandists may have exaggerated its actual importance, the incident at San-yuan-li did indeed provide an early warning that Western discipline and technological superiority did not necessarily guarantee military success.

IV

For a great power seeking to justify the imposition of a particular order on others (as the British did on the Manchus or as NATO did on Yugoslavia), having another state as adversary is of inestimable value. Today, however, the worst, or at least the most complicated dangers in the world exist where states have failed and where chaos, organized crime, and terrorism have supplanted the civil order. This problem of failed states poses a problem not only for the West but also for the inheritor states of the former Soviet Union—the fate of Chechnya from 1996 to 2000 being an awful warning of this possibility. Likewise, in the Middle East, the greatest threat to U.S. interests derives not from conventional conflict between regional powers—not even an attack by a resurgent Iraq—but from internal upheaval that might destabilize key allied regimes.

In this sense, NATO coerced Yugoslavia into surrendering Kosovo only because Yugoslavia retains the characteristics of a modern state, not least of all a disciplined army and police forces under the effective control of a semi-autocratic president, Slobodan Milosevic. NATO needed the Serb leader in order to claim its victory. When Milosevic decided to call the war off—not because Yugoslavia was unable to resist further, but for his own political reasons—Yugoslav forces obeyed, and promptly withdrew from Kosovo.

Had the Serb effort to ethnically purify Kosovo relied on a mass movement supported by autonomous militia groups under local warlords, bombing bridges, factories, and TV stations in Belgrade would not, in all likelihood, have produced decision. And once "strategic" bombing had failed, what options would NATO have had available? The laws of war prohibit the indiscriminate bombing of villages and concentrations of people or livestock—although Western scruples in this regard may well prove short-lived when truly important national interests, or the lives of numerous Western soldiers are at stake. The only recourse for NATO in Kosovo under these circumstances would have been either political compromise involving the partition of Kosovo or all-out invasion. An invasion employing NATO ground troops would have been politically unpalatable. An invasion relying on the KLA as proxies would have made NATO morally complicit in the conduct of its partner. As with the U.S.-supported Croat army in 1995 or Israeli-supported Christian militias in Lebanon in 1982, a KLA bent on liberating Kosovo would have simultaneously engaged in atrocities against the Serb civilian population—of the kind which accompanied the actual NATO occupation, but on a much larger scale.

While NATO's victory in Kosovo undoubtedly qualifies as an impressive achievement in the history of warfare between states, it therefore provides no answers whatsoever therefore for two other forms of armed conflict: wars against peoples in arms and wars against decentralized, anarchical, or "tribal" societies. Nor, of course, does the Kosovo experience provide ready answers for the dilemmas involved in occupying, administering and policing recalcitrant areas.

An English wit once wrote that you should never trust a corporation, since it possesses "neither a body to be kicked, nor a soul to be damned." However great their apparent military advantage, Western nations will be hard-pressed to impose their will on nonstate actors that possess neither infrastructure to be destroyed nor economies to be strangled.

Thus, in a decade that began on a triumphal note with victory over Iraq and ended with another over Yugoslavia, it is the military event sandwiched between these two victories—the debacle of Somalia—that should command attention. During the urban fighting in Mogadishu, American tactics, weaponry, intelligence and above all political analysis proved wanting. Somalia also demonstrated the limits of Western humanitarian concern and military self-restraint in actual combat. In the famous firefight that cost the lives of 18 of their comrades, American troops killed a far greater number—at least 500—of Somali civilians, including many women and children.[6]

After the firefight, Ambassador Robert Oakley promised Somali leaders that failure to release a captured American pilot would mean that U.S. forces would obtain that release forcibly, "The minute the guns start again," Oakley threatened, "all restraint on the U.S. side goes. Just look at the stuff coming in here now. An aircraft carrier, tanks, gunships . . . the works. Once the fighting starts, all this pent-up anger is going to be released. This whole part of the city will be destroyed, men, women, children, camels, cats, dogs, goats, donkeys, everything. . . . That would be really tragic for all of us, but that's what will happen."[7]

The point is not to criticize the way in which the United States used or threatened to use firepower in Somalia. In the last resort soldiers, like any human beings faced with death, will fight with all the means available, and the second duty of commanders—after mission accomplishment—is to the lives of their own men. Rather the point is that the brutal fight in Mogadishu should be a most searing reminder that orderly, "sanitized," limited war such as the kind NATO fought over Kosovo has been very much the exception historically and is likely to remain the exception in the future.

To emphasize that Kosovo not Somalia is the anomaly, we need only note that other instructive failures both preceded and followed the victories of 1991 and 1999. American intervention in Lebanon in 1982, like Somalia, led to dangerous mission creep. This in turn alienated much of the local population, drew U.S. troops into local ethnic conflict, and finally exposed them to a devastating terrorist attack. In Kosovo, efforts by NATO peacekeepers since the war's end to protect the local Serbian minority and to create a democratic, let alone a multi-ethnic Kosovo, have failed. As of August 2001, NATO has only very partially succeeded in blocking armed Albanian attacks from Kosovo first into Serbia proper, and then, much more dangerously, into Macedonia. The KLA retains a major armed presence in northern Albania, which NATO can do nothing about. As a result, NATO will sooner or later be faced with a set of choices every one of which will involve a measure of moral disgrace and political humiliation.

V

The alternation between overall military dominance, local defeats, and permanent, intractable problems has prevailed throughout Western military history over the past 500 years. Indeed, in each of the three great military revolutions of this period, a similar pattern has repeated itself. Given sufficient technological superiority, Western powers can defeat non-Western states with relative ease. Once their leaders of those states accept defeat, the war ends. Perhaps even more importantly, the bureaucratic institutions and habits of mass obedience inculcated under the former order enable the conquerors to administer the defeated states to the West's advantage.

The situation is vastly different with tribal and semitribal societies whose social disciplines are not based on submission to state authority or laws given from above, but on forms of "ordered anarchy"—where no permanent centralized authority exists, and where no "army" that can surrender exists, only local volunteers without uniforms or regular units, fighting on the basis of blood, personal, or religious allegiance.

Not only have Western militaries found it far more difficult to defeat such societies (at least without slaughtering much of the "civilian" population in the process), but officers and officials of modern states often have the very greatest difficulty understanding how such societies work, and devising even theoretical means of dealing with them. This was true of the Russian officials who planned the intervention in Chechnya in December 1994—and no less true of the American officials in Somalia who devised the war to get Mohammed Farah Aidid. Although describing Somalia, the anthropologist I. M. Lewis makes a point applicable to many similar societies:

> Like many pastoral nomads who range far and wide with their herds, the Somali have no indigenous centralized government. And this lack of formal government and of instituted authority is strongly reflected in their extreme independence and individualism. Few writers have failed to notice the formidable pride of the Somali nomad, his extraordinary sense of superiority as an individual, and his firm conviction that he is sole master of his actions and subject to no authority save that of God. If they have noticed it, however, they have for the most part been baffled by the shifting character of the nomad's political allegiance and puzzled by the fact that the political and jural unit with which he acts on one occasion, he opposes on another.[8]

When it comes to identifying the complex clan, family, religious, personal and opportunistic allegiances of ordinary Somali fighters, intelligence satellites or spy-planes are of limited utility.

A striking passage by the Russian anthropologist Sergei Arutiunov about Chechen society runs on similar lines:

> Chechnya was and is a society of military democracy. Chechnya never had any kings, emirs, princes or barons. Unlike other Caucasian

> nations, there was never feudalism in Chechnya. Traditionally, it was governed by a council of elders on the basis of consensus, but like all military democracies—like the Iroquois in America or the Zulu in southern Africa—Chechens retain the institution of military chief. In peacetime, they recognize no sovereign authority and may be fragmented into a hundred rival clans. However, in time of danger, when faced with aggression, the rival clans unite and elect a military leader. This leader may be known to everyone as an unpleasant personality, but is elected nonetheless for being a good general. While the war is on, this leader is obeyed.[9]

In the late eighteenth and early nineteenth centuries, the Russian imperial army had won a whole string of victories over the Turks and various European rivals. It even fought Napoleon to a standstill; but it took decades to subdue comparatively tiny numbers of Chechens and other tribesmen in the mountains of the Caucasus. Even today such societies retain a remarkable capacity to mobilize formidable powers of armed resistance, even though lacking the formal institutions and cadres of "classical," mid-twentieth-century insurgencies, as exemplified by the Viet Cong or the Algerian FLN. Thus, faced with Russian aggression in 1994, Chechens once again rose to the occasion with a war effort spontaneously generated by Chechen society.[10]

Such successful opposition could exist even very close to the most developed states of the day: the British state did not succeed in "pacifying" the Gaelic clans of Scotland until after the Jacobite revolt of 1745, and then only by repressive measures the savagery of which prefigured that of the antipartisan wars of the twentieth century. This long British failure was due not only to the rugged terrain of the Highlands, but equally importantly to the clans' mixture of highly decentralized authority with fanatical loyalty to the clan chiefs. As a result, British authorities could rarely be entirely sure that an apparent ally would not change sides at a crucial moment; nor without massive repression could they force the highlanders to accept the authority of the new British state.

Similarly, in sixteenth-century Ireland, the establishment of British state authority was made extremely difficult not just by Irish resistance, the growing religious divide between Irish and English, and the wildness of the country, but also by the division of Irish authority into clans (or "septs"). Moreover, according to Irish tradition, the leadership of these clans did not pass from father to eldest son. The new head of the clan was elected by the clan's leading men.

In many ways, this was a curse for Irish society, sparking endless conflicts and feuds and undermining the resistance to the English. However, it was also a curse for the authorities in London and Dublin, who would extract allegiance from one chieftain only to find later that the clan had rejected the chieftain's son as successor and had renounced the treaty. British and American authorities faced this same problem in their dealings with Native American tribes. In both cases it contributed to their perception of Irish and Indian "treachery."[11]

In all these cases, nominally backward societies gained strengthen not just from ethnic and cultural loyalties but also from a profound attachment to an ancient way of life menaced by modernizing forces. When I first went into Afghanistan with the anti-Soviet Mujahedin in the late 1980s (as a journalist for the *Times* of London, based in neighboring Pakistan), the first thing to strike me in the "liberated areas" was the complete absence of all the institutions and visible symbols of the state: not a policeman, not a telephone or power line, not a court, not an office, not a doctor. As I wrote in the *Times* in February 1989, from the province of Nangrahar:

> In the Afghan countryside, the state and its symbols have vanished with a completeness almost inconceivable to the Western mind. There are no civil servants of any kind—not even a postman—and their symbol, the astrakhan fur hat, seems unlikely ever to return . . .
>
> With the Russians gone, the conflict will slip back to what it was before they intervened—a war by the bulk of the Afghan people against the modern Afghan state, as taken over by the Communists.
>
> Most people in the provinces always hated the modern and modernizing state . . . . It appeared to them chiefly in the guise of the conscripting officer, the ruthless bureaucrat, the brutal policeman, and the corrupt, savage, incomprehensible and atheistical legal system. It represented an assault on their religious and tribal traditions and on their idea of freedom. And unlike in Europe, it brought them very little of prosperity or progress and even on occasions destroyed what little they had.
>
> In return, the people have swept the state away, with all its works, and all its empty promises.[12]

VI

Afghanistan in its time brought both British and Soviet armies to grief. Almost simultaneously with the beginning of the First Opium War, a British army entered Afghanistan to install its own preferred claimant to the throne of Kabul and to create a bulwark against the Russian expansionism into Central Asia. But unlike China, where the defeat of the emperor's army and navy led to a settlement with the imperial government and an end to war, in Afghanistan—in the 1840s as in the 1980s—the multi-headed tribal and religious resistance could not be defeated in this way. There was, in fact, no unified enemy authority with whom to arrange a peace. And unlike the unarmed and generally passive Chinese peasantry, the Afghan tribesmen—like Somalis and Chechens, among others—were (and are) fierce fighters. Honoring warfare, they were trained from an early age to fight without mercy and equipped with weapons that (like the kalashnikovs and rocket-propelled grenades employed by partisan forces today) may not have been the most modern but were eminently well-suited for the preferred Afghan style of warfare.

In China, British officers at the time recognized the complete impossibility of invading and occupying the inland provinces, given the huge size of their territories and populations and the very small size of the British army and its Indian auxiliary troops. Fortunately, there was no need to do so. Once the British demonstrated their ability to move at will down China's rivers, and menaced the capitol, Beijing, the will of the Chinese government collapsed.

In Afghanistan too, the British did not have remotely enough troops to garrison the whole country. By late 1841, the force based in Kabul consisted of only one British and three British Indian infantry battalions and a single cavalry regiment, with other "armies" in Kandahar and Jalalabad. Although the British attempted to recruit local Afghan allies, relying on financial subsidies and allegiance to the local British puppet, Shah Sujah-ul-Mulk, the attempt failed. The presence of "infidel" troops in Muslim Afghanistan whipped religious leaders and their followers into a frenzy. As so often in such situations—one thinks of U.S. support for the Shah of Iran—British support for Shah Sujah undermined rather than enhanced his standing in the eyes of his own people. The British could not check atrocities by Shah Sujah's followers against their personal and political enemies. Liaisons between British officers and Afghan women infuriated the (male) population of Kabul. The British alienated a key ally—the Khan of Khelat—by holding him responsible for acts of banditry by his followers that he could not have prevented even had he wanted to, and ended by deposing and killing him. And finally the British government of India—under pressure from the government and parliament in London to economize—refused funds necessary to strengthen the British camp at Kabul and cut the subsidy to the tribes who controlled the British lines of communication.

The result of all this was the defection of the British allies, a general rising, an appallingly bungled attempt to retreat from Kabul across the mountains in midwinter, and the destruction of the entire British force. In addition to all their other failings, the British army had encumbered itself with an immense train of camp-followers, servants, and officers' luxuries—resembling the present-day U.S. Army in its insistence on deploying with all the comforts of home.[13]

Later that year, 1842, a much stronger British army returned to recapture Kabul and wreak revenge on its inhabitants: but the larger lesson had been learned. Never again did Great Britain permanently station troops in Afghanistan, or attempt to reduce its rulers to the completely subservient condition of the British Indian princes. Instead, the British exerted its influence over Afghanistan through "indirect" means. This approach saved the British from further disasters and the draining financial and human costs of an endless war of occupation; but it also meant that throughout the entire period of the British Empire in India, Afghanistan remained a constant security problem.

Although British authorities worried about Afghanistan providing a corridor for a Russian invasion of India, the real threat was quite different. As a practical matter, the security problem emanating from Afghanistan was twofold: It took the form of anti-British jihads stoked by local Muslim religious leaders (like the "Fakir of Ipi") and raids launched into British territory by tribal "bandits." British troops guarding the Afghan frontier tried various different responses to these dangers: the use of elite, locally-recruited troops (the famous Scouts and Guides) to seize individual troublemakers, the aerial bombardment of villages and flocks, and even full-scale punitive expeditions. The impact of all these responses—few of which were constrained by concerns about human rights—tended to be limited and above all temporary.[14]

In dealing with Afghanistan, British authorities found that it was largely pointless to pressure the government in Kabul to play a helpful role—for the simple reason that the government did not control its own territory and its own subjects in the frontier areas.

This same problem exists today. Chechnya provides an example. When Moscow pulled its troops out of Chechnya in 1996, the Yeltsin government decided to withdraw completely rather than leaving a security force along the Terek River. The government based that decision on the expectation that General Aslan Maskhadov, the former Soviet artillery colonel turned Chechen commander with whom Russia had negotiated, would prove to be a moderate and effective leader—someone who would keep order and with whom Moscow could deal on a pragmatic basis.

Unfortunately, while Maskhadov did indeed win presidential elections in January 1997, the destruction, militarization and brutalization caused by the war, together with the traditional Chechen aversion to authority, made it impossible to create an effective Chechen state. Instead, Chechnya became the base not only for international Islamic revolutionaries, but also for a great wave of kidnapping and raiding into surrounding Russian territory that claimed more than 1300 victims among Russians, Daghestanis and Ingush as well as a variety of Westerners.

In August 1999, Chechen and Islamist fighters launched a major incursion into the neighboring republic of Daghestan aimed at driving Russia from the region and creating a larger Islamic state. Russian pressure on Maskhadov to act proved ineffective since he did not in fact control the situation within Chechnya. That fall, Russia once again invaded.[15]

Even if, as appears likely, Russia succeeds in reconquering and occupying Chechnya, Moscow will find itself presiding over a bitterly discontented region and forced to deal with a long-running terrorist threat. The casualties inflicted by Russian bombardment of Chechen towns have alienated even Chechens who were thoroughly fed up with the anarchy and religious extremism of the years between 1996 and 1999—just as the civilian casualties inflicted by U.S. troops in Mogadishu infuriated even Somalis who loathed General Farah Aidid.

Because thousands of miles of ocean separate Somalia from the territory of the United States, the Americans at least had the option of abandoning Somalia. For Russia in Chechnya that option does not exist.

VII

If one of the lessons of Chechnya is the difficulty a modern state faces in dealing with an anarchic society that works by different rules, the other is the crucial importance of terrain. This lesson is, as already noted, a very old one.

Today, however, this lesson has taken on a new and sinister importance. For while in the nineteenth century Chechen fighters would hole up in the forested foothills, in the latest wars the key battles took place in the city of Grozny. As the Russians—and the Americans in Mogadishu—have learned at great cost, urban environments are the most difficult and dangerous of all battlefields even for modern armies with overwhelming firepower. Faced with brave, determined enemies armed with relatively primitive weapons, even modern tanks and armored personnel carriers can easily become death traps for their crews.[16]

Fighting in cities almost inevitably exacts a heavy toll in civilian casualties—around 100 for every U.S. military casualty during the battle for Manila in 1945, for example.[17] Even though U.S. doctrine now in theory at least eschews the kind of massive bombardment to which Manila was subjected, the sheer killing power of even small contemporary weapons platforms suggests the likelihood of similar civilian casualties in urban battles today—with Mogadishu a case in point. Writing about the Korean War, David Rees summed up the Western tradition this way: "At the heart of the West's military thought lies the belief that machines must be used to save its men's lives; Korea would become a horrific illustration of the effects of a limited war where one side possessed the firepower and the other the manpower."[18]

The Israeli army faced this dilemma when it invaded Lebanon in 1982. The PLO could not face them in the open field or even in the mountains, and instead retreated to Beirut and other cities. When the Israelis' heavy firepower caused heavy civilian casualties, they drew international condemnation. When they used infantry and suffered comparatively heavy casualties of their own, the result was domestic criticism and demoralization.[19]

Yet no army—least of all that of the world's hegemonic superpower—can assume that it will not have to fight in cities. Whereas in 1950, there were only 50 cities in the world with more than 1,000,000 people, today there are more than 300, with 25 cities claiming a population that exceeds 10,000,000. By 2025, 60 percent of the world's population will live in large cities, according to recent projections. As Stephen Metz has written, "The Army must be prepared to deter or defeat a cross-border invasion by another state, but if that is all it can do, it risks becoming the twenty-first-century equivalent of a sixteenth-century armored knight." [20] Today, as an ever increasing proportion of the world's population lives in ever larger cities, it would be simply ludicrous to draw up any military strategy that did not include urban warfare as a major component.

In January and February 1995, I witnessed the Russian assault on Grozny from both sides of the lines, and gained a vivid impression of the extreme difficulty and ugliness of urban warfare. At a lower intensity of violence, this had already struck me when I reported on ethnic violence in Karachi in 1989, and the way in which the Pakistani troops were swallowed up in the giant, featureless slums. During the Soviet occupation of Afghanistan, as I learned during my visits there, the Russians and their Afghan Communist allies never did succeed in controlling large areas of the suburbs of Kandahar and Herat. Their only recourse was to destroy these areas with artillery—after which Mujahedin sniped at them from the ruins.

In particular, what struck home in all these places was the huge number of troops needed to isolate, attack, and establish even a semblance of control over even a medium sized city like Grozny (which in 1989 had a population of just under 400,000)—unless, that is, the attacking troops are ready to accept the kind of casualties suffered in World War II by German troops attacking Stalingrad or Soviet units attacking Berlin.

A young Russian private named Valery Kukayev gave me a vivid picture of urban warfare conducted by armies trained for maneuver warfare. Describing the fate of his company of the 65th Motorized Infantry during the initial Russian attack on Grozny, he said:

> The commanders gave us no map, no briefing, just told us to follow the BMP in front, but it got lost and ended up following us. By morning, we were completely lost and separated from the other units. I asked our officer where we were, he said he didn't know—somewhere near the railway station. No, he didn't have a map either. We were told to take up defensive positions, but it was hopeless—the Chechens were all around us and firing. There was nowhere to take cover, because they were everywhere. I asked for orders from our company commander, Lt. Chernychenko, and they told me he'd already run for it. Then we tried to escape. That was when I was wounded, by a sniper—I'd got out of the BMP to try to find a way out.

Before mocking Russian incompetence and unpreparedness, it is worth remembering that in October 1993 in Mogadishu, the U.S. reaction force trying to locate the crew of one of the downed helicopters also got lost several times, despite being guided by a command-and-control helicopter above.[21]

The realities of urban warfare mean that the fog of war remains to a considerable degree impenetrable even to the latest technology. This is especially true in the shambolic, faceless, endlessly repetitive cities of the "Third World," where often no street names (and certainly no street signs) exist. Anyone who has experienced the frustration of spending hours searching for a house or flat at night in Delhi or Karachi understands this—and that is without the added strain of people shooting at you.

To the extent that the U.S. military is attempting to learn the lessons of Grozny and Mogadishu, that effort has taken the form of a search for technological fixes that will, in the words of one senior American officer with whom I spoke, make urban warfare "fast, clean and painless, just like current U.S. military operations on open terrain."

Thus, the Army and Marine Corps' Joint Advanced Concept Technology Demonstration has identified the following capabilities (among others) as ones towards which U.S. forces should be working in the field of urban warfare:

1) the ability to identify and discriminate between combatants and noncombatants at greater ranges and during all conditions;
2) the possession of vision equipment allowing all soldiers to see at all times (day, night, in basements/tunnels, through smoke, etc.);
3) the ability to produce maps and distribute them down to at least squad level within 6 to 12 hours of notification;
4) the possession of a soldier-portable, intelligence collection and dissemination tool to conduct remote, route/area/building reconnaissance, ideally incorporating through wall and countersniper sensors;
5) the possession of recoilless, hand-held projectiles capable of piercing walls and armor (a "bunkerbuster");
6) the possession of thermal, electronic and visual "badges" to mark all friendly soldiers;
7) the possession of nonlethal weapons for use in peacekeeping and police operations, and for storming buildings that may contain civilians.[22]

An Integrated Helmet Assembly Subsystem (IHAS) already exists, allowing the individual soldier to see computer-generated data, maps, and imagery, including pictures from a camera. This will enable the soldier to see and fire around corners. Much thinking is also going into the creation of small robots both for intelligence and fighting in urban terrain.

Whatever the utility of individual items that emerge from this project, the overall approach displays a dangerous degree of wishful thinking. To begin with, there is a real risk that a mixture of the strain of combat and the sheer complexity of the equipment will overwhelm the ordinary soldier. In the words of one British officer with urban combat experience, "They'll be so busy looking into the computer screens in their helmets that they won't notice when someone creeps up behind them and hits them on the head." He pointed out that commanders of armored vehicles have long been equipped with numerous vision and sensory devices—and in the British case, still prefer to take the risk of sticking their heads out of the hatch to see what is happening. Talk of this kind also ignores the way that commanders too can be overwhelmed by sheer volume of information. If, as is often the case, the chain of command has also become disrupted, the result can be a confusion that, because it has its roots in essentially human limitations, technology cannot remedy. Episodes during the Rangers' fight in Mogadishu illustrate this to perfection.

Secondly, the technology that aims to distinguish between combatants and non-combatants is very much at the wish-list stage. From this point of view, the introduction of robotic devices could represent a step backwards, since it is not clear how these could be prevented from killing everything in their path, or even—if they malfunction—turning on their own side, electronic "recognition devices" notwithstanding. Moreover, the technology for these is in fact still embryonic.

Above all, much of the U.S. military literature on future urban warfare seems to assume two things. The first is a really remarkable level of leadership ability and courage on the part of junior officers, non-commissioned officers, and even privates. The courage expected is both physical and in a sense moral—the courage to operate in near-physical isolation or in very small groups.[23]

This has indeed always been a feature of urban warfare. In the words of Marshal Vasily Chuikov, commander of the defense of Stalingrad, "In street fighting a soldier is on occasion his own general." A critical failing of the Russians in Grozny in 1995 was the poor quality of their junior leadership, and the acute demoralization of their individual soldiers. These, however, are essentially traditional military qualities, not provided for under the heading of technological or robotic development.

The other assumption pervading U.S. literature on urban warfare is the tendency to underestimate the potential tactical skill of the enemy while greatly exaggerating the capacity of U.S. troops on the ground. Thus the principles set out by Marine analysts for the Active Urban Defense of a city by U.S. troops are very close to those actually employed by the Chechens in Grozny. This assumes a hardly credible level of local knowledge, fanatical determination, and courage among the U.S. troops concerned. Such qualities might be forthcoming in the unlikely event that like the Chechens, U.S. troops were fighting an invader of their country, in the streets of Los Angeles or Chicago. These qualities are unlikely to be present to the same degree in U.S. soldiers fighting in Baghdad or Kabul.

Finally, U.S. planners are in my view hopelessly overoptimistic about the prospects for minimizing civilian casualties by the use of "nonlethal" weapons. As Major John Schmitt has written, "The idea of using nonlethals to incapacitate everyone and then sorting things out once everyone is "down for the count" greatly oversimplifies the problem and betrays an imperialistic high-handedness that will be politically unviable in many situations." On the whole, the U.S. approaches to future urban warfare are characterized—if only unconsciously—by what has been called "Technological Superiority Theory" rather than "Mental Agility Theory."[24]

VIII

Urban combat against well-armed and fiercely committed, but politically amorphous bands constitutes the kind of warfare that over the next two generations will pose the greatest challenge to Western armed forces. By contrast, major wars between the West and large opposing states are less likely. The drubbing administered to the Iraqi and Yugoslav national infrastructures will have had their effect. Unless the United States hopelessly mismanages relations with Russia, China or both, it is difficult to see why these or other states would risk directly confronting U.S. military power.

For a long time to come, the enormous superiority of American technology and military spending will, in this limited sense, make conventional war "obsolete." Despite Chinese alarm over the demonstration of American military prowess in Kosovo, China for a long time to come will possess neither the technological nor the financial resources to exploit the "Revolution in Military Affairs" so as to pose a really serious challenge to the United States in high-tech warfare.[25]

Failing some truly absurd American provocation—for example, supporting full independence for Taiwan or a Ukrainian move to expel Russia's Black Sea Fleet from Sevastopol—Chinese and Russian national elites are unlikely to risk their national infrastructures, and no less importantly, their own positions and wealth on so hazardous a gamble as war against the United States. On the American side, ever since Vietnam the inclination to court a major war has been limited by a fear of casualties and well-founded doubts about the American public's ability to stomach operations in which the United States itself has not been directly attacked and vital U.S. interests are not at stake. For years to come, the more immediate threat to the U.S. military will come not directly from existing states, but from within states, as those groups who have failed to benefit from the new world economy express their frustration by rising up against their own rulers, venting their anger against ethnic neighbors, or trying to create a radical new order.

At times, the United States will find itself drawn into these conflicts because of regional sensitivities—in Central America and the Caribbean, for example. At other times, it will intervene because critical interests are at stake, as for example, with the oil-producing states of the Persian Gulf. In other instances, intangibles may propel the U.S. to intervene—to shore up American credibility or to sustain U.S. claims to global leadership.

Critics will say that the United States can always avoid such conflicts by simply refusing to get involved.[26] But to assume that this will always be possible suggests an attitude of profound complacency. In the eyes of future generations, a nation willing to spend tens of billions of dollars to create a missile shield that saves North Korea from committing suicide, while failing to prepare for urban and partisan warfare, is likely to be regarded as at least irresponsible if not altogether paranoid. Apart from anything else, such a view assumes that our leaders will exercise unerring judgment and never engage in seemingly safe and limited military deployments that turn out to have unforeseen consequences—a naive assumption, given the historical record.

The further spread of terrorism will only serve to increase the likelihood of such interventions, especially if—as seems all too possible—at some stage terrorists gain access to weapons of mass destruction. The existence of states acting as bases for terrorism has already led the United States in the last two decades to bombard Libya, Afghanistan, and Sudan. This is the underside of the "global village": it spawns universal threats, thereby creating the requirement for universal policing.

As the brutal, chaotic, and menacing aftermath of the war in Kosovo suggests, the possession of superior air power does not necessarily equip a nation to keep order in that global village. In that regard, the intellectual and cultural weaknesses of Western armed forces in general, and U.S. forces in particular, are acutely relevant, whether they are the reluctance to suffer casualties among ground troops or to use ground troops to inflict heavy casualties on civilians—as may well be unavoidable on occasions.[27]

At the very least, some pretty tough, consistent and lengthy policing may be necessary. Where a tradition of socially sanctioned violence and theft is present in both parts of an ethnically mixed society, the only way of containing this in a moderately equitable way is sustained policing by an outside power. But for this to work, a whole series of factors have to be present, which the United States seems unwilling to countenance.

In the first place, the outside power has to be actually in control of the police forces and other authorities concerned and capable of handing out real rewards and punishments. It needs to maintain a sufficient number of its own men on the ground, speaking a local language and understanding local society. Given the general U.S. assumption that globalization means that the rest of the world is gradually becoming more American, U.S. forces are not likely to make the effort to become sufficiently conversant with other cultures.

Secondly, the presence of the outside power has to appear pretty much eternal—or at least it must appear that way to the local population. The mere discussion of "exit strategies"—much less publicly declared deadlines for withdrawal—signals to adversaries that they need simply bide their time.

Thirdly, the outside policing force, to be effective, will have to adopt methods very different from those common to modern Western societies. In circumstances where criminality is ethnicised and enjoys communal protection, pursuing individual perpetrators may be worse than useless. It may therefore in the end be both more effective and less provocative to resort to collective punishment; not mass executions or the burning of villages, but fines, confiscations, and restrictions on movement.

For obvious reasons, it is extremely difficult for U.S. (or European) armed forces of today to fulfill such requirements.

IX

The remarkable American reliance on air power stems at least in part from a determination *not* to become bogged down in such situations—to police the world but to do so on the cheap. This is not a new phenomenon. In the days of empire, whenever possible, European colonial powers used professionals—drawn from the expendable underclass and led by a largely hereditary caste of officers—rather than conscripts in their colonial campaigns. The determination to sustain the empire at minimum cost to the nation explains the creation of the French Foreign Legion in the nineteenth century and the retention of the British Gurkhas into the twenty-first. There was always a strong feeling that conscripts could only legitimately be used close to home and in wars for the defense of the homeland. It helps explains why despite much saber-rattling, no major European powers ever went to war with each other over colonial possessions in Asia or Africa (with the partial exception of the Crimean War). As a reflection of Western social, political, and cultural reality, the aversion to casualties in distant operations is nearly inevitable. The only difference today is that the aversion to losses in far-off operations now applies to professional soldiers as well (though less so in Britain than America).

But the concentration on aerial warfare suggests trends that go beyond and are more worrisome than the fear of casualties alone. One such trend is an aversion to combat itself, reflected in the belief that judiciously administered punishment (or even the prospect of punishment) along with skillful diplomatic signaling can bring an adversary to terms. Hence, the expectations in Brussels and Washington that three or four days of NATO bombing would surely suffice to force the Serbs to evacuate Kosovo.

Even more significant is the desire to impose order on warfare—to bring precision, predictability, and control to the use of force. Many—perhaps most—soldiers have always resisted the notion that war *by its very nature* is chaotic, filled with chance, and, at a certain level, unfathomable. For while this truth is acceptable to the freelance warrior, it goes against the entire spirit of the organized, "rational" military machine. Today, the age of the computer and so-called information revolution combines with these traditional bureaucratic and hierarchical elements of Western military culture to foster expectations that war can now at long last be tamed. This tendency may well be particularly pronounced among American officers, and is likely to get worse as more and more of the senior ones are drawn from the ranks of the technicians rather than the units "at the sharp end." For example, former U.S. Air Force Chief of Staff General Ronald Fogleman has declared that "in the first quarter of the twenty-first century you will be able to find, fix or track, and target—in near-real time—anything of consequence that moves upon or is located on the face of the Earth."[28]

But while a career spent ascending the ranks of the military bureaucracy in peacetime may equip a man for the technical and organizational aspects of warfare, it does not provide adequate psychological and intellectual preparation for command in the Mogadishus or Groznys that define much of the future of warfare. Such a career path tends to diminish a capacity for flexibility and improvisation, and to encourage a preference for what Andrew Bacevich has called "stylized warfare." While such warfare may make its appearance every generation or so—as in the Gulf War of 1991—the record of military history *since* Desert Storm, to include the war over Kosovo, suggests that other contingencies are far more commonplace as well as more perplexing.[29]

X

This then would seem the greatest threat: not major battles in the open field, where electronic intelligence and accurate firepower will give the United State huge advantages; but the America's global aspirations leading to the commitment of U.S. forces to occupy territories, and above all great cities, in the face of a bitterly hostile population and amidst a mixture of cultural ignorance, poor intelligence, racist hostility, brutality, and demoralization that affect its own forces and civilian population. Such conflicts could not in themselves lead to major physical defeats for U.S. forces, nor are they alone likely to destroy American global hegemony. But moral defeats like Somalia, and the losses and the moral squalor of such conflicts could over time undermine the will of the American people to play a global role. And if anger at a bungled and brutal American occupation encouraged massive terrorist attacks on the continental United States, it could inflict terrible harm on the American people.

Most of the thinking being done by the U.S. armed forces is wholly irrelevant to such conflicts, and the lessons learned from Kosovo have been entirely the wrong ones. The chief result, as evidenced by the 2000 military budget and the proposed reforms of Defense Secretary Donald Rumsfeld, appears to have been even more spending on the airforce and high technology. This spending has gone in part to "smart" weapons, which however useful against enemy armor in the open field, are next to useless in cities and in partisan warfare. The "lesson" of Kosovo has also translated into further development of the joint strike fighter, a weapon designed to fight above all against sophisticated, well-trained, large scale enemy air forces of a kind which simply do not exist in the world today.

Meanwhile, the limited contingent of U.S. troops on the ground in Kosovo are discovering that they lack both the numbers and the determination to prevent ethnic cleansing by the victorious Albanian majority, or even adequately to patrol Kosovo's border with Serbia proper and, even more importantly, with Macedonia. To accomplish the tasks those soldiers actually face, horses and mules would be more useful than additional smart weapons, fighters, and main battle tanks.[30]

At the time of writing, there are several potential scenarios in Kosovo and the wider Balkans that could lead either to a humiliating and disastrous NATO withdrawal or a dangerously increased NATO presence in the whole region: Relations with the Albanian majority could breakdown entirely, leading to attacks on NATO forces supported by segments of the local population. KLA incursions into neighboring Macedonia have spurred an Albanian revolt there and may lead to the collapse and partition of Macedonia. Bloody Serbian terrorist attacks on U.S. troops could prompt either a hasty Somalia-style pull-out or a U.S.-led invasion of Serbia proper. A unilateral Montenegrin declaration of independence could provoke a Serb intervention there, leading to civil war and a NATO military invasion and occupation undertaken in the midst of a largely hostile Montenegrin Serb population.

Such conflicts are exactly the kind that will pose the greatest threat to Western armed forces in the decades to come. They are unlikely, even theoretically, to end in American victory through new technology or the adoption of grand new strategic theories. They will demand stamina, casualties, ruthlessness and adaptability. In the end the lessons most useful in such conflicts are likely to be ancient ones: know thy enemy, despise not thy enemy, and pick thy battles with care. Or in the words of Ecclesiastes, the preacher who was also a king and military leader: "I returned, and saw under the sun, that the race is not to the swift, nor the battle to the strong . . . but time and chance happeneth to them all. For man also knoweth not his time: as the fishes that are taken in an evil net, and as the birds that are caught in the snare; so are the sons of man snared in an evil time, when it falleth suddenly upon them."[31]

Notes

An abridged version of this chapter appeared in the winter 2000–2001 issue of *The National Interest*.

1. John Keegan, "How We Beat Milosevic," *Daily Telegraph* (London), 12 July 1999. For a more skeptical view, see Alexander Nicoll, "The Lingering Question," *The Financial Times* (London), 1 July 1999.
2. See Edgar Holt, *The Opium Wars in China* (London: Putnam, 1964), p. 91, and Maurice Collis, *Foreign Mud* (London: Faber and Faber, 1946), pp. 253–61.
3. Holt, p. 111; Lieutenant John Ouchterlony, *The Chinese War* (London: Saunders and Otley, 1844), pp. 98–99.
4. Moreover, there is strong evidence to suggest that Yugoslav ground forces in Kosovo suffered most of their losses when the Kosovo Liberation Army (KLA) launched an offensive over the mountains from Albania. They forced the Yugoslavs to concentrate against them and thereby expose themselves to NATO fire. In other words, to the extent that NATO did defeat the Yugoslav army as such, the victory was not due to airpower alone. Lieutenant Colonel Price T. Bingham, "Rapidly Stopping an Invasion," *Strategic Review*, Fall 1998.
5. For San-yuan-li, see Frederic Wakeman Jr, *Strangers at the Gate: Social Disorder in South China, 1839–61* (Berkeley: University of California Press, 1966), pp. 11–21. For Chinese accounts, see Arthur Waley, *The Opium War Through Chinese Eyes* (London: Allen and Unwin, 1958).
6. Captain Kevin W. Brown, "The Urban Warfare Dilemma," *Marine Corps Gazette*, January 1997.
7. Mark Bowden, *Black Hawk Down* (New York: Atlantic Monthly Press, 1999), pp. 327–28. A less colorful account in reported speech is to be found in Oakley's own description of developments in Somalia: John L. Hirsch and Robert B. Oakley, *Somalia and Operation Restore Hope: Reflections on Peacemaking and Peacekeeping* (Washington, D.C.: United States Institute of Peace, 1995), p. 131. See also Patrick J. Sloyan, "How the Warlord Outwitted Clinton's Spooks," *Washington Post*, 3 April 1994.
8. I. M. Lewis, *Understanding Somalia: Guide to Culture, History and Social Institutions* (London: HAAN Associates, 1993). Quoted in Hirsch and Oakley, p. 4.

9. Sergei Arutiunov, "Ethnicity and Conflict in the Caucasus," in *Ethnic Conflict and Russian Intervention in the Caucasus*, ed. Fred Wahling (Institute for the Study of Global Conflict and Cooperation, University of California, San Diego), p. 17.
10. This is not simply an "Old World" phenomenon. The Spanish conquistadors managed in a very few years to subjugate the great Aztec and Inca empires—and then spent several centuries attempting to subdue comparatively tiny numbers of primitive Yaquis, Apaches, and Araucanians in the deserts of northern Mexico and the freezing wastes of southern Chile.
11. For a recent survey of European wars with "primitive" peoples, portrayed as far as possible from the side of the resistance, see Mark Cocker, *Rivers of Blood, Rivers of Gold: Europe's Conflict with Tribal Peoples* (London: J. Cape, 1998); for the "Indian wars" in North America, see Armstrong Stanley, *European and Native American Warfare, 1675–1815* (London: UCL Press, 1998).
12. *Times* (London), 7 February 1989.
13. Patrick Macrory, *Signal Catastrophe: The Story of a Disastrous Retreat from Kabul, 1842* (London: Hodder and Stoughton, 1966); Lady Sale, A *Journal of the Disasters in Affghanistan, 1841–2* (London: Murray, 1844). For the general background of British Afghan policy, see Malcolm Yapp, *Strategies of British India: Britain, Iran and Afghanistan, 1798–1850* (Oxford: Clarendon Press, 1980), and David Gillard, *The Struggle for Asia, 1828–1914: A Study in British and Russian Imperialism* (London: Methuen, 1977).
14. For a late-nineteenth-century British campaign against a religiously inspired tribal rising by a young officer who participated, see Winston S. Churchill, "The Malakand Field Force," in his *Frontiers and Wars* (New York: Harcourt, Brace and World, 1962), pp. 17–130.
15. For the background to the invasion, see Anatol Lieven, "Nightmare in the Caucasus," *The Washington Quarterly* (winter 1999).
16. For a description of the battle for Grozny in January 1995, see Anatol Lieven, *Chechnya: Tombstone of Russian Power* (New Haven: Yale University Press, 1998), pp. 108–17, and Carlotta Gall and Thomas de Waal, *Chechnya: calamity in the Caucasus* (New York: New York University Press, 1998), pp. 204–27.
17. See Keith William Nolan, *Battle for Hue: Tet, 1968* (Novato, Calif.: Presidio Press, 1983).
18. David Rees, ed., *The Korean War: History and Tactics* (London: Orbis, 1984).
19. Mark Hewish and Rupert Pengelley, "Warfare in the Global City," *Jane's International Defense Review*, June 1998.
20. Stephen Metz, "The American Army in the 21st Century," *Strategic Review* (fall 1999).
21. Bowden, *Black Hawk Down*, pp. 160–64.

22. See International Institute for Strategic Studies, "The Future of Urban Warfare," *Strategic Comments* 5, no. 2 (March 1999); "Non-Lethal Weapons Bestow Particular Advantages in MOUT," *Jane's International Defense Review*, June 1998; and "MISER Permits Engagement from Confined Space," *Jane's International Defense Review*, September 1998.
23. See Lieutenant General Paul K. Van Riper, USMC, "A Concept for Future Military Operations on Urbanized Terrain," *Marine Corps Gazette*, October 1997 (special supplement), and Colonel Randolph A. Gangle, "The Foundation for 'Urban Warrior,'" *Marine Corps Gazette*, July 1998.
24. Major John F. Schmitt, USMCR, "A Critique of the Hunter Warrior Concept," *Marine Corps Gazette*, June 1998.
25. Paul Dibb, "The Revolution in Military Affairs and Asian Security," *Survival* 39, no.4 (winter 1997–98).
26. David Tucker, "Fighting Barbarians," *Parameters* (summer 1998).
27. See John A. Gentry, "Military Force in an Age of Cowardice," *The Washington Quarterly* (autumn 1998).
28. Quoted in Michael O'Hanlon, "Can High Technology Bring US Troops Home?" *Foreign Policy* (winter 1998–99).
29. Andrew J. Bacevich, "Preserving the Well-Bred Horse," *The National Interest* (fall 1994).
30. Indeed, in 1946 a British officer attempting to prevent rural massacres by Hindus and Muslims in India expressed regret that the British Indian army had scrapped its horse cavalry units.
31. Ecclesiastes 9:11–12.

5 Kosovo and the Moral Burdens of Power

Alberto R. Coll

Beyond its military and political dimensions, the war in Kosovo was filled with large and daunting moral complexities. The purpose of this essay is to examine these in light of the responsibilities the United States faces today as the world's preeminent power. The essay will analyze the moral ends for which United States and its allies carried out the Kosovo operation, the means by which they conducted it, and the war's consequences for the international system and its evolving norms of state behavior. The essay also will explore the degree to which the Kosovo operation yields insights for future statesmen committed to using American power in a morally responsible fashion. While this writer agreed with the decision to intervene militarily in Kosovo, the other side of the debate will be presented in this essay in order to give readers the opportunity to reach their own conclusions.

We must begin, as future historians no doubt will, by noting the strategic context in which the United States and its allies undertook the Kosovo operation. In 1999 the United States stood at the apex of its military, economic, and political power. At no time before in its history had the United States found itself so strong, in both absolute and relative terms, and so unopposed by any potential rival or challenger. The American economy, in the midst of an unprecedented expansion powered by huge productivity increases, generated by the revolution in information technologies, was the envy of the world. American society was recording 30-year lows in crime and unemployment. Militarily, the United States was outspending Russia, China,

Great Britain, France, Italy and Spain combined, and U.S. military forces were unmatched in their capabilities, technological sophistication, and global reach. Politically, the United States was acknowledged by all, and feared by some, as the world's hegemon. The United States either controlled outright or exercised decisive influence over all of the world's leading political and financial institutions, including the United Nations, NATO, the World Bank, and the International Monetary Fund. The only power that historically would have had the ability and the inclination to frustrate NATO's actions in Kosovo, Russia, was politically and economically weak and ultimately dependent on Western goodwill. Throughout the crisis, it could play no more than a mildly obstructionist role and, in the end, it encouraged Serbia to give in to Western demands.

American primacy in the 1990s gave free rein and heightened impetus to a series of long-held American beliefs about the historical role of the United States in the world. These beliefs, commonly grouped in recent decades under the rubric of Wilsonianism, have been an important strand of the American political psyche since the country's earliest days. In its barest outlines, Wilsonianism holds that the United States is a unique society destined by Providence to lead the rest of the world to a future of freedom, democratic equality, and harmony.[1] Wilsonianism is exceptionalist, universalist, and messianic. It is exceptionalist to the degree that it posits that the United States is different from other nations, and that it has a unique historical mission. It is universalist in that it maintains that the liberal Western understanding of liberty, democracy, and equality, notions of what constitutes a legitimate polity, and definitions of human rights are desirable across the entire range of global cultural and religious differences. And it is messianic in that it holds that America's historical mission is to promote, not only by example but also by energetic action, these values around the world. A vibrant force in American foreign policy for much of the twentieth century, Wilsonianism entered a particularly vigorous phase during the years of the Clinton presidency.

Several developments illustrate the resurgence of Wilsonianism in the 1990s and the degree to which it helped to set the stage for the Kosovo intervention. First, Wilsonian rhetoric found renewed favor among American leaders, with frequent references by President Clinton and Secretary of State Albright to the United States as "the indispensable nation." National Security directives and State Department documents became steeped in grandiose language about America's responsibilities to promote global democratization and human rights. The State Department established an "Assistant Secretary of State for Democracy," and the creation of a similar office within the Department of Defense was averted only by the narrowest of margins after a tough bureaucratic fight. Second, within the executive and legislative branches there was a massive urge to impose diplomatic and economic sanctions, or strengthen existing ones, on many countries. While in a handful of cases, such as Iraq, North Korea, and Libya, the sanctions were related to national security concerns, most were imposed on the basis of human-rights violations. As of early 2001, the United States maintained diplomatic and economic sanctions on some 75 countries, compared to fewer than a dozen countries subject to sanctions by the United Nations. Almost half of the 125 unilateral economic sanctions imposed by the United States since World War I took effect between 1993 and 1998.[2]

The revival in Wilsonian rhetoric and the use of sanctions as a foreign policy instrument were coupled with several major interventions in which the United States deployed military power to restore order and to promote Wilsonian goals. The most notable of these were in Somalia (1992–93), Haiti (1994) and Bosnia (1996–the present). Like the subsequent intervention in Kosovo, the interventions in Haiti and in Bosnia combined security and humanitarian objectives, whereas the Somalia operation was almost purely humanitarian in character. It is impossible to understand the context of the Kosovo operation without some discussion of the three major interventions that preceded it.

When the Bush administration launched the Somalia operation in its last days in office, it conceived it as a narrow humanitarian intervention to end the famine scourging the country, and was intent on withdrawing U.S. forces as soon as it achieved this objective. The Clinton administration, prodded by its then Ambassador to the United Nations, Madeleine Albright, broadened the mission's goal to include supporting the United Nations agenda for rebuilding the country's political and economic institutions and creating a more democratic and prosperous Somali society. This expansion of the original objectives brought the United Nations and the American government into conflict with Somali warlord and political leader Mohammed Farah Aidid, who sought to take control of the country. For several months in the summer and fall of 1993, American military forces were openly at war with Aidid and his partisans. In October of that year, after a violent clash in which U.S. forces killed several hundred Somalis and suffered 18 killed in action, the Clinton administration, under pressure from Congress and the American public, abruptly terminated U.S. participation in Somalia and shortly thereafter withdrew all U.S. forces.

Several key facts stand out about the Somalia episode. First, even though there were no important U.S strategic interests at stake, the Clinton Administration embarked on an ambitious "nation-building" mission from which it withdrew only in the face of strong U.S. domestic opposition. Second, although one of the intervention's declared goals was to improve the lives of the Somali people, it encountered fierce resistance from significant elements of the Somali population and its political elites, and in due course UN and U.S. forces wound up taking the lives of several thousand Somalis and inflicting considerable material damage. While it is also true that, thanks to the U.S.-UN intervention, the Somali famine came to an end and some 10,000 lives were saved, the overall moral picture was one of considerable ambiguity.[3] Ironically, smarting from criticism of its handling of Somalia, the Clinton administration refrained the following year from intervening in Rwanda, where again there were no security interests at stake, but where a modest U.S.-European military involvement might have stopped a genocide that took more than half a million lives.

Next on the road to Kosovo came Haiti, which, in the wake of a military coup against the elected government of President Jean Bertrand Aristide, verged on political and economic chaos. With the Haitian economy in 1994 groaning under the weight of U.S.-imposed "pro-democracy" economic sanctions, violence between security forces and pro-Aristide elements escalating, and the number of Haitians fleeing their homeland mounting daily, the Clinton administration decided to intervene militarily on both security and humanitarian grounds. Internal unrest, accentuated by the military junta's illegitimacy and its authoritarian and corrupt practices, was provoking an exodus of Haitian migrants to American shores. The Clinton administration considered this exodus destabilizing for the Caribbean region and for the southern United States, especially for the populous and politically influential state of Florida. To this security-related concern was joined the Wilsonian goal of promoting Haitian democracy and a more prosperous and equitable Haitian society. In contrast to the U.S. operation in Somalia, the U.S. occupation of Haiti generated no opposition, but the results were equally ambiguous, politically and morally. When the last American troops left in 1999, Haiti was no closer to true democracy, social stability, or economic prosperity than it had been five years earlier.

In Bosnia, the United States carried out another military intervention in which security goals were joined to humanitarian ones. The Bosnia intervention had two principal objectives: to strengthen NATO and European security through the enforcement of the 1995 Dayton Accords settling the war in Bosnia-Herzegovina, and to promote order and stability within Bosnia by preventing further human-rights violations, including acts of war and genocide against any ethnic or religious minority groups. The Clinton administration persuaded Congress to support the intervention, at least half-heartedly, with the rationale that the American effort would enhance U.S. influence in NATO and Europe at a time of growing reassertion of European independence, and that it would stop the massacres of innocent Bosnians dominating the evening news. The intervention appealed to large numbers of internationalists of all stripes: conservatives and liberals, idealists and realists, Cold War warriors and Wilsonian crusaders, many of whom saw it as an instrument for promoting American security interests while accomplishing worthy humanitarian ends.

As of this writing, a large contingent of U.S. troops remains in Bosnia and progress in the implementation of the peace settlement has been glacially slow. Yet, under the shadow of the American peacekeepers, human-rights violations have ceased; a semblance of order, stability, and normal economic activity has returned to the country, and there is a glimmer of hope that over time a durable peace may emerge. In Bosnia, as in Haiti, the American military entered the country with the approval of the relevant political authorities and major political factions, and this helped to insure little violent opposition to the American presence and thus hardly any U.S. casualties. This also meant that, in both cases, the American intervention, even if it did not accomplish the wholesale restructuring of society hoped for by some of its more ardent Wilsonian advocates, at least had the salutary effect of ratcheting down the overall levels of violence.

To what degree did the Kosovo intervention differ morally from those that had occurred in the Clinton years? While Haiti and Bosnia resemble Kosovo in their underlying mix of security and humanitarian objectives, neither Bosnia nor Haiti took the form of a full-fledged war against an established government and its military forces, as was the case in Kosovo. In fact, Kosovo can be considered the first war of humanitarian intervention ever carried out by the Western liberal powers. This is its salient characteristic, and the main reason its moral complexities were numerous, and its implications for the future exercise of American power in a morally responsible manner so significant. Looking over the course of the last hundred years, never before had the Western powers used force for ostensibly humanitarian purposes, whether in Katanga in 1961 or in China's Boxer Rebellion of 1908, *except* for the purpose of rescuing nationals. Never before had the West carried out a full-scale war against an established state, as it did in Kosovo, for the sake of protecting the rights of a foreign people with whom it had no ethnic, religious, or political ties.

Ius ad Bellum: Was it Right to Undertake the Kosovo Intervention?

An analysis of Kosovo's moral complexities and their long-term implications for the morally responsible use of American power must begin by asking whether the United States and its allies were morally justified in undertaking the intervention. Was it right for NATO to unleash a full, violent war against Serbia? To address this question requires, in turn, asking a series of related subquestions that are part of common moral reasoning and intrinsic to the Western philosophical and political tradition within which American public life and discourse continue to be embedded. They are questions that seem to come naturally to anyone inquiring into the rightness of a decision to resort to the highly destructive instruments of war. In the West's history these questions have come to be known collectively as "just war theory." This term is perhaps misleading because the word "theory" implies a high degree of abstraction, an artificial flight from natural human moral reasoning and discourse into the realm of formalism. But the questions at the heart of just-war theory are neither artificial nor abstract. They are quite "natural" questions that a reasonable human observer would ask when placed in the position of having to analyze the moral rightness of the resort to war.[4]

Just-war theory evaluates the rightness of a war by examining two dimensions: the rightness of the decision to wage war (*ius ad bellum*), and the rightness of the means by which the war is conducted (*ius in bello*). We will examine these two in order, first looking at the rightness of NATO's decision to employ force as an instrument of policy to compel Serbia to stop its massive human-rights violations against the Albanian Kosovars. The related subquestions that come naturally to mind, and that are also part of just-war theory are as follows. First, was there sufficient cause to justify NATO's resort to force—in other words, were the evils being perpetrated by Serbia in its province substantial enough to justify the violence, deaths, and destruction entailed in war? One way of putting this question is to ask whether the object of the intervention was of sufficient moral worth to outweigh the evils likely to be generated by the use of force. Second, did NATO have lawful authority to engage in war against Serbia, and what was the source of that authority? Third, was there a reasonable chance of success? Fourth, did NATO exhaust all reasonable peaceful alternatives prior to waging war—in other words, was war truly the last resort?

One word of caution is necessary at this point. This writer does not see the just-war tradition as a simple formula that consistently provides clear-cut answers to the moral dilemmas posed by the use of force. Even though some writers treat just-war reasoning this way, others see it instead as a series of broad guidelines or principles that help policymakers discern the moral reasonableness of a particular resort to war but never provide the equivalent of scientific certainty or precision. Under this latter view, the just-war tradition is useful, not so much because it supplies definitive answers, but because it forces decision makers to ask a series of tough questions and to engage in the kind of careful deliberation that can clarify the moral costs and benefits of alternative policy choices and, in some cases, lessen the likelihood that some terrible crimes will be committed. Applying just-war criteria to the use of force in Kosovo may not tell us beyond a shadow of a doubt whether NATO was right or wrong in doing what it did, but it will clarify the issues that demand attention in order to reach one's own conclusions.

Was There Just Cause?

Were Serbia's acts against the Albanian Kosovars on such a scale as to justify NATO's use of force? The immediate justification for the war was the recrudescence in 1998 and 1999 of Serb violence against the ethnic Albanians, apparently calculated to drive most of them out of Kosovo into Albania. It was similar to the "ethnic cleansing" that the Bosnian Serbs, with the full backing of Slobodan Milosevic, had carried out against the Muslims in Bosnia. In 1989, aware that Yugoslavia was on the verge of breaking up along ethnic lines, Milosevic had reversed Marshal Tito's policy of granting considerable autonomy to the Kosovars and opted for a policy of centralization and tighter control. The Albanian Kosovars resisted this new policy. Milosevic's policies spurred the rise of several new Kosovar nationalist groups, the more moderate ones insisting on a return to autonomy, the more radical ones such as the Kosovo Liberation Army (KLA) agitating for full independence. As Slovenia and Croatia broke away from Yugoslavia in 1990 and the war in Bosnia broke out, Milosevic's energies became focused away from Kosovo, where an uneasy calm punctured by sporadic low-level violence prevailed. In its closing days, the administration of George H. W. Bush warned Serbia that "in the event of conflict in Kosovo caused by Serbian action, the United States will be prepared to employ military force against the Serbs in Kosovo and in Serbia proper."[5] It is not altogether clear why the elder President Bush chose to draw the line in Kosovo when he failed to do so earlier in Bosnia. But there was a belated recognition that Milosevic had to be stopped from further depredations, coupled with fear that a Serb-Kosovar war would destabilize the Balkans beyond the breaking point and draw into the conflict Greece, Bulgaria and Turkey with potentially devastating consequences for European peace and NATO's continued viability.

When in 1999 President Bill Clinton made good his predecessor's threat, the chief NATO powers—the United States, Great Britain, France, and Germany—offered several reasons for their military intervention in Kosovo. First, NATO sought to stop ongoing human-rights violations against the ethnic Albanians, including ethnic cleansing and killings of those who resisted or were considered KLA sympathizers. These human-rights violations were significant in their number and severity, and they had increased throughout 1998 and early 1999. Second, NATO feared the destabilization of southeastern Europe if the situation in Kosovo further deteriorated. The flow of refugees from Kosovo into Albania, Bosnia, and Macedonia was rising sharply, affecting the internal stability of those states. If the strife in Kosovo continued to worsen, outside powers might step in, provoking a wider conflict. From the time Milosevic stepped up repression against the ethnic Albanians in 1998 to the end of hostilities following NATO's intervention, approximately one million refugees fled Kosovo, and another 300,000 to 500,000 remained as internally displaced persons within Kosovo.[6] Third, NATO members wanted to avoid a repetition of the earlier events in Croatia and Bosnia, and were eager to establish a precedent by indicating to Milosevic that they would not tolerate his policy of fanning ethnic strife to establish a Greater Serbia. The NATO powers also claimed to be establishing the broader precedent that such aggressive behavior would not be tolerated anywhere in Europe.

Thus, a cluster of three reasons supported the intervention, all of them adding up supposedly to sufficient justification. The first cause was *humanitarian*, the second one was grounded in regional *security*, and the third one could be called *normative*, that is, related to upholding the norms and precedents necessary to maintain a humane and peaceful international order. Did all these justify the war? Did they outweigh all the evils and disorders that a war was likely to set in motion? This writer believes that they did. The scale of human-rights violations was sufficiently high, the regional security problem generated by these violations sufficiently severe, and the need to uphold normative standards compelling enough to add up to a justification for military action.

Yet debate on this critical question has not stopped, and it is useful to consider some of the arguments against NATO intervention. Critics maintain that none of the justifications given, either individually or combined, amounted to a just cause for war. First, the comparative scale of repression in Kosovo did not differ appreciably from other cases—for example, Turkey's treatment of the Kurds and Guatemala's abuse of its own indigenous peoples—where it never occurred to the United States government to carry out a military intervention on behalf of the victims. Moreover, critics argue that in Kosovo some of the acts of violence classified as Serb human-rights violations were either legitimate acts of war against the violent terrorist KLA paramilitary forces, or else unfortunate and unavoidable by-products of the war with the KLA.

Second, critics argue that the Kosovo conflict posed no real threat to regional security. In fact, not only was there no serious risk of the war spreading, but it was NATO's military intervention that raised such risks dramatically by antagonizing Russia in an area of great sensitivity to Russian interests and prestige, by raising the tempo of ethnic cleansing and overall violence, by increasing refugee flows, and finally through the bombing of the Chinese embassy. While the ongoing conflict between Serbs and Albanians in Kosovo posed a risk of escalation, the best way to contain the conflict was not to turn it into a full multistate war but through diplomacy.

Critics likewise dismiss the normative justification for intervention. They argue that the Serb-Albanian conflict in Kosovo did not affect the normative foundations of international order because it was a domestic conflict within a recognized nation-state. Encouraging further negotiations among the concerned parties, perhaps under the auspices of the United Nations, was the appropriate course of action. Moreover, the NATO intervention established several morally and legally noxious precedents. First, internal strife in a weak and isolated country such as Serbia can be a handy excuse for meddling by outsiders, using humanitarianism as a pretext. Under this precedent, dozens of countries around the world could find themselves at the receiving end of a humanitarian intervention by more powerful, self-interested neighbors. Second, by acting militarily without UN authorization, NATO undermined the United Nations's credibility and authority and created a precedent giving regional organizations wide latitude to intervene militarily. This undermines international order and morality because regional organizations such as NATO and the OAS are generally less impartial than the United Nations—they tend to be dominated by the stronger regional powers that belong to them. Far from strengthening the normative pillars of international order and morality, the Kosovo intervention visibly weakened them by pushing the world in the direction of the rule of the weak by the strong.[7]

It is hardly surprising that the issue of whether there was sufficient cause to intervene provoked controversy. This has been the case with most wars throughout history, even many that in retrospect appear to have been clear-cut cases of justifiable wars. While the Kosovo military intervention garnered the support of many countries, it did not attract the more solid international consensus the Persian Gulf War enjoyed. This, too, should not be surprising. The principle that no country should be allowed to invade and occupy another sovereign state unless attacked is deeply rooted in international law and morality as one of the basic safeguards of international order. States perceive this principle as clearly in their interests, as an indispensable guide to survival in an anarchic world. On the other hand, states are highly suspicious of the concept of humanitarian intervention. There are few countries in the world, including the United States, which at some point in their history have not committed serious acts of violence against minorities in their midst. Whereas the principle at stake in the Gulf War was supportive of state power, and hence enjoys the support of most states in the international system, the principle of humanitarian intervention is threatening to many states and is viewed skeptically by most governments.

The inherent suspicion with which most governments view humanitarian intervention explains why the concept disappeared from the practice of international law at the end of the seventeenth century and did not enjoy a revival again until the last decade of the twentieth. What international law theorists of the nineteenth and early twentieth century called "the right of humanitarian intervention" was a desiccated, shrunken version of the real thing; it referred only to the right of states to rescue their own nationals. The idea that states had a right to rescue other peoples from the depredations of their own rulers, advocated by such early international legal theorists as Aquinas, Vitoria, Suarez, and Grotius, ceased to be a living element of international law and practice by the late seventeenth century in tandem with the end of the wars of religion and the consolidation of the secular nation-state system.[8] It was roundly dismissed by Vattel and his positivist successors in the nineteenth century, and remained an unfashionable viewpoint for most of the twentieth.[9]

There were two main reasons why the almost absolute ban on humanitarian intervention that dominated international law throughout the twentieth century crumbled over the last decade. First, there was the collapse of the Soviet Union and the emergence of an international system in which the United States and its allies hold a preeminent position, together with great freedom of action to carry out such interventions as their interests dictate or their publics demand. Second, the conceptions of state sovereignty underlying the older absolutist position are no longer as credible. In our crowded, highly interdependent planet, certain human-rights outrages that decades ago could be coldly ignored as a state's domestic matter no longer are truly domestic because they affect the stability and welfare of neighboring countries, as well as the normative fabric of international society. A number of human-rights advocates, mostly Western, believe that the end of the Cold War and the erosion of state sovereignty brought about by the forces of globalization offer an unparalleled opportunity to create a new world order that safeguards the rights of individuals and minority groups against governmental abuse. Such advocates hailed the United Nations action against Iraq in 1990–1991, the subsequent efforts to protect the Kurds and Shiites in that country, and the interventions in Somalia, Haiti, Bosnia, and Kosovo as flawed but positive harbingers of a changing international order in which the claims of state power and sovereignty will yield before those of a global community of human rights and interdependent moral obligations.

But the collapse of the old consensus against humanitarian intervention has not been followed by a new consensus. International opinion today ranges widely on the issue of the legitimacy of humanitarian intervention, with support for the revived concept coming mostly from a handful of powerful Western countries and their allies. Support for, or opposition to, the concept seems to depend on the circumstances of the particular case and on the strategic interests of each state. At one end of the spectrum are the United States and Tony Blair's United Kingdom, eager to reserve as much freedom of action as possible for future interventions, especially if carried out by NATO. Strategically, the United States sees itself as the guarantor of international order, the great power that must be ready to intervene anywhere, anytime, when others cannot or will not do so. A muscular Wilsonianism demands this freedom of action, as also does a calculated realpolitik. Meanwhile, Great Britain sees its strategic interests as closely bound with those of the United States and with an activist NATO role that enables the British to play one of their strongest cards in Europe: their robust military capabilities relative to those of other European states. Next on the intervention spectrum are states such as France and Germany. The French are suspicious of excessively elastic pro-intervention criteria that might legitimize what they see as American hegemonic pretensions. For their part, the Germans want to avoid situations in which Germany will act militarily outside its borders without a clear international mandate.

At the other end of the spectrum are the most vocal opponents of loosening the crtieria for humanitarian intervention. As one might expect, these include some of the weakest states in today's international system or those that have the most to lose from a resurgent American Wilsonianism. Cuba fits the first category, China and Russia the latter. For the Cubans, NATO's intervention in Kosovo, devoid as it was of a Security Council mandate, opened the door for bolder U.S. action around the world, including the Western hemisphere and someday, possibly even Cuba. Russia and China have large minorities in their midst, such as the Chechens and Tibetans, against whom they are prepared to use force on a massive scale in order to preserve national territorial integrity. They have nothing to gain and much to lose from more flexible standards for humanitarian intervention.

In the end, the arguments for or against a broader concept of humanitarian intervention seem to be dictated, not so much by their legal or moral persuasiveness, as by the strategic perspective and self-interest of each state. This also means that no solid consensus is likely to emerge. For the foreseeable future, the five Security Council members will remain divided, with the Western powers far more willing to countenance a more activist position than either Russia or China will support. Like the other four powers on the Council, the United States will focus first on its specific strategic responsibilities as it decides which interpretation of the rules to support, rather than its responsibilities to international law in the abstract or even to international morality.

Thus, the answer to the question whether there exists a new right of humanitarian intervention is complex. The Western powers insist that such a right is indeed beginning to emerge, while China, India, Russia, and much of the developing world reject the notion. Undoubtedly, the conviction that such a right exists is much stronger today than at any previous time in the last three centuries. If the international distribution of political, economic, and military power continues to favor the United States, Europe, and Japan, the right of humanitarian intervention will continue to enjoy its current resurgence. But any future assertions of this right will be resisted by a large number of states, including some with substantial military clout. If a prospective humanitarian intervention threatens to escalate into a serious conflict with a large- or medium-size military power, the odds are that the Western powers will not undertake it. If, on the other hand, the intervention is directed against a weak or isolated state such as Serbia that is unable to defend itself or to call upon a powerful ally to do so, the Western powers will be more likely to intervene.

Did NATO Have Lawful Authority?

Did NATO have lawful authority to engage in war against Serbia, and what was the source of that authority? In light of the preceding discussion, it is clear why those states that oppose the revival of humanitarian intervention will insist that, even in the most egregious cases of human-rights violations, a humanitarian intervention against a sovereign state requires the full backing of the international community, meaning, at a minimum, authorization from the United Nations Security Council. According to this viewpoint, only the United Nations commands sufficient legitimacy, universality, and impartiality to legitimize an act so extreme as the resort to war. While regional organizations carry enough authority to promote the peaceful settlement of disputes, they are not sufficiently impartial to authorize the use of force because they tend to be dominated by the strongest regional powers, and they lack mechanisms to protect weaker member states.

The opposing viewpoint, with which this writer agrees, contends that in the real world United Nations consensus is extremely difficult to achieve. No matter how hideous its human-rights violations, a state will almost always be able to find a patron in the Security Council willing to cast its veto on that state's behalf to protect it against a humanitarian intervention. In the case of Kosovo, Serbia found two such friends in Russia and China, both of which would have vetoed any United Nations resolution authorizing the use of force. If we are not prepared to acknowledge the legitimacy of humanitarian intervention by regional organizations or even individual states in cases of extreme human-rights violations, we will have a world in which such violations will take place with impunity while the international community stands by helplessly. Such an outcome is highly subversive of world order and human decency. Princeton philosopher Michael Walzer has put the case for this viewpoint eloquently:

> It was the Vietnamese who stopped Pol Pot in Cambodia, the Tanzanians who stopped Idi Amin in Uganda, the Indians who ended the killing in East Pakistan, the Nigerians who went into Liberia. Some of these were unilateral military acts, some (the Nigerian intervention, for example, and now the campaign in Kosovo) were authorized by regional alliances. Many people on the left yearn for a world where the United Nations, and only the United Nations, would act in all such cases. But given the oligarchic structure of the Security Council, it's not possible to count on this kind of action: in most cases on my list, UN intervention would have been vetoed by one of the oligarchs. Nor am I convinced that the world would be improved by having only one agent of international rescue. The men and women in the burning building are probably better served if they can appeal to more than a single set of firefighters.[10]

NATO argued that it had lawful authority to intervene on the basis of several grounds. First, the conflict's refugee flows, interethnic violence, and human-rights violations seriously affected regional stability in an area immediately adjacent to NATO. European security, broadly defined to include economic and social stability and containing the risk of conflict escalation, was at stake. In the face of likely United Nations inaction, NATO had the right to address this security threat. Second, NATO had lawful authority because it was sufficiently impartial. The NATO powers insisted that they were not pursuing an anti-Serbian crusade. They offered to take into account legitimate Serbian interests by specifying at the Rambouillet conference that Kosovar autonomy, not independence, would be the basis of any settlement; that the KLA and other Kosovar factions would have to disarm; and that Serb historical and religious shrines in Kosovo would be fully protected and controlled by Serbia under any autonomy scheme. The NATO powers also argued that they were willing to let Russia play a constructive role in their dealings with Serbia, though they also made it clear that they would not allow Russia to obstruct a humanitarian intervention. Third, NATO claimed that it had lawful authority because it was intervening on behalf of principles of human rights and international order fully compatible with those of the United Nations Charter. NATO's action would strengthen those principles, not only in southeastern Europe, an area of vital concern to NATO, but elsewhere in the world.

As with the debate on whether there was sufficient justification to intervene, the debate on whether NATO had lawful authority has remained inconclusive, shaped more by the interests and perspectives of the state making the argument than by the intrinsic legal and moral foundations of the argument itself. While NATO members and most Western authors are convinced that NATO had lawful authority, a large body of opinion in much of the non-Western world led by China and India strongly disagrees. This divergence of viewpoints seems unavoidable, if unfortunate. From the perspective of creating a more humane international order, it would be best if a solid consensus developed legitimating humanitarian intervention in cases of outrageous human-rights abuses. Two key elements of such a consensus would be *standards of impartiality* and *practical mechanisms for implementation.* These standards are unlikely to emerge anytime soon. UN Secretary General Kofi Annan has described the problem at the heart of the debate:

> Kosovo has cast in stark relief the dilemma of what has been called humanitarian intervention: on the one side, the question of the legitimacy of an action taken by a regional organization without a UN mandate; on the other, the universally recognized imperative of effectively halting violations of human rights with grave humanitarian consequences. The inability in the case of Kosovo to unify these two equally compelling interests of the international community—universal legitimacy and effectiveness in defense of human rights—can only be viewed as a tragedy.[11]

Was There a Reasonable Chance of Success?

The use of power in a morally responsible manner requires that close attention be paid, not just to one's good intentions, but also to the practical realities of acting on them. Good intentions that are carried out ineptly, or that result in evil consequences, are morally questionable. In the real world, of course, these are precisely the kinds of situations that even well-intentioned statesmen have to deal with most of the time: either policies that are difficult to implement well or actions that, no matter how skillfully implemented, will produce, along with some good, a great deal of evil as well. How did NATO and its key military power, the United States, do in Kosovo with regard to this calculus?

From the outset, the question was not whether NATO would prevail militarily but whether it would achieve its political objectives at a reasonable cost. These objectives were to stop the ongoing human-rights violations, end all violence in Kosovo, and facilitate a settlement of the conflict along the lines of the Rambouillet conference. In the end, NATO achieved these only partly, and at a much higher cost than anticipated. The question presenting itself is whether the alliance's leaders should have foreseen the difficulties they would encounter in achieving their objectives and, if so, whether they still should have gone forward with the military intervention.

First, did NATO's leaders err strategically and morally by failing to anticipate that the commencement of military operations against Serbia would lead the Serbs to step up the pace of ethnic cleansing, thereby increasing violence and human suffering dramatically? It was reasonable to expect that, in a conflict as charged with hatred as that between Serbs and ethnic Albanians, an effort to help the latter would also trigger massive reprisals against them, especially because the Serbs could not strike back at NATO itself.[12] And if there was a reasonable possibility that this would happen, the problem was compounded by NATO's obvious inability to respond, unless the Alliance was willing to use ground forces, something which would carry its own set of serious risks and disadvantages. Thus, the moral score is mixed. On the one hand, it is fair to charge NATO with a degree of strategic and moral turpitude to the extent that its intervention worsened considerably the very outrages it was meant to halt. But on the other hand, NATO eventually did put a stop to Serbian depredations against the ethnic Albanians.

NATO only partially achieved its two other objectives: to end all violence in Kosovo and to facilitate a settlement of the conflict along the lines of the Rambouillet conference. Following the withdrawal of Serbian forces from Kosovo in the wake of NATO's victory, a wave of violence by ethnic Albanians against Serbs broke out, and NATO proved unable to control it for a period of time. Though not on the same scale as Serb abuses against the Albanians, the abuses suffered by the Serbs were massive and resulted in the flight of 250,000 Serbs and Gypsies from Kosovo.[13] Eventually, NATO asserted its control and an uneasy peace ensued, although to this day sporadic acts of violence against Serbs continue in spite of NATO's best efforts to suppress them.

Two years after the NATO intervention, the Kosovo conflict remains far from settled. Intransigent ethnic Albanians, spearheaded by the KLA, insist on independence, while the Serbs vow never to accept such an outcome. The democratic election in the fall of 2000 of Vojislav Kostunica to the presidency of Yugoslavia, and the advent to power of a noncommunist Serbian government, may open up some space for a peaceful compromise between the more moderate elements on both sides. But one should not be too optimistic. In the wake of the atrocities committed prior to, during, and after the war, NATO's objective of an autonomous Kosovo that remains part of Serbia, where Albanians and Serbs can live together peacefully, seems increasingly elusive. Yet, for now, NATO has no option but to maintain its occupation force in Kosovo, including the large American contingent. To withdraw it in the absence of a settlement agreed to by all the major parties would mean a return to civil strife.

In retrospect, NATO underestimated the difficulty of achieving a lasting settlement of the Kosovo conflict through military means. Stopping the anti-Albanian human-rights abuses, and even most of the open violence between both sides, was something that military force could achieve, however slowly. But force has not been able to bring all the enemies to the peace table to agree on a comprehensive solution to the Kosovo problem. Political and religious animosities are too strong, and historical memories too long. While this could have been foreseen prior to the war, it was a probability that NATO's leaders chose to ignore given how morally and politically unpalatable it seemed to them to refrain from intervening altogether. In light of Milosevic's intransigence and the quickening pace of ethnic cleansing by early 1999, the choices facing NATO were less than perfect. Had NATO chosen not to act, the Serbs would have succeeded in driving a large proportion of Albanians from Kosovo permanently, at a high cost in human lives and suffering. In acting militarily, NATO could at least stop human-rights violations, level the playing field within Kosovo itself between the Serb and Albanian factions, and create the conditions for a reasonably humane settlement of the conflict down the road.

Was War the Last Resort?

Did NATO exhaust all realistic peaceful alternatives prior to unleashing its military might? NATO imposed stringent economic sanctions on Serbia and put enormous diplomatic and political pressure on it to alter its policy in Kosovo. It appears that Serbian leader Slobodan Milosevic miscalculated NATO's resolve to use force and decided he could ignore NATO's non-military measures. By the time Milosevic realized that the NATO powers meant business, it was too late for him to compromise without forfeiting his domestic political credibility. This in turn suggests that Milosevic's authoritarian personality, his inability to assess realistically his chances, and the closed nature of his regime may have left NATO no reasonable alternative by early 1999 but to go to war. It is always plausible to argue that NATO could have persisted longer in using non-military means, and that perhaps Milosevic eventually would have given in, at least on the demand of protecting the human rights of the Albanian Kosovars. But this argument ignores the fact that, while the NATO powers waited, the onslaught in Kosovo would have continued. While the resort to war entailed human costs, so did inaction. In the end, one is left with as much ambiguity on this issue as with the previous ones. While the critics insist that NATO acted too fast and hard, NATO's defenders argue, with considerable plausibility, that the alliance had exhausted all realistic options short of force to achieve its humanitarian and security objectives.

Ius in Bello: Did NATO Use the Right Means in the Conduct of its War?

No matter how worthwhile the cause, states also have an obligation to use the right means in waging war. They have a moral obligation to wage war consistent with certain principles, and to refrain from certain practices. A just war must be fought justly. In the Western tradition, this dimension of the moral rightness of fighting a war is known as *ius in bello*. The two key elements of *ius in bello* are *proportionality* and *discrimination*. Proportionality is not "tit-for-tat." It is a subtler calculus that requires that the means employed, and the violence they generate, be roughly proportional to the evils the war sets out to eradicate. To take one example: Serbia's acts against the ethnic Albanians would not have justified Dresden-type terror bombing raids on Belgrade costing tens of thousands of lives. Even less would it have justified NATO's resort to nuclear weapons.

Discrimination is the requirement that military forces refrain from targeting noncombatants. In most wars, discrimination is more honored in the breach than in actual practice. Yet, tenuous as its hold is, and as contrary as it is to the claims of military necessity, discrimination is a vital barrier that helps to keep wars from pushing to the outer limits of barbarism to which they naturally tend. The foremost problem in applying the principle of discrimination is what is known as *collateral damage*, the harm that ensues to non-combatants as a result of military operations directed against seemingly legitimate military, industrial, and economic targets. Even in the age of precision weapons, smart bombs stray on hospitals, schools, and foreign embassies. Attacks on military installations and war-related factories kill innocent civilians who live and work nearby.

Worse yet, given the nature of modern warfare and its close dependence on economic, industrial, transportation, communications, and energy infrastructure, many of the targets that a belligerent will attack because of their close relationship to the war effort are also targets the destruction of which will cause untold suffering to the adversary's civilian population. A key example in both the Gulf War and the Kosovo intervention was the electrical grid, considered essential to the effectiveness of the Iraqi and Yugoslav military and therefore a legitimate military target. In both cases, attacks on the electrical grid caused enormous harm to the civilian population by hampering the functioning of hospitals, public utilities, and water-purification systems.

NATO's difficulties in fighting a proportionate and discriminate war against Serbia were compounded by several factors, all of them related to the democratic character of NATO's societies. Chief among these problems was the aversion to casualties. Democratic societies are willing to endure high numbers of casualties if the interests at stake are significant, especially if they confront a serious threat to their survival or to major tangible economic or strategic interests that the public can readily understand. But when it comes to interventions that the public perceives as mostly humanitarian, and only indirectly related to security interests, public tolerance for casualties is minimal. It took the loss of 18 U.S. soldiers in Somalia to convince the American government to end its intervention. In the subsequent interventions in Haiti and Bosnia, even though the security interests involved were more apparent than in Somalia, the Clinton administration still conducted its military operations with extreme care to avoid American casualties. In Kosovo, the same administration feared that even minimal losses would cause public support for the operation to crumble. President Clinton's situation was not helped by the fact that the opposition party controlled the

Senate and the House, and that a number of prominent congressmen immediately went on record to question and oppose the intervention. Among the various candidates for the Republican presidential nomination, only two, George W. Bush and John McCain, spoke in support of the administration's decision to intervene. A number of commentators have noted the discrepancy between NATO's lofty rhetoric justifying the Kosovo intervention and the unwillingness of NATO leaders to ask even the smallest sacrifices of their peoples.

The United States's aversion to casualties, shared in varying degrees by all of its NATO partners, complicated allied efforts to fight the war proportionately and discriminately.[14] Several examples illustrate this. From the outset, the NATO commander made it clear that this would be exclusively an air operation. When bombing alone proved inadequate to stop the ethnic cleansing, critics began to clamor for the introduction of Apache attack helicopters and ground troops. The debate continues to this day on whether this would have been a wise thing to do. Assuming that the forces could have deployed in a timely fashion (not an easy thing to do given the Cold War characteristics of the U.S. Army), ground troops would have put an end to Serbian atrocities more quickly and would have sent a powerful signal to Milosevic regarding NATO's will to prevail. But there would have been two serious drawbacks. First, sending in ground troops would have antagonized Russia, potentially destabilizing the government of Boris Yeltsin and fraying Russia's ties to the West. Second, in ground combat, NATO would inevitably have suffered casualties.

The Clinton administration, along with the rest of the allies, decided after a great deal of intra-allied debate and skirmishing, to persevere in the use of air power alone. While one may disagree with this decision, it is possible to see why reasonable people could have arrived at it. The grave error was to announce the decision in public, and to insist that under no circumstances would NATO change its strategy in the future. Doing so gave Milosevic a green light to continue Kosovo's accelerated ethnic cleansing, and led him to hope, mistakenly as it turned out, that the alliance, unwilling as it was to incur any serious costs for its campaign, might give up if the Serbs hung on long enough. Yet the reason President Clinton made the public announcement, and insisted on the unchangeable character of allied strategy, was to reassure the U.S. public and prevent Congressional opposition to the intervention from gathering momentum. Thus did an aversion to casualties lead the NATO powers to conduct the war in a way that undermined the allied objectives of a swift end to the violence and human-rights abuses in Kosovo. The announcement also lengthened the war itself by feeding Milosevic's intransigence and his erroneous assessment of Western political will. The cost of maintaining public support for the war within the NATO powers was to increase innocent suffering in Kosovo and Serbia proper as the war dragged on longer than necessary.

There was another unfortunate consequence of the aversion to casualties. Reliance on air power alone meant that for NATO to compel Milosevic to accept its terms it had to attack targets of value to the general civilian population, and it had to conduct those attacks in a way that placed non-combatants at risk. For example, even though the most appropriate targets would have been the Serbian military and security forces in Kosovo providing the support for ethnic cleansing, NATO found itself able to do little damage to these forces. Its air campaign failed, for example, to destroy Serbian armor or infantry units. Not only did NATO limit itself to air attacks, but to avoid casualties commanders restricted their missions to high altitudes. The Serbs took advantage of this by hiding their forces, complicating NATO's efforts to hit them. After several weeks of the most intensive bombing campaign recorded in Europe since the Second World War, NATO had managed to destroy only a small handful of tanks and had inflicted minimal casualties on Yugoslav infantry and paramilitary units.

Thus, the alliance turned its attention to Serbia's overall economic, industrial, transportation, communications, and utilities infrastructure. Targeting them just might put sufficient pressure on Milosevic to give up. Moreover, attacking the civilian infrastructure became NATO's only option given its unwillingness to use ground forces, Apache helicopters, or low-altitude bombing missions. Yet, these attacks also ran counter to, and severely undermined, NATO's political objectives of ending the war in Kosovo quickly, facilitating a long-term peace settlement, and encouraging Milosevic's replacement by a democratic Yugoslav government. At the same time that NATO was urging Serbs to overthrow Milosevic and opt for Western-style democracy, the alliance was raining bombs on Belgrade and making life miserable for millions of innocents. Although the attacks hurt the civilian population, they did not do much damage to the Milosevic regime. In some ways, they strengthened Milosevic by giving him nationalist, patriotic ammunition while leaving his forces in Kosovo with impunity to continue their ethnic cleansing campaign. Far from shortening the war, the NATO strategy lengthened it unnecessarily. Moreover, the destruction of civilian infrastructure will slow down considerably future efforts to build an economically prosperous, democratic Serbia.

Morally, one of the great contradictions involved in NATO's conduct of the war was its tacit decision to value the lives of its soldiers above those of the enemy's non-combatants, including even those ethnic Albanians on behalf of whom NATO launched its humanitarian intervention. Yet this is not altogether new. Governments at war routinely design military operations to reduce casualties among their own forces at the expense of increasing non-combatant deaths and suffering on the enemy side. In the Kosovo War, however, this otherwise routine practice seemed jarring given the supposedly humanitarian nature of the intervention. Speaking in their own defense, NATO leaders argued that the bombing campaign against Serbia's infrastructure was carried out with as much precision as possible, with the objective of destroying material targets but sparing human lives. It was the best they could do, they claimed, to avoid the collapse of public support that would have ensued had NATO itself suffered casualties.

Finally, one of the more tantalizing moral questions NATO faced as it fought the war was whether it should target President Milosevic with a view to killing him. There were those who argued at the war's outset that Milosevic, as commander in chief of the Yugoslav military, was a legitimate target. They also pointed out that Milosevic was the main culprit of the war and the chief obstacle to its settlement; hence, targeting Milosevic seemed more justifiable than targeting thousands of innocent Serbs.

Proposals to target Milosevic ran counter to a centuries-long Western tradition that has looked askance at killing heads of state during wartime. Only during that bitterest of total wars, World War II, did this tradition weaken when Allied leaders contemplated assassinating Adolf Hitler.[15] At the height of the Cold War, neither the Americans nor the Soviets attempted to kill the other side's political leaders, though they did not apply this prohibition to political leaders of smaller countries that might defect to the rival alliance. In the early 1960s, the U.S. government attempted several times to assassinate Fidel Castro, and the Soviet Union murdered Imre Nagy, who was acting as head of the Hungarian government following the November 1956 revolution. In 1975 President Ford signed an executive order forbidding any U.S. government agency from carrying out assassination attempts against foreign heads of state, thereby vindicating the honored tradition of refraining from such acts. The tradition, however, suffered setbacks subsequently when the United States targeted Libya's Muammar Ghaddafi in 1986 and Iraq's Saddam Hussein in 1991, in both cases unsuccessfully.

On balance, the traditional prohibition on killing heads of state is still strong. During the early stages of the Kosovo intervention NATO rejected calls to target Milosevic. But as the ethnic cleansing campaign in Kosovo intensified and Milosevic showed no signs of giving up, NATO decided to step up its air attacks against high-profile political targets. Eventually, NATO attacked the key government-controlled television station in Belgrade as well as one of Milosevic's better known residences. By then Milosevic knew that he was likely to be targeted and was careful about his whereabouts. NATO never succeeded in killing him, and it appears that NATO never really tried—the attack on his residence was more symbolic than substantive. It was not intended to kill him but to let him know that NATO was serious about achieving its objectives, and that in the end NATO would hold him personally responsible for war crimes in Kosovo.

The Kosovo War raises the question of whether the new kinds of weapons associated with the "Revolution in Military Affairs" impose a qualitatively new set of moral obligations. The availability of precision weapons has raised expectations about the feasibility of minimizing collateral damage. And with those higher expectations has come a higher moral standard, with the more technologically sophisticated Western powers expected to use high precision weaponry in such a way as to keep civilian casualties to a minimum. At the same time, however, Western public opinion has come to expect that the new kinds of weapons also make it possible to avoid casualties among one's own soldiers. Thus, two new sets of moral expectations are at play: a reduction in enemy civilian casualties, and a reduction in casualties among one's own military forces. These two sets of expectations are not easy to reconcile. In Kosovo, the tension was resolved in favor of minimizing losses among one's military forces. This implied refraining from using ground troops or Apache helicopters, flying bombing missions at high altitudes, and focusing on the destruction of military-industrial-infrastructure targets most susceptible to air attack.

One should not read too much into the ostensible requirement to keep enemy civilian casualties low. That requirement is likely to hold only so long as the war is short, its objectives limited, and the enemy unable or unwilling to deliver a major blow to U.S. and allied forces. If any one of those three conditions were to change, public opinion in Western countries would likely support less discriminate strategies that might increase the pressure on the enemy to give up. Had Milosevic persisted longer, or had he used missiles or weapons of mass destruction against NATO forces, there would have been considerable pressure within NATO countries for an even more intense bombing campaign even if it meant larger numbers of Serb civilian casualties.

Implications for the Morally Responsible Use of American Power

America's unchallenged global power at the opening of the twenty-first century has prompted many to argue that the United States today enjoys a unique opportunity to fulfill the Wilsonian dream of remaking the world in America's image. Among conservatives, the argument has been made most forcefully by William Kristol and Robert Kagan of the Project for the New American Century, and among liberals by former Secretary of State Madeleine Albright. As they see it, the United States and its allies are strong, the enemies of liberalism are on the defensive, and there are plenty of opportunities where a limited investment of American resources can make a substantial difference. The world may never again be so pliable, and action now may help to move at least some regions of the world in directions more congruent with long-term American interests and values.

Assuming that this is, indeed, a historic opportunity for the United States to advance liberal democratic values, how can the United States do so in a morally responsible fashion? Thucydides' *History of the Peloponnesian War* poignantly reminds us of the follies and hubris of which even the greatest, most exalted democracies are capable in peace and war. Like Athens in its golden heyday of the Periclean Era, the United States today faces great dangers as well as great opportunities. The opportunities to use its power to accomplish good are matched by the dangers that the United States will wield its power irresponsibly, thereby diminishing its credibility and undermining the very values it seeks to spread. The Kosovo intervention amply illustrates this quandary.

The Kosovo intervention highlighted some of the political and moral complications that an overly passionate embrace of Wilsonianism can produce. By supporting and leading NATO's intervention in Kosovo, the United States went on record in favor of a world of dissolving sovereignty barriers, a world in which notions of an international moral consensus can override the claims of individual nation-states. This development is a double-edged sword. On the one hand, American statesmen cite the world's growing interdependence and the decline of state sovereignty when they push the American agenda on trade, democratization, and human rights, especially in places where doing so serves the interests of the United States or involves minimal costs. But the Wilsonian appeals seem hypocritical, and undermine American credibility, when the United States resists the Wilsonian logic on issues where its application does not serve America's own interests.

President George H. W. Bush's rhetoric about a "New World Order" and his successor's humanitarian interventions have raised expectations that the United States will strengthen the norms of an international community. But recent American decisions to vote against an International Criminal Court, to refuse to ratify the Comprehensive Ban Treaty, and to maintain sanctions on Cuba with the support of only two other UN members send a different message. They suggest that the United States brandishes Wilsonianism selectively, on the basis of considerations as pragmatic or cynical as those of any other country in the world. This would not be so bad if American leaders in the Wilsonian tradition were not also insisting so earnestly that America is not just another great power, but a uniquely benevolent nation destined by history to lead the rest of the world toward a new moral order. What damages American credibility is not that the United States acts in accordance with its interests, but that it claims to be more disinterested than anyone else. There is a marked discrepancy, for example, between the vigorous American demands that Milosevic be tried by the Hague Tribunal for his crimes in Bosnia and Kosovo, and the equally dogged U.S. refusal to accede to the creation of an International Crimes Tribunal.

The Kosovo intervention also provided reminders that humanitarian interventions are not risk-free. The costs of Kosovo easily could have been much higher. Assume that Slobodan Milosevic, whose military forces were not being seriously damaged by NATO's air campaign, had decided not to yield. Eventually, NATO would have had to use ground troops. In spite of mounting casualties, NATO would have had to persevere, even as domestic opposition to the intervention increased. Assume also that Russia, seeing its credibility at stake, had dispatched forces to create a "cordon sanitaire" on the Kosovo-Serbia border, or within Kosovo itself, to prevent NATO forces from pushing far into either Kosovo or Serbia. These developments were well within the realm of the possible and suggest how quickly the Kosovo intervention could have escalated into a broader conflict that, at a minimum, would have done lasting damage to Russia's relations with Europe and the United States.

Kosovo also suggests that, although Wilsonianism and the concept of humanitarian intervention bound up with it seem attractive options for a powerful United States, their practical application can be morally troubling. As pointed out earlier, the advanced military technologies associated with the "Revolution in Military Affairs" gave NATO the unusual option of fighting the war solely from the air without having to put combat troops on the ground. This had several regrettable consequences. First, because NATO was not incurring any significant risks or losses, it was difficult for the public to appreciate what was really at stake in the conflict. The public, in fact, was prepared to "cut and run" at any moment if the military operations did not go well. There was a morally absurd contrast between the high-sounding rhetoric of Western leaders about the mission's idealistic goals, and the costs they and their peoples were willing to pay to attain these goals.

Second, the alluring prospect of fighting without casualties meant that NATO was willing to proceed deliberately, thereby permitting the Serbs ample time to complete their campaign of ethnic cleansing. During the long weeks of the air campaign, the Serbs moved ruthlessly to uproot as many ethnic Albanians as possible. Along with the ethnic cleansing went an unprecedented degree of rape, looting, and murder. In initiating force against Serbia, NATO should have contemplated the possibility that, with their backs against the wall and little to lose, the Serbs would be tempted to destroy the Albanian presence in Kosovo once and for all so as to make an Albanian-free Kosovo an irreversible fait accompli. NATO's failure to anticipate this development, and even worse, its failure to act once it became apparent that it was happening, was morally irresponsible to a high degree.

Third, the seemingly "cheap" option of fighting a war without casualties may have profound long-term systemic consequences, as Carl Cavanagh Hodge persuasively has argued.[16] The notion of "war without casualties" has chipped away at the firewall laboriously built up throughout the twentieth century against the casual use of military force. To the extent that they view Kosovo as a "success," political leaders may come to view the use of force through air power as a sanitized instrument of statecraft requiring few moral scruples and no international sanctioning.

The breakdown of the firewall poses long-term dangers to the stability of the international system. Any use of force, no matter how sanitized, carries a high risk of escalation. It was Clausewitz who, almost two centuries ago, recognized that even limited wars, those conflicts in which "the statesman seeks to turn the terrible two-handed sword that is war into the lightest rapier, fit only for thrusts and parries," can degenerate into bitter, all-out general war as the passions of the people are aroused and outside parties intervene.[17] While the risk of such escalation may have been low in Kosovo, it will not always be so. Inevitably, as enthusiasm for "casual war" or "sanitized war" spreads, some statesman somewhere is bound to miscalculate its consequences, and what was conceived as a self-contained conflict will escalate and draw in great power antagonists. The Viennese statesmen who contemplated a limited punitive strike against Serbia in 1914 had no idea of the global conflagration they were about to kindle.

At a higher level of analysis, Kosovo offers us some general reminders for the United States at a time when its power, and therefore its moral obligations, have never been greater. The exercise of power in this broken world, even for the noblest values, is bound to be a messy affair, full of paradoxes, unintended consequences, ample doses of inconsistency and hypocrisy, and ultimately falling considerably short of expectations. That said, hopes that the United States will use its power responsibly should entail several things.

First, a restoration of rhetorical modesty is necessary. There is no escaping that the United States, exceptional as it is in some ways, is still a fallen, sinful society, to use the language of Christian realism with which readers of Reinhold Niebuhr and Herbert Butterfield are familiar. We are as eager to put our interests at the center of our global agenda as any other state, and as easily able as anyone else to deceive ourselves about the extent to which our interests correspond with those of the rest of the world. One problem with Wilsonianism is that its proponents tend to forget this and become seduced by their own rhetoric. Our allies and friends are prepared to respect us when we make a case for policies that benefit us as well as them, but our sanctimony erodes our credibility and elicits their resentment when we speak as if our actions are guided entirely by disinterestedness. The language with which a great power speaks, as Theodore Roosevelt well understood, is central to its leadership. More often than not, Wilsonian rhetoric weakens rather than enhances our leadership through its hubris and self-righteousness, though this is far more obvious to the rest of the world than it is to us. A sense of modesty would help to counteract this weakness.

Second, in future humanitarian interventions American statesmen will need to consider more rigorously whether the ends to be achieved are worth the destruction caused by war, and whether the constraints of "sanitized war"—war fought solely through long-range precision strikes—are suitable to the war's particular political objectives. Even if one agrees that NATO was right to fight the Kosovo War exactly as it did, on future occasions, given the nature of the enemy's strategy or U.S. political objectives, the United States will not always have the option of fighting a "casualty-free" war. On those occasions, it will be incumbent upon American leaders to understand the limits of "sanitized wars," lest they employ means that are inappropriate, impossible, or counterproductive to the moral goals and political objectives being pursued.

Does NATO's Kosovo War of 1999 suggest the creation of a new set of international norms? It is difficult to determine the extent to which Kosovo may be a harbinger of future humanitarian wars as opposed to being an isolated incident. Two or three decades from now, Kosovo may appear as a significant milestone in the evolution of international politics, law and morality in the post–Cold War world. Or it may be seen instead as an aberration, an episode that, controversial though it was, remains unique. Only time will tell. In either case, Kosovo will claim significance because of the moral and political debates surrounding it, debates about what kind of international society the United States and its allies ought to nurture, who should make its rules, and how the rules should be enforced.[18]

The debate generated by the Kosovo intervention revolves around two conceptions of international order, each of which has profound implications for future American foreign policy. One side of the debate argues that Kosovo embodies a new trend in international politics, in which a few states, often led by the United States, will undertake joint military action to prevent aggression and extreme human-rights violations. Intrinsic to America's moral responsibilities as a great power is the obligation to shape the norms of international society. This obligation includes the use of American economic, political and military power to help move international society in the direction of greater security and respect for human rights. Occasionally, a humanitarian intervention supported by America's full military might will be necessary to uphold these values.[19]

On the other side of this debate are those who view the Kosovo War as bad news. These critics divide into two camps. Among American conservatives, there are critics who insist that Kosovo, insofar as it is a precedent, is an insidious one. The United States should be careful not to associate itself with the notion of a world of dissolving sovereignty barriers, lest this notion come back to haunt it in the form of future restraints on American unilateralism. According to this argument, humanitarian interventions such as those in Kosovo are not only wasteful and distracting from America's core strategic priorities. They also give the misguided impression that the United States supports the establishment of some form of transnational normative system, under UN or NATO sponsorship, that will ultimately trump American sovereignty and hem in American power.[20]

A second camp of critics make a different set of arguments. On the American left are those who claim that Kosovo's precedent is bad, precisely because it endows America with dangerous prerogatives. In this view, the Kosovo intervention gives the United States wide latitude to interfere in the internal affairs of other states and the excuse to maintain the world's mightiest military establishment.[21] According to these critics, Kosovo also feeds American exceptionalism and perpetuates the bogus notion of the United States as a uniquely benevolent, disinterested power. For these critics, the Kosovo intervention was tainted because it was led by the United States; a humanitarian intervention sanctioned by the United Nations could well have been legitimate and appropriate.

Whether Kosovo turns out to be an aberration or the start of a powerful new trend in world politics, the United States and its allies will confront future humanitarian crises that invite intervention. As they ponder such situations, American statesmen would do well to keep in mind the moral complexities surrounding Kosovo. The key will be not to draw simple lessons from NATO's apparent success, but to reflect soberly on the risks, ambiguities, and shortcomings. Great care will be necessary in determining whether military force is the best instrument to right the evils in question. Much deliberation will be needed to calculate whether the good produced by the forcible intervention will outweigh the totality of human, moral, and economic costs. In addition, American leaders will confront the conundrum of fighting with due regard to the principles of proportionality and discrimination while treating the avoidance of friendly casualties as an important goal but never an absolute one. As the chief provider of forces for such an operation, the United States will exercise decisive influence on the type of strategy that is adopted. One of America's responsibilities will to avoid a repetition of some of the more unfortunate aspects of the Kosovo campaign. Good intentions are not enough. Equally important will be competence, foresight, avoiding the hubris to which our technology makes us so vulnerable, and not underestimating the adversary. In other words, those who claim to use military force for good ends have a moral responsibility to use force wisely, and this includes taking into account the irrationality, unpredictability, and the Clausewitzian fog and friction that make war a less than perfect instrument of politics. This kind of strategic humility will be essential to the morally responsible use of American power in a new century.

Notes

1. For discussions of the intellectual origins of Wilsonianism, see David M. Fitzsimons, "Tom Paine's New World Order: Idealistic Internationalism in the Ideology of Early American Foreign Relations," *Diplomatic* History 19, no. 4 (fall 1995): 569–82; and Walter MacDougall, *Promised Land, Crusader State: The American Encounter with the World Since 1776* (Boston, Mass.: Houghton Mifflin, 1997).
2. "Powell Intends to Curb US Use of Diplomatic Sanctions," *Los Angeles Times*, 22 January 2001, p. 1.
3. For the controversy surrounding the estimates of lives actually saved, see Coll, *The Problems of Doing Good: Somalia as a Case Study in Humanitarian Intervention* (New York: Carnegie Council on Ethics and International Affairs, 1997).
4. For two classic discussions of "just war theory" and the just-war tradition, see Paul Ramsey, *The Just War: Force and Political Responsibility* (Princeton, N.J.: Princeton University Press, 1968) and Michael Walzer, *Just and Unjust Wars* (Cambridge, Mass.: Harvard University Press, 1977).
5. "Bush Warns Serbs Not to Widen War," *New York Times*, 28 December 1992.
6. William Joseph Buckley, ed., *Kosovo: Contending Voices on Balkan Interventions* (Grand Rapids, Mich.: William B. Eerdmans, 2000), p. 4.
7. See the Melian Dialogue at the end of Book 5 of Thucydides' *History of the Peloponnesian War*.
8. For a discussion of the classic theory of humanitarian intervention as developed by Vitoria and Suarez in the sixteenth century, see Alberto R. Coll, *The Western Heritage and American Values: Law, Theology and History* (Lanham, Md.: University Press of America, 1982).
9. For a comprehensive discussion of the question of humanitarian intervention from different historical and philosophical perspectives, see Laura W. Reed and Carl Kaysen, *Emerging Norms of Justified Intervention* (Cambridge, Mass.: American Academy of Arts and Sciences, 1993). The ethical issues in the contemporary debate over the place of humanitarian intervention in American foreign policy are reviewed most lucidly in Michael J. Smith, "Humanitarian Intervention: An Overview of the Ethical Issues," *Ethics and International Affairs* (1998): 63–79.

10. Michael Walzer, "Kosovo," *Dissent* (Summer 1999), reprinted in William Joseph Buckley, ed., *Kosovo: Contending Voices on Balkan Interventions* (Grand Rapids, Mich.: William B. Eerdmans, 2000), p. 335.
11. "Secretary-General Presents His Annual Report to General Assembly," UN Press Release SG/SM/7136, GA/9596, 20 September 20 1999, cited in Richard J. Goldstone, *Kosovo: An Assessment in the Context of International Law,* Nineteenth Morgenthau Memorial Lecture on Ethics and Foreign Policy (New York: Carnegie Council on Ethics and International Affairs, 2000).
12. See Craig R. Whitney (with Eric Schmitt), "NATO Had Signs Its Strategy Would Fail Kosovars," *New York Times,* 1 April 1999, p. A1.
13. Buckley, *Kosovo,* p. 9.
14. Among the NATO powers there was a "spectrum of hawkishness" regarding their willingness to suffer casualties, with the British government being the most outspoken in favor of the use of ground troops, and the United States and Germany at the other end of the spectrum opposing any measures that might raise the risks. For an interesting study on the issue of casualties and public opinion, see Charles K. Hyde, "Casualty Aversion: Implications for Policymakers and Senior Military Officers," *Essays 2000: Chairman of the Joint Chiefs of Staff Strategy Essay Competition* (Washington, D.C.: National Defense University Press, 2000), pp. 1–16.
15. The successful American plan to kill Admiral Yamamoto in 1943 did not violate the taboo against killing heads of state. Yamamoto was a senior military commander, not Japan's political leader.
16. Carl Cavanagh Hodge, "Casual War: NATO's Intervention in Kosovo," *Ethics and International Affairs* 14 (2000): 39–54. See also the interesting discussion by Martin Cook in the same volume, "'Immaculate War': Constraints on Humanitarian Intervention," 55–66.
17. Carl von Clausewitz, *On War,* Book 8, ed. and trans. Michael Howard and Peter Paret (Princeton, N.J.: Princeton University Press, 1976), p. 606.
18. For a discussion of this debate in the context of the views of the new Bush Administration, see James Traub, "Downsizing Foreign Policy," *New York Times Magazine,* 14 January 2001, pp. 28–34.
19. For articulate presentations of this viewpoint, see Richard N. Haass, *The Reluctant Sheriff: The United States After the Cold War* (New York: Brookings Institution Press, 1997); Chester Crocker, "The Lessons of Somalia," *Foreign Affairs* (May–June 1995); and Andrew Natsios, "Humanitarian Emergencies and Moral Choice," *American Purpose* (Winter 2000).
20. For an exponent of this viewpoint, see Marc A. Thiessen, "When Worlds Collide," *Foreign Policy* (March–April 2001): 64–74.
21. Noam Chomsky, *The New Military Humanism: Lessons from Kosovo* (Monroe, Maine: Common Courage Press, 1999).

6 Neglected Trinity: Kosovo and the Crisis in U.S. Civil-Military Relations

Andrew J. Bacevich

I

In the annals of U.S. military history the war for Kosovo stands out as a singularly peculiar episode. Among other things, the war produced more than its share of "firsts." It was, famously, the first war that U.S. forces fought to its conclusion without sustaining a single combat casualty. Indeed, for the policymakers who conceived Operation Allied Force and the commanders who directed it, minimizing the risk to allied soldiers seemingly took precedence over both their obligation to safeguard Serb noncombatants and their interest in protecting the ethnic Albanians whose plight provided the ostensible rationale for intervention.[1] American officials described that intervention as a *moral* imperative. Yet before the conflict had even ended observers were wondering if the United States had turned moral tradition on its head, with combatants rather than noncombatants provided immunity from the effects of fighting.[2]

Reflecting in part this pronounced sensitivity to casualties, Kosovo was also the first American conflict in which the commander in chief at the very outset offered public assurances that the adversary need not fear suffering the full weight of U.S. military power. As the bombing commenced, President Bill Clinton on March 24, 1999 told the nation and the world, "I do not intend to put our troops in Kosovo to fight a war." By foreclosing the option of introducing ground troops, the president made it unmistakably clear that NATO would restrict itself to conducting a standoff war. Hallowed bits of military doctrine—for example, the supposed requirement to "close with and destroy the enemy"—did not apply.

The overriding priority assigned to force protection inevitably called into question other presidential statements, namely, that crucial U.S. interests were at stake in Kosovo and that the United States and its allies were determined to "persist until we prevail."[3] The circumspect language employed to explain NATO's military objectives did little to help. "Our goal is to exact a very high price for Mr. Milosevic's policy of repression," Mr. Clinton announced during the war's first days, "and to seriously diminish his military capacity to maintain that policy."[4] Commanding the world's most capable military machine, backed by a formidable array of allies, the president studiously refrained from suggesting that NATO sought anything so definitive as the actual "defeat" of Yugoslavia.

Such radical departures from military convention—renouncing the most ordinary instruments of combat, reviving the long-discredited principle of gradual escalation, avoiding any mention of victory as an objective, indeed, avoiding the term "war" altogether—distressed senior American military officers, already leery of deepening the U.S. involvement in the Balkans. So the war for Kosovo also broke new ground in the swiftness with which it exposed rifts between senior soldiers and their civilian masters. As soon as it became apparent that the campaign would last beyond the four or five days initially expected, leaks emanating from the Pentagon were signaling the military's extreme dissatisfaction with the way that civilians were orchestrating the war against Yugoslavia.[5]

Even the campaign's ultimately successful outcome did not restore civil-military comity. Indeed, Kosovo prompted complaints of civilian interference—voiced openly by serving officers—not heard since Vietnam. A widely circulated postmortem prepared by Admiral James O. Ellis, commanding U.S. naval forces in Europe, lamented that an otherwise well-executed air campaign had been "politically constrained." Among the adverse effects, according to Ellis, were a tendency toward "incremental war" and excessive concerns about collateral damage. Political considerations had also needlessly complicated efforts to implement "NATO out-of-charter operations."[6] Similarly, in a postwar interview, Lieutenant General Michael C. Short, who directed the air war, complained of being "constrained in this particular conflict to an extraordinary degree." Political restrictions had prevented Short "from conducting an air campaign as professional airmen would have wanted to conduct it."[7]

In fairness to Short, civilian intrusion into operational matters did, in certain respects, recall Vietnam. Before striking targets in Serbia deemed especially sensitive, military commanders found themselves obliged to gain clearance from high-ranking civilian officials, including in some instances Clinton himself. Throughout the campaign, according to the *Washington Post*, "Generals raced across the Potomac River with satchels of targets to get the White House to approve the next night's work." Among senior military officers, the perception of civilian meddling roused unhappy memories. Short, himself a veteran of the Vietnam War, worried about getting "into something like the Rolling Thunder campaign, pecking away indefinitely" while public support gradually ebbed away.[8]

Whether or not civilians were guilty of inappropriate meddling, senior officers could justifiably conclude that in the Clinton White House their own professional counsel was not in high demand. Whatever their actual opinion of the advice rendered, every president since World War II has made a point in times of crisis of "consulting" with the Joint Chiefs of Staff. Throughout the Cold War, the image of a grim-faced commander in chief surrounded by beribboned four-stars as he announced some portentous new decision had been a stock part of American political theater. Here too Kosovo marked a departure, ringing down the curtain on this hoary old tradition.

Rather than consulting the Joint Chiefs collectively, Bill Clinton relied for professional advice (as he had in lesser military contingencies throughout his presidency) almost exclusively on the chairman of the Joint Chiefs of Staff—in 1999, General Henry H. Shelton. A seasoned and dutiful soldier, Shelton is by all reports not the type to make waves. Described by one newspaper as "the general who speaks when spoken to," he possesses little of the flair, political savvy, or media presence of a Colin Powell—indeed, the Clinton administration may well have appointed him for that very reason. With a compliant Joint Chiefs of Staff chairman reportedly "unwilling—or unable—to air the Pentagon's misgivings about the war," the White House managed the campaign according to its own lights.[9]

Kosovo may well have sealed the demise of another tradition as well, one stretching across a bloody century in which Americans frequently found themselves called upon to fight, but in which the United States itself was spared the direct experience of war. As a matter of course, throughout that century, whenever American soldiers ventured into harm's way American journalists went with them, not infrequently at considerable personal risk. Charged with explaining war to readers largely insulated from its impact, the very best reporters did so by documenting the experience of their fellow citizens in military service—flesh-and-blood Americans with actual names and real hometowns. On behalf of a worthy cause, the vivid and intimate reporting of an Ernie Pyle or an A. J. Liebling helped sustain popular support for the war effort, forging a bond between citizens and soldiers. In the case of a more dubious enterprise, press coverage could undermine that support, as Pyle's successors did in bearing witness to the experience of American soldiers in Vietnam. In every case, however, by reporting the war from the field, journalists made it next to impossible for those on the home front to ignore or take for granted the sacrifices of those actually doing the fighting.

Not so with the war for Kosovo. In this conflict, citing security concerns, senior commanders restricted the journalistic coverage of the war, thereby erecting a barrier between those serving in the combat zone and those following the war from the comfort of their living room.[10] Interviews with pilots flying combat missions over Yugoslavia were kept to a bare minimum. Personal information such as names and hometowns was off-limits. This did not mean that the war went unreported. But instead of American soldiers themselves framing the story, attention shifted to the relentlessly upbeat news briefings conducted in Washington or Brussels and to the suffering of ethnic Albanian refugees or of Serb civilians victimized by errant allied bombs (neither of which corroborated official claims that all was well).

To the extent that journalists were permitted to glimpse American servicemembers "in action," their reports did little to promote understanding, much less empathy. A revealing wartime dispatch in the *New York Times* typifies the result. Visiting the destroyer *Gonzales*, periodically lobbing cruise missiles toward Serbia from its station in the Adriatic, the *Times* reporter discovers there "the face of modern warfare: antiseptic, distant, impersonal." A montage of accompanying photos shows various American sailors—all of them nameless—"pumping iron" in the ship's exercise room, taking a smoke break below decks, posing in dress uniform for cruise-book portraits, and gazing at "a buffet that could be in Las Vegas as easily as the Adriatic."[11] Who are these people? Where do they come from? What precisely are they contributing either to preserving U.S. national security or to the eradication of ethnic cleansing? Why should we care about them? On these matters, the reader—and perhaps the reporter as well—remains unenlightened.

Another factor further complicated the average citizen's efforts to make sense of Kosovo. Signposts of sound thinking once deemed authoritative, whatever one's political persuasion, now pointed every which way. In the overlapping worlds of intellectuals, pundits, and political ideologues, disagreement over the most fundamental questions—whether the war was moral or immoral, necessary or unnecessary, a success or a failure—demolished longstanding alignments and overturned views once deemed sacrosanct. The result was not simply that hawks and doves reversed their usual roles. The war for Kosovo scrambled the political line-up, creating odd alliances between figures who had stood for decades on opposite sides of the barricades. Old radicals like Tom Hayden, archconservatives like Patrick Buchanan, and libertarians like Ted Galen Carpenter all railed against "liberal humanitarian imperialism run amok." On the Right, Trent Lott, the Senate Majority Leader, called on President Clinton to "Give peace a chance." On the Left, Todd Gitlin, veteran of the 1960s antiwar movement, enthused about the potential uses of American military power. "Just wars are not only possible, but legion," he proclaimed.[12] Meanwhile, David Rieff, a journalist of impeccably Left liberal pedigree, could be found doing a passable imitation of Henry Kissinger: "you send your F-15 to help the Kosovars and what it does is it blows up a bunch of children in a hospital. It is inevitable. That's what war is. We've made a lot of claims for ourselves, for our societies and for our moral aspirations. But without force or the threat of force, they're hollow ideas."[13]

By the time the war finally wound down in June, Americans had effectively decided that it no longer merited their attention. When in the weeks following the end of hostilities the air squadrons that carried the brunt of the fight rotated back from the war zone, their return failed to cross the threshold of newsworthiness. If newspapers reported the troops' homecoming at all, they did so via brief, colorless wire service dispatches, buried in the inside pages. Sports teams that *lose* the Super Bowl or the NCAA basketball championship receive a warmer welcome upon returning home than did the Americans who *won* the war for Kosovo. In present-day America, even the runner-up in a major sports competition qualifies as a celebrity. In contrast, the aviators who conducted—and won—the air campaign against Yugoslavia remain even today shrouded in anonymity. Indeed, the war for Kosovo also broke new ground by being the first American conflict not to produce a single bona fide hero.[14]

Even the campaign's chief architects reaped few of the accolades that normally accompany victory. Publishers suppressed any impulse to pony up a Schwarzkopf- or Powell-style advance for the wartime recollections of General Wesley K. Clark, the officer commanding all NATO forces. Indeed, when in the war's immediate aftermath General Clark appeared in Washington, he found himself not basking in the adulation proffered by a joint session of Congress but being grilled by notably frosty members of the Senate Armed Services Committee.[15] Soon thereafter, Clark was, if not exactly sacked, shoved unceremoniously into early retirement. Voices protesting the ingratitude implied by his treatment were notable by their absence. As for the triumphant commander in chief, far from being rewarded with a "bounce" in the polls, Bill Clinton actually saw his approval rating dip.[16]

In the end, Kosovo qualifies as peculiar because as "a war waged from 15,000 feet and fought mainly for humanitarian principles" it failed to engage the passions of the people.[17] For most Americans, Kosovo was a *distraction* and not really a very important one at that. In the 1990s, the nation's real business lay precisely where Calvin Coolidge had located it in the 1920s. As if to emphasize that point, during the 78-day campaign the Dow Jones industrial average not only broke 10,000 points for the first time, but continued to advance through the 11,000 point barrier. Thus, when the war finally concluded, the nation showed no inclination to organize tickertape parades to celebrate "V-K Day." Befuddled, impatient, and slightly embarrassed, Americans instead gave a sigh of relief, purged from memory the odd bits of knowledge acquired about Serbia and its history, and gratefully turned their attention back to more important things.

II

Yet however peculiar Kosovo appears when contrasted with previous episodes in American military history, it is not simply a momentary aberration, a lapse never to be repeated. Nor does it signify an abrupt departure from established practice. On the contrary, for all of its apparent novelty, the war for Kosovo offers the fullest expression yet of changes in U.S. national security policy that had been underway throughout the decade following the end of the Cold War.

As Eliot A. Cohen suggests elsewhere in this volume, the campaign waged for Kosovo reveals the outlines of a "new American way of war," heralding the role of U.S. military power in the aftermath of the Cold War. The purpose of this essay, which builds on Cohen's thesis, is threefold. First, it identifies the origins of this new style of warfare, attributing it to a seemingly incompatible mix of large strategic aspirations and formidable domestic constraints, largely cultural in nature. Second, it argues that efforts to reconcile this disparity between strategy and culture have necessitated a profound realignment in the relationship between the state, the military, and the American people. That is, instituting a new way of war has entailed a commensurate transformation of civil-military relations. Finally, it suggests that national security policies based on this new civil-military paradigm are inherently flawed and are likely to prove unsustainable if not downright pernicious.

More broadly, the essay takes issue with the tendency, increasingly prevalent since Operation Desert Storm, to neglect the nontechnological dimensions of war. If anything, the war for Kosovo—reputedly won by air power alone—has reinforced this inclination to see armed conflict largely as the application of advanced technology. Americans take comfort from such a view: sustaining the nation's technological edge—in intelligence collection and analysis, command and control, strategic mobility, and long-range precision strike—will seemingly guarantee continuing U.S. military supremacy with minimal exertion and sacrifice. But such expectations are dangerously misleading.

Such, at least, is the view implied by the greatest Western philosopher of war, Carl von Clausewitz. In his classic work *On War*, Clausewitz all but ignored technological considerations, identifying instead three distinct but intertwined "tendencies" that govern armed conflict. Together, according to Clausewitz, these three tendencies—reason, primordial violence, and chance—comprise a "remarkable trinity." Conceiving through careful deliberation the ends that necessarily guide the conduct of war is, according to Clausewitz, the province of the *state* and its political leadership. War implies the use of force in pursuit of those ends. Force derives its efficacy from the passions of the *people*. The creativity required to harness that violence to policy—and to do so despite the physically and psychologically daunting reality of combat—defines the realm of the *army* and its commander. To wage war effectively—and by extension to create sound military institutions—the elements of this trinity must exist in harmony with one another. According to Clausewitz, students of warfare who disregard any of the three or who impose a fixed and arbitrary relationship between them misconstrue the nature of their subject. A military policy that neglects the relationships embodied in Clausewitz's trinity courts disaster.[18]

Formulated in an age when kings and emperors still dominated politics, Clausewitz's insight becomes even more pertinent in an age of democracy and for a democratic superpower such as the United States. Indeed, far more than any other factor, the changing nature of this coupling of state, people, and army accounts for the rise and fall and restoration of American military power during the momentous half-century that began when Germany invaded Poland and ended with the fall of the Berlin Wall. During the first decade of the new era that began with the end of the Cold War, further changes in that relationship—largely unnoted—are reshaping the character of U.S. military power.

To understand the significance of those changes requires a basic understanding of the history of American civil-military relations.

The theme of the earliest (and longest) chapter of that history was antimilitarism. A suspicion of things military formed part of the American birthright, predating even the founding of the republic. Among the Founders, the belief that standing armies were antithetical to liberty was commonplace, hence, the preference for relying chiefly on politically reliable *citizen*-soldiers rather than regulars to defend the nation. That belief persisted for generations. Among Americans generally—pragmatic, individualistic, and (to a degree) egalitarian—the professional soldier's taste for pomp, hierarchy, and iron discipline was anathema. The approach to civil-military relations devised in response to these considerations was based on the principles of wariness and strict supervision. The objective was less to provide for effective military policy than to guarantee absolute civilian control. Consistent with the terms of this model, the United States had habitually maintained in peacetime the smallest possible regular army, confined the officer corps to the periphery of public life, and relied on a militia of dubious military value as the chief instrument for national defense. To the extent that officers occupied themselves with activities related to national development—exploring the West, building canals, and developing railroads and harbors—they earned the gratitude of their fellow citizens. But gratitude was not to be confused with status or clout. This republican model of civil-military relations served the United States well through 1898 and survived even during the period following World War I.

The coming of World War II spelled the demise of this republican model. A relationship based on an instinctive aversion to all things military did not suit the needs of an industrialized democracy compelled to raise a massive military establishment. Even before the United States entered the war, statesmen like Henry L. Stimson and generals like George C. Marshall were collaborating in the creation of a new liberal democratic model of civil-military relations. The guiding principles of this new model were respect and reciprocity. The new compact served purposes that extended well beyond the immediate needs of national defense: It succeeded because it worked to the mutual benefit of all three elements of Clausewitz's trinity.

For example, the "way of war" to which the United States subscribed throughout the conflict not only provided a suitable means to achieve victory, but also meshed precisely with the important political and social priorities. To defeat Nazi Germany and imperial Japan, the United States created military forces suited for decision-oriented, machine-age warfare—campaigns and battles waged by vast fleets of tanks, warships, and combat aircraft. Fielding armies and fleets large enough to permit the United States to fight on several fronts simultaneously demanded an unprecedented mobilization of the nation's industrial and human resources. Notably, to satisfy the services' enormous manpower needs, that mobilization relied on conscription, initiated well before U.S. entry into the war and endorsed by the people with only the barest hesitation.

Adhering to a strategy of abundance (when possible equipping other nations to shoulder the brunt of the actual fighting), the United States achieved victory with relatively few casualties. No less important, the transformation of the United States into the "arsenal of democracy," from which there flowed a torrent of weapons, munitions, and supplies needed to fight, fueled an economic boom. On the American home front, military Keynesianism restored prosperity.

By 1945, its enemies crushed, its allies exhausted, the United States had ascended to a position of dominance rare in recorded history. This marked an astonishing turnaround. During the decade prior to war, the Great Depression had threatened the legitimacy of the political order in the United States. Bolshevism on the Left and fascism on the Right posed ideological challenges that called into question the viability of liberal democracy. Although Franklin Roosevelt's New Deal had stanched the economy's downward spiral, it had not produced recovery. As a result, the government that led the nation into war in December 1941 did not enjoy an excess of credibility. Within four years, wartime achievements—not only in battle, but also on the factory floor—had restored confidence in American institutions and in the American elite that presided over those institutions.

In this and other ways, the methods chosen to conduct World War II found favor with the American people. That was hardly an accident. In crafting the policies that would guide the war effort, senior leaders, both civilian and military, did so with one eye fixed on public opinion. The problem was to keep the people engaged in supporting the war without exacting more from them than they were prepared to offer. "A democracy cannot fight a Thirty Years War," General Marshall warned.[19] Like Roosevelt himself, Marshall understood the imperative of ending the war quickly and decisively while sparing Americans unnecessary sacrifice for what was, after all, a "foreign" war.

Among other things, those directing the war effort reassured the majority that military necessity would not become a pretext for radical social experiments. The world's greatest democracy, the United States in the 1940s was also a society in which white male Protestants wielded power and in which distinctions, especially those based on race and gender, mattered. Although the war did generate demands for change, political and military authorities did their best to preserve the social status quo ante bellum. By 1940, the era of reform had ended, Roosevelt himself offering his assurance that "Dr. New Deal" had retired in favor of "Dr. Win-the-War." Apart from creating a handful of Negro combat units, the army resisted the efforts of those hoping to use the war to advance the cause of civil rights. The armed services remained rigidly segregated, with African Americans largely relegated to menial service support duties. Notwithstanding unprecedented wartime opportunities for women both in and out of uniform, men at least understood these to be emergency measures, not a permanent transformation of gender roles. And indeed, when the war ended, women for the most part reverted to their traditional status. Millions of returning male vets reclaimed the best jobs and, propelled by the G.I. Bill's generous educational benefits, joined the expanding ranks of the upwardly mobile, white-collar, suburban-bound middle class.

Because it had satisfied the disparate interests of the state, the people, *and* the military during World War II, this new civil-military compact endured beyond 1945. Underpinning that compact was a tax that before 1940 Americans would have found inconceivable and unacceptable: a permanent peacetime draft.

Restored following the war after only the briefest interruption, conscription provided the foundation of postwar U.S. national security policy. It also extended through the first decades of the postwar era the liberal democratic model of civil-military relations forged during the war. As was the case during the war, the reciprocal relationship worked to the mutual benefit of all parties concerned.

From the point of view of the officer corps, the draft imparted predictability and stability to the military's connection to state and people. Assuring the armed services that they could draw as needed on the pool of the nation's best and brightest young men, conscription also provided a hedge against misuse by a reckless government or abandonment by a feckless polity. From the point of view of those formulating U.S. strategy, the draft provided the muscle to pursue the ambitious policies of the immediate postwar and early Cold War eras—and it implied popular support for those policies.

But in acceding to this arrangement, the people exacted a price. Included in that price were several expectations. First, Americans assumed that these citizen-soldiers would be used sparingly. Their primary purpose was to prevent the occurrence of war, not to engage in constant campaigning. Second, if U.S. interests required those soldiers actually to fight, the people expected that the war would be brief, decisive, and conducted far from America's shores. Third, in anticipation of such contingencies, government was to amass weapons and materiel sufficient to insure that the next war, whenever it occurred, would be fought with the same emphasis on avoiding unnecessary American casualties that had characterized the U.S. approach to World War II. Not incidentally, this requirement to stockpile and modernize a great arsenal would also reduce the danger of returning to the hard times of the 1930s—defense spending continuously priming the pump of economic expansion.

The arrangement did not survive without missteps or without its critics. In its eagerness to bring the Korean War to neat and rapid conclusion—consistent with popular expectations and past military practice—the Truman administration in the fall of 1950 permitted an overconfident Douglas MacArthur to push beyond the 38th parallel toward the Yalu. The result was a war larger, longer, and bloodier than Americans were prepared to accept. Truman's miscalculation earned Democrats a sharp rebuke. In 1952, the people elected the first Republican president in two decades—a general who promised to extract the U.S. from a war that promised to continue without end.

Calculating but prudent in his approach to statecraft, Dwight D. Eisenhower hewed closely to the terms of the civil-military compact. There would be no more Koreas on his watch. Nor, as a result, would there be any demands by a people exhausted by war for the United States to revert to isolationism. Gratified that the new president had promptly ended the fighting in Korea, Americans acceded to Eisenhower's determination to maintain

U.S. commitments abroad. Throughout his two terms, without complaint or controversy, a continuous flow of draftees—even Elvis—rotated to Europe and the Far East, pulled their hitch, and came home. Meanwhile, defense plants from Long Island to southern California churned out a never-ending stream of fighters, bombers, tanks, and guided missiles. With defense priorities dictating the allocation of research dollars, institutions of higher learning happily crowded around the bountiful government trough. Among the few who worried about the potentially insidious consequences of this cozy arrangement for American democracy was Eisenhower himself. Two terms as commander in chief had convinced the former general that the United States was at some risk of becoming, whether due to malice or inadvertence, a garrison state. In his farewell address to the nation, Eisenhower warned his fellow citizens about the dangers of a "military-industrial complex." But few heeded his words. The immediate and tangible benefits for all concerned—corporations, labor unions, universities, the entire national security apparatus—trumped the concerns of the outgoing president.

III

Despite its apparent durability, the civil-military equilibrium bred of the Second World War and sustained through the 1950s collapsed soon thereafter. The implications for American military power and policy were catastrophic.

The proximate cause of that collapse was Vietnam. Cast in terms of Clausewitz's trinity, Vietnam was a conflict in which the state flagrantly violated its covenant with both people and army. Civilian officials responsible for formulating policy, abetted by ineffectual military advisers, perpetrated a crisis in U.S. civil-military relations without precedent. By the end of the 1960s, the trinity lay in shambles.

Vietnam became the "Thirty Years War" that George Marshall had warned against, an amorphous, protracted war of attrition, conducted with little immediate prospect of achieving a decisive outcome. Lyndon Johnson and his advisers concluded that the best way to wage a conflict of indeterminate length was to *avoid* rousing the passions of the people. To the maximum extent possible, they wanted to disguise the realty of the war by insulating the home front from it effects. Hence, the administration rejected Pentagon recommendations in favor of mobilization, refusing to call up the reserves and placing the entire burden for fighting the war on active duty forces.

In the combat zone, campaigns orchestrated by commanders schooled in the arts of conventional warfare relied on the abundance of materiel (and firepower) that had become an American hallmark. But the enemy refused to fight on American terms, shrewdly exploited the self-imposed restrictions to which U.S. forces adhered, and exacted a gruesome toll in casualties, both American and Vietnamese.

At home, defense contractors worked overtime to replace the fighter-bombers and helicopters lost in combat, but instead of promoting prosperity, increased military spending—combined with Johnson's refusal to choose between guns and butter—produced by the early 1970s deficits, inflation, and economic stagnation. To the manifest unhappiness of the American people, Vietnam brought the postwar boom to an abrupt end. Nor did the administration even succeed in keeping war away from America's shores: By 1968, opposition to Vietnam had fueled a level of civil unrest, frequently violent, not seen in a century.

For the military itself, as the war dragged on from one year to the next, Vietnam became a nightmare. The United States Army, with the largest contingent engaged, suffered the most acutely. By the early 1970s, the Army teetered on the verge of disintegration. In Vietnam itself, combat refusals and attacks by soldiers on their own leaders ("fraggings") became commonplace. Throughout the service, problems of drug abuse and racial animosity raged all but out of control. Basic discipline broke down.

Even with conscription still in place, the people began severing their links to the military. Avoiding the draft lost its stigma; subverting it acquired a certain fashionability. By implication, only the morally inert or the politically unenlightened would submit to the directives of the selective service system in support of a pointless war. Thus, by the time Vietnam was winding down, the great American middle class had all but opted out of military service—a process acknowledged and affirmed in 1970 when President Richard Nixon announced plans to terminate the draft altogether. Henceforth, the United States would rely for its defense not on citizen-soldiers drawn from throughout American society, but on an "All Volunteer"—that is, professional—force.

Yet for all the stresses induced by Vietnam, the war alone cannot explain the full extent of the civil-military estrangement symbolized by Nixon's decision to terminate the draft. The story had another dimension. Unlike Korea—the so-called "Forgotten War" that even now appears historically disembodied—the Vietnam war occurred in the midst of (and itself helped to spur) a cultural revolution of extraordinary scope and intensity. Beginning in the mid-1960s, that revolution transformed manners, morals, and mores throughout the West but most particularly in the United States. That upheaval also provoked resistance, touching off a fiercely contested "culture war." At the heart of the culture war were (and are) two radically divergent views of what "The Sixties" signified. To some, the period fostered a new spirit of liberation, exposing the repressive underpinnings of American life and promising justice to oppressed minorities, especially blacks and women. To others, it meant, as Gertrude Himmelfarb recently observed, "the collapse of ethical principles and habits, the loss of respect for authorities and institutions, the breakdown of the family, the decline of civility, the vulgarization of high culture, and the degradation of popular culture."[20]

Already reeling from the war itself, the United States military found itself battered further still by this cultural revolution. For partisans on both sides of the cultural divide, the soldier became an invaluable symbol and military policy a battleground in which to fight out their differences.

For the Left, the military provided a palpable representation of all that they scorned. Military institutions were impersonal, uptight, authoritarian, bureaucratic, and resolutely male. They served as instruments of American imperialism abroad and government oppression at home. Military life itself—implying the loss of individual identity and the submission to authority—was the polar opposite of cool.

In the eyes of the Right, the military represented a last bastion of order, tradition, patriotism, and respect for basic national institutions—all of which the 1960s had seemingly swept away. Conservatives saw in the soldier's calling the best hope of preserving from complete extinction virtues like honor, courage, self-discipline, and self-sacrifice. Inveterate cold warriors understood (correctly) that attacks on the military were attacks on the anti-Communist crusade, to which they remained passionately committed.

Thus did the military become an object of intensely partisan struggle. After Vietnam, the old pretense that matters pertaining to national defense remained above mere politics now became a complete fiction: Henceforth, everybody knew that controversies revolving around nominally military questions contained a political subtext. Deciphering that subtext was impossible without reference to the ongoing culture war.

In this environment, preliminary efforts to reconstitute a viable trinity foundered. Moving beyond the war was not just a matter of soldiers knocking the mud off their boots and getting back to work. The task at hand was to rebuild U.S. military institutions from the bottom up and to do so in the teeth of the barely disguised hostility of American elites and despite the bone-deep weariness of the American people who were sick and tired of Vietnam and all its works. And despite, too, the fact that the officer corps came home from Vietnam nursing its own feelings of resentment and alienation.

Recruiting jingles proclaimed that "The Army Wants to Join You." But the sort of people the army wanted couldn't imagine wanting to join the army or any of the other services, for that matter. In the 1970s, those who did enlist tended to be those with few other options. The military effectively found itself the employer of last resort.

Yet despite such troubles—today largely eradicated from national memory—the seeds of recovery were being planted. Ignored by the media, unnoticed by their fellow citizens, a counterrevolution of sorts, instigated by soldiers, was laying the foundation for the revival of American military power. The aim of this counterrevolution was to *restore* what Vietnam had destroyed. By returning to the old strategy of containment and by redirecting its attention to a more familiar form of war, the military sought to regain a semblance of institutional stability and to reestablish its relevance. Ultimately, soldiers sought to repair their estrangement from American society, which had been a by-product of Vietnam.

Having had a bellyful of fighting guerrillas, military leaders after Vietnam reconfigured the services into instruments for large-scale, mechanized conventional conflict. Their intent was by no means to raise forces that reckless policymakers could then expend in further Third World crusades. Rather, they proposed to revert to the core mission of the Cold War: deterring Soviet aggression in "the Central Region." The Pentagon consciously designed the post-Vietnam force structure so that active duty forces would depend on the reserves for certain critical support functions, thereby making it next to impossible for a president to order any large-scale intervention without at least partial mobilization. Soldiers calculated that such a mobilization would proceed only if the intervention itself enjoyed popular support, thereby reducing the danger of being abandoned as they had been (in their own view) in Vietnam.

All of these preliminaries occurred before Ronald Reagan became president. Indeed, all of the major reforms of the post-Vietnam era—the overhaul of operational doctrine, the innovations in training, the design of new weapons like the Abrams tank—predate the Reagan era, as does reversing the post-Vietnam decline in military spending. It nonetheless remains true that but for the contribution of President Reagan himself, efforts to revive American military power may well have come to naught.

Without doubt, Reagan facilitated that revival by boosting defense spending to unprecedented peacetime levels. Yet his most important contribution was to restore to reasonable health the civil-military relationship that Vietnam had ruptured. Reagan repaired the bond between the military and society. Exuding optimism, he lifted the country out of its post-Vietnam funk. Lavishing soldiers with affection and entrusting to them the task of thwarting Soviet aggression, Reagan validated the Pentagon's determination to redefine its raison d'être: standing athwart the Fulda Gap rather than vainly chasing pajama-clad guerrillas. The people, still harboring their visceral dislike for communism and rankled by Vietnam era scapegoating of soldiers, applauded. More substantively, their sons (and now increasingly their daughters) found reason to serve in uniform: by the mid-1980s, the shaky experiment in creating an all volunteer force appeared headed for success. Patriotism had become respectable again. Being a soldier became hip.

Even without conscription, Reagan reactivated the liberal-democratic civil-military compact that had governed the immediate postwar era. Apart from the single, disastrous lapse of Beirut, he was careful to abide by its conventions. There would be no Vietnams on Reagan's watch. On that score, both citizens and soldiers could rest easy. The Reagan administration publicly committed itself to a demanding set of prerequisites—codified in the Weinberger doctrine—that would govern its use of force. Meanwhile, as had been the case in World War II, a revival of military Keynesianism energized the economy and fostered a renewed sense of national well being.

In short, bountiful defense budgets alone did not produce American military preeminence in the 1980s. Military power in a democracy is not simply a product of money or technology. Whether through instinct, reasoning, or the advice of wise counselors, Reagan grasped that nurturing sound military institutions and using military power effectively demanded the active engagement of the people. He secured the people's support by restating with conviction simple truths: that communism was a great evil, that the Soviet Union threatened American security and values, and that the United States was not condemned to inevitable and irreversible decline. To these—which until the deluge of the sixties had seemed self-evident—he added one notion that was uniquely his: that the Cold War was not something to be managed, but to be won.

To be sure, Reagan could not repeal the cultural revolution. As a result, his views did not go down well among the sophisticates in the prestige media or in faculty lounges. But throughout his presidency—that revolution's Thermidor—they resonated on Main Street.

Reagan's own election to a second term, the election of George Bush as his designated successor, and victory in the Cold War all seemingly validated Reagan's achievement. The result—demonstrated most vividly, after Reagan had left office, in the Persian Gulf War—was a Clausewitzian trinity of surpassing robustness. For a brief moment, the policy objectives of the state and the capabilities of the military appeared to align precisely. And the new professional military establishment to which the United States had committed itself—its members now universally referred to as "the troops"—became also at one and the same time a people's army.

IV

But the Reagan restoration has proven to be strikingly ephemeral. In the comparatively brief interval between Operation Desert Storm in 1991 and Operation Allied Force in 1999, the liberal democratic covenant between state, people, and military has once again come unglued, this time in all likelihood for good. A new civil-military arrangement has evolved, one that reflects the prevailing values of a different time—the age not of Ronald Reagan but of William Jefferson Clinton.

The geopolitical upheaval caused by the end of the Cold War, a redefinition of U.S. grand strategy, and a novel conception of warfare that itself is a product of powerful technological and cultural influences have all contributed to this transformation. Whereas the old liberal democratic covenant operated on the principle of reciprocity, the new arrangement adheres to the nostrums of a new age, one that is postliberal, postindustrial, postmodern, and postheroic. In Kosovo this new "trinity" was fully on display for the first time.

Devising this new postliberal model of civil-military relations ranks among the least recognized accomplishments of the Clinton presidency. But the achievement, if not necessarily salubrious, is a genuine one.

Clinton the master politician accurately gauged—indeed, in his own personal conduct, exemplified—the temper of his times. Better than any other player on the national political stage, he understood what Americans want, how much they will pay, and what they will put up with.

Meanwhile, Clinton the statesman—schooled in his duties through intensive on-the-job training—recast the nation's strategic purposes. Contrary to the assertions of critics who complained of a decade of drift, the president outlined an ambitious project that both departs from the obsolete pattern of the Cold War and yet maintains continuity with the underlying thrust of twentieth-century U.S. foreign policy. He articulated a clear vision of what the world of the twenty-first century should look like and within that vision allotted to the United States a role worthy of a superpower. Moreover, speaking from his Bully Pulpit, he explained with almost mind-numbing frequency the assumptions and principles that underlie that grand strategy.

Finally, Clinton the commander in chief fashioned a doctrine for employing American military power that bridges the gap between his grand strategic objectives and the public's limited willingness to exert itself on behalf of those objectives. The military component of Clinton's strategy requires minimal blood and only modest treasure—indeed, the cash flow on balance may be positive. And it does not unduly tax the nation's attention span. Finessing the deficit between ends and means, the new postliberal civil-military relationship that Clinton ushered into existence seemingly reconciles the irreconcilable. For this achievement, Bill Clinton, in his own way, deserves to rank alongside FDR and Reagan as one of the most influential commanders in chief in modern American history.

This achievement is not without considerable irony. Indeed, at the outset of his first term, as evidenced by the fiasco over gays in the military, Bill Clinton seemed oblivious to the very concept of civil-military relations. Tone-deaf to military culture and unimpressed by the military's longstanding exercise of professional autonomy, the newly inaugurated Clinton apparently took for granted that as commander in chief his authority was absolute. He issued orders. Soldiers obeyed. Although the Pentagon signaled frantically the officer corps' unwillingness to accept a repeal of the ban on gays serving openly in the military, the newly inaugurated president ignored that warning. The upshot was a public spectacle in which Clinton and the top brass came precariously close to toppling the carefully erected edifice of constitutional precepts, traditional prerogatives, and mutual self-restraint that sustains civilian control. Embarrassed, Clinton cut a deal and acceded to the phony "don't ask, don't tell" policy.

Clinton's first year in the White House provided a similar education regarding the use of force. The president had been in office less than five months when he first ordered U.S. troops into action—a cruise missile attack against Baghdad in June 1993. Yet in many respects, his (vicarious) baptism of fire occurred later that year. In the same month that he pummeled Baghdad with missiles, Clinton quietly launched a quasi-covert war against the Somali warlord Mohamed Farah Aidid. In October of that year, Clinton's war careened out of control. A bungled raid in downtown Mogadishu resulted in a fierce firefight between U.S. forces and Somali militias. By the time it ended, American helicopters had been shot down, a pilot was being paraded in captivity, and 18 U.S. Army rangers lay dead. The political outcry in Washington was immediate and deafening.

In responding to this crisis, Clinton displayed all of the instincts for self-preservation for which he became rightly known. He assigned primary blame for the debacle to the United Nations. To placate an infuriated Congress, he offered up as sacrificial lamb his own secretary of defense, Les Aspin. And he wisely cut his losses, ordering U.S. forces to terminate their mission in Somalia and come home. Being bloodied by General Aidid did not diminish the president's propensity to employ coercion, as subsequent events in Haiti, Bosnia, Iraq, Sudan, Afghanistan, and Kosovo would show. But there would be no more Mogadishus on his watch.

From the gays-in-the-military debacle and the bloody encounter with General Aidid, Clinton took away important lessons. He would, henceforth, avoid ruffling the military's feathers and give wide berth to African warlords. But conclusions drawn from those two episodes also contributed directly to the larger task that he faced as commander in chief, namely to adapt U.S. national security policy more generally to the perplexing conditions that he encountered as the first genuine post–Cold War president. On that score, Clinton's critics fail to give him the credit he deserves.

In the eyes of his admirers, Ronald Reagan won the Cold War. By extension, in bringing about the downfall of communism, Reagan gets credit for furthering the global spread of market principles. But Reagan did not succeed in winning the culture war or even in rolling back the torrent of cultural change unleashed by the sixties. Indeed, the fact that the electorate in 1992 chose (in the formulation of a U.S. Air Force major general) a dope-smoking, skirt-chasing draft dodger to lead the nation illustrates that the values of the cultural revolution emerged unscathed from the ostensibly conservative decade of the 1980s. In short, the situation that Clinton inherited from his Republican predecessors was one in which the Right had won decisively the argument over economics and in which the Left had prevailed in matters of culture. Free enterprise and the politics of personal liberation had both triumphed.

This result was a new zeitgeist, one that the Cold War had kept in check but that sprang loose as Bill and Hillary proudly marched down Pennsylvania Avenue at their first inaugural. Profit, lifestyle, and radical individualism became the dominant values of Bill Clinton's America. Exploiting a revolution in information technology, more Americans made more money than ever before. It was money they intended to enjoy. Autonomy, extravagance, self-gratification, and tolerance were in. Accountability, austerity, self-denial, and being judgmental were definitely out. Rights proliferated. Responsibilities shrunk. As postmodern precepts such as deconstruction and multiculturalism seeped from the academy into the public square, old distinctions blurred: between men and women, good and evil, reality and fiction, truth and falsity, freedom and responsibility, art and exhibitionism. As the president himself suggested, even the meaning of the word *is* could no longer be taken for granted.

All of this provoked dismay and even outrage in some quarters. So-called "virtuecrats" worried about the collapse of American civilization and grew apoplectic at the lubricious antics of Clinton himself. But the American people—at least the dwindling proportion of the electorate able to motivate itself to go to the polls—expressed their approval of Clinton's stewardship, awarding him in 1996 a second term. Despite evidence of the most egregious presidential misconduct, efforts to remove Clinton from office in 1999 left the majority of Americans unmoved.

In the age of Clinton, the traditional martial virtues—honor, courage, and self-discipline—were notable by their absence, both in the culture at large and in the person of the commander in chief. This shortfall would not matter if the United States were a small nation comparable, say, to Switzerland or if the end of the Cold War had prompted it to become once again a "normal nation," chiefly preoccupied with cultivating its vast North American homeland.

But returning to the normalcy of pre-1940 America was simply out of the question. The foreign policy establishment that greeted Clinton when he arrived in Washington in 1993 refused categorically to accept any diminution of the global role to which the United States had become accustomed during the Cold War. Although the former Arkansas governor did not claim prior membership in that establishment, he could not afford—or was unwilling—to ignore its requirements, any more than he could ignore those of teachers' unions or the Black Caucus.

From the perspective of the foreign policy elite, Clinton's chief responsibility as president was to formulate a strategy of sufficient grandeur to justify America's continuing status as the World's Only Superpower—something to replace the outmoded concept of containment. Always a quick study, Clinton gamely rose to the occasion and soon enough was mouthing phrases about America's indispensability and its inescapable obligation to lead, codewords signaling his support for activist policies aimed at perpetuating U.S. global preeminence.

A handful of skeptics suggested that the cultural fabric of postliberal America seemed rather poor stuff with which to sustain such a policy.[21] Such concerns did not deter the majority of foreign policy experts, whatever their political inclination. Operation Desert Storm and the collapse of communism had convinced the Left and the Right of the superiority of American power. But Clinton understood that the skeptics were on to something. He knew—or during his first painful year in office had learned—that if the United States would not return to normalcy neither did it possess the capacity to engage in any great crusades: Neither the people nor the military had the stomach for the sacrifices that such crusades would entail. If the Clinton years have produced a broad domestic consensus in favor of a quasi-imperial role, a tacit corollary of that consensus was that the United States must gain and maintain its global hegemony without tears.

V

The twin phenomena identified by the Clinton administration as the cornerstones of its post–Cold War grand strategy reflect this requirement. Amidst all the confusing welter of change, the president and his chief lieutenants identified two developments that really matter: the information revolution and the process of globalization. These two all but inseparable factors, the administration believed, were transforming the international order. As such, they were creating vast new opportunities while imposing on the United States new responsibilities to exercise leadership.

The defining quality of the order resulting from this transformation is openness. Under the impact of technological change, according to Mr. Clinton, "the blocks, the barriers, the borders that defined the world for our parents and grandparents are giving way."[22] As they fall, there is emerging, in the words of Madeleine Albright, a world of "open markets, open investment, open communications and open trade."[23]

Openness will permit—indeed, is already permitting—the creation of wealth on a scale hitherto unimaginable. In explaining the stakes in Kosovo, the president described "a new century and a new millennium where the people in poor countries all over the world, because of technology and the Internet and the spread of information, will have unprecedented opportunities to share prosperity."[24] Indeed, thanks to the information revolution, "we clearly have it within our means to lift billions and billions of people around the world into a global middle class and into participation in global democracy."[25] As that remark suggests, a more prosperous world points inevitably toward a more democratic world. Given the administration's belief that "democracies do not go to war with one another," a more democratic world will in turn be more peaceful as well.[26]

For all of its apparent novelty, little of this strategy of openness was substantively new. Certainly, the foreign policy pronouncements issuing from the Clinton administration would be of little surprise to Charles Beard, eminent historian of an earlier generation, or William Appleman Williams, his intellectual heir. Both had identified the quest for a world open to U.S. economic activity as the overarching theme of American diplomacy.[27] The strategy of openness revives that theme.

Yet much as Beard and Williams had both argued, American enthusiasm for openness is by no means an exercise in altruism. In the eyes of the Clinton administration, globalization became, for the United States itself, an imperative. A failure to create an open order would imperil America's own well being. According to Albright, "our own prosperity depends on having partners that are open to our exports, investment, and ideas."[28] Or as Clinton himself bluntly put it, "Growth at home depends on growth abroad."[29] Indeed, given "the inexorable logic of globalization," as the president declared just prior to the war for Kosovo, "everything, from the strength of our economy to the safety of our cities, to the health of our people, depends on events not only within our borders, but half a world away."[30] With so much at stake, insuring the success of globalization became a vital U.S. interest.

According to administration spokesmen, "the President's strategy for harnessing the forces of globalization" aimed to make the promise of a peaceful, prosperous world a reality.[31] Topping the agenda of that strategy was trade liberalization—hence, the priority assigned to the North Atlantic Free Trade Agreement, the World Trade Organization, economic engagement with China, and the 200-plus trade agreements that the administration touted among its proudest achievements.

But the strategy has an important political aspect as well. Openness does not imply anarchy. As the chief proponent of globalization, the United States is also its midwife, responsible for insuring adherence to established norms of behavior and for comporting itself such that no nation questions its prerogative to do so. As Secretary Albright remarked, the United States must serve as the "organizing principal [sic]" of the new global system.[32]

Yet as events obliged Mr. Clinton to admit, "globalization is not an unmixed blessing."[33] The prospect of joining a global middle class—saturated with American pop culture, American tastes, and the American preoccupation with lifestyle—does not elicit universal delight. Globalization has evoked backlash by "forces of destruction"—terrorists, rogue states, drug cartels, and religious extremists who "find opportunity in the very openness, freedom and progress we cherish."[34] The result is conflict, amorphous, protracted, and bitter. Thus, according to the president, as it entered the new millennium, the United States found itself engaged in "a great battle between the forces of integration and the forces of disintegration; the forces of globalism and the forces of tribalism; of oppression against empowerment."[35] Kosovo became only the latest skirmish in that larger struggle.

As the U.S.-led intervention in Kosovo suggests, for all of the administration's emphasis on international economics, its strategy contained a vital security component. American military power is essential to the prospects of globalization. Without it, the misguided and the malicious will wreak havoc. Stability will erode. Progress toward openness will stall. Barriers will go back up. Assertions by American officials that the United States alone is equipped to preside over the global order will ring hollow.

Thus, whereas in former times wariness of becoming entangled in foreign wars was a hallmark of American statecraft, in an age of globalization, any disturbance anywhere demands the attention of the United States. As one senior Clinton administration official admitted in a moment of candor, "I am not sure there is such a thing as a foreign war anymore."[36]

The operational implications of converting the American military into an adjunct to globalization loom large. Soldiers themselves have obscured those implications by clinging to an identity that has long since become anachronistic. Although soldiers insist that they remain "warriors" who exist to "fight and win the nation's wars," the frenetic military history of the 1990s—a single, brief, prematurely terminated war followed by a nearly continuous stream of "operations other than war"—tells a different story. Today's G.I. functions in practice as a member of an armed constabulary that exists to nudge others into conformity with the American vision of a well-ordered planet and to punish (usually from a safe distance) those with the temerity to challenge that vision.

Indeed, the principles governing the Clinton administration's use of force had little to do with war as traditionally conceived: Globalization is, after all, making war as such obsolete. Under the terms of the Clinton doctrine, the United States wields military power not to defeat adversaries but as part of an effort to "shape" the international environment.[37] Policing and punishment have supplanted the pursuit of victory as the primary purpose of military action. Publicly announced objectives that are intentionally spacious (obliging transgressors to "pay a price" has become a favorite) permit maximum creativity when evaluating the outcome of any military operation.[38] Vaguely defined objectives also permit political leaders to extricate themselves altogether at the first hint of quagmire—declaring success all the while. When administering punishment—whether against rogue states like Iraq and Yugoslavia or against alleged terrorists in Sudan or Afghanistan—the Clinton doctrine eschewed full-fledged campaigns in favor of brief, measured ripostes. The idea was not to achieve decision, but to signal, warn, contain, or punish, or at least to avoid the appearance of weakness and inaction. Limited numbers of cruise missiles or air strikes with precision guided munitions were usually deemed sufficient to make the point. When policing—as, for example, in Haiti or the Balkans—the standard practice was to intervene massively and to tailor the mission so as to minimize exposure and commitment. In all cases, casualty avoidance ranked as a paramount measure of success.

VI

The liberal democratic civil-military compact forged in World War II reflected not only the requirements of war in an industrial age but also a particular set of socioeconomic and cultural imperatives. The same holds true for the postliberal covenant that has supplanted it: it manifests the new American way of war. It also testifies to changes in the nation's aspirations and character.

To the casual observer, the implications of the transformation may not be immediately self-evident. The survival—and skillful manipulation—of familiar symbols and rituals convey the impression that traditional civil-military arrangements remain intact. In the manner of his predecessors, President Clinton still placed wreaths at the Tomb of the Unknowns, visited U.S. troops abroad on Thanksgiving, and on occasions of state routinely praised their dedication and patriotism. Artifacts of military professionalism remain much in evidence. Distinctive uniforms, insignia of rank, service ribbons, recruiting slogans, and the presence of military color guards at football games all suggest continuity rather than change. As reflected in opinion polls, popular regard for "the troops" remains at or near Gulf War levels.

These vestiges of past practice conceal the extent to which a fundamentally new relationship has supplanted the "trinity" with which Americans are familiar. The connecting tissue in the old liberal democratic relationship—underpinning policy and essential to the actual conduct of war—was popular support. During World War II and through the Cold War, the engagement of the people lent credibility to the policies devised by the state—or, as in the case of Vietnam, undermined that credibility. The people provided the human and material resources that created effective military institutions—or, as was the case during the years immediately following Vietnam, withheld those resources with severely adverse consequences. In contrast, the new postliberal relationship obviates the need for popular support altogether, insulating both U.S. policy and American military power from the vagaries of a fickle and moody public. Decoupling the people from military affairs is its primary purpose.

Its primary purpose but not its sole one: The postliberal system of civil-military relations also seeks to reduce the influence of soldiers. Having long since concluded that "diplomacy and force are two sides of the same coin," President Clinton knows that coercion is integral to his efforts to pry open the world.[39] The flowering of American aspirations to global hegemony no longer permits the United States to turn a blind eye to crises that in an earlier era would have been dismissed as not our affair. Instead, political elites persuade themselves that the nation has essentially no choice but to become involved, if only to demonstrate leadership or prevent the erosion of American credibility.

But coercion is not to be confused with waging war, which entails huge risks and all too often produces unintended and highly disruptive consequences. As envisioned by Mr. Clinton and his advisers, the use of force was to be calibrated, judicious, and precise. Above all, whereas war implies a sharing of authority between policymaker and generals, force as an instrument of diplomacy would become exclusively the province of the statesman, with soldiers reduced to the role of mere ordnance deliverers.

The essential ingredient in the new civil-military relationship—rendering both popular support and professional military advice moot—is technology.

Much as information technology fuels hopes for globalization and expectations of continuing U.S. economic dominance, so too does technology infuse the Clinton doctrine for the use of force and the civil-military relationship that supports that doctrine. High-tech military capabilities—to strike with accuracy and impunity, to anticipate and parry attack—reduce the uncertainty formerly inherent in the use of force. Technology largely obviates the need for sacrifice. It seemingly permits the United States to pursue global policies without subjecting the home front to the unwelcome dislocations of large-scale armed conflict—political protest or economic instability, for example. In short, technology enables the United States to use its military power to sustain American hegemony without the necessity of fighting messy old-fashioned wars. As a bonus, technology even facilitates efforts to align American military institutions more closely with advanced thinking on sensitive issues such as gender and sexual orientation.

The best illustration of the postliberal civil-military relationship in action is the Clinton administration's *other* war of 1999, the yearlong bombing of Iraq.

What war? In the administration's view, needless to say, the ongoing hostilities against Iraq, launched in December 1998 with a four-day air offensive known as Operation Desert Fox, failed to qualify as actual war. Indeed, the White House barely acknowledged that military action continued thereafter. This, despite the fact that, in the twelve months *after* Desert Fox, U.S. and British warplanes unloaded nearly 2,000 missiles and precision-guided bombs against several hundred targets scattered throughout Iraq.

According to administration officials, the aim of U.S. policy was to contain Iraq and prevent it from acquiring weapons of mass destruction, while ultimately removing Saddam Hussein from power. Observers might expect, therefore, that a year's worth of bombing would have pounded weapons research facilities, military headquarters, key government installations, and presidential palaces—in the jargon favored by air power advocates, "all that the regime holds dear."

Such was not the case. Principles of the schoolyard rather than principles of war governed the campaign: It was a game of tit-for-tat. Iraqi air defenses "painted" or otherwise challenged aircraft flying daily patrols in the Northern or Southern No-Fly Zone. Using this pretext, allied bombers flying at high altitudes retaliated against radar sites, surface-to-air missile batteries, and command centers, targets that shared one thing in common: They were all remote from Baghdad. The result testifies to the proficiency of American airmen—tens of thousands of sorties flown without a single loss—but there is no evidence that the attacks caused Saddam to lose sleep, literally or figuratively.

Yet as a demonstration of postliberal civil-military relations, the Persian Gulf conflict of 1999 was a rousing success. Administration officials labored assiduously to deflect scrutiny from Mr. Clinton's stealth bombing campaign. To their delight, Congress, the media, and the military all played along, permitting the administration a free hand.

As with every other U.S. military operation launched since the Persian Gulf conflict of 1990–1991, the Persian Gulf conflict of 1999 proceeded on executive authority alone, Congress tacitly accepting the administration's thesis that the clashes in the skies over Iraq did not require legislative sanction. The Republican majority did not even motivate itself to ask what the nation had gotten in return for the billion or so dollars expended in support of this operation.

News organizations likewise largely ignored the resumption of hostilities against Iraq. A brief report buried in the inside pages of the *New York Times* makes the point. The headline reads "Iraq: U.S. Bombs Again," that slightly weary "again" hinting at the incident's failure to qualify as genuinely newsworthy. The wire service dispatch that follows—barely a single column-inch in length—reinforces that interpretation. Repeating the mutually contradictory claims of the Iraqi News Agency (civilians attacked) and U.S. military spokesmen (military targets destroyed), it conveys the impression that the incident merits scant attention. Thus cued, the American people responded accordingly: They remained oblivious to what had become a stealth war.

Meanwhile, although the bombing of scattered Iraqi installations, by any standard measure of effectiveness, was pointless, senior military leaders themselves found no cause for complaint. Flying live-fire missions beyond the reach of Iraqi defenses provided American pilots with a welcome opportunity to enhance their skills. Commanders and staffs gained invaluable operational experience. Aging stocks of munitions were expended and then replenished with the latest that money can buy. Back in the Pentagon, arguments for additional force structure or for new weapons systems accrued.

Best of all, no one got hurt—at least not on our side. Even after Clnton had departed the White House, squadrons continued to deploy, rotate home, and prepare to deploy again, their movement like their operations all but unnoticed by the public.

In the skies over Iraq, the postliberal system of civil-military relations functioned precisely as intended. In the interest of freeing policymakers from constraints, the system delivered two essentials: acquiescent citizens and compliant soldiers. With the American people increasingly inured to the use of force, with American soldiers dutifully pushing the buttons that put bombs on target, this new "trinity" offers the prospect of compensating for the disparity between the nation's quasi-imperial grand strategy and its singularly nonimperial culture.

VII

A new strategic azimuth, a new doctrine for the use of American military power, a radically altered climate of civil-military relations: each of these, prominently on display during the war for Kosovo, deserves to be ranked among the foremost accomplishments of the Clinton presidency. To a far greater degree than the signature issues of the 1990s—health care, welfare reform, public education, the environment—they are likely to form an enduring part of the actual Clinton legacy.

None of the three has attracted the attention it deserves. For critics interested in scoring partisan points, bashing the administration for having failed to devise a coherent strategy is far more gratifying than tracing the connections (and noting the contradictions) between American actions and the rationale for those actions offered by the White House or the State Department. Similarly, lambasting Bill Clinton for amateurism or incompetence in his various military adventures is easier than identifying the patterns of behavior that constitute, for better or worse, a new American doctrine for the use of force. Thus, the failure of most commentators in the aftermath of Kosovo to gauge its true importance as a watershed in U.S. military history. No sooner had the last bomb fallen than Operation Allied Force faded into the crowded tableau of military adventures in which the United States had engaged since the end of the Cold War.

Given the habitual inclination of most Americans to take civil-military matters for granted, it comes as no surprise that this dimension of the story likewise escaped notice. Yet for a democratic superpower, reconfiguring the connection between state, people, and army must inevitably have profound consequences. Indeed, as Kosovo suggested, the postliberal model of civil-military relations is deeply flawed. It is incompatible with traditional military professionalism and it poses an unacceptable risk to democratic practice.

As noted above, President Clinton's grand strategy of hegemony through globalization requires coercion but has no place for real war. But the obsolescence of war portends the obsolescence of officership as a profession. Indeed, with the end of the Cold War, the delegitimization of "the art of war"—begun in 1914, seemingly validated by the events of August 1945, but then held in abeyance—has resumed with a vengeance. In a society in which the professions generally are suffering a loss of prestige and authority, the notion that the "management of violence" constitutes a distinctive field of endeavor to be mastered only through lifelong study no longer commands automatic assent.

Where does that leave soldiers?

With war no longer the chief reason for their existence, they are hard pressed to sustain the claim that the business of soldiering constitutes a unique calling, guided by its own values and nurturing its own culture. As a result, military service is in danger of becoming, as the distinguished sociologist Charles Moskos has suggested, just another job, subject to the societal norms that govern other occupations.

Thanks to a long string of embarrassing incidents—beginning with the infamous Tailhook convention of 1991—the services themselves have managed to increase the pressures to adhere to those norms. Revelations about the predatory sex life of the Air Force's first woman B52 pilot, boorish drill sergeants hitting on female recruits at Aberdeen, the U.S. Army's top NCO hauled into the dock for sexual harassment, general officers being disciplined for sleeping with the wives of their subordinates: These public relations disasters not only demolished cherished images of the military as a repository of rectitude and propriety but undercut the Pentagon's efforts to sustain even minimal claims to autonomy.

For cultural progressives, these incidents have been a godsend. Forced onto the defensive, the services spent the 1990s appeasing their critics, in particular by striving to demonstrate enlightened attitudes regarding gender.[40] In the traditionalist camp of the culture war, such efforts triggered concerns about the "feminization" of the armed forces.

Although these concerns are not entirely misplaced, they miss the heart of the matter. The real problem is not the military's prospective emasculation but its inability to identify *any* persuasive rationale for maintaining a distinctive ethos. Adherents of the old school may still *recite* hallowed soldierly values—manliness, courage, discipline, sacrifice, self-abnegation—but the society from which the military fills its ranks no longer *assents* to those values. Certainly, most members of the elite, increasingly innocent of first-hand military experience, no longer connect such values to the actual role of present-day soldiers. A recent report in the *New York Times* makes the point. Struggling to explain the renewed popularity among soldiers of a Vietnam-era novel that is a tract on behalf of military traditionalism, the *Times* correspondent discounts the phenomenon as simply "nostalgia for simpler days with obvious heroes and villains . . . when 'duty, honor, and country' *really was* the soldier's calling."[41]

If indeed nostalgia is all that sustains the residual identification with the military ethic, then the profession's days are numbered. Young Americans of the current generation who choose to serve—themselves products of a culture that cherishes individual autonomy and lifestyle above all else—are not prone to nostalgia and differ little from their counterparts who stay back in the neighborhood. When today's soldiers deploy to keep the peace in Kosovo or to rebuild shattered nations like Bosnia-Herzegovina, they expect that the "neighborhood"—pizza places, video arcades, and cable television—will accompany them. The terms of the soldiers' implicit contract with their employer have changed accordingly.[42]

As traditional military culture erodes, other potentially perverse "values" fill the void. In the eyes of some analysts, the extraordinary sensitivity to casualties—so vividly on display during the Kosovo war and as prominent among senior officers as among their civilian counterparts—is itself "corrosive to the professional military ethic," endangering ancient principles such as the primacy of mission accomplishment.[43] The aversion to casualties may likewise reflect a growing aversion to risk of any kind. For those hoping to get ahead in today's military, "zero defects" is the rule—a precept more conducive to careerism than to leaders gutsy enough to ask tough questions of civilian officials inclined to view force as an all-purpose remedy to political predicaments.

Most troubling of all, the erosion of received values is also undermining old taboos that obliged soldiers to remain above politics. For generations, nonpartisanship formed an integral part of officership. Eminent soldiers like George Marshall thought it improper even to vote. Evidence suggests that such attitudes are on the wane. Today's officer corps has become consciously "conservative" in its outlook and identifies itself with the Republican Party.[44] This trend, if unchecked, suggests that the military may well become just another interest group like big business or big labor, wooed by opposing political factions and placing its own parochial concerns above the nation's.[45]

If the postliberal approach to civil-military relations weakens the second element of Clausewitz's trinity, by negating the traditional basis of military professionalism, it has had an equally damaging impact on the third element, excluding the people from a direct and active role in military affairs. The predictable result is a popular indifference that is manifesting itself in several ways. Members of Congress and their staffs are increasingly uninformed about and uninterested in military matters—except for hot button issues related to the culture war. Other institutions such as the prestige media or universities treat military subjects as hardly worthy of serious attention. (Again, the culture-war exception applies—the *New York Times* will interest itself in the rigor of boot camp only to the extent that it relates to the preservation of gender-integrated training).

For members of the elite, security, which in the liberal democratic era implied the citizen's obligation to contribute to the nation's defense, becomes in the postliberal age yet another function best satisfied by outsourcing. It is something that *they* do for *us*. Meanwhile, the plain folk, no fools, express their own indifference in a way that strikes directly at the very lifeblood of the armed services: They chose not to serve. As a result, the vaunted all volunteer force today faces the imminent prospect of running out of volunteers.[46]

Whether America's new technology-dependent way of war, vividly displayed in Kosovo, will suffice to create and maintain the global democratic imperium envisioned by Bill Clinton remains to be seen—although on that score the difficulties caused by an adversary as puny as Yugoslavia offer scant cause for optimism. No doubt the conduct of that war—at once pusillanimous and needlessly brutal—would have left Clausewitz for one appalled.

The thought of offending the sensibilities of a long-dead German soldier-intellectual is unlikely to trouble most Americans. When was the last time that Germany got a war right? Yet the trinitarian arrangement accompanying this new approach to employing American military power—a state with an appetite for empire, an exceedingly powerful army shorn of professional restraint, a self-absorbed and apathetic citizenry—would also likewise appall Americans whose views once commanded respect: soldiers like Washington, Marshall, and Eisenhower. That Americans have so casually discarded *their* views regarding the difficulty of balancing politics, military power, and liberty may yet prove our undoing.

Notes

1. In the end, according to estimates by journalists, "NATO killed about as many civilians as military personnel." Dana Priest, "France Played Skeptic on Kosovo Attacks," *Washington Post*, 20 September 1999, p. A1.
2. Jean Bethke Elshtain, "Whose Lives Are We Sparing?" *Washington Post*, 16 May 1999, p. B3.
3. Bill Clinton, "Statement by the President," 5 April 1999.
4. Quoted in Tim Weiner and Jane Perlez, "How Clinton Approved the Strikes on Capital," *New York Times*, 4 April 1999, p. 7.
5. Bradley Graham, "Joint Chiefs Doubted Air Strategy," *Washington Post* 5 April 1999, p. A1; Michael Hirsh and John Barry, "How We Stumbled Into War," *Newsweek*, 12 April 1999.
6. Admiral James O. Ellis, "A View from the Top." This undated briefing prepared in the immediate aftermath of Operation Allied Force provides lessons learned from the perspective of the officer commanding both U.S. naval forces in Europe and all NATO forces in Southern Europe.
7. John A. Tirpak, "Short's View of the Air Campaign," *Air Force* 82 (September 1999).
8. Dana Priest, "United NATO Front Was Divided Within," *Washington Post*, 21 September 1999, p. A1.
9. Steven Lee Myers and Eric Schmitt, "War's Conduct Creates Tension Among Chiefs," *New York Times* 30 May 1999, p. A1. Only on June 3 did the president even go through the motions of meeting with the Joint Chiefs as a group—a session widely interpreted as intended to provide political cover to permit Clinton to reverse his prohibition on the use of ground troops.
10. Jason DeParle, "Allies' Progress Remains Unclear as Few Details Are Made Public," *New York Times*, 6 April 1999, p. A10.
11. "Impersonal War On the Adriatic," *New York Times*, 9 April 1999, p. A10.
12. Patricia Cohen, "Ground Wars Make Strange Bedfellows," *New York Times*, 30 May 1999, p. wk5.
13. Interview with Margot Adler, "All Things Considered," National Public Radio, 29 June 1999.
14. The one breach in the Pentagon's policy of anonymity produced not empathy but embarrassment. The American public did become familiar with a specific handful of soldiers in the war zone, namely the three unfortunate G.I.s who were captured in Macedonia and incarcerated in Belgrade. The U.S. Army's

ill-advised decision to shower these soldiers with decorations upon their release provoked loud guffaws and contributed to the impression that the military was engaged in an attempt to manufacture heroes.

15. John Donnelly, "Air War Leader Greeted Coolly by Senators," *Boston Globe*, 2 July 1999, p. A1.
16. John M. Broder, "Laurels Elude President As Public Judges a War," *New York Times*, 22 June 1999, p. A22.
17. Carla Anne Robbins, "To All but Americans Kosovo War Appears A Major U.S. Victory," *Wall Street Journal*, 6 July 1999, p. A1.
18. Carl von Clausewitz, *On War* (Princeton: Princeton University Press, 1976), p. 89.
19. Quoted by Barbara Tuchman, *The American People and Military Power in an Historical Perspective*, Adelphi Papers, 173 (London: Institute for Strategic Studies), p. 6.
20. Gertrude Himmelfarb, *One Nation, Two Cultures* (New York: Alfred A. Knopf: 1999), p. 20.
21. Samuel P. Huntington, *The Clash of Civilizations and the Remaking of World Order* (New York: Simon and Schuster, 1996), pp. 301–308; James Kurth, "The Real Clash," *The National Interest* 37 (fall 1994): 3–15.
22. Bill Clinton, "American Security in a Changing World," Washington, D.C., 8 January 1997.
23. Madeleine K. Albright, "Address to the Milwaukee Business Community," Milwaukee, Wisc., 2 October 1998.
24. "Clinton's Speech on Kosovo: 'We Also Act to Prevent a Wider War,'" *New York Times*, 2 April 1999, p. A11.
25. Bill Clinton, "Remarks by the President to the Council on Foreign Relations," 14 September 1998.
26. Madeleine K. Albright, "Remarks and Q & A Session," Howard University, Washington, D.C., 14 April 1998.
27. Charles A. Beard and Mary R. Beard, *The Rise of American Civilization*, vol. 2 (New York: Macmillan, 1930), pp. 490–95; William Appleman Williams, *The Tragedy of American Diplomacy*, 2d ed., rev. (New York: Dell, 1972), *passim*.
28. Madeleine K. Albright, "Confirmation Hearing," 8 January 1997.
29. Bill Clinton, "Remarks by the President to the Council on Foreign Relations," 14 September 1998.
30. Bill Clinton, "Remarks by the President on Foreign Policy," San Francisco, Calif., 26 February 1999.
31. "Press Briefing by National Security Advisor Sandy Berger," Rio de Janeiro, Brazil, 15 October 1997.
32. Madeleine K. Albright, "Remarks and Q & A Session," Howard University, Washington, D.C., 14 April 1998.

33. Bill Clinton, "Remarks by the President in Foreign Policy Speech," Mayflower Hotel, Washington, D.C., 7 April 1999.
34. Bill Clinton, "American Security in a Changing World," Washington, D.C., 5 August 1996.
35. Bill Clinton, "Remarks by the President to American Society of Newspaper Editors," San Francisco, Calif., 15 April 1999.
36. Deputy Secretary of Defense John J. Hamre, "The Future of the U.S. Military Presence in Europe," Chicago, 4 August 1999.
37. The concept of using military power to "shape the environment" now permeates Pentagon documents. Senior military officers routinely cite it as a priority mission. See, for example, General Henry H. Shelton, "Surviving Peace," Harvard University, 11 December 1997.
38. "Clinton's Speech on Kosovo: 'We Also Act to Prevent a Wider War,'" *New York Times*, 2 April 1999, p. A11.
39. Bill Clinton, "Helping Write 21st Century International Rules," National Defense University, Fort McNair, Washington, D.C., 29 January 1998.
40. Stephanie Gutmann, "Sex and the Soldier," *The New Republic*, 24 February 1997, p. 19.
41. Elizabeth Becker, "Military Goes by the Book, but It's a Novel," *New York Times*, 16 August 1999, p. A15. Emphasis added. The novel is *Once an Eagle* by Anton Myrer.
42. By the year 2000, the U.S. Army at least had seemingly capitulated to the trend toward of individual autonomy, choosing a new recruiting slogan—"An Army of One"—in part because it conveyed the sense that military service offered an attractive avenue for "self-actualization." James Dow, "Ads Now Seek Recruits for 'An Army of One,'" *New York Times*, 10 January 2001, p. A1.
43. Peter D. Feaver and Christopher Gelpi, "A Look at Casualty Aversion," *Washington Post*, 7 November 1999, p. B3.
44. Tom Ricks, "Military Is Becoming More Conservative, Study Says," *Wall Street Journal*, 11 November 1997, p. A20.
45. The Republican Party already views the military as a constituency to which it lays claim. In another sign of the changing civil-military climate, the Republican National Committee now takes out ads in service-oriented newspapers attacking the commander in chief by name for having "damaged our military's readiness and hurt troop morale" and calling on soldiers to vote for the GOP. See the full-page ad entitled "Keeping the Commitment: Republicans Reverse Years of Military Neglect," *Air Force Times*, 13 December 1999, p. 57.
46. In the fiscal year ending in September 1999, the Marine Corps alone of the four services met its recruiting goal without compromising its standards—this despite the fact that the Pentagon is now spending $1.8 billion annually on recruiting. Andrea Stone, "Paying High Price for Preparedness," *USA Today*, 22 October 1999, p. 18A.

7 Revolution Deferred: Kosovo and the Transformation of War

Michael G. Vickers

I

In the decade since the Persian Gulf War, public debate over defense issues in the United States has been sporadic, diffuse, and generally desultory. To the extent that military matters have engaged the attention of citizens, discussion has tended to focus on issues such as the proper uses of force, on allegations of sagging combat readiness, and above all on social issues, especially those relating to gender and sexual orientation.

Among specialists, however, a different debate has occurred, one that has been continuous, narrowly focused, and intense. For a small but influential core of soldiers, defense analysts, and journalists, one issue above all others has dominated the defense agenda throughout the 1990s: the Revolution in Military Affairs (RMA). In the eyes of its adherents, the RMA constitutes the latest in a series of military revolutions—periods of profound change in military affairs that render obsolete existing means for conducting war. Earlier revolutions—for example, the industrialization of warfare in the nineteenth century or the emergence of naval air power and armored warfare between the world wars in the century just concluded—brought to the battlefield new technologies. The RMA promises to do so as well. But a military revolution is not exclusively a technological phenomenon nor does it occur instantaneously. The change entailed by a genuine revolution is also conceptual and social. Over a period of years or decades it transforms warfighting concepts, challenges traditional military organizations and bureaucracies, and generates radically different demands for human and material resources. In its simplest terms, the RMA is the military revolution of the information (and biotech) age, one that entails the adaptation of military institutions to the imperatives, opportunities, and dangers peculiar to that age. This essay explores the connection between the RMA debate and the war in Kosovo.

When the Cold War ended and victory in the Persian Gulf endowed the United States with the mantle of "world's only superpower," Americans found themselves in the possession of a force already exhibiting incipient RMA capabilities—stealth, precision-guided munitions (PGMs), and all-weather imaging satellites, for example. Yet the military establishment that existed in 1991 remained for the most part an artifact of the industrial age, albeit one that was magnificently trained and equipped. With the demise of the Soviet Empire, that force had both accomplished its primary purpose and largely outlived its usefulness. As even the most ardent fans of that force recognized—even General Colin Powell, then serving as the immensely influential chairman of the Joint Chiefs of Staff—the end of the Cold War demanded a "new" military.[1] America's need for military power had by no means diminished, but henceforth that power would respond to a different set of circumstances. The only questions concerned the extent and character of the change required.

In the decade that followed, a succession of high-profile commissions and study groups—beginning with the Bush administration's "Base Force" plan of 1991 and continuing through the Bottom-Up Review, the Commission on Roles and Missions, the National Defense Panel, and the first Quadrennial Defense Review—convened to chart a path toward defense reform. Along the way, each attempted to take the measure of the RMA and to assess its implications for the United States. To take Pentagon claims at face value, the result of this process was to win the military itself over to the imperative of transformation—fundamental institutional change. Senior leaders in each of the services fully embraced the need to transform Cold War–era forces. In documents such as Joint Vision 2010 and Joint Vision 2020, the imperative of "revolutionizing" the armed forces became official doctrine. Well-funded initiatives such as Army XXI—creating ground forces for a "digital battlefield"—seemingly affirmed that transformation was well underway. Indeed, those serving in uniform during the first decade of the post–Cold War era—a time of dizzying change and ceaseless activity producing an extraordinary outburst of interventionism abroad—could be forgiven for concluding that something akin to a revolution had indeed occurred.

The Kosovo war of 1999 offers an opportunity to take stock of defense reform. In that conflict, with only a handful of exceptions, U.S. forces performed to a very high standard. Yet the war against Yugoslavia shows that defense transformation has stalled. Despite a decade's worth of exertions, the process of adapting the U.S. military to the post–Cold War security environment has achieved disappointing results. If anything, the gap between actually existing capabilities and existing or emerging requirements looms larger than it did a decade ago. A decade of talk about an RMA had done remarkably little to bring it to fruition. Although Kosovo showcased some RMA-like capabilities on the part of the United States, the chief lessons of that conflict lie in what it tells us about the institutional impediments to a real transformation of the American military.

II

At one level, Operated Allied Force would seem to affirm that U.S. military dominance remains as great at the end of the 1990s as it was at the beginning of that decade. The United States and its NATO allies prevailed at minimal cost. Although the war was not without its well-publicized miscalculations and missteps—NATO underestimated Serb determination, failed to anticipate certain enemy actions, and committed egregious blunders such as bombing the Chinese embassy—these could be attributed to the fog and friction inherent to war. The fact of the matter is that NATO won and did so quite handily. A related fact of equal significance is that in conducting the war U.S. forces carried the lion's share of the burden and American air power enjoyed a near monopoly on the capabilities that finally delivered victory.

Yet if Operation Allied Force qualifies as a legitimate success, it offers little cause for complacency. Victory in this very small war against a small, backward country without powerful friends willing to act on its behalf was never seriously in doubt. A war pitting the United States and its NATO allies against the rump of Yugoslavia is the equivalent of a preseason scrimmage pitting a top NFL team against a high school squad. However scrappy and determined the high schoolers, the outcome of such a contest is foreordained, whether the NFL team is at the top of its form or merely starting to get in shape.

The security environment that is evolving in the aftermath of the Cold War confronts the United States with three, distinctive requirements, two of them glimpsed, however imperfectly, in Kosovo. The first of these involves maintaining an edge in military capability over potential peer competitors—not necessarily states of equivalent wealth and military capacity (there are none), but those like China that can, in the not too distant future, pose a serious military challenge, much as Japan did in the 1940s. This is the arena of long-term, high-technology competition in areas such as missile defense or maritime and space supremacy. By and large, Kosovo had nothing to do with this requirement.

The second requirement is the need to project superior military forces to critical regions such as Europe, the Persian Gulf, and Northeast Asia. The aim is, of course, chiefly to deter adventures such as Saddam Hussein's invasion of Kuwait in 1990, or Slobodan Milosevic's assaults on the non-Serb components of the disintegrating Yugoslav republic in the ensuing decade. But should deterrence fail—and clearly, throughout the 1990s it often did—the United States must be able to win its wars in a manner peculiar to the new international political environment, at extremely modest cost to itself in terms of military losses, and almost equally limited losses to enemy civilians. Many of these constraints have grown over time: They now seem to include, for example, a regard for the physical environment after the conduct of military operations.

The third requirement stems from the nature of conflict after the Cold War, and above all from the proliferation of ethnic and civil wars, the fraying and even collapse of fragile state structures, and the ready availability of military hardware to all kinds of substate entities. Whether it is called peacekeeping, humanitarian intervention, or (perhaps a more honest term) imperial policing, this function sets its own peculiar operational imperatives for vigilance, safety of both troops and civilians, and duration.

The three kinds of forces suggested by this analysis do not necessarily resemble one another. A space-dominance force, for example, would have little to offer a peacekeeping operation, although satellites might provide some useful support to such a force. The nonlethal munitions required to restrain crowds, or the identification technology useful in keeping track of individuals in an occupied population, might offer little for a mid-intensity conventional operation such as Kosovo. In all three cases, however, military technology, if properly fit into the right kinds of organizations and using the right kinds of operational concepts, should make modern armed forces look quite different from their predecessors of twenty or thirty years ago.

The Kosovo war shows that, despite all of the rhetoric about defense transformation in the 1990s, and despite all of the quasi-imperial experience of the same decade, the United States military lags far behind in developing the capabilities demanded by these requirements. Indeed, there is some danger that the success of the Kosovo war, inelegant though it might be, will impede rather than enhance the momentum for serious military reform.

III

As a measure of U.S. progress in perpetuating the dominance it enjoyed at the end of the Cold War, Kosovo serves, in some respects, as a classic "precursor war"—a conflict hinting at the potential of transformational change, even if it did not manifest that change fully. During Operation Allied Force, that potential was apparent in the performance of a variety of RMA-related systems, chief among them long-range precision strike weapons, advanced reconnaissance platforms, and techniques for conducting information warfare.

Thus, for example, the 49 sorties flown by the B-2 stealth bomber during Operation Allied Force constituted the first ever large-scale effort to mount a long-range, precision-strike offensive from a secure base on American soil.[2] Beginning on the first night of the war, the B-2 smashed Yugoslav command bunkers, radar installations, communications sites, bridges, arms factories, and other heavily defended targets. Continuing a practice first evident during the Persian Gulf War, for the first 58 days of Operation Allied Force only stealth aircraft—B-2s and F-117s—were used over the enemy capital.[3] Although the B-2 flew only 1 percent of all NATO sorties, it accounted for 11 percent of the bombs dropped during the campaign. The aircraft's precision targeting system produced a higher percentage of targets destroyed per target attacked than any other aircraft.[4] According to the campaign's senior air commander, Air Force Lieutenant General Michael Short, the B-2 with its all-weather satellite-guided bombing system was the "greatest technology success story of Operation Allied Force."[5] NATO Supreme Allied Commander General Wesley Clark concurred, testifying that the B-2 was "the key weapons system for continuing to bring pressure to bear on the enemy, and was an absolutely critical ingredient of success."[6]

Operation Allied Force also saw the introduction of several new PGMs, continuing the trend away from traditional "dumb" bombs. During Operation Desert Storm, PGMs had comprised a mere 7 percent of total munitions employed. For the air campaign in Kosovo that figure increased to 35 percent. Since the Gulf War, U.S. reliance on conventional PGMs to attack military and strategic targets has increased by an order of magnitude.[7] In four of the five most recent U.S. power projection operations, PGMs accounted for more than 60 percent of the total ordnance employed. (See Table 7.1.)[8]

During Operation Allied Force, cruise missiles further cemented their role, along with stealth aircraft, as weapons of first resort. U.S. forces used Global Positioning System–guided Tomahawk Land Attack Missiles (TLAMs) to attack nearly half of all government, military, and police headquarters, air defense systems, and electric power grids that were hit throughout the war. When NATO targeted the high rise that housed the Socialist Party headquarters and state-run television in Belgrade, it did so by programming eight TLAMs to strike precise aim points on the sixth floor and roof in order to disable the building's primary fire-sprinkler system. The building burned for three days. Nor were cruise missiles employed only against large fixed facilities. Twenty-six TLAMs, including 10 with sub-munitions, were also used against 18 mobile targets during the conflict. In all, U.S. surface ships and submarines fired 218 Tomahawk cruise missiles against 66 Serb targets. Approximately 181 hit their intended target.[9]

In addition, with the initial combat employment of the Joint Direct Attack Munition (JDAM), the war for Kosovo further accelerated the shift toward all-weather, GPS-guided munitions.[10] The $14,000 JDAM outperformed laser-guided bombs and cruise missiles that are 10 to 70 times more expensive, and became the weapon of choice for the most sensitive targets. For example, B-2-delivered JDAMs took out the Danube River bridges in Novi Sad that had defied laser-guided strikes.[11]

During Operation Allied Force, Unmanned Aerial Vehicles (UAVs) came of age. The near-continuous surveillance of Yugoslav field forces that they provided to NATO included extensive monitoring of the forced evacuation of ethnic Albanians. UAVs probed Serb air defenses, scouted attack and escape routes, identified targets, and performed battle damage assessment. They conducted electronic eavesdropping, served as airborne communica-

TABLE 7.1 Trends in PGM Use

Operation	TLAMs Expended	CALCMs Expended	Short Stand-Off/ Gravity PGMs Expended	Unguided Munitions Dropped	Percent Conventional Precision Strike
Deliberate Force— Bosnia, August–September 1995	13	33	662	318	69
Desert Strike— Iraq, September 1996	31	13	0	0	100
Desert Fox— Iraq, December 1998	330	90	230	250	72
Infinite Reach— Sudan/Afghanistan, August 1998	79	0	0	0	100
Allied Force— Kosovo, March–June 1999	218	111	≈7,700	≈15,000	≈35

SOURCE: Internal CSBA Research based on multiple sources

tions relays, and jammed Yugoslav communications. Had the war lasted a few days longer, the Air Force would have used UAVs mounting laser designators to pick out Yugoslav military targets.[12] The Pentagon even gave consideration to using an armed Israeli UAV to attack Yugoslav air defenses.[13]

Operational Allied Force also witnessed the first combat use of computer-network attack tools by the U.S. military. An information operations (IO) cell reportedly launched attacks against the command and control infrastructure supporting Serb air defenses. Part of the effort involved manufacturing false radar images and signal-intelligence intercepts and inserting them into the Serb air-defense system.[14] Only a small portion of the offensive information-warfare "toolbox" was apparently used, however. According to one senior U.S. commander, "Properly executed, IO could have halved the length of the campaign. . . . All the tools were in place . . . [but] only a few were used."[15]

Complementing these limited information warfare attacks, the United States for the second time in a decade employed specialized warheads to disable a nation's electrical grid. Electronic power distribution munitions containing spools of fine, electrically conductive filaments wreaked havoc on Serbia's electrical power infrastructure, to include both power generating stations and transformer yards. Conductive filaments shorted out high voltage lines and caused five power grids to fail, cutting off electricity to 70 percent of the country.[16]

Submarines played a limited role in Allied Force, but still managed to deliver 25 percent of all cruise missiles launched during the 78-day campaign—a six-fold increase over the 1991 Persian Gulf War.[17] One sub, the USS *Miami*, made history of sorts by conducting Tomahawk launches successively against Iraq in Operation Desert Fox and against Yugoslavia in Operation Allied Force.[18]

Yet if Operation Allied Force affirmed the potential of certain RMA capabilities, it also revealed the extent to which several others were in very short supply. At the time of the war for Kosovo, only nine B-2s had been outfitted to full operational ("Block 30") configuration. During the campaign, the Pentagon's total inventory of critical munitions such as the conventional air-launched cruise missile (CALCM) and the JDAM fell below one hundred. To enable U.S. forces to prosecute their war against Milosevic, the Pentagon found itself obliged to raid munitions stockpiles of commands in other regions of the world.[19] According to Duncan Hunter, chairman of the House Armed Services Committee's Subcommittee on Military Procurement, Kosovo showed that the Pentagon's procurement of PGMs is not keeping up with the growing U.S. appetite for using them.[20]

Finally, with respect to Kosovo as a test case for evaluating U.S. efforts to sustain global military dominance, what did not happen during this eleven-week precursor war is as important, if not more so, than what did occur. In contrast to any future peer competitor worthy of the name, the rump state of Yugoslavia lacked the capability of placing the American homeland at risk. It was unable to challenge U.S. access to forward bases or to outer space. It could not threaten American control of the sea. To state the matter bluntly, the Yugoslavia that managed to hang on for 11 weeks provides at best a weak surrogate for the sort of military power that the United States must be able to defeat and would prefer to overawe.

IV

Casting the war for Kosovo as a surrogate for imperial policing produces conclusions that are more troubling still. Like it or not, the lion's share of responsibility for imperial policing will fall to the service that has traditionally in U.S. history served as a military constabulary—the United States Army. Just as the army in the nineteenth century pacified the West, at the dawn of the last century governed Cuba and the Philippines, and after World War II occupied Germany and Japan, so too the army of the post–Cold War era is fated to assume similar responsibilities. Events in Somalia, Haiti, and Bosnia within the last decade, and in Kosovo itself in the war's aftermath, make that abundantly clear.

Yet the actual war over Kosovo shows how slow the army has been to grasp the full implications of its new/old role. Converting the army of the Cold War into an effective instrument for imperial policing also requires transformation, albeit of a different sort than that required to exploit the RMA. The army's embarrassing contribution to Operation Allied Force shows how far that service lags behind in effecting the necessary change.

The war over Kosovo can be viewed as an episode in imperial policing in this sense: The massive violation of international norms posed by the Yugoslav campaign of ethnic cleansing—a campaign that allied air power failed to check—required a ground presence to provide immediate, effective protection to the afflicted Kosovar Albanian population. That portion of the army agile enough to deploy on short notice to the theater of operations—

traditional light infantry—lacked survivability. Sending the 82d Airborne Division (or for that matter U.S. Marines) to the rescue would have entailed the risk of substantial U.S. casualties. Neither political nor military authorities in Washington were willing to accept that risk. Yet when the Pentagon at the urging of the Supreme Allied Commander Europe attempted to improvise a force with more muscle, the result was a full-fledged fiasco. Task Force Hawk, the army's much ridiculed effort to deploy an attack-helicopter task force to the war zone, fell victim to inadequate technology, poor operational readiness, and a long-standing institutional propensity, in the words of former Chief of Staff General Dennis Reimer, "to go in a little too heavy." The result was a mix of tragedy and farce.

To support and protect a mere 24 AH-64 Apache attack helicopters, the army determined that it was necessary to deploy a grand total of 6,200 troops. To provide this contingent with the wherewithal it required, the army shipped 26,000 tons of equipment to a staging area in Albania. Doing so consumed 550 C-17 sorties and cost $480 million. The cargo included more than a dozen 70-ton M1A1 tanks—too heavy to use on most Albanian roads—42 Bradley fighting vehicles, and 24 Multiple Launch Rocket Systems with extended-range, Army Tactical Missile System missiles. To preside over this arsenal, the army cobbled together a tactical headquarters that itself required the shipment of 20 five-ton Expando vans from Germany. The army also shipped 190 containers of ammunition, and enough repair kits to support twice the number of Apaches actually deployed. Thirty-seven other utility helicopters—Blackhawks and Chinooks—rounded out this mammoth task force.

Fabricating a base from which this force could operate posed further challenges. Transforming the tiny airfield at Rinas, Albania, into an adequate facility required 667,000 square meters of rock fill and 58 specially designed landing pads. Self-deploying the Apaches from their base in Germany alone took 12 days. When they arrived, they were not ready for combat. Sixty-five percent of the pilots had fewer than 500 flying hours under their belts.[21] None were proficient in flying with night-vision goggles.[22] With the Joint Chiefs doubting the wisdom of the operation and the army warning of heavy losses if the Apaches went into combat, it is hardly surprising that the task force assembled over a period of weeks at such great expense never got into the fight. The protection that U.S. forces offered to the hapless victims of ethnic cleansing was limited to receiving the survivors into refugee camps.

V

The limitations of the force with which the U.S. went to war in Kosovo—measured against the requirements of either global power projection or imperial policing—reflect both the lingering legacy of the Cold War and also the outcome of the post–Cold War drawdown. In this as in other respects, Operation Allied Force resembled Operation Desert Storm, the Gulf War of 1991. In both cases, the military's chief reaction to the conflict was a mixture of satisfaction at a predetermined success and irritation at not having had even more of a free hand at using the full-range of capabilities at its disposal. Although the Pentagon throughout the 1990s repeatedly touted its commitment to "revolutionary" change, and although a decade of experience with peacemaking, peacekeeping, and humanitarian intervention has reacquainted American soldiers with the demands of imperial policing, the services have clung whenever possible to the Cold War status quo. At best, the services have pursued a "revolution without pain" that leaves core platforms intact and attempts to preserve familiar organization, procedures, and war-fighting concepts. The army won't relinquish its heavy tanks. The navy won't give up its carriers. And the air force continues to insist that short-range, manned fighters constitute the real essence of air power.

Consistent with this preference for the familiar, the allocation of defense resources emphasized consumption over investment throughout the 1990s. From the peak year of the Reagan buildup (FY 1985) to the war in Kosovo, annual investment spending plummeted from $184 billion to $92.1 billion. In the meantime, funding for operations and support (which includes operations and maintenance, personnel, military construction, and family housing) declined by little more than a fifth, from $252.4 billion to $200.5 billion.[23] Making matters worse, the preponderance of research and development since the end of the Cold War has gone to completing the development of systems devised during (and for) the Cold War or to making incremental improvements to systems already fielded.

For example, the centerpiece of the Pentagon's current investment program is the planned purchase of three new tactical fighters: the Air Force F-22, the Navy F/A-18E/F, and the Joint Strike Fighter. Current plans call for the purchase of 339 F-22s, 548 F/A-18E/Fs, and 2,852 Joint Strike Fighters (1,763 for the Air Force, 480 for the Navy, and 609 for the Marine Corps).

Development and procurement costs for the three aircraft are projected to total a jaw-dropping $340 billion.[24] Other big-ticket purchases include the construction of three new aircraft carriers at a cost of some $18 billion, some 30 Virginia-class attack submarines at nearly $2 billion each, and a fleet of 458 V-22 Osprey tilt-rotor, vertical-takeoff and -landing aircraft at a cost of $35 billion. The army meanwhile plans to replace most of its existing inventory of helicopters with a fleet of 1,213 Comanche helicopters for $35 billion, and to upgrade its arsenal of heavy artillery with 480 Crusader self-propelled howitzers, bigger than the guns they replace and priced at $11 billion. Five separate theater-wide missile defense systems, expected to cost in excess of $40 billion, are also in the works.[25]

As this emphasis on short-range manned aircraft, massive aircraft carriers, and heavy artillery suggests, from both strategic and budgetary perspectives the Pentagon's actual investment plan will go further toward perpetuating the existing force structure than toward transforming it. Even at that, the total cost of the wish list assembled by the services exceeds by $40–50 billion or more *per year* the amount of funding currently projected to be available.[26]

To a remarkable extent, the RMA-relevant systems showcased over Kosovo barely managed to avoid being "crowded out" of 1990s defense budgets in favor of "legacy" modernization. The size of the B-2 fleet, a hotly debated issue since the end of the Cold War, offers a case in point. In 1981 the Reagan administration first established the projected size of the B-2 fleet at 132 aircraft.[27] A month after the fall of the Berlin Wall, Secretary of Defense Richard Cheney ordered a review of four major aircraft programs, among them the B-2. While the review classified the B-2 chiefly as a nuclear-armed bomber, Secretary Cheney also speculated that "the B-2's conventional capabilities will become increasingly important as forward forces decline and the need for rapid-decisive global power projection increases."[28] Still, in April 1990, for fiscal and political reasons, Cheney reduced the planned B-2 buy to 75 aircraft. A little over a year later, the number slipped even further. Influential members of the House of Representatives, led by Rep. Ron Dellums (D-Calif.) and Rep. John Kasich (R-Ohio), capped the B-2 program at a paltry 20 aircraft, despite a plea from President George H. W. Bush.[29]

Politics, not defense requirements, produced the decision to cut the B-2 force to 20.[30] Top military and defense officials at the time and ever since assailed the decision as ham-handed and illogical. According to former Air Combat Command commander General John Loh, "we got to 20 not because it was the right number; we got to 20 because it was the minimum number to provide an operational capability."[31] But such a capability would indeed be no more than minimal.[32]

Operation Desert Storm seemingly demonstrated the requirement for a robust force of stealthy long-range bombers. Yet studies sponsored by the Clinton administration repeatedly reaffirmed the decision to limit the B-2 fleet to 20 (now 21) aircraft. To reach their conclusion, however, these studies relied on unrealistically optimistic assumptions about warning time, American access to forward bases, and the feasibility of swinging forces between theaters. Analyses undertaken beyond the administration's aegis, it should be noted, came to sharply different conclusions. For example, the 1997 Independent Bomber Force Review chaired by former National Security Adviser Brent Scowcroft argued that in the uncertain security environment of the twenty-first century the U.S. requirement for long-range air power will, if anything, increase. The panel recommended congressional funding of at least nine additional B-2s (adding an additional squadron to the two currently in the force structure). It also suggested that Congress create an air-force command responsible for long-range strike operations.[33] The review concluded, "With no funding, no modernization plan, and no evident concern for their absence, the bomber force faces inevitable extinction."[34]

Hostility to the B-2 may well be sharpest within the air force itself. That antagonism, according to the Scowcroft Commission, stems in no small measure from bureaucratic politics. The ascendance of "fighter generals" over "bomber generals" since the 1980s has greatly weakened institutional support for long-range bombers.[35] Thus, whereas in 1950 the ratio of fighters to bombers in the U.S. inventory was 2:1, by 1995 it had grown to 16:1.[36] The ratio of fighter investment to bomber investment is projected to increase by more than an order of magnitude from FY 1998 to FY 2003 (3.5:1 to 37.5:1). Development of a follow-on to the B-2 is not scheduled to begin until 2019, with procurement deferred until 2034.[37]

As with the B-2 bomber, the tale of UAV development by the Department of Defense is one of half-hearted support and squandered opportunity. The United States currently has two promising UAV programs under development: the Global Hawk high-altitude, long-endurance UAV and the Unmanned Combat Air Vehicle. The RQ-4A Global Hawk is to replace the U-2, a manned long-range, high-altitude reconnaissance aircraft now four decades old.[38] Global Hawk is expected to have a range of 14,000 miles and to fly at an altitude of more than 65,000 feet, transmitting images of ground targets via satellite. Global Hawk is currently projected to cost $15.3 million each, far less than a U-2.[39] The spy plane demonstrated its potential in a recent exercise, flying a 28-hour, trans-Atlantic mission and transmitting imagery directly to U.S. forces in the field.[40] The non-stealthy Global Hawk, however, cannot penetrate denied air space. In short, it is susceptible to being shot down. Yet a high-altitude, long-endurance UAV with a stealthy design, the "Tier III," died at the hands of budget cutters early in the Clinton administration.

The only other surviving major UAV initiative is the Unmanned Combat Air Vehicle (UCAV), a stealthy, 26-foot-long, boomerang-shaped craft being developed by Boeing.[41] UCAV will have a range of 1,000 miles, be able to fly 550 miles per hour, and carry up to a dozen 250-pound bombs. It will be controllable either via AWACS aircraft or ground station. At $10 million per plane, it is projected to cost about two-thirds *less* than the Joint Strike Fighter while possessing comparable strike capabilities.[42] Development costs are projected to be orders of magnitude less.[43] Initial fielding of the UCAV is currently projected after 2010.[44]

But if UCAV survives that long the credit will go less to the Pentagon than to the system's congressional promoters. In the year 2000, the chairman of the Senate Armed Services Committee, Senator John Warner, proposed a goal of making one-third of operational deep-strike aircraft unmanned within ten years.[45] Warner has his work cut out for him. As a senior defense official noted, "assimilating new technologies is very difficult for a very structured organization, especially if those technologies are somewhat threatening to the organization."[46] To an air force whose founding identity revolves around manned flight, UAVs and UCAVs pose such a threat.

The submarine offers a third case demonstrating the obstacles impeding defense transformation. In one sense, of course, the sub is an unlikely symbol of revolutionary change: It has formed an essential part of the fleet for decades. Yet if reconfigured to perform new roles, this familiar type of warship offers a readily available means to improve RMA capabilities—especially for long-range attack of land-based targets. One promising idea entails the conversion of four Ohio-class, Trident nuclear ballistic missile submarines (SSBNs)—designed to deliver strategic nuclear weapons—into SSGNs or platforms for delivering conventional munitions. The START II Treaty already requires the United States to reduce its Trident fleet from 18 to 14 boats. When the navy begins decommissioning these submarines beginning in FY 2003, they will each have 20 years of operational life left. Converting the boats to SSGNs would entail retrofitting their 24 ballistic missile launch tubes to accommodate 154 cruise missiles (22 tubes with 7 missiles each) and up to 66 Navy SEALs or other commandos. The net cost of conversion would be between $500 million and $1 billion per boat.[47]

The SSGN would carry more Tomahawks than any other currently existing platform. It would also deliver them far more economically than other platforms. With a total of four SSGNs available, two would be deployed at any given time. The unknown presence of an SSGN might help catch an enemy unawares, and the SSGN's ability to "ripple fire" all 154 missiles in six minutes would have potentially devastating effects. The SSGN would also facilitate large-scale special operations. Having a stealthy platform capable of firing several dozen Tomahawks, according to Clinton administration Secretary of the Navy Richard Danzig, would, in turn, free up attack subs and other assets from the hard-pressed surface fleet for other missions.

Nevertheless, as with the B-2 and UAV, the SSGN faces significant opposition. Within the Navy's surface warfare community, many see it as a threat to the next generation of destroyer, the DD-21. Whether or not the SSGN ever makes the leap from concept to reality stands as another measure of the Pentagon's ability to distance itself from the status quo.

VI

The point is not that building more B-2s instead of new types of short-range fighters, favoring unmanned over manned aircraft, or transforming a handful of SSBNs into SSGNs will alone secure long-term U.S. military dominance. Indeed, as expressions of the RMA, these particular systems represent at best the preliminary outlines of a revolution still very much in the making. Rather, the point is that the shilly-shallying, hesitancy, and niggardliness that have characterized the Pentagon's embrace of even these readily available RMA capabilities testifies to the larger obstacles to genuine defense transformation. If the United States fails to overcome those obstacles, it risks forfeiting to others—powers less wedded to industrial-age conceptions of warfare—advantages that the RMA offers.

Although the dimensions of a fully mature RMA are at present only dimly seen, it holds the promise of capabilities that within a decade or two will make even the most advanced, cutting-edge weaponry of the 1990s seem out of date. Those capabilities include: space-based radar satellites that can track moving ground targets; ground- and air-based radars that can "see through walls"; sophisticated information warfare tools; non-lethal weapons based on directed energy (e.g., high-power microwaves) or biotechnology; advances in miniaturization leading to micro-UAVs and micro-satellites; stealthy, information-intensive ground forces that rely heavily on robotics; and the development of sea-control techniques employing extended-range, anti-ship missiles, stealthy, weaponized UAVs, land-based over-the-horizon radars, and ocean-surveillance satellites. The continued evolution of the RMA and the diffusion of RMA capabilities can no more be averted than could the nuclear arms race following Hiroshima. Barely recognized by most Americans, a competition to exploit the RMA's military potential for political advantage is now well underway.

The record of reform in the 1990s—and, more particularly, the way that the military has chosen to interpret the "lessons" of Kosovo—underscores the reality that it is by no means a foregone conclusion that the United States will prevail in this competition. For the most part, the Pentagon concluded that Operation Allied Force produced few lessons worth noting, certainly none that required any rethinking of service-procurement plans. Victory over Milosevic affirmed the Pentagon's sense of complacency. It reinforced the military's conviction that all would be well if only a post-Clinton presidency would bump up the aggregate level of defense spending, thereby permitting the services to follow through on plans to restock their arsenals with next-generation aircraft carriers and fighter planes.

There is one exception to that statement. Coming out of Kosovo, the United States Army found itself face-to-face with irrelevance and declared that it had "gotten the message." In short order, the army jettisoned its ill-advised Army XXI project—little more than an effort to add a gloss of information technology to a conception of mechanized warfare dating back to the 1930s —and embarked on a new initiative to create lighter, more-mobile forces. This marked a radical change of course for the army. It remains to be seen whether this new initiative will produce forces able to satisfy the full range of high-end power-projection challenges and imperial policing burdens facing the army. Still, this one service at least deserves credit for its willingness to reexamine hitherto sacrosanct assumptions. Absent such willingness, defense transformation will remain a chimera.

Why should Americans care? Do not the easy triumphs of Operations Desert Storm and Allied Force, bookends on the decade of the 1990s, indicate that all is well? One might respond that, in war, smugness sooner or later gets its comeuppance: In 1870, a highly professional French army, armed with a superior rifle and prototypical machine guns, was soundly whipped by a German army that had achieved unprecedented standards of operational excellence; in 1942, American and British pilots were amazed to find themselves pitted against a Japanese air force qualitatively superior to their own; in 1973, cocky Israeli tankers paid a heavy price at the hands of semi-literate Egyptian peasants whom they had crushed with ease only six years earlier. History is replete with such surprises.

In the case of present-day America, the potential outlines of such a surprise are already visible. These include a China investing heavily in weapons aimed at neutralizing American aircraft carriers and surface warships; lesser antagonists looking to weapons of mass destruction or relatively primitive missiles to deter U.S. intervention or intimidate American allies; and guerrillas and terrorists becoming ever more skillful at operating in urban and semi-urban environments. These antagonists understand America's strengths and weaknesses—its impatience, its open if complex decision-making system, its reluctance to suffer or inflict heavy losses. Only the most sanguine temperament would assume that no opponent, or collection of opponents, will figure out ways to bypass America's strengths and capitalize on its weaknesses.

In the end, the impetus for challenging old assumptions about defense may have to come from outside the armed services. Based on a very preliminary reading of events, the administration of President George W. Bush, especially Bush's secretary of defense, Donald Rumsfeld, seems to appreciate that point. Shortly after taking office, the new Bush administration dashed the hopes of military leaders (and many Republican supporters) by announcing that it had no intention of requesting an immediate boost in defense spending. Rumsfeld insisted that before entertaining requests for a possible budget increase he would conduct a comprehensive review of strategic requirements, a review driven from the top rather than cobbled together so as to satisfy the niceties of interservice consensus. This approach offers cause for hope that Rumsfeld is aiming for more than cosmetic change. But the actual conclusions reached by that review, and Rumsfeld's capacity to implement them, remain to be seen. Neither the services nor their allies in Congress and within the defense industrial sector are likely to relinquish their hold on the past without a fight. But if the United States continues to defer the transformation required both for global dominance and imperial policing, it may well find that the war over Kosovo ends up being the last "easy win" it enjoys for some time.

Notes

1. Colin Powell, *My American Journey: An Autobiography* (New York: Random House, 1995), pp. 435–58.
2. The aircraft were refueled in the air twice on the way to Kosovo, and an additional two times on the return leg.
3. Bill Sweetman, "B-2 Is Maturing Into A Fine Spirit," *Jane's International Defense Review*, May 2000. While pilot error appears to have been the principal cause of the F-117 shootdown—the bomb door was reportedly left open between target runs, causing the aircraft's radar cross section to increase substantially—the plane's "first generation" stealth technology, now some twenty years old, is increasingly vulnerable to long-wave, early-warning radars.
4. Frank Wolfe, "Pentagon Report Lauds B-2; Notes Shortfalls," *Defense Daily*, 16 February 2000, p. 6.
5. Paul Richter, "B-2 Drops Its Bad PR In The Air War," *Los Angeles Times*, 8 July 1999, p. 1.
6. Tony Capaccio, "U.S. Won't Order More Northrop B-2s, Stevens Says," *Fort Worth Star-Telegram*, 2 July 1999.
7. On PGM trends and information operations, see Andrew Krepinevich and Robert Martinage, "Transforming Strategic Strike Operations" (Washington, D.C.: Center for Strategic and Budgetary Assessments, 2001).
8. Totals exclude PGMs used in Operations Southern and Northern Watch, which are still ongoing. As of summer 1999, PGMs comprised 86 percent of the weapons used in Northern Watch and 100 percent of those used in Southern Watch.
9. Bryan Bender, "Tomahawk Achieves New Effects In Kosovo," *Jane's Defence Weekly*, 19 July 2000, p. 3.
10. B-2 stealth bombers were the only aircraft configured at the time to drop the new bombs. A total of 656 JDAMs were expended during Allied Force.
11. Patrick Ryan, "The Bargain Basement Bomb," (Long Island) *Newsday*, 14 November 1999, p. 23. JDAM development was spurred by failures during the Persian Gulf War, where sandstorms and smoke from oil fires foiled some laser-guided bomb strikes, and by the desire to reduce costs. JDAMs also permit bomb release from much higher altitudes, enhancing aircraft and pilot survivability. Alas, not all JDAM achievements during the Kosovo war fell on the positive side of the ledger. It was a JDAM that took out the Chinese embassy in downtown Belgrade.
12. David Fulghum, "Kosovo Conflict Spurred New Airborne Technology Use," *Aviation Week & Space Technology*, 23 August 1999, p. 30.
13. Bryan Bender, "Cold War Treaty Could Block Future US Weapons," *Jane's Defence Weekly*, 20 October 1999. The United States refrained from using a

bomb-dropping UAV—the "Harpy" on loan from Israel—because of concerns that doing so might violate the Intermediate Nuclear Forces Treaty with the former Soviet Union. The State Department subsequently determined that weaponized, *reuseable* UAVs are not cruise missiles and, as such, would not violate the treaty.

14. David Fulghum, "Yugoslavia Successfully Attacked by Computers," *Aviation Week & Space Technology*, 23 August 1999, pp. 31, 34. See also David Fulghum, "Telecom Links Provide Cyber-Attack Route," *Aviation Week & Space Technology*, 8 November 1999, p. 81, and Bob Brewin, "Kosovo Ushered in Cyberwar," *Federal Computer Week*, 27 September 1999, p. 1.
15. Andrew Rathmell, "Information Operations—Coming of Age?," *Jane's Intelligence Review*, May 2000, p. 52.
16. See David Fulghum, "Electronic Bombs Darken Belgrade," *Aviation Week & Space Technology*, 10 May 1999, pp. 34–36, and "Russians Analyze U.S. Blackout Bomb," *Aviation Week & Space Technology*, 14 February 2000, p. 59.
17. Andrea Stone, "Request For Subs Could Spark Defense Battle," *USA Today*, 8 March 2000, p. 22A. The 25-percent figure includes British as well as U.S. attack submarines.
18. Richard Newman, "The Navy Weighs A Potent New Weapon," *U.S. News & World Report*, 28 February 2000.
19. Bryan Bender, "US Weapon Shortages Risked Success In Kosovo," *Jane's Defence Weekly*, 6 October 1999. Laser-guided bombs and the AGM-130 television and infrared-guided missile were among the weapons transferred from other commands.
20. Sheila Foote, "Services Reviewing Requirements For Preferred Munitions," *Defense Daily*, 20 October 1999, p. 1.
21. "Army Hunts For Answers As Apaches Fail In Kosovo," *Baltimore Sun*, 16 July 1999.
22. Dana Priest, "Army's Apache Helicopter Rendered Impotent In Kosovo," *The Washington Post*, 29 December 1999, p. 1. During the three weeks of training with night-vision goggles to prepare for operations in mountainous terrain, accidents killed two Apache pilots.
23. Steven M. Kosiak, *Analysis of the FY 2001 Defense Budget* (Washington, D.C: Center for Strategic and Budgetary Assessments, February 2000), Appendix: Table 4. All figures are in FY 2001 dollars.
24. Steven M. Kosiak, *Options for U.S. Fighter Modernization* (Washington, D.C: Center for Strategic and Budgetary Assessments, September 1999), p. 4.
25. Cost estimates are derived from DoD Selected Acquisition Reports and other sources. Theater-wide missile-defense programs include a Patriot upgrade (PAC 3), Navy Area Defense, Navy Theater-Wide, Theater High Altitude Air Defense (THAAD), and the Airborne Laser.

26. For additional details, see Michael G. Vickers and Steven M. Kosiak, *The Quadrennial Defense Review: An Assessment* (Washington, D.C.: Center for Strategic and Budgetary Assessments, December 1997).
27. President Ronald Reagan, Remarks and a Question-and-Answer Session with Reporters on the Announcement of the United States Strategic Weapons Program, 2 October 1981, in *Public Papers of the Presidents: The Administration of Ronald Reagan, 1981* (Washington, D.C.: U.S. Government Printing Office, 1982), p. 879.
28. Richard Cheney, in House Armed Services Committee, Hearings, *National Defense Authorization Act for Fiscal Year 1991—H.R. 4739*, HASC No. 101-45, 101st Cong., 2nd sess., p. 790.
29. President George Bush, Address to the American Defense Preparedness Association, 9 July 1991.
30. A test-flight vehicle was later upgraded by the Clinton administration, bringing total force size to 21 aircraft—16 in operational units and 5 for attrition reserve and training.
31. General John Loh in House National Security Committee Hearings, *National Defense Authorization Act for Fiscal Year 1996—S.1124 (H.R. 1530)*, HNSC No. 104-4, p. 1219. The House Armed Services Committee had originally tried to cap the B-2 fleet at 15 aircraft, which would have yielded just one squadron of no more than 11 combat-ready aircraft—enough, according to General Loh, for a limited operation like the 1986 raid against Libya, but little else.
32. Secretary of the Air Force Donald Rice in House Armed Services Committee Hearings, *National Defense Authorization Act for Fiscal Year 1993*, HASC 102-41, p. 235.
33. *Scowcroft Independent Bomber Force Review*, p. 17, reproduced in *Congressional Record—House*, 23 June 1997.
34. Ibid., p. 3.
35. A 1995 survey of 283 serving air-force generals revealed that nearly 60 percent had some background in tactical aviation, while a little more than 10 percent had an association with the bomber force. Among the 10 four-star generals, none had a bomber background, while 9 had experience in tactical aviation. Cited in Andrew Krepinevich, *The Air Force of 2016* (Washington, D.C.: Center for Strategic and Budgetary Assessments, 1996), p. 19.
36. Barry Watts, "The Air Force in the Twenty-First Century," in *The Emerging Strategic Environment*, ed. Williamson Murray (Westport, Conn.: Praeger, 1999), pp. 183–217.
37. U.S. Air Force, "Air Force White Paper on Long-Range Bombers," 1 March 1999, p. 10.
38. Among the payloads the Global Hawk will carry is an advanced synthetic-aperture radar system, capable of 1-ft. resolution. A Global Hawk flying over

Philadelphia will be able to take targetable images of the Pentagon. Global Hawk's radar will also have a ground moving-target indicator capability. See David Fulghum, "UAV To Carry U-2 Recce Unit," *Aviation Week & Space Technology*, 15 May 2000, pp. 28–30.

39. Christian Lowe, "Global Hawk Costs Soaring," *Defense Week*, May 1, 2000, p. 6.
40. Timothy Gaffney, "Pilotless Spy Plane, Crosses Ocean," *Dayton Daily News*, 18 May 2000, p. 1E.
41. The UCAV has been unofficially dubbed the "Uncounted Air Vehicle." Air-force officials are wrestling with ways of forming two UCAV squadrons without having them count against the service's authorized limit of 20 fighter wings.
42. Dave Moniz, "Air Force's Pilotless Bombers To Be Tested Next Year," *USA Today*, 21 August 2000, p. 8A.
43. The UCAV is currently a $110-million technology-development program. Cost savings would also accrue from operations. The air force currently spends about $2 million for initial training of each pilot, and about $1 billion a year to keep 2,000 F-16 pilots trained and ready for their job. See Paul Richter, "Pilotless Plane Pushes Envelope For U.S. Defense," *Los Angeles Times*, 14 May 2000, p. 1.
44. Boeing, the prime contractor, estimates that engineering and manufacturing development would take six years and would involve eight flight-test vehicles. Production of 202 UCAVs (enough for nine squadrons) could begin as early as 2013. At any given time, 80 percent of the UCAVs would be in storage, with the other 20 percent undergoing maintenance or training. Mark Hewish, "Coming Soon: Attack of the Killer UAVs, *Jane's International Defense Review*, September 1999, p. 36.
45. "Warner: Speed Development of Unmanned Combat Systems," *Defense Daily*, 9 February 2000, p. 1. The air force is conducting experiments to adapt Predator as a weapons carrier—in part, it seems, to head off congressional pressure for more spending on UCAVs. "Air Force Plans Demonstration Of Predator's Ability To Drop Bombs," *Inside the Air Force*, 26 May 2000, p. 1.
46. Christian Lowe, "Pentagon Drafting Master Plan For UAVs," *Defense Week*, 17 July 2000, p. 1.
47. Rick Newman, "Navy Sizes Up Tomahawk Tridents," *Defense Week*, 28 February 2000, p. 1.

Index

Abdullahi, Khalifa, 100
abundance, strategy of, 163
AC-130U gunships, 18
Afghanistan, 112, 117; British and, 108–109; Russia and, 107
Ahtisaari, Martti, 19, 20
aircraft: B-2 stealth bomber, 8, 193, 196, 200–201; B-52 bomber, 18; bombers versus fighters, 201; under development, 201–202; F-22 stealth fighter, 119; F-117 stealth fighter, 8, 193; F/A-18E/F fighter, 8, 193; Joint Strike Fighter, 199; RQ-4A Global Hawk, 201–202; Tier III, 202; U-2, 201; *see also* helicopters
aircraft carriers, 200
Air Force, U.S., 53
Air-Land Battle Doctrine, 88
air-to-air missiles, 8
air warfare, 82–83; ascendance of, 53–54; civilian populations and, 83; controlling rogue states with, 85; drawbacks of, 55; future of, 87; against guerillas, 87; Kosovo war and, 83, 84–87; as paradigm for 21st century, 98; traditional use of, 53
Albright, Madeleine, 8, 28, 61, 68, 125, 126, 147, 176
anarchy, "ordered," 105
Annan, Kofi, 138
antiaircraft artillery, 14
Apache helicopters, 143, 146; deployment of, 198
armed forces, U.S. *See* military, U.S.
Army, U.S., 16; policing role of, 197
Army of Northern Virginia, 39
Army of the Potomac, 39
Army Tactical Missile System, 198
Army XXI project, 190, 204
Arnold, Gen. Henry H. ("Hap"), 41
Arutiunov, Sergei, 105
Aspin, Les, 173

assassination. *See* heads of state, assassination of
Athens, 147

B-2 stealth bomber, 7–8, 193, 196; debate about, 200–201
B-52 bomber, 18
Balkans: Balkan Wars, 73–74; crisis of 1914, 47; Europe, Middle East and, 74; as NATO test, 76–78
Baltic states, 80
"Base Force" plan, 190
Beard, Charles, 176
Becevich, Andrew, 119
Beirut, 99, 170; *see also* Lebanon
Belgrade, bombing of, 12
Berger, Samuel R. ("Sandy"), 9
Blackhawk helicopters, 198
Blair, Tony, 12, 134
Bogart, Humphrey, 99
Bolshevism, 163
bombs: cluster, 12 (*see also* Joint Standoff Weapon); laser-guided, 8; satellite-guided, 8; *see also* precision-guided munitions
borders, elimination of, 69
Bosnia intervention, 126, 128–129, 131; exit strategy from, 49; NATO's role in, 77
Bottoms-Up Review, 190
Bradley fighting vehicles, 198
Bragg, Gen. Braxton, 38
Britain, 134; Afghanistan and, 108–109
Broz, Josip. *See* Tito, Marshal
Buchanan, Patrick, 159
Bulgaria, Russia and, 89
Bunting, Josiah, 40
Burnside, Gen. Ambrose, 39
Burundi, massacre of Hutus in, 80, 81
Bush, George H. W., 45, 49, 148, 200
Bush, George W., 143, 205
Butterfield, Herbert, 150

CALCMs. *See* Conventional Air-Launched Cruise Missiles
Carpenter, Ted Galen, 159
Casablanca (film), 99
casualty avoidance, 12, 59, 118, 148–149, 155; air warfare and, 54; erosion of war objectives and, 144; ground forces and, 82, 148; liberal democracies and, 85–86, 142; as measure of success, 178; perversity of, 184; public opinion and, 142–144; reasons for, 55–56
CBS-TV, 13
Chancellorsville, battle of, 42
Chechnya, 72, 80, 99, 102, 110–111; bombing of Grozny, 91; lessons of, 113; Russian failure in, 114–115; society of, 105–106; urban warfare in, 111, 112
Cheney, Richard, 200
Chernomyrdin, Vladimir, 16, 19, 20
China, 108; embassy bombing and, 92; Korean War and, 88; Kosovo war and, 135; liberal globalism and, 71–72; reaction to Kosovo war by, 9, 92
Chinese embassy, bombing of, 19, 53, 92, 132, 191
Chinook helicopters, 198
Chirac, Jacques, 12, 20
Chuenpi, second battle of, 100
Chuikov, Marshal Vasily, 114
CINCPAC. *See* Pacific Command, commander in chief of the
CINCs. *See* commanders in chief
CINCSOUTH. *See* Southern Command, commander in chief of

cities, growth of, 111
civilian casualties. *See* collateral damage
civil-military compact. *See* civil-military relations
civil-military relations, 56–58; after Vietnam, 168–169; after World War II, 164–175; Bill Clinton and, 171–175; changing of, 58–59; crisis over Vietnam and, 166–167; flaws in new model of, 183; popular indifference to, 185; principles of, 44–45; prior to World War II, 162–164; public opinion and, 179; purposes of changes in, 179; Ronald Reagan and, 170; technology and, 180; weakening military role in, 179–180
civil rights, World War II and, 164
Civil War (U.S.), 38–39
clans, 106–107
Clark, Gen. Wesley K. (Supreme Allied Commander Europe [SACEUR]), 3–5, 9, 19, 193–194, 198; collateral damage and, 15; early retirement of, 159–160; escalation rationale of, 17; General Short and, 28–29; role in Kosovo war of, 57
Clausewitz, Carl von, 43, 49, 149–150; "trinity" and Persian Gulf war, 171; "trinity" of armed conflict, 161, 185
Clinton, William J., 13, 125, 131, 160, 176; approval of targets and, 12; characteristics of presidency of, 174; as commander in chief, 173–174; escalation of war and, 10; ground troops and, 8; liberal globalism and, 68; military tradition and, 179; political skills of, 171; public statements on Kosovo, 19, 46–47, 49–50, 155
cluster bombs. *See* bombs, cluster
coalitions: political legitimacy and, 51–52
Cohen, Eliot A., 160
Cohen, William, 8, 11, 28
Cold Harbor, battle of, 39
Cold War, 60, 61, 65, 73, 82, 170, 173; aftermath of, 134; coalitions and, 52; rationale for U.S. conflict during, 80–81; U.S. grand strategy during, 64, 66
collateral damage, 19, 22, 142, 146; concerns about, 4–5, 7, 11, 12, 14–15, 24, 28
Combat Air Vehicle, Unmanned, 201
Commanche helicopters, 200
commanders in chief (CINCs), 56; Chairman of the Joint Chiefs of Staff and, 59; rise in power of, 58
Comprehensive Ban Treaty, 148
computer-network attack tools, 196
Congreve rockets, 100
conscription, 163, 166; end of, 167; peacetime, 164–165
Contact Group, 1, 2
Conventional Air-Launched Cruise Missiles (CALCMs), 8, 21, 196
Coolidge, Calvin, 160
Crimean War, 118
Croatia, 131
cruise missiles, 8, 21–22, 194, 196, 203
Crusader self-propelled howitzers, 200
Cuba: Kosovo war and, 135; sanctions on, 148
cultural revolution, 168; Ronald Reagan and, 173
Czech Republic, 75

Danube River bridges, 194
Danzig, Richard, 203
Defense, Secretary of, 56
Defense, U.S. Dept. of, 6
Defense Panel, National, 190
defense reforms, 190–191; impediments to, 199, 203; Kosovo war and, 191, 193; need for, 189; post-Cold War U.S. security requirements and, 192
Defense Review, Quadrennial, 190
defense spending, 163, 165–166; investment and consumption, 199–200; review of strategic requirements, 205; under Ronald Reagan, 170; wish list versus available funds for, 200
Dellums, Ron, 200
Democracy, Assistant Secretary of State for, 125–126
democracy, promoting. *See* Wilsonianism
diplomacy, 118; military power as, 179–180
Djakovica-Decane incident, 15, 16
Doolittle, James ("Jimmy"), 41
draft, military. *See* conscription
"dumb" munitions, 53–54

Eastern Orthodox countries, opposition to liberal globalism of, 71
Eisenhower, Dwight D., 165–166
electronic power distribution munitions, 196
Ellis, Adm. James O., 156
Emancipation Proclamation, 38
end state. *See* exit strategy
English language, 52
escalation: Bill Clinton and, 10; General Clark and, 17; gradual, 156
ethnic cleansing, 2, 8–9, 11, 73, 197; inability to prevent, 120; Kosovo war and, 139, 149, 198; reverse, 84
European Command, commander in chief of (CINCEUCOM). *See* Clark, Gen. Wesley K.
European Union, 19
exit strategy, 44, 48–49, 117

F-22 stealth fighters, 199
F-117 stealth fighters, 8, 193
F/A-18E/F fighters, 199
Fallaci, Oriana, 50
Farah Aidid, Mohammed, 105, 110, 126, 173
Farah Aidid, Muhammed, 54
fascism, 163
Flexible Anvil "Limited Air Response," 1–2
Fogelman, Gen. Ronald, 119
foreign policy, U.S.: Clinton and, 174–175; debates in U.S. about, 151; openness, 67, 68, 175–177
Forward Maritime Strategy, 88
France, strategic interests of, 135
Franz Ferdinand, Archduke, 73
Fredericksburg, battle of, 39
free trade. *See* trade, free
French Foreign Legion, 118

GATT. *See* General Agreement on Tariffs and Trade
gays in the military, 172, 173
General Agreement on Tariffs and Trade (GATT), 65
Germany, strategic interests of, 135
Ghaddafi, Muammar, 146
Gitlin, Todd, 159

global economy, 66–67, 69, 70
globalization, 134, 175; democracy and, 176; dominance through, 183; forces against, 177; military power and, 177, 179; U.S. influence and, 176–177
Global Positioning System, 53, 194
Goldwater-Nichols Department of Defense reorganization act, 56–58
Gonzales (destroyer), 158
grand strategy, U.S.: in 21st century, 65–70; the Balkans and, 73–74; compared to 19th century Britain, 85; dominance through globalization, 183; history of, 64–65; Kosovo war and, 93; military strategy in, 69–70; opposition to, 70–72; post-Cold War, 175–177; redefinition in 1990s of, 171; retaliation as part of, 70; transformation of, 66–69
Grant, Ulysses S., 39, 41
Great Depression, 163
great schism, 71
ground combat, 3, 8, 82, 139, 143, 155, 197; advances in, 55; deployment of troops for, 198
Group of Eight, 20
Grozny. *See* Chechnya
Guatemala, 132
guerilla warfare, 73
Gurkhas, British, 118

Haiti intervention, 47, 126, 127
Hamburger Hill (Vietnam War battle), 55
Hamre, John, 17
HARMs. *See* high-speed antiradiation missiles
Harper's Ferry, 38
Havel, Vaclav, 68–69
Hayden, Tom, 159
heads of state, assassination of, 145–146
helicopters, U.S. Army, 19, 55; *see also* Apache helicopters; Blackhawk helicopters; Chinook helicopters
Herat, 112
high-speed antiradiation missiles (HARMs), 8, 22
Himmelfarb, Gertrude, 168
History of the Peloponnesian War (Thucydides), 147
Hobbes, Thomas, 48
Hodge, Carl Cavanagh, 149
Holbrooke, Richard, 2, 3, 28
humanitarian intervention, 68–69, 81–82, 126, 127–128; arguments against, 151–152; concensus for, 138; future of, 83, 150–152; grounds for, 136–137; history of, 133–136; Kosovo war and, 79–83, 128–129; weaker nations and, 135–136; *see also* Bosnia; Haiti; Somalia
human rights, 68, 70; violations of, 1; *see also* individual rights; universal rights
Hungary, 75
Hunter, Duncan, 196–197
Huntington, Samuel, 71, 72
Hussein, Saddam, 28, 44, 54, 146, 180–181
Hyacinth, HMS, 99

IHAS. *See* Integrated Helmet Assembly Subsystem
IMF. *See* International Monetary Fund
Inchon, 88
Independent Bomber Force Review, 201
India: liberal globalism and, 71–72

individual rights, 68
Indonesia, 81
information economy, 66–67
information revolution, 175–176
Integrated Helmet Assembly Subsystem (IHAS), 114
"Interim Agreement for Peace and Self-Government in Kosovo," 78; *see also* Rambouillet Conference
International Criminal Court, 148
International Criminal Tribunal for the Former Yugoslavia, 19
International Monetary Fund (IMF), 64–65, 70
Internet, 15
Ipi, Fakir of, 109
Iran, 74
Iraq, 74, 81; continued bombing of, 180–181; Kurds in, 80; massacres in, 81
Iraq News Agency, 181
Ireland, British and, 106–107
Isandlwana, 99
Islamic countries, opposition to liberal globalism of, 71
Israel, 74; invasion of Lebanon, 111
ius ad bellum, 129; *see also* Kosovo war, moral rightness of
ius in bello, 129; elements of, 141

Jackson, Jesse, 19
Jackson, Thomas J. ("Stonewall"), 41
Jacobite revolt, 106
JDAM. *See* Joint Direct Attack Munition
Johnson, Lyndon, 45, 166
Joint Advanced Concept Technology Demonstration, 113
Joint Chiefs of Staff, 16, 56, 57, 157
Joint Direct Attack Munition (JDAM), 21, 194, 196
Joint Standoff Weapon, 21
Joint Strike Fighter, 199
Joint Vision 2010, 190
Joint Vision 2020, 190
journalists, restrictions on, 158
Jovanovic, Zivadin, 15
Jumper, Gen. John, 3, 13
"just war theory," 129–130

Kagan, Robert, 147
Kandahar, 112
Karachi, ethnic violence in, 112
Kasich, John, 200
Keegan, John, 19, 98
Keynesianism, military, 163, 170
Khelat, Khan of, 108–109
King, Adm. Ernest, 41
Kissinger, Henry, 50
KLA. *See* Kosovo Liberation Army
Korean War, 111, 165; U.S. strategy in, 86, 88
Kosovar Albanians, 14, 47, 80, 197; attacks on Serbs by, 139; ethnic cleansing of, 2; Milosevic's policies and, 130–131; violence against, 1, 2
Kosovo, refugees from, 131
Kosovo Liberation Army (KLA), 11, 17, 18, 104, 120, 131, 132, 140; counteroffensive of, 19; disarming of, 137
Kosovo war, 142; actual American purposes of, 48; aftermath of, 140; air power and, 63; alternate scenerio of, 148–150; alternatives to surrender in, 103; arguments against, 132–133; Chinese reaction to, 92; conduct versus results of, 143–147; defense reforms and, 191, 193; ethnic cleansing and, 139, 149, 198; failures of, 104; as first

humanitarian war, 69, 128–129; as last resort, 140–141; lawful authority for, 130, 136–138; lessons of, 119–120; moral rightness of, 128–136, 141–147, 145; NATO justification for, 129–132, 137–138; objectives of, 139; place in history of, 151; as precedent for Russian military action, 91; restriction on journalists during, 158; results of, 50; Russian reaction to, 89; stated objectives of, 46, 49–50, 156; strategic context of, 124–125; traditional war and, 45–46; UN consensus for, 136; uniqueness of, 93; U.S. grand strategy and, 63–64; U.S. rationale for, 76–78; U.S. role in, 57; *see also* Operation Allied Force
Kostunica, Vojislav, 140
Kristol, William, 147
Kuan T'ien-p'ei, Adm., 99
Kukayev, Valery, 112
Kurds, Turkey and, 132

Lazarevic, Maj. Gen. Vladimir, 19
Lebanon, 104; *see also* Beirut
Lee, Robert E., 39, 41, 42
Leviathan (Hobbes), 48
Lewis, I.M., 105
liberal globalism, 68, 70–72; *see also* grand strategy, U.S.
Libya, 117
Liebling, A. J., 158
Lincoln, Abraham, 38–39
Loh, Gen. John, 200–201
Lott, Trent, 159

M1A1 tanks, 198
MacArthur, Gen. Douglas, 42, 88, 165
Macedonia, 47
Marine Corps, U.S., 41
market principles, 173
Marshall, Gen. George C., 162, 164, 184
Maskhadov, Gen. Aslan, 110
massacres, state-organized, 73, 80–81; after Cold War, 81; during Cold War, 80–81; *see also* ethnic cleansing
McCain, John, 9–10, 143
McNair, Lt. Gen. Leslie, 39–40
MEAT. *See* Munitions Effectiveness Assessment Team
"Mental Agility Theory," 115
Metz, Stephen, 111
military, U.S.: changes in tradition of, 157; civilian wariness of, 162; Clinton legacy on, 182–183; dissatisfaction among, 156; embarrassments in, 183; gays and, 172, 173; military culture, erosion of, 183–184; as police force, 178; politics and, 184–185; post-Vietnam reforms of, 169; role of today's soldiers in, 177–178; women in, 183, 185
military budget. *See* defense spending
Military Policy of the United States, The (Upton), 45
military power: globalization and, 177, 179; as instrument of diplomacy, 179–180; as shaper of international environments, 178
Military Procurement, Subcommittee on, 196–197
Milosevic, Slobodan, 2, 3, 9, 25, 28, 46, 54, 79, 130–131, 141, 143, 144; attacks on interests of, 17; indictment of, 19; NATO victory and, 102; as potential target, 145;

Milosevic, Slobodan (*Continued*)
Russia and, 20; Serb protests against, 17; strategy of, 13–16
missiles: air-to-air, 8; Army Tactical Missile System, 198; Conventional Air-Launched Cruise (CALCMs), 8, 21, 196; cruise, 196; high-speed antiradiation (HARMs), 8, 22; mobile SA-6 (SAM), 14, 22; SA-2/3, 22; Tomahawk cruise, 8, 21–22, 194, 203; Tomahawk Land Attack Missiles (TLAMs), 194
mobile SA-6 missile (SAM), 14, 22
Mogadishu. *See* Somalia intervention
Monroe Doctrine, 64
Montenegro, targets in, 4, 12
morality. *See* Kosovo war, moral rightness of
Moskos, Charles, 183
Mujahedin, 112
multiculturalism, 67, 68
Multiple Launch Rocket Systems, 198
munitions: amount used in Kosovo, 20; *see also* precision-guided munitions (PGMs)
Munitions Effectiveness Assessment Team (MEAT), 25
Murphy, Vice Adm. Daniel J., 5, 15
Muslims, in Russia and Serbia, 90

NAC. *See* North Atlantic Council
NAFTA. *See* North Atlantic Free Trade Agreement
Nagy, Imre, 145
national security policy, U.S., evolution of, 160
nation-state, weakening of, 67–68
Native American tribes, U.S. and, 107
NATO, 1, 2, 47, 48, 52, 57, 64, 131, 134, 135, 139, 141, 156; 50th Anniversary Washington Summit of, 16, 75, 76, 84; approval of targets by, 11–12; enlargement of area of jurisdiction of, 83; future Balkan scenerios and, 120; ground operations and, 15–16; lack of political consensus among, 4; OPLAN 10601, 3; peacekeeping forces of, 20; Russia and, 20; United Nations and, 133; U.S.-desired changes in, 74–76, 77; *see also* Kosovo war, NATO justification for
Nemesis, HMS, 100
New Deal, 163
Newshour, 8
New York Times, 158, 181, 184, 185
Niebuhr, Reinhold, 150
Nimble Lion, 3, 4
Nixon, Richard M., 167
North Atlantic Council (NAC), 2, 10, 16–17
North Atlantic Free Trade Agreement (NAFTA), 177
North Atlantic Treaty Organization. *See* NATO
Novi Sad, 194
nuclear deterrence, 69–70
nuclear weapons. *See* weaponry, nuclear

Oakley, Robert, 103
OAS. *See* Organization of American States
offensive tactics, 41
Omdurman (battle), 100
On War (Clausewitz), 161
open society, 67, 68, 70, 175–177
Operation Allied Force, 2, 191; aircraft used in, 7–8, 16, 18; air sorties in, 21, 22; army's role in, 197; changes in tactics in, 3; civilian casualties in, 15, 22; compared to Persian

Gulf War, 199; conclusion of, 21–26; constraints on targets in, 24; damage assessment in, 23 table, 24–26; evaluation of, 26–29, 138–147; expansion of targets in, 16–17; failures of, 28–29; four "Ds," 6; initial target groups in, 6; Kosovo Liberation Army and, 19; lack of allied consensus in, 84; maintaining the coalition during, 51; Pentagon's conclusions about, 204; Phase 1, 7–10; Phase 2, 10–12; Phase 2a, 12–13; Phase 3, 16–20; planning for, 3–7; political considerations of, 5; reporting of, 158; requirements for, 4; Serbian casualties in, 100; statistics on, 21–26; targets of, 17, 22; technology use in, 193–197; weaponry in, 21–22, 193–198; weather and, 12, 15; *see also* Kosovo war
Operation Deliberate Force, 14
Operation Desert Fox, 180
Operation Desert Storm. *See* Persian Gulf War
Operation Horseshoe, 2, 11, 14, 54; *see also* ethnic cleansing
Operation Matrix, 17
Operation Restore Hope. *See* Somalia intervention
Opium War, First, 99–100, 101–102, 108
Organization of American States (OAS), 64
OSCE. *See* Security and Cooperation in Europe, Organization for

Pacific Command, commander in chief of the (CINCPAC), 58
Palestine Liberation Organization (PLO), 111
Panama, U.S. invasion of, 47
Patten, Gen. George S., 40
peacekeeping. *See* NATO, peacekeeping forces; policing, "imperial"
Pentagon, 198
Periclean Era, 147
Perry, William, 49
Pershing, John J., 41
Persian Gulf War, 5, 21, 28, 40, 45, 53, 88, 119, 133, 142, 161, 201; Clausewitzian trinity and, 171; precision-guided munitions in, 194; stated objectives of, 44; U.S. strategy and, 86
PGMs. *See* precision-guided munitions
"Phased Air Campaign," 1
PLO. *See* Palestine Liberation Organization
Poland, 75
policing, "imperial," 192, 197–199, 204; requirements for, 117
postmodern society, 66–67, 68
Powell, Colin, 40, 53, 57, 59, 88, 170
power, exercise of, 48
precision-guided munitions (PGMs), 8, 12, 21, 53–54, 100, 120, 180, 190; comparative use of, 195 table; in Persian Gulf War, 194; shortage of, 197
prisoners, U.S. Army, 19
Project for the New American Century, 147
Protestants, liberal globalism and, 71
public opinion, 146–147, 55, 98, 143–144, 160; apathy of, 159; Vietnam War and, 167; World War II and, 164
punishment, collective, 117

Pusan Perimeter, 88
Putin, Vladimir, 90
Pyle, Ernie, 158

Racek massacre, 2
Ralston, Gen. Joseph, 27
Rambouillet Conference, 2, 50, 78, 79, 137, 139; "Interim Agreement for Peace and Self-Government in Kosovo," 78; "Status of Multi-National Military Implementation Force," 78
Reagan, Ronald, 169–171; civil-military relations and, 170; cultural revolution and, 173; defense spending and, 170
realist internationalism, 82
Rees, David, 111
refugees, Kosovar, 131
Revolution, American, 41
Revolution in Military Affairs (RMA): impediments to, 199, 203; need for, 189–190; submarines in, 202–203
Rieff, David, 159
risk, aversion to, 84
RMA. *See* Revolution in Military Affairs
Robertson, George, 10, 26
Roles and Missions, Commission on, 190
Rolling Thunder campaign, 157
Roman Catholics, liberal globalism and, 71
Roosevelt, Franklin D., 68, 164
Roosevelt, Theodore, 150
RQ-4A Global Hawk (aircraft), 201–202
Rumsfeld, Donald, 205
Russia: Afghanistan and, 107; Chechnya invasion and, 110; collapse of Soviet Union, 134; Kosovo war and, 135; opposition to liberal globalism by, 71; reaction to Kosovo war by, 9, 89–91; Serbia and, 89–90; strategic position of, 125; support for Serbs and, 16; the West and, 90–91
Russo-Turkish war, 89
Rwanda, 46, 127; massacre of Tutsis in, 81

SA-2/3 (missile), 22
SACEUR. *See* Clark, Gen. Wesley K.
SAM. *See* mobile SA-6 missile
sanctions, as foreign policy, 126
San-yuan-li incident, 101–102
Schmitt, Maj. John, 115
Schultz, George, 44
Schwarzkopf, Gen. Norman, 57, 59
Scotland, British and, 106
Security and Cooperation in Europe, Organization for (OSCE), 70
Security Council, United Nations, 1, 136; opposition to war in, 92; resolution 1199 (UNSCR 1199), 1
Senate Armed Services Committee, 160
septs. *See* clans
Serbia, Russia and, 89
Serbs: Austrian-Hungarian ultimatum to, 78–79; Kosovar Albanians and, 130–131 (*see also* ethnic cleansing); tactics of, 13; violence against, 139
73 Easting (Persian Gulf War engagement), 55
Shalikashvili, Gen. John, 49
SHAPE, 16
Shea, Jamie, 18
Shelton, Gen. Henry H., 6, 8, 11, 57; reticence of, 157

Sherman, Gen. William Tecumseh, 40
Short, Lt. Gen. Michael C., 18, 156, 193; disagreement with Clark and, 4–5, 10–11, 28–29; NATO strategy criticized by, 27; rules of engagement revised by, 17; strategy of, 14
Slovenia, 131
"smart" weapons. *See* precision-guided munitions
Smith, Adm. Leighton ("Snuffy"), 58
Snowcroft, Brent, 201
Snowcroft Commission. *See* Independent Bomber Force Review
Solana, Janvier, 2, 3, 9, 12, 15, 17, 28, 60
Somalia intervention, 46, 47, 54, 99, 110, 111, 126–127, 142; intelligence lacking in, 103–104; lessons learned from, 113, 173; local society and, 105; planned exit strategy in, 49; urban warfare in, 112–113, 114
Southern Command, commander in chief of (CINCSOUTH), 58
sovereignty, state, 78–79, 147–148; diminishing of, 67–68; moral obligations and, 134; U.S. loss of, 151–152
space satellites, 192
Spanish-American War, 76
SSGNs (non-nuclear submarines), 202–203
Stalin, Joseph, 73
Stalingrad, 112
START II Treaty, 202
State, Dept. of (U.S.), 74, 125–126
state sovereignty. *See* sovereignty, state
Stimson, Henry L., 162
Stoddard, William, 39
"Strategic Concept, The," 75–76; 1999 update of, 84
Strategic Studies, International Institute for, 26
submarines, 196, 202–203; Virginia-class attack, 200
Sudan, 117; Christians in, 80; massacres in, 81
Sujah-ul-Mulk, Shah, 108
Summers, Col. Harry, 19, 42
Supreme Allied Commander Europe (SACEUR). *See* Clark, Gen. Wesley K.
Supreme Headquarters Allied Powers Europe. *See* SHAPE
Syria, 82

Tailhook convention, 183
"Taiping" rebellion, 101–102
Taiwan, 92
Talbott, Strobe, 19
Task Force Hawk, 55, 198; *see also* Apache helicopters
technological advances, moral obligations and, 146
"Technological Superiority Theory," 115
technology: Kosovo war and, 193–197; reliance on, 161
Terek River, 110
terrain. *See* urban warfare; war, old style, importance of terrain in
terrorism, 116–117
Tet Offensive, 88
Thucydides, 147
Tibet, 72, 80, 81, 92
Tier III aircraft, 202
Times, (London), 107
Tito, Marshal (Josip Broz), 73, 130
TLAMs. *See* missiles, Tomahawk Land Attack Missiles

Tocqueville, Alexis de, 64
Tomahawk missiles. *See under* missiles
TORCH landings, 39
trade, free, 69; *see also* global economy; globalization
trade agreements, 177
Trident nuclear ballistic missile submarine (SSBN), 202
Truman, Harry, 165; Truman Doctrine, 73

U-2 aircraft, 201
UAVs. *See* Unmanned Aerial Vehicles
UCAV. *See* Unmanned Combat Air Vehicle
Ulundi (battle), 100
United Kingdom. *See* Britain
United Nations, 70; rebuilding Somalia and, 126; *see also* Security Council, United Nations
United Nations Convention on the Prevention and Punishment of the Crime of Genocide, 80
United States: changing military strategy of, 87–89; foreign policy debates in, 151; foreign policy of, 48; future threats to, 116; grand strategy of (*see* grand strategy, U.S.); hypocracy of, 148; as imperial state, 48; international organizations and, 64–66; military vulnerability of, 205; moral obligations of, 150; as part of coalition, 50–52; role in Kosovo war, 21, 57; strategic context of, 134–135
United States European Command, 3
universal rights, 68
Unmanned Aerial Vehicle (UAV), 194, 196, 201–202
Unmanned Combat Air Vehicle (UCAV), 202
Upton, Maj. Gen. Emory, 44–45
urban warfare, 99, 111–115; advisories on, 113; technology for, 114

V-22 Osprey tilt-rotor verticle-takeoff and -landing vehicles, 200
Vietnam War, 45, 46, 48, 157, 166–168; reporting of, 158; U.S. bombing in, 86–87; U.S. strategy in, 88
Volage, HMS, 99

Wald, Maj. Gen. Charles, 51
Walzer, Michael, 137
war, old style of: anarchic or tribal societies and, 105–113; British 19th century style and, 86; controllability of, 118–119; decisiveness in battle during, 41–42; importance of terrain in, 111; reporting of, 157–158; risk of escalation and, 149–150; technological superiority in, 99–100; Western imperial style of, 98–100; Western vulnerability in, 101
war, old U.S. style of, 38–46; actual practice of, 45–46; air warfare and, 53; bloodlust in, 40; four qualities of, 40–46; Kosovo war and, 45–46; politics and, 49
war, post-Cold War style of, 46–52; air warfare and, 53–54; constraints on, 192; future of, 59–61; minimizing losses in, 54; peacekeeping functions and, 192; rise of the commander in chief in, 58; "sanitized," 151; shift from civilian control and, 58–59; urban warfare, 99, 111–115; U.S. methods of, 86; vague objectives in, 178
Warner, John, 202

Washington Post, 58, 157
Washington Treaty, 76
weaponry, 8; delivered by U.S. in Kosovo, 21; "dumb" munitions, 53–54; future of, 203–204; nuclear, 98; planned purchases of, 199–200; technological advances in, 53–54, 115–116; *see also* missiles; precision-guided munitions; *individual* weapons
Weinberger, Caspar, 42
Weinberger doctrine, 42–44, 170; lapses from, 49; liberal elite and, 82
Westmoreland, Gen. William C., 88
Williams, William Appleman, 176
Wilson, Woodrow, 68
Wilsonianism, 125, 135, 147; American actions and, 148; moral ambiguities of, 149; revival of, 126; rhetoric of, 150
World Bank, 70
World Trade Organization (WTO), 70, 177
World War II, 39, 112, 162–164; civil rights and, 164; U.S. strategy in, 88
WTO. *See* World Trade Organization

Yeltsin, Boris, 9, 143
Yugoslavia, Federal Republic of (FRY), 1; after Tito, 73–74; civil war in, 73; extent of destruction in, 17–18; Integrated Air Defense System (IADS), 6; reaction to NATO bombing by, 10; U.S. interests and, 77; weakness of, 197; World War II and, 73
Yugoslav military: claims of civilian casualties by, 15; dissent among, 17; war statistics of, 22; withdrawal of army by, 19

Zululand, 99